"Swish" Nicholson

"Swish" Nicholson

A Biography of Wartime Baseball's Leading Slugger

ROBERT A. GREENBERG

McFarland & Company, Inc., Publishers
Jefferson, North Carolina, and London

LIBRARY OF CONGRESS CATALOGUING-IN-PUBLICATION DATA

Greenberg, Robert A., 1952–
  "Swish" Nicholson : a biography of wartime baseball's leading slugger / Robert A. Greenberg.
      p.   cm.
  Includes bibliographical references and index.

  ISBN-13: 978-0-7864-3274-5
  softcover : 50# alkaline paper ∞

  1. Nicholson, Bill, 1914–[1996.]   2. Baseball players — United States — Biography.   I. Title.
  GV865.N487G74   2008
  796.357092 — dc22   [B]   2007040804

British Library cataloguing data are available

©2008 Robert A. Greenberg. All rights reserved

No part of this book may be reproduced or transmitted in any form or by any means, electronic or mechanical, including photocopying or recording, or by any information storage and retrieval system, without permission in writing from the publisher.

Cover photograph: Nicholson connecting at Wrigley Field in his final season as a Cub, 1948 *(courtesy of Emily Joiner)*

Manufactured in the United States of America

McFarland & Company, Inc., Publishers
  Box 611, Jefferson, North Carolina 28640
  www.mcfarlandpub.com

Acknowledgments

I am indebted to many people for their assistance with this project, which had its genesis during the early 1970s. At that time, I was a student at Washington College, intrigued to learn that a former major leaguer had been born, bred, and still lived in Chestertown, Maryland. Though I never had the opportunity to meet Bill Nicholson, throughout the years I found myself collecting articles about him that appeared from time to time, in the local papers and college publications.

The decision to write the book came nine years after the ballplayer's death. Most of Nicholson's contemporaries were, unfortunately, deceased. Luckily, he provided an expansive oral history in 1983 to Marge Fallaw, of the Kent County Historical Society, describing his early life in Chestertown, and his big league career. He was also interviewed by several authors researching biographies of other players from the wartime era, including Norman Macht, who—fortunately—still possessed the cassette tape of *his* interview 20 years later.

At the time of his death, Nicholson resided with his stepdaughter Emily Joiner and her husband Alan in the farmhouse at Broad Neck. It was my good fortune to have their cooperation and support from the first. Emily, Alan, and their family (including, but not limited to, John Curlett, Priscilla Curlett Whiting, Julia Curlett Stap, Caroline Thompson, Charlotte Curlett, and Ben Joiner) could not have been more accommodating, beginning with our initial meeting at the farmhouse. They graciously lent me memorabilia of "Mr. Bill," including photographs and letters, and were a ready source of information about his life after baseball. They made me feel almost like a part of the family, and I appreciate their kindness.

Other current and former Kent Countians were generous with their time, as well. Thanks to Margo Bailey, mayor of Chestertown, and Elmer Horsey, the former mayor; his wife, Joan Horsey; Mackey Dutton; my former college librarian, Miriam Ford Hoffecker; Stefan Skipp; and Harrison Vickers. The late Hurtt Deringer — who confided to me, before his untimely death, that he'd hoped to write this biography — spent several hours one winter's day at the local Dunkin' Donuts expounding on the virtues of his boyhood idol, Swish Nicholson.

Coach Ed Athey provided a wealth of information about Tom Kibler, and even lent me a videotape of the testimonial dinner held to honor Nicholson in 1991. Bryan Matthews, athletic director at Washington College, provided access to old photographs of Nicholson and Kibler. Marcia Landskroener, editor of the *Washington College Magazine,* published an excerpt from this book, causing several people with information about Nicholson to contact me. Jennifer Bershon, the college's registrar, assisted me in obtaining Nicholson's academic transcripts from 1931 through 1936. The staff at the Clifton E. Miller Library allowed me to view old copies of the *Elm, Enterprise, Transcript,* and *Kent County News,* and the employees of the Alumni House provided unfettered access to old yearbooks.

Former major league players and coaches Phil Cavarretta, Randy Gumpert, Maje McDonnell, Pete Naktenis, the late Buck O'Neill, Andy Pafko, Robin Roberts, Bobby Thomson, and Bill Werber responded to my requests and patiently answered all of my questions. Special thanks go to Marge Fallaw and Norman Macht, whose interviews with Nicholson have been a most valuable resource. I am grateful for the help of Emily Adams, Jane Bristoll, Roger Miller, Meg Nichols, Pamela Yerkes Soutter, Lisa Sparacino, Betty Beck Welton, the staff at the Madison Reading Room in the Library of Congress, and the Kent County Historical Society, not to mention ardent Swish Nicholson fans Bill Mortell, Jim Revord, Bill Stone, and Paul Wysard.

The two days I spent at the National Baseball Library, at the Hall of Fame in Cooperstown, New York, were simply not enough, and the staff — especially John Horne — was most gracious and helpful. So were staff members at Old St. Paul's Church in Fairlee; the Sudlersville Library, and — just down the street — the Jimmie Foxx Museum. Many thanks to the folks at the Philadelphia A's Historical Society — particularly David Jordan — in Hatboro, Pennsylvania, who've kept alive the legacy of the long-departed Mackmen.

University of Maryland librarian Anne Turkos provided me with yearbooks, articles, and programs from Shoremen-Terrapins football games. Membership in the Society for American Baseball Research (SABR) enabled me to review newspaper accounts of virtually every major league game Nicholson played. Several SABR members, including Mark Millikin, Marty Friedrich, Richard Hamilton, and Bill Deane took the time to e-mail or write me about my book, and I appreciate their thoughtfulness and assistance. *Retrosheet* enabled me to check, and double-check, scores and standings from 60 years ago, in the flash of a keystroke.

Charlie Berry, Washington College '36, shared an encyclopedic knowledge about his *alma mater*'s athletic program in the years 1932–36, and I enjoyed our periodic telephone conversations.

Finally, this book could not have been written without the guidance and support of my wife, Jill. Her patience, energy, research assistance, and computer savvy were absolutely *nonpareil*. This project is as much hers as mine. She, and our three children Jamie, Sara, and William, stood with me at the beginning of the journey, and at its end.

For Mom

Table of Contents

Acknowledgments — v
Introduction — 1

1. ♦ On Fancy Farm — 5
2. ♦ Three Sport Man — 17
3. ♦ Return from Annapolis — 35
4. ♦ Mr. Mack and the A's — 44
5. ♦ Life in the Bushes — 55
6. ♦ Back to the Big Leagues — 72
7. ♦ Catalina to Chicago — 78
8. ♦ The Last Prewar Season — 92
9. ♦ Baseball, As Usual — 102
10. ♦ Coming Into His Own — 115
11. ♦ "Swish" and His Fans — 124
12. ♦ The Supreme Compliment — 132
13. ♦ The Year of the Billy Goat Curse — 145
14. ♦ Benched — 162
15. ♦ The Cubs in Decline — 172
16. ♦ Farewell to the Windy City — 181
17. ♦ The City of Brotherly Love — 189
18. ♦ The Whiz Kids — 200
19. ♦ The Giants Win the Pennant — 208

20 ◆	Shakeup on the Phillies	213
21 ◆	Is There Life After Baseball?	218

Epilogue 233
Appendix — Bill Nicholson's Regular Season Career Statistics and World Series Record 237
Chapter Notes 239
Bibliography 251
Index 255

Introduction

Maryland Route 213 meanders south from the main highway, through picturesque Centreville and, five miles beyond, tiny Church Hill. The road bisects the flat Eastern Shore countryside, crossing six more miles of corn, soybean, and wheat fields, before houses and small businesses signal the motorist's arrival in Chestertown.

The Chester River soon appears, muddy green in color, traversed by a two-lane bridge that has existed, in roughly the same location, for two centuries. Just beyond the river, parallel to it on either side of the span, lies a row of stately residences fronting on Water Street. Several of these homes date from the era when Chestertown, seat of Kent County, was a vibrant port in colonial Maryland.

Cross Street is two blocks west. There, next to the town hall and visible from the road, stands a six-foot bronze statue of a baseball player. He is finishing a swing of his bat, gazing in the direction of a ball he has powerfully struck, as it soars majestically towards some hypothetical right field fence.

The batter was born and raised on his family's farm, near Chestertown. After high school, where he was a standout on the baseball team, he enrolled in the local college, and learned to play football. So quickly did he adapt to the game that he was selected as an all–Maryland performer by his junior year. The baseball squad, on which he starred, defeated much larger and better-equipped university teams from Maryland, Penn State, and George Washington.

While still a college junior, he was signed by Connie Mack's Philadelphia Athletics, for whom he played — sparingly — upon graduation. Three seasons in the minors transformed him into a hustling, hard-nosed competitor, who played on the last pennant-winning Chicago Cubs team in 1945. On the downside of his career, he stepped into the role of pinch-hitting elder statesman for the Philadelphia Phillies "Whiz Kids" of 1950. With the looks of a matinee idol and the physique of a weight lifter, the bronzed batter was a player of enormous popularity, and the game's greatest power hitter during World War II.

Weakened by disease, he retired from baseball after the 1953 season, to return to his home town and work at a variety of jobs, before he resumed life as a farmer. In many ways, his tale is one of tragedy. He was predeceased by his two brothers, two wives, and two sons, who were his only natural children. He struggled with diabetes for nearly fifty years, suffering recurrent seizures as he aged.

By birth, he was William Beck Nicholson. Legions of National League baseball fans, however, knew him as "Swish," for that was the sound that was heard as his bat whipped through the air of big league ballparks, often with disastrous results for opposing pitchers. To the people of the community where he returned after baseball, however, he remained simply "Billy Nick," a quintessential son of the Eastern Shore: rugged, independent, and forever bound to the small town in which he was born and where he died.

A major leaguer during parts of three decades, Nicholson's slugging feats were legendary. He hit four home runs in four consecutive at-bats against the New York Giants in 1944, to culminate a weekend during which he blasted five homers in seven times at the plate, and six such clouts over the space of 40 hours. After witnessing this display, and afraid to face him in his last time up, the Giants intentionally walked Nicholson *with the bases loaded*, a tribute so extraordinary that it did not happen again for more than 50 years — when Barry Bonds received the same treatment.

He is one of only two major league players — Pittsburgh Pirates Hall of Famer Roberto Clemente being the other — to come within inches of hitting the distant center field scoreboard at Chicago's Wrigley Field with one of his prodigious circuit clouts.

Nicholson was the first National Leaguer to lead the league in both homers and RBIs in consecutive years, a feat he accomplished in 1943 and 1944. Paradoxically, when his 1945 offensive production fell off, some National League pitchers were terrified, viewing the streak-hitting outfielder as a time bomb in the Cubs lineup, ready to explode at any time. So befuddled by his slump were sportswriters covering the team in 1945 that any sustained period of offensive production by the slugger sent them scurrying to their typewriters, to proclaim that Nicholson had finally emerged from his batting funk. Sadly, he never again achieved the hitting prowess that had so terrorized National League hurlers before 1945.

Exiled to Philadelphia after the end of the 1948 campaign, he became "Papa Nick," a steadying influence on the Whiz Kids, who won the National

League pennant in 1950. He was in a Chicago hotel in 1949 when his Phillies roommate, Eddie Waitkus, was shot and nearly killed by a "Baseball Annie." The incident provided the inspiration for a novel called *The Natural*, later made into a popular motion picture starring Robert Redford.

Yet, several years before his death in 1996, Nicholson told a visitor to his farm outside Chestertown that he felt forgotten, and insisted that few people in the community were even aware that he once played major league baseball. As late as 1990, when he was inducted into the Chicago Sports Hall of Fame, he told a reporter: "The news was most welcome, because I thought I was just another forgotten ballplayer." That assumption, of course, was belied by the town's dedication of the statue in his honor in 1992.

There was nothing complex about the man. Bill Nicholson was no different from many who came of age during the Depression. Born to a farm family, he learned early that nothing of value was attained without hard work. So it was that, during his professional career, Nicholson made sure that no one outworked or outhustled him. He played hurt, and he played while he was seriously ill, without alibi or complaint. He competed in four All-Star games and one World Series; only serious illness and a recent hospitalization prevented him from playing in a second. There were dizzying accomplishments over which to exult, and abysmal slumps that were stoically endured.

After his playing days were over, his marriage ended in divorce, and eventual estrangement from his two natural children. Though he found a loving and loyal wife and stepchildren in later years, Nicholson was plagued by health problems that depressed him, made travel difficult, and sometimes prevented him even from leaving his house.

It is hoped that those readers who were previously unfamiliar with the life and career of this once-famous, but now largely forgotten, star will gain an appreciation for his professionalism and the caliber of his play, on some particularly dismal teams. Cubs rooters of the '40s and Phillies fans of the early '50s will, of course, need no introduction to Swish Nicholson, the self-effacing slugger of their youth. Here is the story of his life.

◆ 1 ◆

On Fancy Farm

Maryland's Eastern Shore is *sui generis*; to hail from the right-hand side of the Chesapeake Bay signifies an independence, and a figurative and literal distance from the hubbub of suburban Baltimore and Washington, D.C. The bay separates the Eastern Shore not only geographically, but socially and politically as well.

Before 1952, when the William Preston Lane Memorial Bridge was built to connect the two shores, the Eastern Shore was isolated from the rest of the state. A traveler who wished to cross the bay from Baltimore or Annapolis either headed around it by highway to the north, or boarded one of several commercial ferries.

Most of the residents of the Eastern Shore worked in agriculture, if they did not make their living on the water. The farmers grew wheat, fruits, and vegetables, and raised livestock; the watermen fished and harvested crabs or oysters. This was especially true in Kent, Maryland's smallest (281 square miles) county, founded in 1642.

Geographically, it embraces an area originally explored by Captain John Smith in 1607. The county is bounded by water on three sides: the Sassafras River to the north, the Chester River to the south, Chesapeake Bay to the west. The state of Delaware is situated on the east. Kent is no city's suburb; by highway, it is nearly equidistant from Philadelphia (85 miles); Washington, D.C. (80 miles); and Baltimore (65 miles), a location befitting its social and political autonomy.

George Washington traveled the highways of Kent County on a number of occasions, *en route* to the Continental Congress in Philadelphia. It was not unusual for him to arrive in nearby Rock Hall on a boat from his home in Mount Vernon, then travel by horseback to his legislative business in the City of Brotherly Love.

The father of his country came to know the area well, and of an institution known as the Kent County School, founded in the 1720s. The Reverend William Smith, a rector of the Anglican Church and close friend of Benjamin Franklin, founded Washington College in 1782, as a successor to the Kent County School. The college owns a distinction no other institution can claim: it bears the name of America's first president by his express consent. General Washington contributed fifty guineas to the school's founding, and served for six years on the Board of Visitors and Governors. Washington College is the tenth oldest college in the country, and the oldest chartered college in Maryland.

As people who make their living from the land and the water surrounding it, Kent Countians are deeply rooted in their community. The Nicholson family is no exception.

"Fancy Farm," located several miles outside of Chestertown, was purchased by Josiah Lusby, Bill Nicholson's great-grandfather, in 1865. It was cultivated by Josiah's lineal descendants until the early 1980s. A three-story house still stands several hundred feet off Earl Nicholson Road, shielded by linden and elm trees. It consists of three sections: the original, pre–1740 dwelling, built of brick and clapboard; a brick central house; and a kitchen/servants' quarters. A bathroom addition was installed on the back of the home in the early 1900s, but there was no electricity until the early 1930s, around the time Bill left home to play professional ball. There were several outbuildings, including a pump house, containing a small gasoline engine to facilitate the flow of water to the house and barn, and a large brick stable.

In that house, while bucolic Chestertown prepared for Christmas, Bill Nicholson was born to Alverta Tylden Beck and Albert Earle Nicholson, on a chilly December 11, 1914.

Family lore holds that baby Bill weighed 13 pounds at birth, although no records survive to confirm or refute the claim. He was Alverta's second child; Albert Tylden Nicholson was almost two years of age at the time of his brother's birth. James Laurence Nicholson — known as "Larny" — would arrive in February, 1916.

After the birth, Alverta became seriously ill with complications that required hospitalization in Baltimore for three weeks, before she was able to return to the farm.

"I was born and raised right there on Nicholson Road, the third farm, and my grandfather [William Thomas Nicholson] lived on the first farm going from Route 20 to Nicholson Road," Bill said. "And we were all farmers at that stage of the game. I don't know what they all were way back there. Some of them were seafaring men, but I guess we've been here a few generations."

Alverta, called "Miss Bertie," and Albert, known as "Earl," were married at Old St. Paul's Episcopal Church on December 5, 1910, by the Reverend Doctor Sewell S. Hepburn. Less than a year earlier, in nearby Church Hill, Reverend Hepburn had presided at the baptism of his granddaughter Katharine, who was destined to become a famous star of the American screen.

At the time of their marriage, Earl was 29 years old, Bertie 27. She was the daughter of James Thomas and Alverta Brice Beck. A kindly and perpetually friendly woman, she was reared on a farm several miles from Fancy Farm. James Beck passed away before the birth of his grandchildren; Alverta Brice Beck lived until 1930.

As a boy, Bill attended Fairlee Elementary School, about three miles from home. The building no longer stands. In good weather, the Nicholson boys walked to school and back home at the

The earliest known photograph of Bill Nicholson, *circa* 1916 (*courtesy Emily Joiner*).

end of the day. In bad weather, they drove a horse and carriage. When they arrived, they unhitched the horse, put her in a shed with plenty of hay, and entered the school. The boys returned home after classes were over.

On occasion, young Bill would accompany Earl to the blacksmith to shoe the horses. Each of them would mount one of the equines, and take another in tow out to Fairlee, at Harry Hoyle's shop, where he would do the job. While in town, they might stop at Bramble's general store to shop for dry goods or supplies. The Nicholsons rarely traveled by automobile, although Earl had purchased a Model T Ford that he occasionally drove.

Sundays were reserved for worship at Old St. Paul's. The ancient church, located several miles outside of Fairlee, was used by British troops as a barracks during the War of 1812. The cemetery on the grounds, surrounded by giant oak trees, believed to date from the late 1600s, is the burial site of many prominent Kent Countians. The Nicholsons were faithful parishoners. Attendance at church was important to Miss Bertie, and she made sure her children worshipped on Sunday. Nicholson remembered: "We went in snow storms and everything else; didn't make much difference.... We'd go in the Dearborn and put blankets over us and that was only on rare occasions, but we didn't miss. I remember I had one of those little pins as a boy for not missing a Sunday for so many years, you know. Had a little pin and then put bars on it every year. Had four or five years of them not missing a Sunday."

The Nicholsons enjoyed wonderful Christmases with huge meals, a tree, and stockings for all the boys. One of the most popular holiday locales for area farmers was Abe Cohen's dry goods and grocery store, just down the street from the church on Sandy Bottom Road. At Christmas time, Abe stocked all the latest toys, along with ornaments and confections like French candy and chocolate drops, to delight local children.

Old St. Paul's was a center for social life in Kent County. On special occasions, the church held festivals for the community, where oysters, crabs, meats, and ham were served by church members. There were also cakes and pies for dessert, all of which could be eaten in the shade of the giant oaks during the warm weather months.

As the children of a farm family, the Nicholson boys were members of the 4-H Club. Every year they could look forward to the annual Farmers' Picnic, sponsored by the Kent County Farm Bureau. Hundreds of area residents came to eat delicious home-cooked foods, see the farm exhibits, and play in ball games and other contests. The Nicholsons were always active participants. Miss Bertie even supervised the turkey calling contest.

The days on the 250-acre spread were long ones for the Nicholson brothers; there were cows to be milked before and after school, and the unceasing chores that are a part of agrarian life. They also helped out when needed on their grandfather's farm. It was during those seemingly interminable days that Bill developed the work ethic that shaped his professional baseball career.

Besides growing crops and dairy farming, the Nicholsons raised turkeys, a lucrative local business. The Maryland Turkey Growers Association of Kent County met monthly, with an eye towards November and December, when market demand was greatest. Out-of-state wholesalers advertised in the local newspapers every spring and summer, seeking plump birds to sell throughout the northeast during end-of-the-year holidays. Young Bill got his fill of the bird, figuratively and literally, and developed a lifelong aversion to eating turkey meat, as a result.

Each of the three brothers had a specialty on the farm. Albert was the stable man, attending to the cows and horses, while Larny — being the most mechanically gifted of the three — was more interested in the operation and maintenance of the equipment at Fancy Farm. Bill preferred to help his mother with her gardening and fruit trees. A prodigious fruit eater, he could down 10 oranges in a single sitting during his years with the Cubs.

Describing the family's life on the farm, Nicholson said: "We had dairy cattle and sold milk, and we had an asparagus patch about six or seven acres, and we grew a lot of tomatoes in those days. We grew the main crop, which was wheat at that time, and corn.... Farming practices were a lot different. When I was a boy, I was a right good size before I ever saw any tractor. We finally had a little Ford tractor with an iron wheel and all we had was horses and mules. Had two big stables for our horses and mules."

The tremendous strength and bat speed Bill exhibited as a professional player was acquired without the assistance of weights or exercise apparatus. His hands and forearms developed by helping to milk the 30 or so dairy cows at Fancy Farm on a regular basis. He was also handy with a pitchfork, lifted and baled hay, and operated heavy machinery and farm equipment.

Threshing of the wheat was a back-breaking job. "We had a big steam engine with a belt on it that ran the thresher, and then they had wagons where the wheat was reaped with a reaper," Bill recalled. "And then they bundled it up and you stacked it, the men stacked it in the fields, and put tops on each little stack all over the field, hundreds of them, thousands of them. And that kept it from the rain. We didn't get many rains then, but you got a few thunderstorms. That kept the rain off it. Some years, when you had a terrible wet spell, why you'd see wheat growing right out of the top, and then you lost all those sheaves on the top. But it took a lot of men to run those kinds of things. They had to haul it with wagons hooked to the thresher. Had two sides and they ran one wagon here and one wagon there, and threw it in the chute that carried it into the thresher. And then you had to have men to bag it up and put it on the truck and somebody to haul it to town. It was a big operation."

The Nicholsons often carried their tomato crop by horse and wagon to nearby Buck Neck, and loaded it on boats destined for canneries in Baltimore. Sometimes the fruit was taken directly to local packers. The wheat was hauled to Chestertown and shipped on Pennsylvania Railroad box cars to buyers in Philadelphia.

All the Nicholson boys were toughened by their work on the farm, but Bill was easily the most athletic of the three. Though Larny was overweight and tipped the scales at well over 300 pounds for much of his life, he was an extremely powerful man. In his youth, he picked up a Ford engine, unaided, and placed it into a farm truck. During Bill's days on the Cubs, his teammates called him "Muscles," impressed by his ability to lift a 100-pound bag of fertilizer with one hand. They were aghast when he informed them that his "little" brother Larny could tote three.

Bill had scant exposure to organized sports before high school. There were no Little Leagues in Kent County in the 1920s. The neighborhood boys would simply congregate out in the field behind Fairlee School, participating in a game played with a softball. As a teenager, Bill competed for a loosely-organized team representing Fairlee against other towns like Worton and Kennedyville on Saturday afternoons. Equipment was rudimentary; farm clothes were the garb. With tongue in cheek, Nicholson remembered the baseball "diamonds" of his early youth, and the perils of playing where livestock had recently trod: "We'd play in the cow pasture mostly.... The grass was cut down, but you'd slide into second base and it might not be second base!"

Bill followed the exploits of major league players by reading the periodicals. "Back when I first came up, there was no radio, so we could only keep track through the newspaper," he explained. "But I can remember listening to the World Series [Yankees v. Cardinals] in 1926."

Fairlee held classes through the seventh grade, after which Bill entered Chestertown High School, seven miles away. The high school building is occupied today by the Kent County Board of Education. By the time high school started, Albert had the use of an old car, in which the boys could travel into town. Bill was a top notch student, who excelled in mathematics. He did not participate on school athletic teams until his junior year, partly owing to his farm chores, but also because he didn't consider himself to be much of an athlete.

Chestertown High was too tiny to field a competitive football team. But, beginning in 1929, Bill played soccer during the fall, basketball in the winter, and — when spring arrived — baseball, until his graduation in June, 1931. It was not unusual for him to run all the way home from school after athletic practices, when there was no other transportation available.

At Chestertown, Nicholson's exploits on the field were a precursor of the success that would be achieved a decade later in major league flannels. He was the starting guard for the basketball team as a junior, and also saw time at center. In an era when teams rarely scored more than 30 points per game, he was known as a tenacious defender, who could accurately shoot the ball when the need arose.

In his first year of high school baseball —1930— it was evident to many that he had the ability to be a special player. A local newspaper carried this item on March 19, regarding the 15-year-old prodigy:

[Chestertown High School Coach W.J.] Stenger believes that in Billy Nicholson he has a coming diamond star. This hefty kid, who also played on the soccer and basketball teams, is a heavy hitter and possesses a gun–like throwing arm.

Though the Chestertonians practiced daily on the field in back of the school, by late April they hadn't played a single game, because local high school administrators were unable to agree upon a schedule. In early May, play finally began against Galena and Rock Hall, the other two county high schools. Notwithstanding Nicholson's two doubles, tiny Galena High won the 1930 county championship game, played at Kennedyville, by a 16–11 count.

When senior year rolled around, Bill was elected captain of the soccer team, for whom he played center halfback. Chestertown cruised to early season wins against Sudlersville (score: 16–0), Centreville (6–0), and Rock Hall (13–0). Finding themselves behind, 2–0, at the half against Elkton, Nicholson and his teammates erupted for 11 unanswered second-half goals to win the game.

Chestertown then bested Oxford, 4–0, to capture the 1930 Eastern Shore Championship on December 5, in a game marred by a near-brawl which broke out among the fans, after a Chestertown player clashed with the Oxford goaltender. The victory earned the Kent squad a berth in the state title game against Hancock, the next week.

The match was held at Centreville, before more than 2,000 animated onlookers. In what was surely one of the most remarkable athletic contests in which Nicholson ever engaged, Chestertown won, 4–3, in four overtime periods. Trailing, 3–0, in the second half, the boys from Kent rallied to tie the game after 60 minutes of regulation play, and then played an additional 40 minutes before the outcome was decided.

By all accounts, the action was furious. The two teams raced up and down the 110-yard pitch, bruised and bloodied. A newspaper correspondent held: "No schoolboy football game was ever as grueling as the soccer battle between Chestertown and Hancock last Saturday." The next week's edition of *The Enterprise* proudly displayed the team's picture on page one, under the headline "Meet the Maryland Soccer Champs," and the boys enjoyed a measure of fame as the first Chestertown High athletic team to win a state championship.

Two weeks after the season ended, basketball practice began. The high school had no gymnasium, and usually practiced and played home games at Washington College. Bill made the team, but played only half the season, the highlight of which came in a 21–19 win over Felton, Delaware, in January. With only a few seconds left on the clock, and the score knotted at 19,

Nicholson got the ball at midcourt, drove to the basket, and sank the winning shot.

In his last year on the baseball team, Bill played the outfield and batted cleanup. The Chestertown nine edged Mardela, 7–6, in Easton, to win the 1931 Eastern Shore high school baseball championship, on June 15. Five days later, however, they were defeated, 11–0, by a scrappy Hyattsville squad in the state title game, played at Elkton. The second baseman for Hyattsville was Harry Clifton Byrd, Jr., son of the University of Maryland football coach. The young Byrd doubled and tripled in the rout. Only one Chestertonian reached second base, and the Kent boys managed but one hit. Nicholson, batting fifth, was blanked in three appearances at the plate, but did have four putouts in center field.

Well-rounded athlete that he had become, Bill also threw the shot for the track team, finishing second in the event at the Delmarva Interscholastic Track Meet, against competition from other Maryland and Delaware schools. If that wasn't enough, he was recruited to play center field for the West Kent team of the fledgling Kent County Amateur League, a four-team loop for high school boys.

Like many players of his era, Nicholson never saw a major league baseball game until he participated in one. Not surprisingly, he had great affinity for fellow Eastern Shoreman Jimmie Foxx, seven years his senior, who was a star for the Philadelphia Athletics. Though Foxx had grown up in nearby Sudlersville, Bill didn't meet him until many years later. "He was my idol as a kid, but he was already a big star in the major leagues when I came along," Nicholson recalled. "I didn't meet him until I was in the minors." They would be teammates, briefly, in 1942 and 1944 in Chicago, at the end of Foxx's storied career.

Nicholson did have the opportunity to see his hero and a group of major league all-stars play an exhibition game at Washington College in October of 1930, after the Athletics defeated the St. Louis Cardinals in the World Series. Surely the 15-year-old high school student could not have imagined he would be playing against some of these pros six years later, and then later alongside the great "Double X."

Apart from his academic and athletic achievements, Bill was quite popular, and never wanted for female companionship. A college classmate, Miriam Ford Hoffecker, was one year behind Bill at Chestertown High. She remembered her relationship with the future ballplayer: "High school ended in the 11th grade in Kent County in those days. I dated Bill in the 10th and 11th grades. We didn't really date just one person like today, but he was the special one."

By his mid–teens, Bill was a strikingly handsome young man, possessed of wavy brown hair parted on the left, twinkling brown eyes, and a broad, dimpled smile that accentuated pearly white teeth. There was a dappling of faint freckles across the bridge of his nose. He was broad-shouldered, with strong wrists and forearms, and an imposing physical presence at just under six feet tall. Nicholson walked with the smooth, slightly pigeon-toed gait common to many athletes.

When he spoke, a listener heard the vaguely southern accent endemic to natives of the Shore, wherein "Baltimore" is pronounced "Bawlamer"; "fire" becomes "far"; and "o"s sound like they have long "a"s in front. Nicholson's was a folksy country dialect, in which one didn't move quickly, but "right quickly." Pronouns were frequently omitted in conversation. "I went to school," was shortened to "Went to school"; "We had a good time," was abbreviated to, "Had a good time."

During the school year, among farm obligations, homework and sports, there was recreation time available to Bill only on weekends. Fridays, he and his buddies might take in a talking picture at the New Lyceum theater on High Street in Chestertown, where for twenty cents one could sit in the balcony to admire Gary Cooper, ogle Jeannette McDonald, or laugh at Buster Keaton, and flirt with the girls. Afterwards, Gill Bros. Ice Cream Factory and Dairy, on nearby Cross Street, was a frequent destination.

On Saturday nights, there might be a party, often at Priscilla Grainger's house off Langford Road, on her family's farm. The guests came with food for all to eat, and someone would bring the newest phonograph records. Miriam Hoffecker remembered that the girls taught Bill and his pals all the latest dances.

Nearby Betterton Beach, located in northern Kent County, where the Sassafras River empties into the bay, was a major resort during the 1920s. Vacationers journeyed from Baltimore and Philadelphia by boat, to enjoy the sun and sand. Boarding houses and hotels bustled during the summer months, as the visitors enjoyed what were billed as "high class moving pictures," bowling, and roller skating at a pavilion called the "Pleasure Pier." Farm families like the Nicholsons had neither the time nor the money to vacation elsewhere during the summer months, and excursions to Betterton were an inexpensive alternative.

There, on Saturday nights during the summer, one could dance to the sounds of local musicians. Miriam Hoffecker, who lived in town, remembered being driven to the dances with Bill in the Nicholson family car; Albert was the chauffeur. Bill had become a good dancer and was always handy around the ladies. Although Miriam insisted she never saw it, he had a streak of mischief in him that surfaced on occasion.

During the Prohibition era, Nicholson and his cohorts sometimes indulged in the consumption of illicit beverages. "We got a quarter on a Saturday night, and we thought we were doing pretty good," Bill said. "After we were 16, we did get a dollar a lot of times on Saturday night. With my first quarter, I generally got ice cream. With a dollar, I'd be wanting to go to Betterton and dance and devil after the girls and, I guess, sometimes sneak a little bit of corn liquor. Up at Betterton, there were so many bootleggers they almost had to keep a tag on to keep from selling to each other. There was whiskey everywhere in Kent County."

Bill told Miriam that one Saturday, tired from the previous evening's activities at Betterton, he was too sleepy to do his chores. He drove the Ford tractor out into the field, turned it off, and decided to take a nap. There he lay sleeping underneath the machine, clad in work clothes. Suddenly, he was awakened by the approach of his father. Thinking quickly, he explained to a surprisingly gullible Earl that he'd been attending to a mechanical problem with the tractor. The prevarication unchallenged, Bill completed the chores, his father none the wiser.

Chestertown was a racially segregated town during Bill's youth. There was a separate educational system for blacks, including Garnett High School, which existed into the 1960s. In the '20s and '30s, race relations on Maryland's Eastern Shore were not much different from those in the deep south. Early in December, 1931, a black defendant awaiting trial on a murder charge was lynched in Salisbury, and an accused rapist in Kent County named George Davis was threatened by white citizens with the same fate. An editorial in the local paper bemoaned the suggestion that Davis could not receive a fair trial in Chestertown, and commented on an offer by a Baltimore City attorney to intercede on his behalf:

> ... Davis, the Kent ravager of motherhood, [was] spirited here and there by Shore police authorities that justice might be done. And all to what end? The chance for a communistic lawyer, interested in the negro law trade because of his connection with a firm dealing in financial loans to negroes, to gain columns of personal publicity at the expense of hampered and delayed justice.

Many of Chestertown's black citizens lived in relative squalor, only blocks away from the fancy homes on Water Street. Other than a select group of professionals like teachers, ministers, and undertakers, most found employment as farmhands, laborers, or servants in the homes of white citizens.

The sheer volume of work on Fancy Farm necessitated the hiring of hands, many of whom were black. In 1920, when Bill turned six years old, four blacks lived in the servants' quarters of Fancy Farm. They were the cook Francis Houston, two hired men — one of whom was named Willie Mays —

and a 12-year-old boy. By 1930, with the advent of the Depression, none of the hired help lived on Fancy Farm, although there were black laborers kept on as employees.

In spite of the fact that he was reared in a segregated community, there is no evidence to suggest that Nicholson was bigoted or racist towards minorities as he matured. He grew up around black people, and played against them on local ball teams. Several Kent County "Negro Nines," as they were dubbed by the local press, provided exceptional competition for white teams. The Chestertown Athletics, featuring a fireballing pitcher named Gibbs, had great success in the early '30s. Several members of the club were students from Garnett. A black outfielder from Kent County was said to possess a throwing arm so accurate that on his relay throw to home, the catcher simply rested his glove on the plate, while the ball plunked right into the pocket.

Bill also faced black players on diamonds in Mexico with the Philadelphia A's, in the minor leagues, and in the National League, at all times without incident. He welcomed the integration of baseball, although he never had a black teammate; the Cubs and Phillies were among the last National League teams to integrate. A year before his death, Bill recounted for a Cubs publication: "I ... played ball against a lot of the colored fellas who weren't allowed in the majors... [T]hey were really good."

He understood the difficulties faced by pioneering black players like Jackie Robinson, and just how good those athletes had to be to make a major league roster. "Robinson was playing in Montreal, and it was a known fact that they were going to bring him up the next year or so," Bill explained. "There was a lot of talk, and a lot of the southern boys didn't like it, you know. And they gave him a hard time, but they gradually brought a few more in. They were all good, seasoned ballplayers. They didn't bring any 'rinky-dinks' in."

When hard times came in the early 1930s, prices for crops went through the floor; the Nicholsons sold their wheat for a trifling thirty cents a bushel. They were the lucky ones; many local farms were in the hands of receivers. A drought during the summer of 1930 exacerbated an already financially precarious time for Kent's farmers, but there was always plenty to eat on Fancy Farm, even if cash money was tight. Besides the produce, fruit, and turkeys grown on the farm, Bill and his brothers hunted for rabbits, quail, and ducks. From the time he was 11 years old, Bill was adept with a hunting rifle. He also enjoyed walking the local streams and catching terrapin, which made an excellent soup. Growing up on Fancy Farm, he developed a lifelong passion for the environment, and in later years worked with conservationists to protect migratory birds and other wildlife.

The Nicholsons always had several dogs, usually English Setters, which were used for hunting. Bill learned from a friend how to train them, and he continued to do so throughout his life. Later, he owned several Labrador and Chesapeake Bay retrievers, and, in retirement, two standard poodles dubbed "Peaches" and "Cha-Cha."

By the time he graduated from Chestertown High School at age 16, Bill had nearly reached adult size. His athletic skills were unrefined, but he caught the eye of Washington College coach Tom Kibler, who frequently officiated at local interscholastic sports contests. Kibler would soon come to be the most influential figure in Bill's early athletic life.

◆ 2 ◆

Three Sport Man

John Thomas Kibler was a man of mythic proportions on the Eastern Shore. Born in 1886 in neighboring Queen Anne's County, he was a former minor leaguer, and teammate of Hall of Famer Frank "Home Run" Baker, from nearby Trappe. Kibler became the athletic director at Washington in 1913, at the tender age of 27, after an incipient professional baseball career was cut short by a leg injury. He left the school briefly to serve abroad in World War I, where he was gassed, and wounded twice in battle. For his actions, he was awarded the *Croix de Guerre*, as well as the Distinguished Service Medal. Upon discharge from active duty, he returned to Chestertown to coach the football, basketball, and baseball teams at the college.

A man of unimpeachable integrity, Kibler was selected as president of the Class D Eastern Shore League in 1936. Seven of its eight teams were affiliated with major league baseball clubs. When it was discovered in 1937 that the Salisbury Indians—who had a working agreement with the Washington Senators—unwittingly used an ineligible player during the season, Kibler ordered the team's 21 victories to be forfeited. This placed him in a ticklish situation, however; the Salisbury team was managed by former major leaguer D'Arcy "Jake" Flowers, one of Kibler's former Washington College players. Kibler was unfazed; he stuck by his ruling.

After Senators owner Clark Griffith accused him of ruining the league by virtue of the forfeiture, Kibler replied: "Mr. Griffith, if we can't play baseball according to the rules of the National Association, let's break up the league." Flowers later said: "I was a little upset at first when the coach deprived my club of 21 games. Sure, I objected, and protested most vigorously, but I knew the old-timer meant just what he said." The Indians went on to win the 1937 Eastern Shore League crown, anyway, compiling a 59-11 record after the issuance of Kibler's edict.

Although he coached several sports, baseball was Kibler's passion. "Yes, it is true that my love for the game amounts to a religion," he mused in 1948. "I'll always be eternally grateful for baseball. I know of nothing outside of religion and education that has more salutary effect on the national character than the national pastime."

Kibler's Washington College basketball teams of the 1920s — known as the "Flying Pentagon"— took on and regularly beat much larger schools, including Temple (his alma mater), Duke, Princeton, Villanova, Maryland, Navy, George Washington, Virginia Tech (then known as "V.P.I."), and Duquesne. By the time he handed the basketball reins over to his successor in 1939, Tom Kibler's teams had compiled a 278-108 record, a .720 winning percentage.

Kibler was short in stature, but powerfully built. He walked with a proud carriage that exuded confidence and authority. He neither smoked, nor drank. "How could I," he would ask, "and then tell my athletes not to?" Possessed with indefatigable energy, he quickly became a one-man athletic department. Besides coaching three sports, he presided over the establishment of a popular and competitive intramural sports program at Washington. In the late '20s and '30s, the school's enrollment was approximately 250 students, of whom roughly two-thirds were men. Considering this comparatively small pool of prospective athletes, it is a tribute to Kibler and his assistant coaches that Washington was so successful at intercollegiate competition.

Community youth also benefited from Kibler's guidance. Once a week, he held an open gymnasium at the college, where he put the boys through exercise routines, supervised games, and distributed the college's second-hand sports equipment, including broken bats and beat-up baseballs. During the Depression, the discarded gear was prized by the lucky recipients, many of whose parents could not afford to provide such luxuries for their children.

Kibler's biggest obstacle to success on the gridiron was the fact that few high schools on the Eastern Shore — from whence many of the college's students hailed — had football teams. For that reason, most recruits were newcomers to the college game, and the results were predictably disastrous.

"In football we have reached the lowest ebb," Kibler told a local newspaperman in 1930. "We have become a doormat for college elevens that should be right in our class. The last time we beat St. John's the students burned down the bleachers. If we could beat them this season, William Smith Hall [the college's main academic building] would be a suitable sacrifice."

Bill came to Washington College in the fall of 1931 on a National Merit Scholarship, which paid his tuition. He lived on the farm, not on campus. At Kibler's urging, he reported for football practice in early September, as the squad prepared for the season opener later that month, against the powerful University of Maryland.

Coach Tom Kibler. One former player said, "He reminded you of Napoleon, and if he placed his right hand over his chest, you would think of Napoleon" (*courtesy Washington College*).

Though Nicholson was inexperienced on the gridiron, Kibler knew he was an exceptional athlete. Bill was brawny and tough, and possessed more than adequate speed afoot, having run 100 yards at just a couple ticks over 10 seconds.

The neophyte Washington team spent two weeks in the broiling summer sun, training under the supervision of Kibler and his assistant George Ekaitis, on the dusty practice field. This was a new experience for many of the freshmen. Daily workouts were intense, occasionally interrupted by Kibler loudly exclaiming "Judas Priest!"— the strongest expletive in his vocabulary — when a player missed a tackle or fumbled the ball. He had difficulty remembering the Christian names of his players, so he devised nicknames to identify them, instead.

Ekaitis was not much older than his charges, having recently graduated from Western Maryland College, in Westminster, where he played quarterback for the legendary coach Dick Harlow. His football acumen was keen, and those in the know claimed that he did not call even one wrong play during his two years as Western Maryland's quarterback.

Besides his prowess in football, the 5' 11" Ekaitis also starred in lacrosse, swimming, and boxing, in which he was a collegiate light-heavyweight champion. A stern taskmaster, he had little patience for players who did not practice with the desired degree of intensity. Many a gridder ran extra laps because of his inattentiveness to Ekaitis' instruction. He was a "man's man," and revered by those whom he coached. Former Washington athletic director and coach Ed Athey played football under Ekaitis in 1946, and said that even at that time, "he looked like he could still play.... No one wanted to disappoint him, for he gave everything to his coaching."

Football was the only fall sport offered for male students at the college and, despite poor teams in several previous years, the games were highly-publicized on campus and in the local newspapers, and well-attended by students and local residents. Bill had never played the sport, and witnessed only one game before he arrived on campus.

Recalling his football indoctrination, he said: "I weighed 197 pounds in those days and I was a right-tough country boy. But I didn't even know what a first down was. When I first saw them bring out the chains, I didn't know what the devil they were."

The Enterprise said of the local youth: "Nicholson ... is taking to football like a duck takes to water. Big and husky Nicholson's one lack is experience." Of course, many of his teammates were in the same boat. A *Washington Post* dispatch on August 23 was, nevertheless, optimistic about the team's 1931 football fortunes:

> [This] season is the first of several years in which the caliber of opponents does not obviously outclass the ability of the local eleven and it is believed Washington will have a chance to garner several victories for the first time in five years.

That prognostication was mistaken, however; the "Maroons" struggled through an 0-9 campaign, during which they were outscored by the whopping margin of 211–13, including seven shutouts. The opening-game loss to Maryland turned out to be the highlight of the season.

The Shoremen had sustained a 60–6 beating in 1930 at the hands of the "Aggies," as Maryland's athletic teams were known until 1932. The tiny Washington College eleven had no business setting foot on the same gridiron with a team from the state university, but the school's athletic department received the princely sum of $500 to serve as Maryland's opening day patsies, and the Shoremen usually played their role well. After the Washington-Maryland rivalry ceased in 1933, the Terrapins held a 19-3-1 edge in the all-time series. The scores from the 1926–1929 games, won by the university, were 63–0, 80–0, 31–0, and 34–7, respectively. Washington hadn't beaten Maryland — which enrolled 1,600 students — since 1911.

A preview of the 1931 contest in the *Post* described Washington's team as "easy meat for the Old Line, although it should improve over its 6-60 showing of 1930." Sixteen-year-old Bill Nicholson, substitute left guard, saw his first gridiron action at the Old Line Bowl in College Park, as his teammates slipped and slid on a rain-soaked field, in a 13–0 loss that was, at least, a moral victory for the Shoremen. The offensive line was composed largely of inexperienced freshmen players, like Nicholson. Maryland fumbled 11 times; eight times a Shoreman recovered the sodden pigskin. Legendary Maryland coach Harry C. "Curley" Byrd was not happy. He sat with a look of concern on his face throughout the game, gripping the side of the bench.

Sportswriter Bob Considine, then a decade away from achieving fame as a columnist ("On the Line with Bob Considine") and war correspondent, covered the game for the *Post,* and thought that "[a] multitude of fumbles did more to hold the Terps in check than did the puerile thrusts and gelatin defense of the visitors."

A reporter for *The Enterprise* had a different spin on the day's activities, though, writing of the David and Goliath contest: "An inspired Washington College football team battled the hefty and veteran University of Maryland eleven inch for inch, foot for foot and yard for yard...."

Washington trailed only 7–0 in the fourth quarter, thanks to the punting of its quarterback, Fritz Reinhold. Three times, in the third quarter, the diminutive back punted the ball to the Terrapins' one yard line. Coach Byrd, whose pregame plans were to play his reserves liberally throughout the contest, did not make even one substitution, so fearful was he of being upset by the undersized Shoremen. In an account written for the *Washington Evening Star* by Byrd himself, he submitted that, "Maryland's game was a distinct disappointment; Washington's all that its supporters could desire, and more."

The 1931 Washington College football squad finished the season with a record of 0-9. Nicholson is third from left, third row. "Moxie" Carey is at bottom left; Coach George Ekaitis at upper left; Coach Tom Kibler at upper right. Three years later the team was undefeated (*courtesy Washington College*).

Several admiring Baltimore sportswriters even took to calling the Shoremen the "Mighty Mites," and the "Fighting Midgets."

Local fans were surprised and delighted by the hometown eleven's effort in defeat. Harrison Vickers, a 15-year-old Chestertown High School student, called the local telephone operator late Saturday afternoon to hear the news from College Park. Anticipating another slaughter, he was stunned when Miss Rachel Willis informed him of the score. He insisted she must be mistaken.

The team traveled to Baltimore the next week, to play Johns Hopkins. In the first quarter, quarterback Ollie Robinson threw a 30-yard touchdown pass to his right end, but the play was called back after an official ruled the receiver stepped out of bounds. The Blue Jays made the only touchdown in the game and won, 6–0. The Shoremen dropped two more games to Swarthmore and Haverford, where the Maroons pushed over their first touchdown of the year.

The next Saturday, at the homecoming game against Mt. St. Mary's,

Nicholson made his first start, at left guard. With 90 seconds remaining in a scoreless game and the ball on the Washington 20, Jerry Giraitis—filling in for the injured Reinhold—punted for the Maroons. The ball thudded off his foot, struck Nicholson in the helmet, and bounced straight up in the air. It was covered by the Mount on the home team's 35. A 15-yard penalty moved the ball to the 20; the Mounties scored a touchdown on the very next play and won, 6–0.

In Philadelphia, against Drexel on October 31, an injury-depleted Washington squad lost, 44–0. Their opponents' offensive line outweighed the Shoremen defensive front by an average of 20 pounds per man. Losses at Albright, 49–6, and a 25–0 shutout at Susquehanna followed, a game quarterback Robinson was forced to miss because of a bout of pleurisy.

The season finale was contested on November 21 at winless St. Joseph's, before a large crowd at cavernous Philadelphia Stadium. The home team's 20–0 victory was their first in two years, but Nicholson's play was the bright spot in another dismal loss. The *Washington Elm*, the student newspaper, observed: "Nicholson, kicking for the first time and playing his best game of the season, displayed an ability that should prove threatening to next year's foes."

After two and one-half months of spartan training that produced only nine consecutive losses, Bill must have been happy to see the season end. Later he would remark, in describing his preference for the diamond over the gridiron: "Football was alright, but it was awful rugged. You took a beating every Saturday whether you won or not. You were sore for a couple of days."

Years after his football days were over, *The Sporting News* reported that Nicholson thought the game of football inadvisable for baseball players, because it made them muscle-bound and diminished their hitting skills.

An "A" and "B" student in high school, Bill struggled academically during his first college semester, receiving a "D" in English, and a "C" in German, although he did earn "B"s in chemistry and history, and an "A" in his strongest subject, mathematics. He was invited to become a member of Alpha Kappa, a local social fraternity, most of whose members lived on campus. He also played on the freshman basketball team. Residing on the farm, however, Nicholson missed out on some of the social activities in which the other undergraduates participated.

He *was* present for the annual freshman vs. sophomore tug-of-war, held at nearby Brook's Mill Stream on October 19, which was followed by a rough-and-tumble mudfight. The frosh—featuring the 195-pound Nicholson and several football teammates—won the contest handily.

Bill managed to improve his grades during the spring semester. If nothing else, he had more time to study, because there was no daily baseball practice; for the second straight year, the college didn't have a team. After compiling a record of 7-4-1 in 1930, the school's athletic council voted to suspend the sport beginning in 1931, ostensibly because of financial woes and scheduling difficulties. Washington College had played the game as far back as 1870, and fielded a team every year since 1889. The local press mourned the passing of baseball at the school; a columnist for *The Enterprise* predicted that the sport would not be revived, despite the fact that "no other college of the size of [Washington] has turned out more first class diamond prospects."

Instead, Coach Kibler assembled a squad to compete for Chestertown, in the local Chesapeake Bay League, coached by Herbert Usilton. Bill played on that team, mostly in right field. He also competed in a few track meets for the college, as a shotputter. The track team, which had been dormant for several years, was coached by the ubiquitous Kibler, of course.

The 1932 edition of the Chesapeake Bay League also featured teams from Rock Hall, Sudlersville, Church Hill, Barclay, and Cecilton. The season began in the late spring and ran into the summer, and included players of varying ages, from older than forty years down to teenagers. The price of admission to the contests was usually a quarter, or so, just enough for the home team to maintain the field, and supply balls and equipment. Early in the season, the Chestertown team was unable to use the college field, which had been taken over by the newly-formed lacrosse squad, and was badly chewed up. Instead, home games were played at the high school field on Washington Avenue. The lack of adequate fencing prevented the collection of an admission fee from all who viewed the action, but there was no alternative home site.

The league season was 20 games long, and divided into two halves. The Rock Hall entry, boasting a loyal and vociferous fan base, dominated the competition. The team's rabid partisans were, unfortunately, prone to berating the umpires when calls didn't go Rock Hall's way, creating resentment from players and fans of the other teams. This poor sportsmanship was a major factor in the league's demise the next year.

Early in May, Chestertown won its opener against Sudlersville, 4–1. Nicholson, patrolling left field, made several key defensive plays to insure the victory. The team did not fare as well thereafter, but Bill's play was drawing rave reviews from local fans and probably some interest from professional scouts. At the beginning of the season's second half in July, Chestertown upset an over-confident Rock Hall club, 8–7, behind Nicholson's three hits, which included a home run. The game was marred by the boorish behavior of the vocal Rock Hall fans, who continually protested the decisions of umpire W.D. Deringer.

Of young outfielder Nicholson, a prescient reporter wrote:

> The Chestertown nine is undoubtedly one of the weakest in the Chesapeake Bay League but at the same time of all the players in the loop it possesses one in Bill Nicholson who has the best future of all in the game if he continues to improve. Big, strong and fast, he is the best looking prospect to play ball in the these parts since [former major leaguer] Roger Smoot toiled for the Washington College team.... Nicholson is a student at Washington College and when Tom Kibler issues the baseball call next spring he will be among the candidates. He could not be in better hands. With three years of training under Kibler any latent ability he may possess will be brought to the fore. Kibler thinks he has a good prospect in Nicholson and will work to get the best out of him. All signs point to a major league star from Chestertown if Nicholson chooses baseball for a stepping stone to a career.

While he was most comfortable in the outfield, injuries and other circumstances sometimes required his services as a pitcher or infielder. "One time, we had three left-hand throwing outfielders and I was a right-hand throwing outfielder, and we had a second baseman who broke his neck," Nicholson recounted. "We had a shortstop that got married, I think, and went on a trip and I had to play those two positions. Then, we had a third baseman who broke his leg, so I played there, all in one year."

Chestertown was eliminated from league competition in late August, but Rock Hall recruited Nicholson to play center field in some non-league games. The team finished its season in early October with a final record of 27-4, although by that time Bill had returned to college and was focused on the upcoming grid campaign.

When Nicholson, still only 17, returned to campus in early September, 1932, to begin football training for his sophomore year, Ekaitis had assumed the head-coaching duties. Like Kibler, Ekaitis had become a very busy man. Besides his football responsibilities, he taught several courses, including a boxing class, and wrote a football column for the *Elm*.

The opening game against the University of Maryland was scheduled for September 24. Curley Byrd, trying to downplay his young team's prospects for 1932, predicted a gloomy autumn in College Park, including the possibility of an opening game loss to tiny Washington College. No one took him seriously.

Despite their enthusiasm, Ekaitis' gridders proved once again that they were nothing but cannon fodder for the yellow-jerseyed Terrapins, who avenged the previous year's "moral victory" by pasting the Shoremen, 63-0, before 3,500 spectators. A verbose *Washington Post* writer described the Maroons, who trailed, 19-0, after the first quarter, as "woefully weak," observing that: "Maryland displayed its superiority in every department of play, sweeping the invaders off their feet from the very start, and hammering away with a terrific bombardment that ceased only with the final whistle." Wearing uniform number 19, Nicholson started at left tackle on offense, and backed the line on defense. The Shoremen's best offensive drive in the game came in the second half, when they advanced to the Maryland 10 yard line, before a 15-yard penalty took them out of scoring range.

Echoing the *Post* account, *Kings of American Football*, a Terrapins gridiron history, said of the rout: "Washington College returned to its role of doormats for the University of Maryland. [Running backs Ray] Poppleton and Norwood Sothoron had sprinting practice as the Shoremen were buried under an avalanche of touchdowns...."

But the *Diamondback*, the university's student newspaper, paid a backhanded compliment to the outclassed Shore eleven, pointing out that they "accepted the massacre stoically." So confident was Coach Byrd of the impending victory that he didn't even show up for the game; he was scouting the Aggies' next opponent, the University of Virginia, while an assistant coach presided over the carnage.

Seven days later, the Maroons traveled to Baltimore to be vanquished by host Johns Hopkins, 21–0, after surrendering two touchdowns in the opening period. Two thousand spectators viewed the shutout at the Blue Jays' Homewood campus. For the first time, however, Nicholson was inserted at a position where he could handle the ball in Ekaitis' single- and double-wing attack. Said the *Elm*:

> Bill Nicholson is being groomed for the fullback position. Playing his first game last week in the backfield, Bill was a continual bitter pill to the Blue Jays. Defensively, he backed up the line in grand style and consequently Hopkins gained little ground after his entrance into the game in the second quarter. This big fellow also shows great promise of becoming a real plunging back....

Slowly but surely, Nicholson was learning how to play the game. His teammates were not surprised. One, Ellery Ward, recalled: "Bill was a big, husky farm boy, and on a football field he could run over you. He didn't know anything about the game when he first started playing, but he was a quick learner. He was well thought of on and off the campus. Everyone knew he was going to be great."

Feeling comfortable in his new role, Bill helped the team gain its first victory since 1929 on October 8 at Gallaudet College's Kendall Green field, 6–0. The next day's *Post* carried this dispatch:

> Jerry Giraitis and Nick Nicholson, a 17 year old, 190 pound fullback, were the sparkplugs in the Chestertown aggregation's attack. Nicholson waded through a

mass of players from the three yard line for the winning touchdown after Giraitis had gone over, only to be called back when both teams were off-side.

The taste of victory was savory, but brief; the next week the Maroons endured a 51–0 beating from Loyola, at Baltimore Stadium. The Shoremen were down to 24 players, owing to injuries and attrition. A *Baltimore Sun* correspondent contrasted the relative sizes of the two teams by remarking in the next day's edition: "Washington was unable to do anything with the Greyhound line. It was like bouncing off a stone wall most of the afternoon."

The first home game, against Susquehanna, was scheduled for October 22. The day before the game, the student body assembled after football practice to cheer on the coaches and players at a pep rally. Then, they paraded downtown, blocking traffic, before finally disbanding. The next day, the Maroon defense played well, but the offense could not put points on the scoreboard, and a 6–0 loss was the result.

The following Saturday, versus Drexel, the Shoremen were on the short end of a 28–13 score, but Bill pushed over his second touchdown of the year. The *Sun* reporter was impressed enough with Nicholson's performance to call him "the individual star of the game."

The Shore gridders traveled by bus to Emmittsburg to play Mt. St. Mary's the next Saturday, leaving early in the morning. The trip should have taken about three hours. When the bus reached Westminster, however, road construction forced the driver to proceed at a snail's pace on the bumpy shoulder all the way to its destination, where the team disembarked just before the scheduled game time. Trailing, 7–6, with five minutes left in the game, the Shoremen fell apart and lost, 19–6, to a team that hadn't won all season.

Three days later, Franklin D. Roosevelt was elected president of the United States, carrying Democratic Kent County by more than 1,400 votes. The president-elect promised a "New Deal" to a country ravaged by the Depression and looking for new leadership.

Football fortunes at the college in Chestertown were unaffected by FDR's ascension. A journey to winless Haverford, on November 12, resulted in the Quakers' first season victory, 7–6. Haverford hadn't even scored a point, before the hapless Shoremen came to town. When the third quarter commenced, the home team was ahead, 7–0. Then, linebacker Nicholson recovered a fumble on the Haverford 40 yard line, leading to Washington's touchdown drive. But the extra point try by luckless Fred Usilton passed under the crossbar by inches.

The inexperienced Nicholson was still a work-in-progress. When running with the ball, he preferred to bowl over would-be tacklers, instead of using his speed to avoid them. Defensively, he was easily fooled by deceptive ball carriers, because of his aggressiveness. But he was improving, game-by-game.

The next week, St. Joseph's notched its first win of the season, 12–7, prevailing in a sea of mud at Chestertown. A driving rain had begun the day before the game, and there were three inches of water on parts of Kibler Field. Burned by two long passes, the Shoremen trailed 12–0, in the fourth quarter. Then, Nicholson caught a short pass and slogged 20 yards to the St. Joseph's 20 yard line before he was pushed out of bounds. Without provocation, a St. Joe's player slugged him after the play ended, resulting in a 15-yard penalty. With the ball on the five, the Maroons were unable to score until — on fourth down — Bill found an opening off tackle, shed the pursuit, and bulled his way into the end zone for the lone Shore touchdown.

United States Senator Daniel O. Hastings of Delaware donated a silver trophy, to be awarded to the winner of the annual University of Delaware-Washington College football tilt. The first Hastings Cup game was held in Chestertown on November 26, 1932, on a windy day that made passing the football virtually impossible.

The Shoremen held closed practices during the week preceding the game. Ekaitis had the varsity run plays against the scrubs, who mimicked Delaware's offense. Then, the scrubs played defense against newly-installed Washington offensive formations.

On game day, when the Maroons emerged from their dressing room in Cain Gymnasium and clomped across a gravel road to the gridiron, they saw the largest audience ever to witness a Washington College home football contest. Estimated at several thousand, the crowd's size necessitated a delay of the game for half an hour so the auto traffic, pouring into Chestertown from the north, could be accommodated. Temporary bleachers had been erected for the Delaware fans, band, and cheerleaders. Cars lined the field, and the stands were quickly filled. Ticket takers were overwhelmed by the sheer number of spectators, so that many got into the game without paying the 75 cent admission fee. It was the coldest day of the year to date, and some chose to remain in their cars, or huddled together on the sidelines.

Midway through the first stanza, a blocked Washington punt resulted in a safety, and a 2–0 Delaware lead. On the last play of the quarter, another Maroon punt was blocked, and Delaware recovered the ball on the Washington one. The Blue Hens ran the ball over for a touchdown on the first play of the second quarter, but missed the extra point.

From the fullback slot, Nicholson had two long runs from scrimmage, penetrating once as far as the Delaware 20 yard line, but the Shoremen were unable to capitalize, even though Delaware was shut out the rest of the way.

After the 8–0 loss, the *Elm* thought Nicholson to be the "outstanding luminary of the day," citing the bruising fullback's numerous runs "through the Delaware line practically unaided."

The Enterprise was also impressed, holding that Nicholson's performance "topped the play of anyone else on the field.... He was finally given an opportunity to run the ball from a position far enough back of the line to give him a chance to get started. And once started he was hard to stop."

Although the 1932 campaign ended with a 1-9 record, four losses were by eight points or less, and Ekaitis' squad could look forward to continued improvement in 1933. Nicholson was selected by the *Baltimore American* as an honorable mention All-Maryland player, along with four teammates.

At football season's end, Bill joined Kibler's basketball squad. As a 6' 0" backup guard, he saw limited action for the 8-9 Shoremen. There were victories over St. Joseph's, Western Maryland (twice), and Delaware (twice), among others, but a loss to Maryland, 35–27, before 1,200 fans at Ritchie Coliseum in College Park, which evened the all-time cage series between the teams at four games apiece.

Nicholson always downplayed his basketball ability, in the "aw, shucks," manner that epitomized his understated nature: "I was never that good in basketball. I played some. I was on the team, but that was actually a few dark years in Washington College's basketball history. They had very good teams, but for a long stretch before I got there."

A special representative of the Gulf Refining Company visited Chestertown on March 2, 1933. He was a large man, 6' 2" tall and more than 200 pounds. His name was Ira Thomas, and he spoke to an assemblage of students and townspeople in the auditorium of William Smith Hall, Washington College's central academic building. He regaled the audience with several humorous baseball stories and lectured the youngsters in attendance on the evils of alcohol and tobacco.

Besides his employment with Gulf, the jug-eared Thomas had another job, with the Philadelphia A's baseball club. The strapping catcher played on four championship teams for A's manager Connie Mack in 1910, 1911, 1913, and 1914. Thomas was one of Mack's favorites, and after the catcher's retirement from the game in 1916, he accepted a scouting position for the club. Thereafter, he was credited with discovering and signing star players such as Hall of Famer Al Simmons, Jimmie Dykes, "Crash" Davis, Elmer Valo, Babe Barna, Wally Moses, Dario Lodigiani, and "Chubby" Dean.

Thomas likely delivered the same speech in William Smith Hall he'd given to many other audiences over the years. He was a teetotaler, he would tell his listeners, as were teammates Stuffy McInnis, Eddie Collins, Jack Barry, and Home Run Baker, all members of the A's famed "$100,000 Infield." "No one can tell me that the fact of their not being addicted to tobacco or liquor in any form hasn't a lot to do with their wonderfully smooth and steady playing," he would explain. "The nerves of the four are absolutely free from the effects occasioned by the use of alcohol or nicotine."

Whether Bill Nicholson attended Thomas' speech is today unknown, but the lives of the baseball scout and the young college outfielder would intersect soon enough.

After a two-season hiatus, the college athletic council voted to bring back intercollegiate baseball in 1933, and a tentative schedule was arranged. In late March, 36 students attended tryouts, which were delayed by bad weather. In the early going, no one looked particularly impressive at bat, although the *Elm* did allow that Nicholson and fellow Eastern Shoreman Hobart Tignor (from rural Nanticoke) "stepped into a couple of Coach Kibler's offerings for long hard drives." But the elation that had prevailed upon reinstatement of the sport to the college athletic program was soon dampened.

By 1933, the spreading national financial panic had resulted in more than 5,000 bank failures. Just before Roosevelt took office in January, many other banks closed their doors to prevent a run on withdrawals.

So it was that on April 1, just before the start of the season, Washington College cancelled most of its home intercollegiate baseball schedule; athletic department funds were unavailable, having been deposited in a bank that was now closed. A planned three-day trip to Pennsylvania to play Dickinson, Susquehanna, and Juniata was shelved. A revised schedule, including two games against Rock Hall (for whom Nicholson had played the previous season in the now-defunct Chesapeake Bay League), the Baltimore Fire Department, and the Easton town team, was hastily arranged. Admission for home games was set at 25 cents.

Team members could still look forward to Wednesday, May 24, however, when they were scheduled to travel to College Park to play the University of Maryland. After that game, they would complete a doubleheader by bussing over to the District of Columbia's Griffith Stadium (home of the American League's Senators), to face George Washington University, in a game under the lights.

With the school unable to afford uniforms, the Shoremen were clad in castoff jerseys scrounged from the International League's Baltimore Orioles. Accustomed to making do with a tight budget, Kibler had a vast network of friends in high places upon whom he could rely to secure used baseball suits. Well into the 1940s, the Shoremen took the field clad in hand-me-downs.

Early in the season, Washington defeated Delaware at Chestertown, by a count of 4–2. Leadoff batter Charlie Berry, the Shoremen's 5' 7", 155-pound freshman shortstop, hit his first collegiate home run, a third-inning solo shot to deep center field. Nicholson, batting fifth and playing center field, had two RBIs. Junior pitcher J. Warren "Moxie" Carey, a lefthander from Rock Hall, fanned 14 Delaware batters, while allowing only three hits. Carey was to have spent the summer of 1931 pitching batting practice for the Philadelphia Athletics, before a dispute over his eligibility arose, and he was forced to return home. Moxie was considered by scouts to be a professional prospect.

Washington split its two-game series with Rock Hall, winning 5–4 (Carey: 16 strikeouts), and losing, 11–9. After the Baltimore Fire Department game was cancelled, the team beat Easton, 4–0. At Delaware's Frazer Field, on May 20, Ira Thomas showed up, to watch Moxie Carey. With the Shoremen making eight errors in the field behind him, the lefty was saddled with the 5–4 loss.

On a sultry May morning, the team climbed aboard a bus which transported them to the Claiborne Ferry in Talbot County, on which they crossed the bay to Annapolis. Then, they drove on to College Park to meet the University of Maryland. By game time, it was a humid 90 degrees. Burton Shipley's Maryland squad, playing its season finale after a four-game winning streak, was as hot as the weather.

The score was 1–1 in the second inning, after left fielder Tignor's solo home run for Washington. Maryland scored again to lead, 2–1, after seven. But a five-run surge off team captain Carey (who signed a professional contract with the Athletics at season's end) sealed a 7–2 Terrapins triumph. Nicholson was hitless in four trips, though he scored a run and had three putouts and an assist in center field.

The Shoremen clambered aboard the bus, in their sweat-soaked woolen uniforms, and headed for Griffith Stadium to face G.W. With the windows wide-open, Bill and his teammates rode through the steamy late afternoon into the District, gobbling down food and refreshment along the way.

The Senators — who went on to win the 1933 American League pennant, before losing in the World Series to the Giants — had played an afternoon game at the stadium, falling to Detroit, 3–1. After the major league contest there was a band competition, featuring local talent, with the Shoremen and Colonials scheduled to face off at 8:00 P.M. Senators owner Clark Griffith's nephew, Calvin (who later inherited the team and achieved local infamy by moving the franchise to Minnesota in 1961), was G.W.'s star relief pitcher. The team was looking to end the season on a winning note, having evenly split their first eight games.

When the Shoremen arrived at the stadium, they must have been awestruck. This park was unlike any in which they had ever played. Emerging from the dugout, the players gazed out at colorful signs plastered over the outfield fences, advertising local businesses, Lifebuoy soap, Dr. Pepper, and Coca-Cola. Right field — Nicholson's favorite target — was only 328 feet down the line from home plate, though topped by a monstrous 30-foot wall. The ballpark had an odd configuration: its outfield was built around several city row houses and a large tree, because the property owner refused to sell his land to Clark Griffith when the stadium was built. As a result, the fence jutted out at a 90-degree angle in deep center field.

As Kibler's team finally took the field for infield practice around 7:30 P.M., the sky overhead was ominous, and a storm threatened. The weather had turned noticeably cooler. A steady drizzle began, and the conditions soon became slick. Shortstop Berry watched as Kibler hit fungoes to third baseman Al Hodgson. Many years later, he still had a vivid recollection of the evening, and the effect the rain had on the abbreviated infield practice.

"Al had never played on a grass infield before, and Coach Kibler was a great fungo hitter," recounted Berry. "He hit those balls hard, and they started skidding on the grass and they were just eating Hodgson up. I was glad the rains came before the ball was hit to me."

Soon, the skies opened up and the field was inundated; the game was washed out. Washington College's long-anticipated finale, under the lights of a big league ballpark, was cancelled and the intercollegiate season ended. Tom Kibler and a tired group of ballplayers reboarded their bus and traveled back to Chestertown.

Bill spent the summer of 1933 away from Fancy Farm for the first time in his life, working for Baltimore Gas and Electric Company in the city on the "steeple jack" crew, and living with his aunt. It was hot and dangerous work, but paid a lucrative $18.00 per week, at a time when many were still standing in bread lines. He said that working in the city "made me love the farm a lot more."

When Nicholson returned to school for his junior year in September of 1933, he did not rejoin Ekaitis' football squad, for his days at Washington College were numbered. Earl and Bertie Nicholson had always encouraged Bill to consider a career as a naval officer. Several Nicholson ancestors were naval men, some of whom reportedly ran munitions to the Confederacy during the War Between the States. Whether Bill wanted to become a naval officer is unclear; he spoke out of both sides of his mouth on the subject. During his career with the Cubs, he told an interviewer that he "wanted to go to

Annapolis more than anything else in the world. I read Navy books, and I suppose I was as salty a kid as there was in Maryland."

In retirement, however, he told Marge Fallaw: "My folks always wanted me to go, but I don't know whether I was so interested or not." Whatever the reason, in 1933 Nicholson secured an appointment to the United States Naval Academy, through the office of Congressman T. Alan Goldsborough, from Maryland's first congressional district.

Bill was to attend a preparatory academy — the Severn School — for one semester, prior to enrollment at Annapolis in the fall of 1934. Concentrating on his studies during the fall semester of 1933 at Washington, he received an "A" and a "B" in his two mathematics courses, an "A" in physics, and "C"s in economics and public speaking. Instead of playing football, Nicholson worked on his basketball game in Cain Gymnasium with assistant coach "Dutch" Dumschott.

On October 21, Bill — along with about 1,500 other Marylanders — attended the inauguration of Dr. Gilbert W. Mead as the 17th president of Washington College. President Franklin D. Roosevelt accepted an invitation to attend the event, along with Maryland Governor Albert C. Ritchie, and Senators Millard E. Tydings and Phillip S. Lee Goldsborough.

Roosevelt arrived early in the day at Godlington Marina on the Chester River, aboard the yacht *Sequoia*, and was driven up Washington Avenue in a convertible, with the First Lady and local dignitaries. Cheering throngs lined the street, and the procession passed in front of young Harrison Vickers' home, escorted by a detachment of Maryland State Police motorcyclists. The president wore a snappy fedora hat and topcoat and waved enthusiastically to onlookers; Vickers could almost reach out to touch him. Roosevelt was enormously popular in Democratic Kent County, and as the teenager watched, he "thought the good Lord himself had come" to town. Even the nominally Republican black citizens were awed by the chief executive's presence.

Once at the college, FDR was awarded an honorary doctor of laws and presented with a photostatic reproduction of the degree conferred upon President Washington in 1789. After the ceremony, Roosevelt delivered an extemporaneous speech, which was broadcast live over the NBC and CBS radio networks to a nationwide audience. The president did not stay for the football game that followed, an 8–0 defeat (again) at the hands of the University of Delaware for the Hastings Cup, this time before an overflow crowd of 3,000, many of whom had remained after the presidential ceremony.

As basketball season neared, Shoreman basketball prospect Nicholson was described by the *Elm* as "a near two hundred pounder possessing plenty of speed, natural ability and willingness...." Playing primarily as a guard, Nicholson was fifth on the team in scoring for the year, despite departing after the first semester for Severn School, and therefore missing half of the season. The cagers finished with a record of 4-10, victories coming against Delaware (twice), Johns Hopkins, and St. Joseph's. In a 44–33 loss to Maryland at Ritchie Coliseum, Nicholson led the team with 14 points. The school yearbook reported that "Nick dropped seven double deckers through the cords, but his teammates were not so successful."

Bill formally withdrew from Washington College on March 1, 1934, to prepare for admission to Annapolis and a career as a naval officer. He spent several months at Severn, whose curriculum was specifically designed to prepare young men for the rigors of the Naval Academy. Physicals for the 550 projected members of the academy's Class of 1938 began on June 7. Soon afterward, future Ensign William B. Nicholson's naval career came to a premature end.

Earl and Larny had driven Bill to Annapolis, said their good-byes, and dropped him off at the main gate. All that remained before admission was the successful completion of a physical examination. After routine optical tests, Nicholson received bad news. He said he never forgot the doctor's words. "I'm sorry, son," the physician told him, "but you're color-blind. The Navy can't take you, and I'll have to recommend your rejection."

Bill phoned home to break the bad news. Earl and Larny then drove back to Annapolis to transport the would-be midshipman back to Chestertown. The course of his life having now been altered, Bill Nicholson abandoned a budding military career for the simple pleasure of playing ball.

◆ 3 ◆

Return from Annapolis

Intending to re-enroll at Washington for the fall semester, Bill spent the summer of 1934 working on the farm, and playing ball for the town team. The local nine competed against outfits from throughout the Shore, including Tilghman, Goldsboro, and Kennedyville, as well as Dover, Delaware, with Nicholson usually patrolling center field. At the end of the season in mid–August, he owned a .375 average, third-best on the team.

When Bill returned to the familiar environs of Washington College in the fall, football prospects had vastly improved. The college game was entering a new era: rules had changed to encourage passing, and the pigskin had been elongated, making it easier to grip. Ekaitis' team was coming off a 2-6 record in 1933, its best in several years, loaded with experienced upperclassmen anxious to commence the season. Few, though, envisioned the glorious autumn that would follow for the little college on the Chester.

The Maroons held an intrasquad scrimmage on October 6; Nicholson was hampered by what the school newspaper described as a "side injury." But when the team opened the regular season against Gallaudet the next week, Bill was back, scoring two touchdowns in a 51–0 rout. Running out of the backfield with 210-pound Wilbert Huffman (a duo the students nicknamed "The Big Berthas"), he sustained another injury, this time to a shoulder, which limited his playing time.

As an institution for the deaf, the Gallaudet team was presented with unique challenges. The quarterback was unable to call signals, and his teammates couldn't hear them, in any event. Instead, the play was communicated in the huddle by sign language, along with the snap count. Once the players lined up, a bass drum was beaten vigorously on the sideline. The Gallaudet players knew, and felt by vibration, the beat on which the ball would be snapped.

Occasionally, Gallaudet fielded a player who wasn't quite as deaf as his teammates. One year, during a game in which the action was particularly fierce, Washington tackle Hobart Tignor stared at his opponent across the line of scrimmage and muttered, "You son of a bitch!" To his surprise, the Gallaudet player fixed Tignor with a steely gaze and replied clearly, "Don't you call me a son of a bitch!"

After their opening game shutout victory, the Shoremen traveled to Homewood in Baltimore for the annual tilt against Johns Hopkins, whom they had never beaten in football. The Blue Jays were smarting from a 7–6 loss to a tough Lehigh team the previous week.

The game was played on an extremely hot day, atop a dry and dusty field. A substantial contingent of Washington students traveled by boat from Kent County's Tolchester Beach to watch, and cheer for the visitors. Sophomore speedster Gibby Young returned an errant Hopkins pass 102 yards for a touchdown, to lead the Shoremen to a 13–0 triumph. After the game, ecstatic Shore rooters—including some faculty members—tore down the goalposts. A student correspondent for the *Elm* wrote, "Our team may be 'farmers,' but we sure showed them we could plough Hopkins under."

The next week, on a rain-soaked field in Emmittsburg, Young scored on a "Statue of Liberty" play against Mt. St. Mary's, and the Maroons filed into the visitors' locker room tied at halftime, 6–6. Team captain Ellis Dwyer was handed a telegram containing a message of support from the student body. After Dwyer read it to his mates, they found new inspiration for the second half. A triple reverse sent Wilbert Huffman over the goal line in the fourth quarter with the deciding tally. The final score was 12–6, and the Shoremen eleven was now a gaudy 3–0.

A thousand rooters showed up for the homecoming tilt with a rugged Susquehanna eleven. Many sported little red "W"s on which was superimposed "Beat Susquehanna," the brainchild of an enterprising student named Louis Goldstein. The pins sold for five cents apiece, to raise money for cheerleaders' uniforms. Bill tallied the only Washington touchdown, on an eight-yard run, and the contest was stalemated at 6–6 late in the game. With only a few minutes remaining, the Susquehanna quarterback attempted a pass that was picked off by Nicholson, and returned deep into enemy territory. Young's end run put the ball on the Susquehanna five. With the screaming crowd anticipating a Washington touchdown, time ran out, and the game ended in a draw.

Ekaitis' squad rebounded the next week with a decisive 39–14 plastering of Haverford. The Shoremen scored in every period, and Nicholson shredded the Quakers' defense, tallying three touchdowns and converting three extra point kicks. Now, only the December 1 Hastings Cup game with

Delaware stood between Washington and the first undefeated football season in school history.

The Blue Hens entered the contest sporting a 4-2-1 record and were much improved from 1933. The game was tight for three quarters, but Washington maintained a 10-7 lead. In the final stanza, however, the Shoremen piled on 19 unanswered points to win the cup for the first time. Employing the kicking skills he had developed on the Chestertown High soccer team, Nicholson booted a second-quarter field goal of 30 yards, and three extra points. He also had a seven-yard touchdown run in the final period. By virtue of the 29–7 rout, the college concluded the most successful grid season in school annals: five wins, no losses, and one tie. Its opponents were outscored, 150–33, and there were two shutouts.

Nicholson's 50 points made him the third-leading scorer in Maryland collegiate football, and the eleventh-best in the east. He was selected by sportswriters as a first team All-Maryland collegiate fullback and linebacker.

The team was celebrated throughout Kent County for its heroics; three banquets were organized to honor the Shore gridders. Several colleges — Gallaudet, St. John's, and Haverford — even dropped the Shoremen from their 1935 schedules, fearful of being beaten again.

Though he won his letter in basketball that winter, Bill was not a regular on Kibler's 1934–35 squad, which finished 10-6. The team had victories over Upsala, Johns Hopkins, Western Maryland (twice), Mount St. Mary's, St. John's College (twice), Swarthmore, and Delaware (twice).

Nicholson's mischievous streak resurfaced during January, 1935, when he was suspended from school for one week, owing to his participation in an impromptu late-night party at a fraternity house, and once again for unbecoming conduct at a dance held in the gymnasium on March 15. Although the infractions appeared to be relatively innocuous, they probably did not endear him to Tom Kibler. Bill's academic performance for the year declined as well. Nevertheless, he ranked 21st academically, out of a class of 57, at the end of his junior year.

The 1934 college baseball nine finished with a record of 3-8-1, while Nicholson attended Severn School. His return to the team in 1935 sparked the Shoremen to a 12-2-1 mark, and the Maryland Intercollegiate Baseball League championship. Among other opponents, the Shoremen prevailed over Delaware, Maryland, George Washington, and Penn State.

Balmy weather in March enabled Kibler's team to get in several weeks of outdoor training. The season began inauspiciously, however, with rainouts against G.W. and Georgetown in mid-April. In the rescheduled G.W. game on April 24 at Chestertown, Bill tripled and homered, in a 6–5 victory. An early season defeat of Maryland was especially sweet.

The Terrapins were sporting a 4-0 record, having swept a doubleheader from Cornell, and single games from Harvard and Michigan, at College Park. They would go on to defeat Virginia, Virginia Tech, William and Mary, Duke, Navy, North Carolina, and Georgetown before season's end.

A copy of the April 8 edition of the *Diamondback* made its way to Chestertown. A student sportswriter unwittingly provided inspiration for Kibler's team, as he previewed the upcoming Maryland-Washington contest:

> Invading foreign territory for the first time this year, the Shipleymen will meet Washington College at Chestertown in a contest which should provide merry entertainment for the Terps. Last year in two games played, Maryland was victorious on both occasions by the score of 9-3.

With the demeaning article fresh in their minds, the Shoremen battled Maryland evenly through the first six innings. The lead seesawed back and forth; it was 4-4, in the bottom of the seventh, when the Shoremen went ahead for good. Nicholson swatted two triples to help the cause. When a ninth inning rally by the Terrapins fell short, Washington emerged with an upset victory, 8-6. The next edition of the *Diamondback* contained nothing more than a line score of the game.

Days later, however, the *Washington Post* described the mood in College Park:

> Maryland has not completely recovered from the shock of losing to Washington College Saturday. The Eastern Shore delegation was known to be strong, but not that strong. The result will bring a favorable reaction, since one defeat does not spoil an entire season.

Sure enough, in the rematch held on May 15, the Terrapins prevailed by a 7-3 count, despite Nicholson's best efforts. The Shoremen only mustered five hits off Vic Willis, son of a turn-of-the-century National League pitcher by the same name. Three of the hits belonged to Bill. He blasted a solo home run, knocked in two, and snared four fly balls in center, confirming the *Elm*'s opinion that "Bill Nicholson seems to be about the most improved batsman on the local squad."

In a 12-0 slaughter at Loyola in early May, Bill was four for five; Tignor, Nicholson, and Huffman homered in succession in the fifth inning, and Bill hit yet another homer for good measure. A 15-4 clobbering of Mt. St. Mary's on May 25 saw cleanup hitter Nicholson go two for five, as the Shore squad scored four runs in the top of the first inning. Although 1935 school baseball archives no longer exist, Nicholson's final batting average for the year, compiled from surviving box scores, exceeded .400. Louis Goldstein, a teammate on the '35 squad who was destined to become Comptroller of Maryland for more than 50 years, summed up Nicholson's season aptly: "When you had a close game and a man on base and Bill came up [to bat], you knew you were going to make the run."

In the season wrapup on May 29, the Shoremen defeated Mt. St. Mary's, 10–4, to clinch the MIBL championship. Nicholson batted cleanup and ignited a four-run second inning rally that pushed his team ahead, 4-2, a lead it never relinquished. Washington's lone tie came in Chestertown against Washington and Lee, the champions of the Southern Conference. That contest was halted after nine innings, with the score knotted at eight, because the visitors had to make travel connections for their return trip.

Nicholson's performance earned him All-Maryland honors, by unanimous vote of the coaches who selected the squad. His team attracted attention from numerous professional baseball scouts during the course of the spring; one, from the St. Louis Cardinals, had his eye on Charlie Berry. Others were impressed by Hobart Tignor. A scout from the Philadelphia Athletics coveted Bill Nicholson: Ira Thomas.

By 1935, the A's were the doormats of the American League. Connie Mack had disbanded his championship club of 1931, for economic reasons. Gone were such stalwarts as Robert "Lefty" Grove, Al Simmons, and Mickey Cochrane. Nicholson's boyhood idol Jimmie Foxx was unloaded at season's end. In their place, Mack had signed young unknowns with names like Vallie Eaves, Wedo Martini, and Earl Huckleberry. The team's financial woes were well-known; Mack was forced to cash out the equity in his life insurance policy in order to meet the club's payroll in 1934.

Mack's interest in recruiting college players was an about-face from the team's policy during its heyday in the late '20s and early '30s. As recently as 1929, Thomas told a reporter that "the college boys just aren't there any more when it comes to playing ball.... A poor boy who wants to play semi-pro ball in the summer to help him earn his way through college is barred by the big universities, who are all bound up by eligibility rules.... The standard of college ball has gone down very low and the alumni have lost interest." The economic woes of the early '30s changed the minds of Mack and his trusted scout, however.

In the spring of 1935, Thomas convinced Nicholson to sign a professional contract, which was not to take effect until 1936, upon Bill's college graduation. Such a procedure was not uncommon at the time, and was perfectly legal; Moxie Carey had signed a similar deal in 1932 with the A's. Nicholson received a $1,000 signing bonus.

Bill was flattered at being considered big league material, albeit unsure of his aptitude for a ballplaying career. "I should have been thrilled, but I didn't know if I was good enough to play with those guys I had watched all my life," he confided. "Couple weeks later, a Yankee scout [Gene McCann, who offered the sum of $5,000, ostensibly unaware that Bill had already signed with Thomas] came through, but I was just as well not going with them, 'cause they had so many good ball players at that time. I would loved to have hit in Yankee Stadium, though. Being a pull hitter, it was ideal for me...."

After the 1935 college season ended, Nicholson spent the summer playing for a semipro team in nearby Federalsburg. When he returned for his senior year at Washington, he wasn't worried about finding post-graduation employment like some of his classmates; he now had the opportunity to earn a living playing baseball.

College teammate Charlie Berry, who also played football and basketball at Washington, was somewhat surprised by Nicholson's signing and his professional athletic success. He remembered the collegiate Nicholson as an amiable partier, who liked to drink and carouse. He also thought Hobart Tignor was a better all-around baseball player, while acknowledging that Nicholson was a speedy center fielder with a good arm, "who could go get the ball." Not unlike other observers, Berry — who served in the military with distinction during World War II — doubted Nicholson would have achieved baseball stardom had it not been for the war.

During the 1934–35 school year, Bill met Nancy Kane, a statuesque Washington College coed from Perryville, Maryland, who was the daughter of a Cecil County doctor. She became the love of his life. Nancy was a young woman of diverse interests. During her four years at the college (1934–38), she played field hockey and basketball, joined a sorority, and was active in several literary and historical clubs.

Margo Bailey, who was married to Bill Nicholson, Jr., for 13 years and later was elected mayor of Chestertown, did not consider her mother-in-law to be a beautiful woman. But, according to Bailey, Nancy carried herself in a way that attracted others, possessing an enthusiasm and lust for life that was always on display.

H. Hurtt Deringer, a journalist who grew up in Chestertown in the '40s and '50s, thought Nancy to be "a very attractive gal, kind of in the Rita Hayworth style, and quite a person." His portrayal was echoed by Bill's cousin, Betty Beck Welton, who described Nancy as "big, tall, and attractive; rather sexy." There was no question, according to Welton, that Nancy was flirtatious and "interested in the men." Nancy was the antithesis of the Bill Nicholson Welton knew, who was somewhat shy and reserved. Nancy and Bill would play these same roles — she the *bon vivant*, he the homebody — until the end of their lives.

3. Return from Annapolis

His white number 23 emblazoned on his jersey, Bill Nicholson struck a menacing pose in the October 5, 1935, edition of the *Elm*. Excitement was building on campus about this year's football team, and the Shoremen were set to build on the previous fall's success.

Washington kicked off the season at Kibler Field against American University, resplendent in new maroon jerseys, with black shoulders, maroon and black socks, and the traditional maroon pants. The game ended in a 41–14 Washington rout, with all of the victors' points coming in the first half. In the first quarter, Bill broke free on a 50-yard run from scrimmage before he was hauled down by A.U. defenders, and caught a touchdown pass from Gibby Young. He also kicked three extra points.

The next week at Swarthmore, Nicholson scored another touchdown in a 13–6 triumph, although his extra point attempt was blocked. On October 19, before a large homecoming crowd that included 1,000 enthusiastic students from Eastern Shore high schools, the Shoremen eleven faced Johns Hopkins.

Although he did not score a touchdown, Bill had a big game on defense and kicked an extra point in a 10–0 whitewash, as the Blue Jays lost to the Shoremen for the second year in a row. Tignor kicked a school-record 44-yard field goal.

Sporting a 3-0 record, the Shoremen appeared to be on the way to another successful fall. But disaster struck for the Maroons in the Hastings Cup game at Delaware. After scoring the first touchdown in the second quarter on what a correspondent described as "sheer speed and power," Bill limped off the field with a sprained ankle, and was unable to return to the game. Without their powerful fullback and linebacker in the lineup, the Maroons went down to defeat, 33–12.

When Nicholson tried to come back the next week against Susquehanna, he ripped off long runs from scrimmage of up to 40 yards. He was hobbled by the lingering injury, however, and the Shoremen lost, 12–0.

He was unable to play against Mt. St. Mary's; Wilbert Huffman, who'd hurt his knee, sat with him. Ekaitis, deprived of the "Big Berthas," spent the week before the game practicing trick plays to employ against the Mounts, but the Shoremen fell, 19–7. Then, the team sustained another defeat in the season finale, 19–3, at the hands of West Chester State Teacher's College, to finish the year at 3-4.

Despite missing much of the season, Nicholson was again honored by Maryland sportswriters, and was named All-League by the Baltimore *Evening Sun*, along with five teammates. He was also selected as an All-State player, with Charlie Berry and two other Shoremen.

Still recuperating from the foot injury, Bill was unable to practice with the basketball team until January, and saw little action once he recovered. The Shoremen won the Maryland Collegiate Basketball Association title, however, compiling a record of 14-7.

Nicholson's last season of college baseball began in April with two rainouts. Graduation losses left the Washington pitching staff thin, with Ed Evans being the only proven starter. An early season loss to West Chester was followed by wins over Johns Hopkins and Loyola. After three games, Bill was hitting .500 with two doubles and two triples.

The end of April brought a 14-1 drubbing of Delaware, and then successive victories over Western Maryland and Lafayette. Losses followed to West Chester, Moravian, and Dickinson, before the Shoremen triumphed over Mt. St. Mary's and St. John's College. Against Mt. St. Mary's, Bill went three for four, and he socked a grand slam homer against St. John's.

The 7-4 Shoremen headed into the annual contest against Maryland with high hopes for another upset. The Terps were 9-5, having vanquished William and Mary two days before, and would go on to win the 1936 Southern Conference championship. Home team Washington pounded out 19 hits, but six errors afield proved to be the Shoremen's undoing, and they lost, 15–13. Nicholson was four for five in the losing effort, with a double and triple, as a Yankees scout watched from the stands. His counterpart in center field for Maryland was beetle-browed and barrel-chested Charlie Keller, from Middletown. By 1939, Keller — nicknamed "King Kong" — was a member of the New York Yankees, with whom he played for 11 years.

After the loss to Maryland, Washington bounced back by administering a 20–4 drubbing to Loyola, during which Nicholson was a perfect five for five at the plate, including a double and a triple. Ira Thomas was in attendance, no doubt satisfied that the star of the game would soon be wearing the royal blue and white of Mr. Mack's A's. Delaware was defeated, 10–5, followed by losses to Mt. St. Mary's (Nicholson: four for four), and Gettysburg.

In late May, in his final collegiate game, Bill batted fifth and homered in an 18–4 romp over Western Maryland, finishing the season with an astounding batting average of .521. For the year, Wilbert Huffman batted .390, Tignor .373, and Berry .322. Despite their purported lack of pitching depth, the Shoremen managed to post a record of 10-7-1, and win the MIBL title for the second straight time.

The college held "Billy Nicholson Day" before the annual alumni game on Saturday, June 6, at 3 P.M. on Kibler Field. In a ceremony at home plate, teammates presented Bill with a traveling bag, crammed with various clothing and toiletries, in anticipation of his departure for the major leagues.

3. Return from Annapolis

Graduation exercises for the Class of 1936 were held at William Smith Hall two days later. College president Gilbert W. Mead presented diplomas to fifty-six graduates (including a Bachelor of Science degree to William Beck Nicholson), and an honorary doctor of laws degree to white-haired Harry C. "Curley" Byrd, now president of the University of Maryland, formerly its football coach. Hobart Tignor won the Simpkins Medal for being the best all-around athlete in the class. He was headed off to Baltimore for a tryout with the International League's Baltimore Orioles, as was second baseman Billy Rinehart, Nicholson's cousin.

Bill ranked 26th in the graduating class. Beneath his photo in the 1936 edition of the school yearbook, the following was noted:

> The old favorite story of the home town boy who made good at college and became the popular hero comes to life in Billy Nick. Why the folks down town would be perfectly content to see him play a football game with only one teammate — to snap the ball back to him. Of course this is a little farfetched, but his being selected on the all Maryland teams will attest of his prowess. Then too, when he wants to be Bill is a good student.

Proud as Earl and Bertie must have been at seeing Bill receive his bachelor's degree, it would be of little practical use to him in the immediate future. No desk job awaited this recent grad; his new office was Shibe Park in Philadelphia, and a paid internship with the Philadelphia A's baseball club.

4
Mr. Mack and the A's

The wizened old manager watched the newest member of the team taking his cuts in the batting cage. The "thwack" of bat meeting ball resounded in the empty ballpark, and several drives disappeared over the right field wall. Two days after college commencement, accompanied by Coach Kibler, Bill Nicholson was working out at Shibe Park for his new skipper, Cornelius Alexander McGillicuddy, popularly known as "Connie Mack." Bill took no fielding practice because he'd injured his ankle during the alumni game. He received treatment from the A's trainer before his workout.

The next day, the ankle felt better and he shagged flies in the outfield, off the bat of an A's coach. He caught every ball hit his way without difficulty. Taking an additional round of batting practice, the Kent rookie deposited another offering into the street. At the conclusion of the session, Bill settled into his new home away from home: a rented room on Lehigh Avenue, several blocks from the ballpark. The cacophony of North Philadelphia's bustling traffic must have made him at least a little homesick for the tranquility of Fancy Farm.

As recorded in the *Philadelphia Inquirer,* Nicholson's Shibe Park practice was "balm to the eye of Connie Mack, who watched him at close range and afterward pronounced him fit to be assigned a locker...." Besides his $1,000.00 signing bonus, Bill was paid a salary of $1,200 for service to the A's during the remainder of the season. The "Mackmen" were down to twenty players (three under the major league limit), and sorely in need of another outfielder after Emil Mailho was optioned to Atlanta of the Southern Association in early June.

The A's were mired in seventh place in the American League, above only the pitiful St. Louis Browns. The team was en route to a 53-100 finish, which would earn them dead last in the standings for the year. By 1936, game attendance had dropped precipitously because of the Depression and the poor quality of the ball club. To prevent fans who resided on 20th Street (which ran behind the right field stands at Shibe Park) from viewing games while perched on nearby rooftops, Mack had erected what came to be known as the "Spite Fence." This was a corrugated metal monstrosity which added 38 feet to the top of the original 12-foot wall from right to center field, and effectively ended freeloading by neighborhood residents and their customers. Some players enjoyed throwing the ball against the "Great Tin Monster" before games just to disturb the neighborhood, as the sound of horsehide striking tin reverberated throughout the vacant stadium.

Connie Mack had been playing or managing professional baseball teams since 1878. The "Tall Tactician," as he was called, hardly looked like a former ballplayer. Mack stood six feet one inches, and weighed no more than 150 pounds. He had a kindly, but gaunt, face topped by thinning white hair, parted in the middle. No detail attendant to the game escaped his notice. From the dugout, clad in a dark business suit, starched collar and tie, he would position fielders with a wave of his rolled-up scorecard.

Dignified and even-tempered, Mack was always in control. Once, he went out to the mound to remove fiery Lefty Grove from the game. As he held his hand out for the ball, the pitcher glared at him. "Go take a shit!," Lefty barked at his manager. Mack fixed his eyes on Grove and continued to hold out his hand. "No, Robert, you take a shit," he calmly replied.

The 1936 A's were composed of fresh-faced newcomers, and a smattering of veterans who had seen better days. A total of 39 players suited up for the team during the course of the year. Pitchers Harry Kelley and Gordon "Dusty" Rhodes—who would lose 20 games on the season—anchored the pitching staff. Lou Finney, Bob Johnson, Pinky Higgins, and Wally Moses were the offensive stars.

By his own admission, Nicholson was frightened at the prospect of competing in the majors. Despite his batting practice success at Shibe Park, he knew he was overmatched against big league pitching: "[In 1936] I hit against some right tough pitchers and I later hit some of them over in the National League, and I later saw some of them in spring training after I got to the majors a few years later," he explained. "I did very well against them, but they were over my head when I first went up there. I hadn't ... walked up to the plate against guys that threw like they did."

After warming the bench for several days, Nicholson's professional debut came on an unseasonably cool Saturday, June 13, in the second game of a doubleheader against the Cleveland Indians, played at Shibe Park. Paid attendance was estimated to be 5,000, but the temperature and misty rain drove all but the hardiest fans from the stadium by the end of the day. The A's won the opener, 7–3, on the strength of Rhodes' six-hitter.

The second game was a blowout, which the A's eventually lost by a score of 19–1. Philadelphia used five pitchers, who surrendered 17 hits, and the Indians scored in every inning except the last. A total of eighteen Athletics saw action. The game was mercifully halted by umpire Cal Hubbard after the eighth because of darkness.

In the bottom of that inning, with one out and the pitcher scheduled to hit, Mack addressed his rookie outfielder: "Nicholson ... grab a bat! You're hitting for Gumpert!" With his white woolen uniform dampened by perspiration and rain, Bill retrieved a bat from the front of the A's dugout, took his practice swings, and strode nervously to the plate to face Cleveland's Johnny Allen, a temperamental righthander with a live fastball. If any of the few remaining fans missed the public address announcement, they would have been unable to identify the pinch hitter; the A's were the only team in the American League without numbers on their backs.

Allen had come over to Cleveland in 1936 from the Yankees, where he'd enjoyed four successful seasons, and went on to finish the year with 20 wins for the Indians. His 165 strikeouts would be second in the league. Nicholson came to know him well over the next decade.

As he dug into the batter's box and prepared to face the veteran Allen, the rookie's right hand gripped the club so far down on the handle that his pinky overlapped the knob. He managed to foul off Allen's first two pitches, but didn't offer at the third one. Hubbard barked him out, anyway. Bill then made the long walk back to the A's bench, while many of the remaining patrons headed to the exits.

The *Inquirer*'s James C. Isaminger recapped Bill's maiden at-bat in the next morning's edition: "In the eighth inning Bill Nicholson, new outfielder from Washington College, in Chestertown, Maryland, had his major league coming out when he batted for the pitcher, but he fell on strikes," one of Allen's five strikeout victims for the afternoon.

June 13 also marked the big league coming-out for 18-year-old Randy Gumpert, who became a teammate of Nicholson in 1938 at Williamsport in the Eastern League, and 22-year-old Pete Naktenis, a lefty speedballer. The lanky Gumpert, fresh out of a Pennsylvania high school, had pitched batting practice to the A's the previous summer. He had early success in '36, before fading.

"Mr. Mack should never have thrown me to the wolves," Gumpert complained. "I wasn't a Bob Feller.... When I first broke in, I wasn't aware that I was pitching against major league ballplayers. Then, when it started to soak in, I think the nerves took over." Banished to the minors in 1937 after injuring his arm during spring training, Gumpert remained property of the A's through 1938, but ended up in the Coast Guard during the war, not to return to the majors until 1946. Although he enjoyed a fine career, he is perhaps best remembered for a day in May, 1951, when as a member of the Chicago White Sox he surrendered the first major league home run hit by Mickey Mantle.

Naktenis, from Duke University, was not impressed by Mack's managerial abilities. "He should have had someone else run the team," he said. "He was a nice man, but over the hill by 1936." Naktenis spent most of his subsequent career in the minors, where he played against Nicholson in the Eastern League during 1938.

With the Chestertonian in uniform, the A's won four of six games. Despite the fact that he'd batted only once, and struck out, a Kent County newspaper claimed, "Many of the sportswriters attribute the improved playing of the A's outfield to the threat of Nicholson's presence."

After the Cleveland doubleheader, the A's went on the road. Nicholson did not play again until June 24, when he pinch-hit unsuccessfully for the pitcher in both ends of a doubleheader at Cleveland. The A's lost each game. By July 5, after another doubleheader loss to the Red Sox, the A's had dropped 12 games in a row, and Nicholson was hitless in seven trips. The best that could be said was that he was gaining experience against some tough pitchers, including Mel Harder of the Indians, Eldon Auker of the Tigers, Bobo Newsome of the Senators, and Wes Ferrell of the Red Sox.

Mack had a working agreement with the Oklahoma City Indians, in the Class A1 Texas League. The A1 classification was the equivalent of today's Triple A; the next stop before the majors—or, in this case, the next step down. The Indians' regular center fielder, Roy Myers, was recovering from a tonsillectomy, and manager Bert Niehoff needed a replacement. The A's optioned Nicholson to Oklahoma City on July 15, hoping to get him some more playing time, and he joined his new teammates in Beaumont, Texas, where they were in the midst of a road swing.

The Indians were fifth in the eight-team league, trailing Dallas, Houston, Beaumont, and Tulsa. San Antonio, Fort Worth, and Galveston brought up the rear. The Texas League was known as a pitcher's league. The great St. Louis Cardinals hurler Dizzy Dean, who'd spent some time in the Texas circuit, thought the caliber of play was high. "I would like to see some of those screwy American League hitters with the swelled heads and the big averages trying to connect with the smart pitching down in the Texas League," he once told a reporter.

When Nicholson arrived from Philadelphia, the southwest was in the midst of a terrible drought. Oklahoma City topped out at 108 degrees on July

18; it was 120 in Alva. Ten persons lost their lives because of the intense heat, and thirsty cattle were dropping dead near dried up water holes. Staple crops like corn, sorghum, and cotton were ruined, wreaking further havoc on the farmers in the Dust Bowl, whose plight would be depicted three years later in John Steinbeck's classic, *The Grapes of Wrath*. Although most of the games were played at night, the oppressive heat and high humidity must have been difficult to endure, even for a Maryland farm boy.

The Indians' roster featured several colorful characters, some with major league experience. They included Paul "Pound 'Em" Easterling, a Texas League All-Star. The 30-year-old Georgian hit .325 for the Detroit Tigers eight years before, and would have two hits in seven times up for Mack's A's in 1938, before his major league career abruptly ended. Pitcher Dick Whitworth was a brakeman for the Southern Pacific Railroad, when he wasn't hurling the horsehide for the Indians. Niehoff, the popular manager, was a lantern-jawed 52 year old, who'd spent time as an infielder on four National League teams during the 'teens.

On a stifling July day, Nicholson made his first minor league appearance, in a 13–6 win over Beaumont. The Exporters featured several future major leaguers on their roster, including catcher Birdie Tebbetts and outfielder Roy Cullenbine. Batting eighth and playing center, Nicholson had two hits in four trips to the plate.

The next day, Niehoff moved Bill up to sixth in the order, and he responded by singling, in another win over Beaumont. After two hitless games, he was two for four in a loss to the San Antonio Missions, driving in a couple of runs.

Barely hitting .200, Nicholson returned with his new teammates to Oklahoma City the day after the Texas League All-Star game, to face the San Antonio Missions. Fifty five hundred packed Holland Field, at 4th Street and Pennsylvania Avenue, to watch the Indians sweep a doubleheader.

With the thermometer touching 100, Bill mustered a hit and knocked in a run in the first game, but was blanked in the second. The correspondent for the *Daily Oklahoman* described Nicholson in the next day's edition as "the new Tribal outfielder who looks good but isn't delivering at the plate...."

At the end of July, the homestanding Indians ran off six straight wins and vaulted into third place. Though Nicholson wasn't producing offensively, Niehoff was nonetheless optimistic. "He hasn't been hitting well because he's new to the lights and trying too hard, but he'll come through," the skipper reassured a reporter. "Just wait until he has had a little more experience. He's a little nervous now, but he keeps his eye on the ball and is taking a good cut."

Soon, Nicholson's spirited play was recognized by the *Daily Oklahoman*, when it ran his picture on the first page of the sports section, under the heading "Our 'Nickie,'" with this caption:

> Whenever a young player steps into the lineup of a ball team, and that team begins to win, the young man must be a pretty fair hand. That has been the experience of Bill Nicholson, new outfielder of the Indians. This is his first bit of organized ball and he isn't knocking down the fences, but he is hustling, and the Tribe is winning with him in the lineup. Which is what really counts.

Defensively, his work was not shabby. Bus Ham, the Indians' beat writer, wrote that the youngster "gets over the ground with a bounding stride, has chased down several blows carrying extra-base tickets, and his throwing arm is strong and true."

Only a couple days later, however, Carl Kott replaced Nicholson in left field. After Kott hit three singles and a triple and reached on a walk against the Houston Buffs, Nicholson was permanently consigned to the bench. His pinch-hit strikeout on August 2 turned out to be his final at-bat in an Oklahoma City uniform.

The Indians were scheduled to leave on an extended road trip, to begin in Dallas on August 10. In 112-degree heat, they defeated the Tulsa Oilers, 10–6, in the final game of a homestand. With the return of the tonsil-less Roy Myers to the lineup, there was no need for a light-hitting outfielder on the upcoming road trip. To save money, Nicholson was sent packing, back to Philadelphia. For Oklahoma City, Bill batted .167 in 48 at-bats. He had no extra base hits.

The A's were in Boston for a series against the Red Sox. Bill stopped off in Chestertown as he prepared to rejoin the team. He complained to the home folks of his difficulty adjusting to night baseball, and attributed his failure at the plate to the artificial illumination.

Returning to the A's, Nicholson's frustration was amplified by the ineptitude of the team for which he played. On a muggy August 15 afternoon, the overmatched A's lost, 16–2, to the mighty Yankees (featuring future Hall of Famers Joe DiMaggio, Lou Gehrig and Bill Dickey, among others) before a small crowd at Shibe Park. Bill batted again for Randy Gumpert in the ninth and struck out, this time against Monte Pearson.

John Drebinger of the *New York Times* wrote the next day that the "woeful Mackmen ... stumbled and fumbled their way all over the field." Despite the heat, Drebinger thought Connie Mack "seemed to wag [his scorecard] with more fervor than ever." Unfortunately, the cardboard was "incapable of stopping a fly ball, putting over a strike, or doing anything else his agile mind would dictate."

Nicholson made his first major league start on August 30, against Detroit, in the second game of a doubleheader. Hitless in two trips to the plate against Tommy Bridges, he reached on an error and scored a run in a 3–2 loss. For the year, Bill appeared in 11 games for the A's, and went to the plate 12 times, striking out on five occasions without getting a hit. Although his playing time was limited, he had the privilege of learning at the feet of the master Mack.

"I'd sit on the bench, and he would talk to me," Bill explained. "And then years later, when I went with the Cubs, we played in an exhibition game and I sat in the hotel and talked with him. He was 74 [years old] in 1936.... I liked him very much. He was a shrewd operator, I'm sure, and he ran his ball club completely. He'd set up there in the dugout and he would move his outfielders and move his infielders, and of course he had coaches who coached his pitching staff and this, that, and the other. And he built great teams. He built great teams a couple of times, and sold them off and started from scratch again. I don't think he ever got the third one. He never got the third great team."

From Mack, Nicholson learned how to play the hitters, and how to get a jump on fly balls: "Just keep your eye on that hitter. And that hitter's bat tells you where you can get a terrific jump on fly balls. Like a righthand hitter hitting one clear down in right field where he would ordinarily pull the ball to left field. Hit one down that corner and I'd catch up with 'em, catch up with all of 'em."

Jess Hill, who played outfield for Mack in 1937, was equally impressed by the old man's knowledge of the game. "Not until I played for Connie Mack did I really learn the art of outfielding," he told an interviewer. "I have been catching more of those line drives in the three months I have played for Connie Mack than I caught in an entire season for Washington and the Yankees...."

Bill Werber, who came to the A's from the Red Sox after the 1936 season, was also impressed with Mack's managerial abilities. "He was a very considerate manager," Werber explained. "If you made a mistake, he didn't bawl you out in front of everyone like [Werber's manager with the Yankees, Joe] McCarthy. After the game, he would tell the clubhouse boy to get you, and bring you into his office. Then, he'd tell you what you did, and ask, 'Next time, will you do it your way or my way?'"

After returning to Chestertown in late September, 1936, Bill spent four-and-a-half months helping out on the family farm. Despite an inauspicious inaugural season, he was invited to spring training with the A's, in Mexico. Ever the penny-pincher, Mack had wangled a deal with the Mexican government to put his team up in Mexico City for the preseason, on the cheap.

Pitchers, catchers and rookies reported several weeks ahead of the rest of the team. Nicholson departed Chestertown for Philadelphia on February 15. The A's train left the North Philly station late in the evening, three days later. Their Pennsylvania Railroad coach arrived in St. Louis on the 19th, where the players transferred to a Missouri Pacific sleeper that took them to Laredo, Texas. From there, the Mexican National Railroad carried them to Mexico City. Upon disembarking at 10:35 P.M., they were serenaded by local musicians.

The veterans, including Werber, who reported later, received no such welcome: after crossing the border into Mexico, while still on board the train, someone stole his cleats and baseball gear.

Because no major league team had previously trained in Mexico, the press devoted extensive coverage to the A's. Connie Mack was even pictured in a zany wire service photo, uncomfortably clad in sombrero and serape, while several players danced around him, under the caption "Connie Mack Goes Latin."

The A's went right to work the day after arriving, reporting to the spacious Parque Delta, where they would train and scrimmage. A herd of sheep and mules had to be escorted out of the playing area by the Philadelphians before practice could even begin. The stadium was in good shape, but center and right fields were vast. Any ball hit over an outfielder's head stood an even chance of resulting in a home run.

Connie Mack was detained in Philadelphia on business, so his son Earl and coach Lena Blackburne directed the initial practice sessions. There was plenty of running in the early going; at the altitude of 7,349 feet, the workouts were grueling. Several other college boys were in camp: Floyd "Eddie" Yount, a righthanded-hitting outfielder from Wake Forest University, and Clarence "Ace" Parker, from Duke University, were chief among them. Parker had just completed his junior year, and begged Mack to take him to training camp. Impressed by Ace's last college season (.347 average, 14 home runs), Mack relented and brought him south of the border. Parker started in right field for much of the exhibition season.

Yount played well throughout late February and early March, but Bill had not yet found his stride. Mack usually sent him into the games around the sixth inning, as a substitute for "Indian" Bob Johnson, in left field.

The *Elm* reported several weeks later on Nicholson's progress:

> Down in the land of chile con carne and the Mexican hairless dog, Bill is knocking the boards off the right field fence with bulletlike drives from the big bludgeon he swings from the left side of the plate ... Nicholson, thus far, has earned the title of "outstanding recruit," conferred by all of the experts that have seen him work.

Clarence "Ace" Parker, Floyd Yount, and Nicholson (left to right) at spring training, Mexico City, 1937 (*courtesy Philadelphia A's Historical Society*).

Others painted a different picture, however. Sports columnist Red Smith wrote in 1953, upon the occasion of Nicholson's retirement from baseball:

> He impressed nobody in training camp. Connie Mack sat on the bench watching him in the batting cage. "Can't understand that fellow," Connie muttered. "He broke the fences down in college." One afternoon, Nicholson and some companions motored to Teotihuacan and climbed the Teocalli, the big pyramid of the sun, and the altitude made Bill's nose bleed. Except for that small incident one might easily forget that he'd been a member of the squad.

Sixty years later, Werber had no recollection of Nicholson even being in camp.

There being no other major league teams south of the border, the A's played primarily against Mexican and Cuban teams. There were games virtually every day, but on Sundays they started early, to accommodate the bull fights scheduled for the afternoon. "Nobody went to the ball game when the bull fights were on, so we played eleven o'clock on Sundays ... eleven o'clock in the morning," recalled Nicholson. "We rooted for the bulls," Werber said.

The A's stayed at the L'Escargot Hotel outside Mexico City, which had

The young flycatcher poses for this publicity shot, 1937 (*courtesy Philadelphia A's Historical Society*).

comfortable accommodations, according to Werber. But several team members came down with ailments attributable to the water and the altitude, including star hurler Harry Kelley, who returned to the States to recover. Even Mack experienced medical difficulties. Just before the team broke camp, he was hit in the right shin with a foul ball. An infection resulted, requiring his hospitalization in San Antonio for several days. Werber had the foresight to purchase a Spanish grammar book before camp, and many of the ballplayers sought him out before going to the restaurants, or other events. When they couldn't understand what was being said, he told them to ask the speaker to slow down: "*Senor, mas despacio, por favor!*"

Mexico was becoming a baseball hotbed, and there were several teams who competed well against the major leaguers, including the "Comintras," a government-sponsored all-star team that beat the A's several times in early games. Many of the Mexican squads featured black players from Cuba, several of whom were quite good.

On Sunday, March 28, just before departing for Texas, the A's were scheduled to play the Mexican All-Stars in Mexico City. When the All-Stars failed to show, a substitute team from the Ford Motor Company played in their stead. They were easily dispatched by the A's, 13–3. Nicholson had a home run, among the 15 A's hits for the afternoon.

As the team barnstormed north by train, Bill saw playing time with the "B" team. He did well against various minor league squads throughout Texas, Arkansas, and Tennessee. The A's departed from St. Louis on April 9, and arrived the next day at North Philadelphia Station, just a few blocks from Shibe Park. There, they played several games against the Phillies, in which Nicholson did not appear.

Disappointing news came on April 14, when Bill was informed that he'd been optioned to the Williamsport Grays, of the Class A New York–Penn League. Upon hearing of the young outfielder's demotion, an inquisitive reporter asked Mack, "Think he has a chance to come back?"

"Oh, you'd be afraid to let a fellow like that get away from you," was the old man's reply. But the Tall Tactician, to his later chagrin, did let Nicholson get away.

In Williamsport, Nicholson began a minor league odyssey that lasted more than two years, riding the buses and trains for hours on end, and playing night games in poorly-lit parks, hoping for the chance to return to Shibe Park. His peregrinations took him from Williamsport to Portsmouth, Virginia, back to Williamsport and then to Chattanooga. Optioned to the minors three times by Mack, he played nearly 400 games, before his sojourn ended with a train ride to Chicago, on July 31, 1939.

5
Life in the Bushes

When Bill Nicholson reported to Williamsport's Bowman Field on April 19, the Grays were already in their third week of spring training. It didn't take long for him to attract the attention of the local media. A sportswriter for Williamsport's *Gazette and Bulletin* declared that the "husky young flychaser ... impressed observers with a sparkling display of both offensive and defensive skill."

Player-manager Ollie Marquardt, a 35-year-old second baseman with major league experience, expected Nicholson to man left field, in a platoon with Floyd Yount, who had also been optioned by the A's. According to this plan, Nicholson would start against righthanded pitchers, and Yount against southpaws.

The Grays were feted at The Lycoming, a local hotel, on the evening of April 21. Club owner James J. Gleason and assorted dignitaries attended the affair; the players were introduced after a speech by the mayor. Baseball fans in this city of more than 54,000, situated on the Susquehanna River, eagerly awaited April 29, when the season would begin with a contest against the Elmira Pioneers. The Grays were still the only game in town; Little League Baseball, now synonymous with the city, would not be founded until 1939.

During the last week of April, heavy rains inundated Pennsylvania, and the Grays repaired to the gymnasium at a local seminary to train. On the 24th, the team bus set out for Johnstown, destined for a two-day exhibition series against the Johnnies, a St. Louis Browns farm club. The trip was a disaster.

First, the Grays' motor coach broke down, and a rickety school bus was hired to take the team the rest of the way. Cold, damp weather forced cancellation of the first game after ten innings, with the score tied at three. On the bright side, Nicholson blasted a home run in his exhibition debut. The next day's contest against the Johnnies wasn't played because of the inclement weather, though, nor was the game scheduled against Lock Haven State Teacher's College.

The day before the season opener, the Grays were finally able to practice on Bowman Field, though the infield was soft and mushy. In an effort to beautify the park, the Works Progress Administration (WPA) provided labor and money to repair the field, paint the stands and scoreboard, and put up new advertisements on the outfield fence.

A parade through downtown Williamsport, featuring the local high school band, signaled the start of Opening Day festivities on April 29. Three thousand fans were expected to view the game on a cool, damp day. The marching band swung by the high school, and the student body followed on foot to the ballpark, where the youngsters were admitted for free.

Bill and his teammates ran onto the field to festive cheering, sporting their white flannel uniforms, with blue pinstripes, a large red "W" on the left breast, and blue and red stockings and caps. After a flag-raising ceremony in center field, the mayor threw out the first ball. Unfortunately, that was the highlight of the day for the home team, as Elmira pitcher Lew Krausse cruised to an 8–1 victory. Bill batted fifth and went hitless.

When the Grays lost again, 10–6, the next day, Nicholson sat on the bench until the seventh inning. He popped up weakly in a pinch-hitting appearance, and then relieved Yount in left field. Two days later, trying to score from third base, Bill was hit in the head by an infielder's errant throw. He fell to the ground, momentarily unconscious, but was revived quickly, and appeared in the next day's game.

Not until May 5 did he finally shine, in a win over the Trenton Senators. Hitless going into the game, his booming two-run homer in the eighth secured the victory and provided a much-needed boost to the young outfielder's confidence.

He followed that performance with another clutch performance on May 9, pinch-hitting a two-run single in the bottom of the seventh, that led to a 12–9 defeat of Elmira, for the Grays' first home win of the year. The next day, he was two for three in a 12–1 loss to the same team, raising his season average to a humble .217.

Just a day later, however, team secretary J. Roy Clunk announced that Bill Nicholson had been released on option to Portsmouth, in the Class B Piedmont League. With a record of 5-7, in fifth place, the Grays badly needed pitching, and the team was "pretty well filled up" with outfielders, according to Bill.

So, on a day when the Spanish Civil War raged, and the lowly A's temporarily gained sole possession of first place in the American League, Bill Nicholson packed his bags and headed to tidewater Virginia, the third stop of his still-brief minor league career.

The Portsmouth Cubs played in the eight-team Piedmont League, at rickety Sewanee Stadium. They were owned by bespectacled Frank D. Lawrence, a local entrepreneur. When Bill arrived on May 12, he was welcomed by player-manager Elmer "Rabbit" Yoter, a wiry ex–major league infielder who'd been searching for a competent center fielder to help his seventh-place squad, losers of four straight games. The Cubs were led by power-hitting left fielder Larry Melville and lefthanded pitcher Harry Brecheen.

In his first game, against the third-place Rocky Mount Red Sox, Nicholson made an auspicious debut, banging out three hits in four trips: a single, double, and triple. The Cubs ended their losing streak with an 8–3 triumph.

After the game, Burke Hewitt, the correspondent for the *Norfolk Virginian-Pilot* observed:

> Nicholson comes from Chestertown, Md., close to the little town where Jimmy [sic] Foxx and Frank Baker, big league heroes, were born. From the looks of Nicholson yesterday it appears as if the area will soon produce another heavy major league slugger.

Within a week, the Cubs had climbed to fifth place, and evened their record at 14-14. During a victory over the Charlotte Hornets on May 21, Nicholson had a homer and three RBIs, to complement Brecheen's work on the mound.

The next night, Bill homered again in the first game of a doubleheader, won by the Cubs. In the nightcap, a wild 14–14 tie suspended by the Sunday blue laws, he hit one more four-bagger, going five for nine on the day.

The Cubs held Ladies' Night on May 22, before 3,000 fans, who were heartened by the team's 10 victories in its last 12 games. This time, Bill bashed a homer in the third inning, helping to defeat the Asheville Tourists, 5–2.

Besides Brecheen, several other 1937 Cubs would eventually play major league ball. They included brash infielder Eddie Stanky and Hank Camelli, a stocky catcher from Massachusetts, who was battling an intestinal illness in May that caused his hospitalization. In his absence, substitute backstop Charlie Schupp was playing behind the plate.

In the second inning of an 11–4 loss to the Winston-Salem Twins, Schupp was hit in the head with a pitched ball thrown so hard that it rebounded into the wire protecting fans in the grandstand. The catcher stayed in the game for awhile, but had to leave two innings later with a headache.

Camelli, recently released from the hospital, was watching the game from the press box. After Schupp's departure, the Cubs were catcherless, so Camelli came down to the field, dressed and caught the remainder of the game. Although he'd lost 15 of his original 190 pounds during the illness, Hank managed to sock a three-run homer, with Nicholson on base, in the sixth inning.

Nicholson was not yet the slugger he would become, but was now playing with confidence. Left fielder and cleanup hitter Larry Melville garnered most of the long ball headlines during the season. Melville hit what was described by the local paper as the longest home run ever hit at Sewanee Stadium on June 3, in a 12–4 win over the Twins. Bill also smacked a two-run shot, in the second inning, to help the slumping Cubs, who'd sunk back into seventh place.

The long bus rides in the Piedmont League took their toll on the players over the course of the season. "Sometimes we'd play a night game in Richmond," explained Bill. "And the next afternoon we'd play in Asheville, North Carolina. Sometimes we just got there in time to get to the clubhouse, put on our suits, and go right out onto the field. Riding and sleeping all night."

Nicholson was, nonetheless, becoming used to the traveling and the pitching. Experiencing his first prolonged period of minor league success, the game had again become enjoyable. In one contest, Bill even caught four fly balls for outs — in a single inning. "The third one was ruled interference [by the catcher], and the batter was given his base," he recounted.

The players looked forward to the homestands, and took advantage of humid Portsmouth's proximity to the Atlantic Ocean whenever possible. "[W]hen we were home I went down to the beach all the time, Virginia Beach and, one stretch we had, several of us got a little cottage down there. My God, it wasn't much money, you know, to get a little cottage. We just had a little shack," Nicholson recalled.

By June's end, the team rose to fourth place. On the 29th, Bill's three-run homer in the seventh helped defeat Rocky Mount, 9–4. The Cubs even managed to beat the Norfolk Tars for the first time in 1937, after a raucous holiday game on July 4. The Tars played their home games at Bain Field, just across the Elizabeth River from Portsmouth, and the teams maintained a fierce rivalry that was often stoked by spirited fans.

Tars manager Johnny Neun was tossed from the Independence Day game, after arguing with popular umpire "Boots" Crowley, a colorful Notre Dame grad and Shakespearean scholar. Twenty-five hundred patrons were on hand, and more than a few of them took umbrage with Crowley's decision to boot the local manager. When the contest ended, Boots and Al Barlick — the field umpire — left the stadium under a police escort, and fans hooted and jeered them as they got into their autos to drive away.

After an 8–3 win over the Richmond Colts on July 7 — in which Bill hit a solo homer into the right field bleachers at Sewanee Stadium — the Cubs were only two games behind second-place Norfolk. Frank Lawrence, sensing his boys had a legitimate chance of winning the Piedmont League pennant, was trying to lure hometown hero Ace Parker from the Southern Association's Atlanta Crackers, where he'd been optioned earlier in the year by Connie Mack. Besides being a valuable player, Lawrence knew Ace would be a box office draw. He'd grown up in the Portsmouth area, where he was an outstanding high school athlete, before going off to play football and baseball at Duke.

While efforts continued to land Parker, the Cubs floundered, slipping to fourth place in mid–July. Norfolk's righthanded screwballer Norman Branch gave Portsmouth batters fits, and he shut them out on July 17, 6–0. Nicholson had one of only four hits for the Cubs, a smash struck so hard that it literally tore the glove off the hand of Tars first sacker Lank Levy.

Within a week, however, the Cubs climbed into second place, behind the Asheville Tourists, by virtue of a doubleheader sweep of Charlotte. Lawrence rued a new development: Ace Parker had been called up to the A's from Atlanta, and would not be returning to Portsmouth any time soon.

Nicholson had the biggest day of his year on July 31, pounding three home runs in a 12–2 slaughter of the Tars, at Bain Field. Brecheen came on in relief of Lefty Donovan in the third inning to claim the victory for the Cubs. The *Virginian-Pilot* reporter was awed by Bill's heroics at the plate:

> His three big blows were titanic swats, two rattling against the stovewood beyond the center wall and the other king of them all, whistling above the right field wall on a bee line. He also hit a single and wound up with a perfect day at bat, four for four, including two walks. He scored four runs.

The Tars got even the next day, with a 6–5, ninth-inning win behind pitcher Hiram Bithorn, Bill's future Chicago Cubs teammate. Trailing, 4–3, in the top of the ninth, a two-run Nicholson homer put Portsmouth ahead, 5–4, but the Tars came back to win in the bottom of the inning. The Cubs nevertheless maintained their second-place standing. Then, Nicholson homered again in the first game of a doubleheader sweep of Charlotte.

Al Schacht, the "Clown Prince of Baseball," entertained the crowd of 4,000 with his zany antics before the next day's game, and even announced the first inning play-by-play over the Sewanee Stadium loudspeaker. Schacht, who was the Boston Red Sox third-base coach the previous year, had retired from organized baseball to become a full-time comic. He was typically attired in a top hat and tails, to go with his baseball pants, socks, and cleats. His act was so popular that within a year he was netting $8,000 for his efforts, much more than he would have earned for serving the Red Sox.

Brecheen won his 15th game, by a 15–5 count, and Nicholson smacked his sixth home run in four days. But pennant hopes faded while August dwindled. Even as Frank Lawrence obtained Ace Parker from the A's, with less than a month to go in the regular season, Portsmouth had sunk to third place.

Parker had a grand start with Connie Mack's club, striking a home run in his first major league at bat, but was now batting only .117 for the seventh place A's. Of the local hero, Lawrence insisted: "Because he comes back to Portsmouth is no indication that he will not make the grade in the major league, but only that he was not ready this year."

In the fall, Parker began what became a Hall of Fame pro football career, with the Brooklyn Dodgers of the National Football League. He hit .230 in 1938 for Mack's A's, but never made it back to the majors, though he played in the minor leagues through 1952.

August 16 was "Ace Parker Night" at Sewanee Stadium, and nearly 3,000 turned out to witness a 5–4 loss to the Rocky Mount Red Sox. In the first inning, Nicholson made a spectacular running catch of a fly ball at the center field wall, then relayed to Stanky, who threw to first to catch the baserunner off the bag for a double play. In the next inning, Bill made another fine catch. Parker was hitless in three trips.

The following evening, however, Ace homered to help beat the Red Sox, 4–2. A newspaper account noted that Sewanee Stadium shook to its foundation, so boisterous was the cheering for the local hero, after his circuit clout. Brecheen notched his 18th season victory. Then, days later, Parker hit a pair of four baggers, earning $10.00 from Portsmouth's city manager, who had a standing offer of $5.00 to be paid to any Portsmouth player who hit a home run. Ace hit his fourth homer in less than a week on August 22, as the Cubs beat Richmond.

Bill learned of his selection as an honorable mention Piedmont League All-Star on August 28, losing out to Kelly Holmes of the Norfolk Tars for first team laurels among center fielders.

When Brecheen earned his 20th win against the Durham Bulls on August 30, 3–1, fewer than 100 spectators were in the stands, and Asheville clinched the pennant a week later. The Cubs' playoff series began against Norfolk on September 14, but it didn't last long. The Tars whipped their cross-river rivals in three straight. Crowds exceeding 3,000 showed up for each contest. Bill was three for four in the first game, with a solo homer, but wasn't much of an offensive threat thereafter.

Connie Mack sent for Parker and Nicholson, so they could finish the season with the parent club. The two reported to the A's after the conclusion of the Piedmont playoffs, but Bill warmed the bench, and never played for Mack again. Still, his Portsmouth performance—.307 average, with 20 home runs — proved to the A's front office that he could compete when given the chance, and boded well for the future.

After a two-year courtship, Bill and Nancy married on December 28, 1937, while she was on a semester break from her senior year at Washington College. The ceremony was held at St. Mark's Protestant Episcopal Church in Aiken, Cecil County, attended only by family members and close friends. Bill's older brother, Albert, was his best man. Afterwards, Dr. Kane and his wife hosted a breakfast for the bridal party, before the newlyweds departed by auto for a brief honeymoon. They returned to live in a small apartment in Chestertown, and Nancy resumed her studies at the college. Based upon his Norfolk performance, the A's decided to return Nicholson to Williamsport for 1938, which was a promotion.

New manager Marty McManus got his first look at the team at their spring training site in Raeford, North Carolina, in early April. The New York-Penn League had been rechristened as the Eastern League. Nicholson and teammate Art McHenry were being counted on to provide the offensive power for the '38 Grays. After beating Kinston of the Coastal Plain League, 7–1, in a late April exhibition game, the team won 14 of 15 games, and there were high hopes for an Eastern League crown.

When the Grays went north from training camp, Bill found lodging at a boarding house in town, next door to Randy Gumpert; he paid $10.00 a week for room and board. Gumpert recalls Nicholson, during this stage of his life, as a good-natured teammate, "happy-go-lucky," but not a drinker or hell-raiser. He was a "wild swinger," according to Gumpert, and his league-leading 97 strikeouts (in 560 plate appearances) attested to that fact.

More than two thousand fans were present on April 27 to watch an opening day loss to Elmira, 6–5. As frequently happened throughout his career, Nicholson was slow to warm up at the plate. But in late May, during a game against the Hazleton Mounts, he swatted a 400-foot home run over the right center field wall that was described as the longest ever hit at the Mounts' park. It cleared the fence on a line drive, with plenty of room to spare.

McHenry, who'd played in the New York-Penn League since 1929, was shipped off to Portsmouth on May 20, but big Babe Barna returned from a pulled leg muscle to bat in the cleanup spot, behind Nicholson. Bill went on a hitting tear to raise his average 100 points — from .288 to .388 — in the space of five weeks in May and June. Though his team languished in seventh place, 10 games below .500, Nicholson was now the fans' darling: "closest to the hearts of the roaring throngs," as a local newspaper characterized him. Five hundred miniature bats, autographed by Bill Nicholson, were given away to children, accompanied by an adult, who came to the June 19 home game against Albany.

Bill impressed not only offensively, but defensively, too. Reporting on a fine fielding play he made early in June, a correspondent wrote:

> Fans are inclined to regard Bill Nicholson as just a ho-hum defensive man in the outfield, but after that sparkling catch in deep center Monday night they'll probably have a different idea from now on. Bill's build makes you think he can't run, but he can really step. That's why he's in center field.

He was batting at a .368 clip on June 15, and leading the league in home runs (12) and runs scored (43). Three days later, Nicholson struck a tremendous drive to right center field, in the third inning of a game against Albany. As the ball crashed into the fence to the right of the scoreboard, a loud report could be heard. Albany outfielder Tony Cotille nevertheless insisted he'd caught the ball on the fly. An argument followed, lasting nearly 10 minutes, after which Nicholson was finally called out by the umpire.

The Albany manager, not content with this favorable ruling, then complained that during the Senators' turns at bat, the Grays' bat boy was replenishing the supply of game baseballs with previously discarded ones. The umpire inspected some of the balls and — apparently agreeing with the Albany skipper — threw a number of them out, while the home crowd booed.

Nancy graduated from college in June, 1938, and soon joined her husband at the rooming house in Williamsport. It was probably lonely for the young bride much of the time: during the season, the Grays traveled more than 5,300 miles, by bus, in a little more than four months. The long road trips took their inexorable toll on Nicholson. His batting average plummeted, until he was down to .304 on July 20. A couple days later, Albany's southpaw Pete Naktenis — who debuted with Nicholson and Gumpert on that rainy June 13, 1936, for Connie Mack's A's — struck out 15 Grays in a 6–1 victory. Bill fanned twice, and every batter who faced the lefty whiffed at least once.

Though he raised his average to .313 on July 27, Nicholson slipped under .300 a week later. A local columnist, who was impressed with Nicholson's speed afoot, had a novel suggestion:

> Bill Nicholson legs it down to first base so fast and is so adept at bunting it seems to a lot of fans that he could easily jump his average 50 points by bunting in the second slot.... The practice would sharpen his batting eye and maybe bring him out of the heartbreaking slough to which he has fallen. It's worth a trial.

The crowning achievement of his season came on August 24, when the local Knotholers Club gave out 100 four leaf clovers to fans, before the game. That evening, for the only time in his career, Bill hit for the cycle: a single, double, triple, and homer. But the season ended disappointingly for the Grays in mid–September. They finished in sixth place, out of the playoffs, which were won by Elmira. Nicholson led the league in home runs with 22, and total bases (280), to go with a .303 batting average and 96 RBIs. Defensively, he paced the circuit in putouts with 305, and tied for fifth among outfielders with 13 assists. He was chosen as an "honorable mention" Eastern League All-Star, along with seven teammates, including Barna, Gumpert, and McManus.

It was a virtual certainty that Bill would get another look from the A's in 1939, but he prepared himself for the possibility that he would not. If he failed to stick with the parent club out of spring training in 1939, it would mark the third time he'd been optioned to the minors, and make him a free agent. He had given baseball his best effort, but was determined to leave the game for another pursuit if he wasn't playing in the big leagues by the end of '39. Early in the year, the Nicholsons learned that their first child would be born in September, providing further incentive for Bill to find a career doing something, somewhere.

"That was my last year, 'cause I was quitting if I didn't get to the majors after that year," he said. "I had plenty of options, I guess.... I'd graduated from college and I majored in ... mathematics. I got A's all the way through college in mathematics."

The Chattanooga Lookouts, of the Class A1 Southern Association, were one of minor league baseball's storied franchises. They were owned by colorful Joe Engel, a former major league pitcher and innovative promoter, alternatively known as the "Barnum of the Bushes," and the "Baron of Baloney." His stunts were legendary: he sold stock in the team on city street corners; dressed up as Napoleon; and held animal races before games, all in an effort to put fannies in the seats. Engel held an "elephant hunt" in center field; he dressed a dozen black Chattanoogans in skimpy attire, to stalk the pachyderms, while hunters with rifles shot blanks into a dummy elephant. The two live elephants who participated in the zany promotion were unharmed. The show drew 15,000 fans to the park, 3,000 above capacity.

On another occasion, Engel offered Dizzy Dean $10,000 to join him in a fist fight at home plate, after the pitcher reneged on a deal to participate in an exhibition game to benefit a poor children's Christmas fund.

Engel had recently purchased the team from Senators owner Clark Griffith; in no time, he obtained Nicholson and $25,000 from the A's in exchange for outfielder Dee Miles. Connie Mack came to regret the trade. He later told Engel: "Joe, I had never seen Nicholson, and they tell me now I made a mistake letting you have him." Having spent six weeks with Bill in

Mexico City a couple years before, it is difficult to fathom how Mack could say he'd "never seen" him; perhaps the old man simply forgot. After Nicholson had become an established National League star, he ran into Mack before an exhibition game. During their conversation, Mack acknowledged, again, his error in letting the slugging outfielder slip through his fingers.

As the newest Lookout, Nicholson earned $250 a month. It was said that the money Engel received upon acquiring and later selling Nicholson kept the club financially solvent for several years.

Engel roomed with the great Walter Johnson, while the two were playing with the Senators. "People used to wonder at our close friendship — said we were so different," he recalled. "Walter didn't drink or smoke and was more or less on the serious side. I liked my fun and as a youngster was something of a hell-raiser. But we just clicked."

In recent times, the Lookouts had not been as successful on the field as they'd been at the gate. In fact, for the past five years, no Chattanooga manager had successfully avoided being fired before the season ended. Determined to reverse this course of events, Engel revamped his team for 1939. Some of the players who reported to player-manager Kiki Cuyler at training camp in Sanford, Florida, were familiar to Nicholson. Hank Camelli, the ironman catcher — who'd come down from the press box to hit a home run with Portsmouth in 1937 — was there. So was Stan Benjamin, from Western Maryland College, against whom Nicholson played in the MIBL.

Bill, who battled weight problems throughout his career, did not report to camp in fighting trim. Early in training, Camelli defended him to questioning reporters. "Nicholson is not swinging well yet, because of a sore side," Hank explained. "Wait until he gets in shape. You are not sure he is fast? I'm telling you, he can fly. He is much faster than you see him here. And wait until you see him, when he's in shape, during the season, come racing home on a close play!"

When the team participated in its first workout at Engel Stadium on April 5, Bill hit two balls out of the park. Viewing early training sessions, however, skeptical columnist Wirt Gammon, writing in the *Chattanooga Daily Times*, expressed his disappointment with Nicholson's defense and speed. "Nicholson has yet to show he is up to Southern League fielding standards. He is still seven or eight pounds overweight," he told readers on April 9.

But Bill won him over several days later during an exhibition victory over the St. Louis Cardinals. Playing right field, he robbed Ducky Medwick of an extra base hit with a one-handed catch in the second inning. "[O]ne of the finest catches ever seen here.... He's okeh out there after that one, and he is still powdering the ball," the now-converted Gammon asserted. Nicholson finished the exhibition season with a .297 average, though he drove in only eight runs in 64 at bats.

The Lookouts opened the season at Ponce de Leon Park against the Atlanta Crackers, losing, 7–1, before more than 15,000 patrons. Two days later, Bill's two-run homer in the third, off Pete Stein, was all Chattanooga needed for a 2–0 victory. One newspaperman described the home run clout as a "Herculean wallop."

With war clouds hanging over Europe, Engel — ever the promoter — commandeered the loudspeaker system at Ponce de Leon, and entertained the fans with this diatribe during the game: "Transatlantic operator ... this is Joe Engel talking from a hick town in Georgia.... I want to talk to a guy who is screwier than I am ... Adolf Hitler!... You meet me at home plate in my ballpark opening day, and I'll punch you in the nose!"

The Lookouts returned home for their first game of the year at Engel Stadium. The park had been constructed in 1929 at the site of the former Andrews Field on East Third Street. It had a seating capacity of 12,000, and what some said was the deepest centerfield in the history of the game — 471 feet to the wall. In left center, there was an inclined stretch of grass with the word "Lookouts" spelled out in bold white lettering. The stadium even featured a delicatessen, and a barber chair to which shaggier patrons could repair during the game for a shave and haircut.

The players donned white jerseys with the team name emblazoned on the front in red, and matching sleeves that made the tops look like vests. Before the home opener, Engel placed this advertisement in the *Daily Times*: "I'm not making any predictions. All I'm saying is: 'Watch our smoke!'"

The only promotion on Opening Day was an appearance by the American Legion Drum and Bugle Corps. But before the next contest, there was a pigeon race. Nicholson had three home runs after seven games, and businessman Engel was already shopping him around. "I'll take $50,000.00 for Nicholson now and not say another word," he told a reporter. "That Brooklyn park [Ebbets Field] is built for him."

Life in the Southern Association was an improvement over Oklahoma City, Williamsport, and Portsmouth. The travel was easier and the accommodations were finer. "You stayed at the good hotels in the Southern League, the better hotels in the towns like New Orleans, Birmingham, and Atlanta," Nicholson recounted.

The team usually traveled by train, and not bus. "We played cards and ate in the diner ... we generally always had a lounge car and we played cards," he continued. "Most of the times in the Southern League, why you were very seldom on the train in the day time. You generally got on at night and go to the next city, and then you'd get off the train and go on to the hotel."

The Lookouts floundered through early May. They sat in eighth place on May 2. As Chattanooga prepared to take on the league-leading Knoxville Smokies that evening, big news came out of New York: Lou Gehrig had ended his 2,130 consecutive-game streak, as journeyman first sacker Babe Dahlgren took his place in the Yankee lineup. Dahlgren and rookie outfielder "King Kong" Keller homered, as the Gehrig-less New Yorkers clobbered the Detroit Tigers, 22–2. Gehrig never played in another regular season game, and, two years later, died of the disease that now bears his name.

Behind Nicholson's three-run homer over the *Chattanooga Times* sign in right field, the Lookouts edged the Smokies, 4–3. In the 10th inning, Bill nailed an opposing baserunner, trying to advance from second on a fly ball to right, with a perfect throw.

Two days later, he tossed another runner out at the plate, tripled, knocked two singles, and drove in four in a 10–5 win over Little Rock. On the occasion of the Lookouts' third consecutive win, this time against Little Rock in 11 innings, Wirt Gammon wrote of Chattanooga's newest star:

> And there you have the star of the game, the man who stars every day, the man who thrives on publicity. The more you write about him, the harder he hits a ball, and goodness knows he swings hard enough now to fell an ox.

The team took its fifth in a row on May 7, in a doubleheader sweep of Memphis, to pull within a half-game of Knoxville. Over the course of the streak, Nicholson was batting at an incredible .700 pace, with 14 hits in 20 at bats. Engel watched from the press box, occasionally dancing, throwing hats and cushions, all the time singing Nicholson's praises.

After Dick Lanahan's no-hitter on May 9, Bill was hitting .392, with six homers and 20 RBIs, and the team had taken seven in a row. The streak reached 11 games before ending with a 5–0 shutout loss to the Birmingham Barons. Chattanooga was now atop the Southern Association standings. Someone figured out that, during their run, the Lookouts had played 84 straight innings, without trailing their opponents.

Despite the team's present showing, Engel — always conscious of the bottom-line — complained about the lack of support at the gate. He must have been heartened, therefore, on May 26, when 14,500 passed through the turnstiles, including 6,000 members of the Knothole Gang, to see a 4–3 victory over the Little Rock Travelers.

To build his fan base, Engel had started the Knothole Gang, for students aged 10–14. To sustain their membership, the youngsters had to maintain a sterling attendance record in public and Sunday school. The group enjoyed great popularity, and helped create a new generation of Lookouts fans.

On the day of the Little Rock game, all mothers of the Knotholers were admitted to the game for free. They led the children — a microcosm of the city's youth — into the park. There were boys dressed in their Sunday finery, while others arrived in caps and overalls. All were treated to a fireworks display before the game. Player/manager Kiki Cuyler even filmed the ceremonies with his motion picture camera.

Nicholson — the hero of many of these boys — treated the crowd to another of his offensive displays. He had three hits, including two doubles, and scored the winning run in the eighth inning with a rolling slide, through the mud, all to the children's delight. Yet another scoring slide, in the fourth inning, was "one of the greatest we ever saw," according to Gammon.

The highlight of the game for the Knotholers occurred in the seventh inning, though, and had nothing to do with Nicholson or his teammates. As rain began to fall, a group of boys suddenly ran onto the field and began to romp around. "...[O]ne little colored boy in snowy white shirt and trousers thought it would be fun to run the bases," Gammon wrote in the next day's paper. "This he did, while the crowd gave him loud applause." Soon, others followed suit, until the grounds were awash with rain-soaked Knotholers, having the time of their lives, slipping and sliding on the field. After a brief delay, order was restored and the game continued.

While the Lookouts chased their first Southern Association pennant since 1932, Chicago Cubs owner and chewing gum magnate Philip K. Wrigley was canvassing minor league rosters for a new outfielder. Wrigley inherited the National League franchise several years before, from his late father William Wrigley, Jr., a popular and generous owner who was beloved by players and fans alike. But the younger Wrigley was not his father, and would come to preside over the gradual demise of the team, despite a pennant-winning season in 1938, and another in 1945.

If nothing else, Phil was proud of his ballpark, Wrigley Field, at 1060 West Addison Street on Chicago's North Side, and spared no expense in furnishing it. He wanted fans to enjoy the stadium's amenities, regardless of the quality of the baseball being played by the home team. To that end, there were brightly-colored pennants fluttering from atop the roof, and seats that were close to the action. In 1937, outfield bleachers and a modern scoreboard in center field were constructed. That same year, 350 Japanese bittersweet plants and 200 Boston ivy plants were purchased to adorn the outfield walls, the first appearance of the greenery that is now synonymous with Wrigley Field.

Transportation to the games was efficient and affordable. Buses and street cars stopped at the park's entrance, and an elevated train ran half a block away. For patrons who chose to drive, parking lots were large and conveniently located. As long as the team was profitable, losing baseball — while not encouraged — would come to be implicitly tolerated by the management.

To boost attendance, Wrigley popularized Ladies' Days, on Fridays, when the fairer sex gained admission to Cubs games at reduced prices. Wrigley correctly deduced that many females would enjoy the contests, and bring their father or boyfriend to the game the next time.

Several major league scouts who frequented Southern Association games had zeroed in on 24-year-old Chattanooga outfielder Bill Nicholson. The Brooklyn Dodgers were interested in signing the free agent, but Chicago had an inside connection: Lookouts manager Kiki Cuyler had patrolled the Wrigley Field outfield for the Cubs from 1928–35. Cuyler had worked diligently with Nicholson, spreading out — and slightly opening — his batting stance. This prevented Bill from lunging at offspeed pitching, which he was wont to do, and made him a more consistent hitter against lefthanders.

Wrigley sent scout Jack Doyle south to look at the young outfielder. But Dodgers general manager Larry McPhail also dispatched his scout, Andy High, who wrote in a report to McPhail: "Has a chance to be a great hitter." This, in turn, prompted Larry to travel to Chattanooga to see the young Marylander for himself. Other teams also sent their scouts to see the Lookouts play, in late June. There were "Chief" Bender of the A's; Hank DeBerry of the New York Giants; Hank Sevareid of the Cincinnati Reds; and Jimmy Hamilton of the International League's Buffalo Bisons. Clark Griffith was also interested in Nicholson; he sent his top talent evaluator, Joe Cambria.

Nicholson's teammates benefited from the interest in him. The play of Stan Benjamin and Babe Barna was also noticed, and the former was signed to play for the Philadelphia Phillies before the season ended. Barna and Nicholson were neck-and-neck for the team home run lead in the early season. At a Shriners luncheon in late June, Cuyler called the two sluggers, "[O]ur powerhouse pair. I refuse to put one before the other."

There are two disparate accounts as to how Nicholson ended up signing with the Cubs. The first was offered by McPhail. In that version, having satisfied himself that Nicholson was a prospect, McPhail approached Engel, and they agreed in principle to a deal that would bring Bill to the Dodgers for $15,000. Then, Engel received another offer, which he couldn't refuse: Wrigley would pay him $35,000, and a player to be named later, for Nicholson. Engel begged McPhail to let him out of their "gentleman's agreement."

The Brooklyn general manager described the scene, and how a future star got away:

> Engle [sic] practically wept. He is operating on a shoe-string.... He wore me down and I told him he'd better make the Chicago deal. Nicholson isn't worth anything like $35,000.00 to us. He isn't ready and we have ball players in the minors who'll be ready ahead of him.

In the second version, recounted by Brooklyn scout Ted McGrew, McPhail called him while he was in Milwaukee. "Stop whatever you're doing, and dash down to Chattanooga. There's an outfielder I want you to see, a fellow named Nicholson," McPhail ordered.

McGrew headed for Tennessee. Just as he arrived at the ballpark, Nicholson hit a home run. Later in the game, he hit another one, and then a double. The portly McGrew bowed to the other scouts, including Doyle. "Gentlemen," he said. "This is a pleasure. I'm glad to see so many of the scouting fraternity here together. I hope you haven't been wasting too much time because McPhail has Nicholson all locked up."

Knowing the Cubs had no chance to outbid Brooklyn for the outfielder's services, McGrew invited Doyle to dinner that evening. "You can't get the player, Jack," offered McGrew, "but you might as well get a dinner out of your trip." Doyle accepted the invitation, but said he first needed to wash up at the hotel. Unbeknownst to McGrew, Doyle surreptitiously called Wrigley from his room and told him Engel would part with Nicholson for $35,000. "Buy him," Wrigley commanded. Doyle thus got his man, and a free dinner, to boot, if this story is to be believed.

Wrigley's account was consistent with McGrew's. "Kiki Cuyler phoned me about this Nicholson," Wrigley said. "He said he had written several letters to Manager Gabby Hartnett about him and had received no answers. So, after he told me how good Nicholson was, I sent a scout down to Chattanooga and later we bought him."

Bill laconically recounted the manner in which he learned of his promotion: "Well, I was at Chattanooga, and all the major league clubs had lots of scouts in the stands. They said most of them were looking at me; I don't know. Well, anyway, I thought I was going to go to Brooklyn, but went home one day and on the radio I heard I had been sold to the Chicago Cubs."

The $35,000 purchase was the most expensive in the history of the Southern Association. When Engel saw Doyle a day or two later, however, he was kicking himself. "I should have gotten $65,000 for him," the Lookouts owner moaned. "Listen, if you want to call the deal off...," he continued. Doyle politely declined Engel's invitation.

Under the terms of the agreement, Nicholson was to report to the Cubs later in the season, but not past August 1, as the Lookouts were short on outfielders. Chicago offered several substitutes, including regular right fielder Jim Gleeson, but all were rejected.

After being officially informed of the deal on June 25, Bill was hitless in five trips, in a doubleheader sweep of the Memphis Chicks. The next day, though, he celebrated by hitting two home runs and a double, driving in four, as the Lookouts beat the New Orleans Pelicans, 6–2, before a "Men's Night" crowd of 11,077. For payment of only a 15 cent "service charge," 10,162 men crowded Engel Stadium, cheering lustily for Nicholson every time he appeared on the field.

Nicholson's clutch hitting did not abate. In the second game of a doubleheader against Birmingham, the Lookouts trailed 5–4 in the ninth, with two out, and two men on base. Alpha Brazle — who'd already lost the first game — was hurling for the Barons. According to an Associated Press dispatch, the Chattanooga fans "looked yearningly toward home plate as big Bill swung his bat. He hit a homer," and the game ended victoriously.

At the end of June, Nicholson was pounding the ball at a .365 clip, to go along with 14 home runs and 59 RBIs. Only two players were hitting for a higher average, and none topped his homer and RBI totals. In a stunning development, however, the Southern Association baseball writers, selecting the league all-star team, omitted Nicholson from the squad. The *Memphis Commercial Appeal* correspondent, David Bloom, didn't think Bill was worthy of all-star consideration, at all. He pointed out that the Lookouts outfielder had only one hit in Memphis and asked: "When is he going to show me something?"

But Bloom's voice was drowned out by a chorus of fans who thought Nicholson's omission was a senseless snub. Acceding to popular sentiment, the league bent the rules and added him to the roster a few days later.

The All-Stars played the league-leading Memphis Chicks on July 6, before a crowd of 9,000. Nicholson started in right field, but was hitless, and popped out with two runners on base in the ninth inning, to end the game. Paul Richards, the manager of the Atlanta Crackers, was still impressed. "He is the best player in this league," Richards insisted.

The Lookouts, who had been in first place since May 29, dropped into second on June 18, and slowly descended the Southern Association standings. Despite the powerful slugging of Nicholson and his roommate Babe Barna, the pitching was shaky. Most upsetting to Engel, attendance was still lagging. "That hurts my pride," the owner lamented. "It makes me feel like getting out of baseball here."

Near July's end, Chattanoogans realized the star outfielder would soon be gone. Before Bill's last scheduled home appearance on July 23, an Engel

Stadium employee warned a local baseball writer: "You had better tell the people to come out and see him Sunday. They will never see him again in the minor leagues."

In his final home appearance, during a doubleheader against the Nashville Vols, Nicholson poled his 23rd four-bagger in a first-game loss. Between the contests, he was honored by his teammates, who presented him with a traveling bag. His hair plastered down with sweat, Bill stood at home plate with a big grin on his face, as he watched the ceremony. The club also gave him a watch, and singer Frankie Mason, from Chicago, sang a song about him over the loud speaker. Fans tossed more than $100 in cash into a barrel under the grandstand for their hero's use. Almost five thousand fans exhausted the concessionaires' food supply before the start of the second game.

Nicholson was touched by the kindness shown to him by the Lookouts' fans, telling Wirt Gammon: "Say, don't you write all this stuff and forget to thank those people who have been so nice to me!"

A local sportswriter named Will Shepherd paid tribute to the departing outfielder in the *Hamilton County Herald*:

> He radiated confidence among the fans. ... [and] proved himself to be a great team man.... He never walked out to his position in right field. He ran. He never walked in to the dugout from his position in the outfield. He trotted in. He did not lean on his bat, but caused his big bat to lean against many balls that landed out of the park.

Nevertheless, there was skepticism among Cubs scouts and manager Gabby Hartnett about whether Nicholson was ready for big league pitching, especially the lefthanded variety. Wrigley overruled them.

For his part, Engel laughed all the way to the bank. Shirley Povich wrote in his *Washington Post* column on July 3 that the owner had turned a $60,000 profit on Nicholson:

> When [Washington Senators owner] Clark Griffith sold the Chattanooga club to Engel, he had his choice of two players then with Chattanooga ... he chose Second Baseman Jimmy Bloodworth and Outfielder Dee Miles and then turned Miles back to Engel ... Miles was sold by Engel to the Athletics last winter for $25,000 and a player in exchange ... the player was Bill Nicholson ... two weeks ago Engel sold Nicholson to the ... Cubs for $35,000 and a player to be delivered later....

Though he missed the last month and a half of the Southern Association season, Nicholson still led the league in home runs (23), total bases (242), and slugging percentage (.632) at the end of the year. When he left them, the Lookouts were in fourth place. His much-lamented departure, however, may have had some beneficial effect, as it spurred his teammates to finish the season atop the Southern Association standings.

6

Back to the Big Leagues

Bill arrived in the Windy City by train on July 31, while the Cubs were playing their minor league affiliate Moline in an exhibition game. Among other news, the morning's *Chicago Tribune* detailed the Germans' plan to overrun Poland. A round-trip flight from Chicago to Seattle cost $160.00, "with complimentary meals aloft." Men's shirts were on sale at a haberdashery on Michigan Avenue, for $1.75. The fourth-place Cubs were imploding, and clubhouse problems — some centering around Hartnett — had surfaced.

Pitcher Larry French was in Hartnett's doghouse. This apparently occurred because French made it known that he preferred to have Gus Mancuso catch the games he pitched, instead of Hartnett. So miffed was French at the treatment he was receiving from Gabby that he paid a visit to Phil Wrigley to vent his anger.

After the Moline game, a still-smoldering French was asked by a photographer to pose with Hartnett, on the way to the train station; he refused. "I feel I can pitch winning baseball, but if the Cubs don't think so I'll be glad to try for some other club," French told reporters.

This spat wasn't the only team problem. *Prima donna* pitcher Dizzy Dean missed the train back to Chicago from Moline, and a taxicab had to intercept it several blocks away, so Dean could board; he was apparently taking a bath in his room at departure, and didn't notice the time. It wasn't the first and it wouldn't be the last occasion on which Dean's behavior would become a distraction to his teammates.

When Bill Nicholson arrived in the Wrigley Field locker room on the morning of August 1, the clubhouse attendant handed him a zipper-fronted flannel Cubs jersey, white with a blue "C" in front, and number eight on the back. A patch on the left sleeve commemorated the celebration of baseball's putative 100th anniversary. Over his sanitary socks, Bill pulled on blue stirrups, with three red stripes and white trim on the bottom, over which came sliding

Having recently arrived from Chattanooga, new Cub Bill Nicholson poses with his Louisville Slugger, 1939 (*courtesy Emily Joiner*).

shorts and white pants with blue piping. After putting on his blue cap with a red "C," he stepped onto the field that was to be his home for the next nine years. Posing for several photographs, including one on the dugout steps with Dean, he talked with reporters, before taking the field. The Philadelphia Phillies were to provide the day's opposition.

With a wad of Beech-Nut chewing tobacco stuffed in his cheek, Nicholson held forth with the writers in the dugout about his forthcoming Chicago debut. "They tell me it's just as easy to hit in the majors as anywhere, if you can hit," he allowed. "I've never played up here, you know. Sat around on the bench for a while with the Athletics last year, that's all. I want to get in there and take a few cuts at this major league stuff."

As game time approached, the mercury hovered near a muggy 90. Seven thousand two hundred ninety shirt-sleeved patrons awaited the opening pitch, including Phil Wrigley, who had attended only a few games that season. Wrigley's relationship with his players stood in stark contrast to that of his late father, who lionized team members.

Nicholson found it curious that Wrigley was so distant. "One time I was going after a fly ball at Wrigley Field, the sun field, right field," he explained. "One of my hinges snapped on my glasses when I flipped them down.... Well, I caught the ball anyway. After the game [Wrigley] sent word for me to bring my glasses up and he'd fix 'em. So that's my only dealing with him. He didn't come to the games very often. They say five or six times a year, so he wasn't very interested in baseball at that time. Later on, they say he got interested in it."

Former Cubs infielder Don Johnson had the same feeling about his employer: "When I joined the Cubs ball club in September of '43, the general manager Jim Gallagher took me down for a luncheon at the Wrigley Building, and introduced me to Mr. Wrigley. Gallagher said to him, 'Mr. Wrigley, this is your new second baseman.' And he kind of looked at me and said 'hi' and then he walked off. I didn't understand that. That was the only time I met Mr. Wrigley."

Wrigley had a rationale for his seeming indifference to the team's plight. "I have only so much time to spare for baseball," he explained. "I can't do the team any good out there watching them play. But I am working from my office to find replacements for the team. That's the reason I haven't seen the boys play a single game this season."

Moments before the start of Nicholson's inaugural game, the beleaguered Hartnett entered the Cubs' dugout, looking around anxiously. "Lose something?" asked starting pitcher Dizzy Dean.

"No, just checking up to see if anyone has gone to see Mr. Wrigley," cracked Hartnett, in obvious allusion to French's recent expression of discontent.

Finally, from his chair next to the backstop, public address announcer Pat Pieper — whose other job was *maitre d'hotel* at a popular restaurant near the ballpark — intoned the starting lineups in his customary fashion. "Tin-shun please! Have your pencils and scorecards ready and we will give you the correct lineups for today's ball game!" After introducing the Phillies, he presented the local team by number, name, and position: "Six, Hack, third base; Four, Herman, second base; Seven, Galan, left field; Nine, Leiber, center field; Eight, Nicholson, right field...."

The next day, the young outfielder's picture appeared in the *Tribune* over the subhead, "Rookie Nicholson Hits a Homer." Reporter Irving Vaughan's characteristically sarcastic *precis* of the day's events follows:

> Mr. Jerome (Dizzy) Dean heard the siren call of the medicine men again yesterday. Mr. Dean, making his first start in six days and apparently getting along nicely, suddenly decided his $185,000 right arm was in no mood for work. So Mr. Dean retired and his Cub mates were so crestfallen over his misfortune that they went on a hitting spree which smothered the eighth place Phillies 6 to 2 in the series opener.

Of Nicholson's Windy City debut, he wrote:

> Another day's development in the Cub family ... was the appearance of Bill Nicholson, who finally arrived from Chattanooga. Bill was dressed up as a right fielder and given a bat. He caught the few fly balls aimed into his territory and put his bat to such profitable use that he notched a homer [into the right field stands, off Kirby Higbe] for the Cubs' sixth run of the afternoon.

After an August 2 rainout, the Cubs beat the Phils again, 9–6, behind Nicholson's three hits (two of which were triples) and two RBIs. The next day, in a 1–0 victory over the Boston Bees, Bill's bat was silent, and he muffed a fly ball in right. With the game on the line in the eighth inning, however, he crashed into the wall to rob Al Simmons of an extra base hit. The *Trib* reporter said Nicholson "pulled it out of the climbing ivy without regard for the brick wall immediately behind the foliage."

Collisions with the right field wall would become *de rigueur* for Nicholson: "I jumped up in the vines and rattled off that concrete wall, but you only do that once in a while, and you get jarred up pretty bad and I got back there and felt that warning track.... And you slow up a little bit.... And sometimes, the game is at stake and it's one of those borderline ones and you still rattle off that wall."

Right field in Wrigley was a "sun field." The Cubs of Nicholson's era played all their home games in the daytime, and the afternoon sun shone almost directly into the right fielder's eyes. High fly balls were visible, but balls hit on a line were problematic. "Yeah, one year I made three errors, and they were all on sun, balls that got in the sun on me and I stayed with them and they hit me," Bill said. "They might even have hit my glove, but I didn't see them. I knew where they were, but I didn't see them. I knew they were right at me or I had to move a couple of steps. You can tell, when you play it every day, when that ball leaves the bat, where it's going to be."

Bill's eighth-inning single knocked in the deciding run in a 3–2 victory over the Boston Bees on August 5; the next day, in a 9–8 loss, he singled, doubled, and tripled. After five days with Chicago, he was hitting .381, with three singles, a double, three triples, and a home run.

The Cubs took 11 of 15 games by August 24, and Nicholson was the catalyst. Skeptical Hartnett was still wary about Bill's ability to hit lefthanded pitching, though, and was not averse to pinch-hitting righthanded Carl Reynolds for the rookie when necessary.

The North Siders climbed to within seven games of first-place Cincinnati on August 27. Nicholson was batting .323, with 20 RBIs in 93 at-bats. By comparison, team RBI leader Rip Russell had driven in 61 baserunners in 404 at-bats.

After Larry French — having patched things over with the manager — won his fifth straight start, over the vaunted Cardinals, 11–3, the team was within 2½ games of second-place.

The Cubs participated in a Larry McPhail–inspired experiment on September 17, in the first game of a home doubleheader with Brooklyn. The Dodgers general manager was granted permission to use special yellow baseballs, which some thought would be easier to see and hit. Nicholson certainly had no trouble hitting them, going two for four with a double, even though the Cubs lost. The next day, Bill became a father. William Beck Nicholson, Jr., known as "Billy," was born back home in Maryland, while his dad stayed in Chicago and prepared to play against the Dodgers.

The team was mathematically eliminated from pennant contention, after a 4–2 loss to Carl Hubbell and the New York Giants at Wrigley on September 20. Against the lefty screwballer, Nicholson bounced to second base three times, before being removed for a pinch hitter.

Chicago briefly reclaimed third-place from the Dodgers on September 27, after a doubleheader sweep over the Pirates. In the first game, Nicholson homered, as did his counterpart in right field, the aging future Hall of Famer Paul Waner.

The regular season ended on October 1, with a 2–1 win over second-place St. Louis. Bill drove in both runs with singles, as Chicago finished in fourth, 13 games off pennant-winning Cincinnati's pace. Despite the club's disappointing 1939 campaign, Nicholson's .295 average and 38 RBIs in two months whetted the appetite of Cubs fans starved for a power-hitting outfielder. There was still baseball left to play before the Cubs players headed home for the winter, however.

The City Series, a post-season contest between Chicago's American and National League clubs, began in 1905 and was played nearly every year at the conclusion of the regular season, unless one of the teams was involved in the World Series. In 1922 it became a best-of-seven affair, and the White Sox nearly always won. When the last series was played in 1942, the Sox had prevailed in 18 of 25, with one tie.

Nicholson had the misfortune of making his City Series debut in the midst of what would become an eight-series losing streak for the Cubs; the team never won a City Series during his stay in Chicago. In 1939, however, they came close.

In the opener, played for the first time at night, more than 42,000 fans at Comiskey Park witnessed an exciting 10–9 Cubs win, in 10 innings. It was Nicholson's ninth-inning home run that tied the score in the top of the frame, forcing the game into overtime.

The following day, the Sox evened the score, but the Cubs won the next two games to go up, 3-1. On the verge of a series victory in the fifth game, the North Siders were five outs away, but somehow managed to lose, 8–5, in 10 innings. Then, they were flattened in the next two contests, 6–1 and 7–1, managing only five singles in the finale at Comiskey Park. Bill batted a lackluster .250 for the series, with three RBIs.

Despite the war raging in Europe at the end of the year, isolationist America seemed to be emerging from the depths of the Depression. The New York World's Fair in Flushing Meadows, Queens, opened to record crowds, and some of its exhibits gave Americans a peek at promising new technologies that would soon alter their way of life. Though wary of potential entanglement in a global conflict, Americans could look forward to the dawn of a new decade.

For Bill Nicholson, who'd finally shown he could play big league baseball, 1940 promised continued success and anticipated stardom.

7

Catalina to Chicago

Gabby Hartnett was a man on the hot seat as his Cubs embarked upon the 1940 season. After the pennant-winning campaign of '38, Phil Wrigley expected a return to the World Series the following year. The team's unsatisfactory fourth-place finish was compounded by Wrigley's dissatisfaction with Hartnett's conduct during the Larry French controversy, and the team's loss to the hated White Sox in the October City Series, after blowing a three-game-to-one lead.

Wrigley was also exasperated by the antics of Dizzy Dean, who had antagonized Cubs players and the press with assorted ailments and complaints, real and imagined, during 1939. Following a lackluster 6-4 season, in which he pitched fewer than 100 innings, Dean was holding out for a higher salary in 1940. Although he signed a contract two weeks into spring training, he was generally ineffective in several appearances. By May he was banished to Tulsa in his beloved Texas League, from whence he would return later in the year.

Gone from the '40 squad were shortstop Dick Bartell and catcher Gus Mancuso. Outfielder Hank Leiber, who led the team in home runs with 24 during the '39 season, was unsigned and holding out for more money. Pitcher Clay Bryant, a 19-game winner in '38, was still nursing a tender arm, having missed much of '39 with the same ailment.

Nicholson was the subject of trade talk throughout the winter "Hot Stove League." One rumor had him and outfielder Augie Galan heading to the Dodgers, in exchange for lanky pitcher Luke "Hot Potato" Hamlin, a 20-game winner in '39. Despite the conjecture, early in the year the Cubs signed Nicholson to a $5,000 contract, with the promise of another $1,000 if he became a regular. By February 25, in the company of Cubs scout Clarence "Pants" Rowland, and veteran players Phil Cavarretta, Billy Herman, Len Merullo, and rookie Bernard Olsen, Nicholson was on board the train for California, and the team's long-time spring training base on Catalina Island.

From 1921 through 1951 (with time out from 1943–45, when wartime travel restrictions necessitated a relocation to French Lick, Indiana), the Cubs spent the early part of spring training on this beautiful island off the southern California coast, 20 miles from Los Angeles.

William Wrigley, Jr. bought a controlling interest in Catalina in 1919. As he developed it, he built a baseball field (whose dimensions were equivalent to those at Wrigley Field), as well as a practice diamond, both of which were surrounded by eucalyptus trees. The players dressed in a locker room at the nearby country club. A small grandstand was erected for the enjoyment of spectators, who could also view the field from the clubhouse patio in left field. Intrasquad games, between the "Regulars" and the "Yannigans," were well-attended by local fans, and vacationers.

Social diversions for the players and their families included dancing, dining, and fishing. Big name bands, like Harry James' and Tommy Dorsey's, would play at the eight-story Casino on the weekends. It was not unusual for movie stars like Cary Grant, Clark Gable, and Errol Flynn to arrive by excursion boat from the mainland. *Mutiny on the Bounty* (starring Gable) was filmed on location at Catalina, and Flynn's reported liaison with a 15-year-old girl became an island scandal.

The Cubs were to train at Catalina for a little more than two weeks, playing intrasquad games, then return to the mainland to make headquarters at Los Angeles' Biltmore Hotel. There they would remain until March 28, playing games principally at Los Angeles' Wrigley Field. Then, they would barnstorm their way back to Chicago by train with the White Sox, stopping in Arizona, Texas, and Kansas along the way. The team was sporting newly-designed uniforms, featuring a sleeveless jersey thought to be less restrictive than the heavy, conventional flannel tops. Nicholson liked the new vest, which had a light white undershirt with loose sleeves to cover the upper arm.

L.A.'s Wrigley Field resembled its more famous counterpart in many ways. The double-decked grandstand was similar to the one in Chicago, and there was the trademark ivy on the walls. One feature, however, distinguished L.A. Wrigley from its midwest cousin: lights, for night baseball. The park's dimensions were ideal for a lefthanded pull-hitter like Nicholson; 339 feet down the right field line. The outfield fence jutted out towards home plate in the power alleys, which were only 345 feet away in left and right center. Behind the fence in right center were bleachers that were an easy shot for power hitters.

Coming off a fine '39 campaign, Nicholson had a notion he could be a starting outfielder in '40. Gabby Hartnett had other ideas, however. The acquisition of diminutive (5'6", 168 pounds) outfielder Dom Dallesandro cast

Nicholson's status in doubt. Dallesandro led the Pacific Coast League (PCL) in '39 with a .378 average, and possessed adequate power at the plate, in spite of his size. A lefthanded hitter with a small strike zone, who could also hit lefthanded pitching, it didn't hurt that Dallesandro would be a box office draw for Chicago's large Italian population, as well.

During Leiber's spring holdout, Nicholson started in right field, and usually batted cleanup, throughout March. He wasn't hitting particularly well, though, while Dallesandro was wearing out opposing pitching. Veteran PCL scribe and longtime Cub-watcher Bob Ray opined in his *Los Angeles Times* column, on March 15, that Dallesandro was a "cinch to hold down a regular outfield job" for the '40 Cubs.

Hartnett was not overly enthusiastic about Nicholson's performance against lefthanded hurlers during the '39 season, when scouting reports suggested that he could be neutralized with a steady diet of inside, shoulder-high fastballs. True enough, Bill loved to turn on inside pitches, often transforming them into majestic clouts over the right field wall. But he was prone to chase balls that were high, and out of the strike zone, which typically resulted in strikeouts. There was no better demonstration of this inclination than his performance against the Dodgers.

Over the years, Bill was a crowd favorite in Brooklyn. Throughout the outfielder's career in Chicago, the Dodgers were managed by Leo Durocher. In his tell-all biography, *Nice Guys Finish Last*, the Dodger skipper — with, perhaps, some degree of exaggeration — revealed his "book" on Nicholson, and how he instructed his pitchers to retire the slugger:

> "Swish" Nicholson [was] a big lefthanded hitter, who was the greatest hitter in the world if you put the ball from his belt on down, and helpless as a babe if you threw him fastballs up and in. The way we liked to pitch him was to get him thinking by starting him off with a slow curve that bounced in the dirt. Boy, he'd step out and pick up a handful of dirt and dig in with his left foot, looking for that slow curve which, of course, he was never going to see again. After that, we pitched him up, up and up. We'd throw him a fast ball across the letters and the whole park would go "Swish" as he swung and missed. The next pitch would be higher — "Swish" — and the third pitch would be — "Swish" — over his head. We struck him out about three times a game, but if you ever made a mistake and got it down, you were lucky if the ball only hit against the fence.

In truth, Durocher and Nicholson belonged to a mutual admiration society, of sorts. In July, 1945, Leo told a gathering at the Touchdown Club in Washington, D.C., that "Nicholson ought to be in a league by himself." He added: "Every time he swings his bat it has a menacing swish, and when he connects he simply flattens the ball. That guy's like a big beast."

For his part, Nicholson thought Durocher to be the best manager against whom he had played. He even named one of his hunting dogs "Lippy," in tribute to Durocher's nickname, "The Lip."

"Durocher always appealed to me," Bill said. "I think he was ... the best manager. Now he might not have been, but to me, looking from my point of view, on his ability to get a lot out of his ball club, out of his bench and his whole club, he might have been the best."

Early in the 1940 exhibition season, Chicago won seven straight games against major league and PCL competition, and nine out of 12. By March 22, Leiber had signed his contract, reportedly for several thousand dollars less than the $17,500.00 he had been demanding. Three days later, in game two of the "Chewing Gum Championship" against the PCL's Los Angeles Angels (also owned by Wrigley), the Cubs lost, 6–3. Nicholson had two of the Cubs' four hits. In the first inning, he broke his bat on one swing, sending the barrel high into and almost over the screen in front of the first base line seats, then fouled a wicked liner that hit manager Hartnett, coaching at first base, just below the ribs, before reaching on a single.

The following day, the Cubs won the rubber game of the Chewing Gum Championship. Then, they beat the White Sox, 10–1, on March 28, with Nicholson hitting a leadoff homer into the top row of the right field bleachers at Wrigley, off future Hall of Famer Ted Lyons. The North Siders boarded Pullman cars to begin the journey to Chicago, arriving in Tucson on March 29, and hurtling on to Phoenix. There, a dozen or so Navajo Indians inducted Hartnett and White Sox manager Jimmy Dykes into the tribe, in a ceremony staged for the press. Hartnett was dubbed "Chief Tomatoface," and Dykes, "Chief Redneck." The Sox won the game that followed, and the next day's contest, as well.

Nicholson had two homers and batted in six runs in a 7–6 victory over the Sox, on March 31. He hit another homer on April 3 in Fort Worth, Texas, in support of pitcher Claude Passeau, but the Cubs dropped a 6–4 decision to the Chisox.

From the time he signed his contract on March 22, Leiber was held out of games as he worked himself into shape. On April 6, however, he was inserted in the lineup as the right fielder. Now he responded with a two-for-four performance, including a homer, as Chicago defeated the St. Louis Browns in Fort Worth, 4–3. Nicholson rode the bench for the entire game, and the next two as well.

As the Cubs prepared for the season, the question mark on the pitching staff was Dizzy Dean, and his physical problems. There was reason for cautious optimism when he made his spring debut on April 8, scattering two hits over five innings against the Browns, in a 15–2 victory. He credited Cubs trainer Andy Lotshaw for his performance and the revitalized feeling in his right arm, drawling: "Doc Lotshaw has brought me back and I hope they keep them specialists away from me."

Andrew Hemmingway Lotshaw was in his twentieth year as the Cubs trainer. Despite the fact that Lotshaw had no medical education, he also trained the Chicago Bears football team. His frequently-bizarre therapies had no medical foundation, but actually seemed to work for some of the players. According to former Cubs infielder and major league manager Gene Mauch, one such remedy was for Lotshaw simply to spit on the injured area. The old trainer also devised a concoction popularly known as "Andy Lotshaw's Body Rub." There is some dispute about the contents of his potion; a prime ingredient was said to be Coca-Cola. Whatever it was left Dean's injured wing lobster-red, but ready to throw.

Lotshaw was from the old school. "The trouble is that the boys are too soft these days," he said in 1937. "Why, when old Andy Lotshaw played ball, the trainers had an easy life. It was nothing for a guy to break his leg sliding into first, and then steal second and third!"

But, twenty-four hours after his victory over the Browns in Topeka, Kansas, Dean left the team, vowing never again to play for Hartnett. Angry because he had been fined $100 for breaking curfew by 45 minutes, Dean threatened to go play for a barnstorming team, where he said he could make more money.

So on April 11, the team arrived in Chicago by train from Kansas City, without its temperamental pitcher. His wife told reporters that, "Gabby Hartnett was absolutely right in fining Diz," and promised that she would persuade him to rejoin the team. Sure enough, he returned a day later, suitably contrite and $100 lighter. A disgusted Wrigley told reporters, "We expect him to be a pitcher from now on, and not a side-show attraction."

By the end of the exhibition season, the handwriting was on the wall: Nicholson, 19 for 84 (.226) would begin the season on the bench, in favor of Dallesandro, who was hitting .362 with one strikeout for the spring. Leiber and Augie Galan would man the other two outfield positions. Some observers thought this was the strongest Cubs outfield lineup since the Kiki Cuyler era of the early '30s.

The North Siders took a train to Cincinnati to open the season against the defending National League champion Reds. Nicholson sat on the bench, as Leiber, Dallesandro, and Galan played the outfield in a 2–1 Cubs loss. On the same day, at Comiskey Park, Cleveland's Bob Feller pitched an Opening Day no-hitter over the White Sox, thus ensuring a glum April 15 for Chicago's baseball fans.

The next day, the North Siders dropped another 2–1 decision in Cincinnati, before 1,536 chilly and damp Crosley Field patrons. The game ended when pinch-hitter Nicholson struck out with runners in scoring position.

After a 3–2 loss to Pittsburgh on April 23, Nicholson was hitless in two at-bats, while his team sat in sixth place with a 2–5 mark. Hartnett announced after the game that he would bench Dallesandro, hitting only .125, along with rookie shortstop Bobby Sturgeon, and first baseman Rip Russell. Galan would shift from center field to left, while Leiber would go to center and Nicholson to right. Bobby Mattick would assume the shortstop duties, with Cavarretta at first.

The reconstituted lineup won the next day, 9–4, against the Pirates. In a last-minute change of plans, however, Hartnett sent Nicholson to left field, not right. It made little difference. He was hitless in five trips, and committed a fielding error.

It wasn't until April 26 that Bill snapped out of his batting doldrums, when the Cubs bested the Reds, 6–2. Before a Ladies' Day crowd of nearly 13,000 at Wrigley, he belted his first of eight career grand slams in the first inning and doubled, to help Claude Passeau earn the victory. Nicholson's blow was only the second Cubs homer of the season.

A modest four-game winning streak ended with a 7–5 loss to the St. Louis Cardinals. Tinkering with his lineup to find a winning formula, *manager* Hartnett decided to bench catcher Al Todd and shortstop Mattick, in favor of *catcher* Hartnett and shortstop Bill Rogell.

The Cubs climbed to third in early May, behind Brooklyn and Cincinnati. Nicholson raised his average to .313, and led the team with 13 RBIs, in only 32 at bats. Leiber was batting .407 to pace the Chicago squad.

Just when a feel-good attitude had started to prevail among team members, the Dizzy Dean saga resurfaced, to the delight of Chicago sportswriters, who knew a good story when they saw one. After being knocked out of the box in the second inning by the Pirates on May 12, Dean barricaded himself in the Wrigley Field clubhouse and wept. A perplexed Hartnett told the press, "It looks like I may have to find another starter." Within days, Dean and still-injured Clay Bryant were on their way to Johns Hopkins Hospital in Baltimore to be examined by an orthopedic specialist.

A dismal May ended with the team dropping six of seven games. Nicholson was still playing left, despite criticism from the *Trib*'s Irving Vaughan that "neither Dom Dallesandro nor Bill Nicholson are satisfactory as left fielders." Vaughan's criticism aside, Dallesandro and Nicholson would play together for seven years, exclusive of Dim Dom's year of military service. Playing center in 1947 — his last season with the club — the tiny outfielder leaped against the wall to spear a fly ball, and became caught in the Wrigley Field ivy vines. Nicholson had to trot over to pull him out.

June began with a 4–3, 12-inning win over the Dodgers at Wrigley. Brooklyn shortstop Pee Wee Reese was carted off the field in the top of the 12th, after being hit in the back of the head by an errant Jake Mooty fastball.

There were usually several beanings at Wrigley each season, attributable to the hitter's vision being limited by the white background in center field. Cubs hitters had complained for years about the difficulty they had seeing pitched balls that appeared to come out of a sea of white shirts just beyond the low center field wall. Nicholson, particularly, was distressed by the sight lines and baffled by management's indifference to the safety of the players.

"When it got warm and the wind blew out, it was so hard to see the ball come out of those white shirts," he complained in 1984. "You were happy to come out of the game healthy. I took one in the head one day there, when I thought the pitcher threw a blank. I still have a small knot on my head today. It didn't make me shy at the plate, but I *did* like to see the ball. They roped it off after I was traded, and it is still that way today."

If Nicholson feared any pitcher, it was Cincinnati's Johnny Vander Meer, who had blazing speed and unpredictable control. "One day, he was pitching," Bill explained, "and was wilder than a jack rabbit, and it was bright and sunny and he was pitching out of those white shirts. And we hadn't gotten a base hit. We got a couple of runs off him, and he had walked the bases loaded again and I was hitting. And he got me three and two, and he reared back and fired. And I never seen the ball, to this day. It just tipped the back of my head as it went by. And we didn't have good helmets, and if he had hit me there, I know he'd have killed me."

Other Cubs of Nicholson's era were concerned about the potential dangers. Phil Cavarretta recalled: "It was very tough to see a white ball coming out of those white shirts, especially in the second game of a doubleheader, when the shadows began to fall. I remember hitting a couple of homers off the Phillies' Robin Roberts in the first game of a doubleheader. In the second, Curt Simmons, I think as a message, threw at me a couple times and just missed me. Then he threw high and inside again. I saw the ball come out of his hand, then lost it. I threw my hand up to protect my face and the ball hit me in the wrist, and fractured it. After that, I complained, and they finally put up a dark background that is still there today."

Popular Eddie Waitkus, traded from the Cubs after the 1948 season, agreed. "Chicago was a grand place to play. The only thing that bothered me was the shirts in center field made a tough background for hitters," he said.

In 1948, a *St. Louis Post Dispatch* correspondent overhead umpire Bill

7. *Catalina to Chicago*

Bill takes his cuts in the cage before a 1940 game, with the omnipresent tobacco chaw firmly planted in his left cheek (*reproduced by permission from National Baseball Hall of Fame Library, Cooperstown, N.Y.*).

Stewart and several Cardinals discussing parks in which hitting was difficult. All agreed that Wrigley Field was the worst. Some even thought it was the reason that Nicholson's skills had seemingly diminished. Stewart said: "I've seen good hitters stand up there at Wrigley Field, well back from the plate, and just go through the motions of swinging three times.... It's easy to lose the ball and get hit by a fast one." He added that he would sometimes look down as the pitcher wound up and then quickly focus his eyes as the ball approached, so as to avoid staring at the white shirts in center field.

Two days after Reese's beaning, Nicholson — who had again been dropped from the lineup — pinch hit a home run off Hugh Casey's 2–1 fastball in the eighth inning, though the Cubs dropped their third game in a row to the Brooklynites, by a 3–2 count.

Reinserted as a regular, Nicholson helped the Cubs patch together a three-game winning streak, hitting two home runs against Philadelphia in Shibe Park on June 6. The next day, Bill represented the team, at the studios of WGN radio, to honor 600 local safety patrols. He was joined at the ceremony by Babe Ruth, and former Cub Rabbit Maranville. A photograph of the three ballplayers, surrounded by the eager youths, appeared in Chicago newspapers on June 8.

In late June, the Cubs remained mired in fourth, seven and a half games out. But Nicholson's booming bat was beginning to attract notice. Even Irving Vaughan grudgingly conceded on June 25: "Nicholson, altho [sic] an easy mark for most of the smart pitchers in the pinches, has been a life saver for a team shy on batting power."

Now playing regularly, Bill raised his average to .315 by June 30, second on the Cubs to Billy Herman's .317. His eight home runs and 41 RBIs topped the team. Cincinnati manager Bill McKechnie, selected to lead the N.L. All-Star team, was also mindful of Bill's recent production at the plate. He added Nicholson to the All-Star squad, in place of Leiber, who had to withdraw from the game because of an infected throat.

Bill boarded a train to St. Louis on July 8, with teammates Larry French and Billy Herman, who had also been selected for the team. The game was played on a sweltering 86-degree Tuesday afternoon, before 32,373 at Sportsman's Park, and ended in a 4–0 National League triumph. The ballplayers' charity fund received a contribution of $42,420.79 from game receipts.

Jimmie Foxx made his final All-Star appearance, wearing the uniform of the Boston Red Sox, and playing against his idol made Nicholson's participation in the game even more special. Bill entered the contest in the second inning, as a defensive substitute for Max West of the Boston Bees. After hitting a first-inning home run that ultimately proved to be the margin of victory, West had been injured when he collided with the right field wall, while chasing a fly ball.

In the third inning, with Cubs teammate Herman on first, Bill hit a fly ball to deep right that was caught by his former University of Maryland rival, Charlie Keller. Herman tagged up and advanced to second on the play. In the fourth, Nicholson snared a fly, off the bat of Joe DiMaggio, for the second out of the inning. In the fifth, Bill again flew to right, before he was replaced by the Giants' Mel Ott in the sixth.

Though he was hitless in the All-Star game, Nicholson's blazing bat continued to wreak havoc throughout the National League. He led the team with a .320 average; his 12 home runs were third in the league, and he was fourth in RBIs, with 55.

The Dodgers-Cubs rivalry reached fever-pitch on July 19, before a large Ladies' Day crowd on the North Side. In the eighth, the Cubs were cruising to an eventual 11–4 rout. Nearly six weeks before, Bill hit an eighth-inning, pinch-hit homer off Brooklyn pitcher Hugh Casey. This day, he blasted one into the right field bleachers off the same hurler, and Leiber followed with a single. When Cubs pitcher Passeau stepped to the plate, Leiber was on second. A wild pitch and a passed ball later, Leiber had scored the Cubs' 11th run.

Plate umpire Tom Dunn later said he heard Durocher give the order to hit Passeau, though he did nothing about it. Sure enough, the next pitch plunked Passeau right between the shoulder blades. Passeau threw his bat in Casey's direction, and both dugouts emptied. With players milling about, Brooklyn's Joe Gallagher jumped Passeau, but was pulled off by Chicago third baseman Stan Hack, who bloodied Gallagher's nose. When order was finally restored, Passeau and Gallagher — but neither Casey nor Hack — were ejected. *Trib* correspondent Edward Burns thought the fight to be "a much better attraction than the usual baseball imbroglio inasmuch as gore was spilled.... Gallagher's gushing puss ... gave color to the occasion."

Interestingly, Casey gained fame the next year for his pugilistic exploits. When the Dodgers went to Cuba for spring training, he was befriended by Ernest Hemingway, who had a home on the island. The author took the pitcher to his house on several occasions, where they would put on boxing gloves. The two would wail away at each other until Hemingway's wife, tired of the racket, would make them leave.

Durocher did nearly anything to help his team win a ball game. Even if it meant stealing the catcher's signs by stationing someone in the outfield with binoculars; berating opposing players with incessant bench-jockeying; or knocking the batter down with a "purpose" pitch, Leo did not hesitate.

Nicholson was a frequent object of Durocher's strategy. "They lowered the boom on me more than any team in the league, Brooklyn," Nicholson related. "And Durocher, mostly, he called for it. He'd say, 'Knock him down.' I seen him over there out of the corner of my eye. I'd reach down, get a little dirt and look at him. And I could see him giving the sign, 'Knock him down!'"

Nicholson with roommate "Smilin'" Stan Hack, at Catalina Island in the early 1940s (*courtesy Emily Joiner*).

With runners in scoring position in one close game, Durocher's Dodgers intentionally walked Nicholson. Instead of throwing four wide pitches, as would customarily be done in such a situation, Hal Gregg threw each pitch shoulder high, and behind Bill's head. Remembering this unique honor, Bill said, "I'd never seen that before the whole time I was in the majors, and I've never seen it since."

Stuck in fourth place, the Cubs were down to 20 players by July 21, owing to injury and illness. Bolstering the roster would have required Cubs management to purchase minor league talent, which owner Wrigley was loathe to do. Nicholson continued to play well, though, and now led the league in RBIs with 62.

It was 106 degrees in the Shibe Park press box on July 30, when Nicholson singled, doubled, and tripled in a 7–5 Phillies victory. But, the next day, left fielder Galan, who was already experiencing a subpar campaign, fractured his left knee cap, running into Shibe's left field wall during another Cubs defeat, and was lost for the season. Thirteen-and-a-half games behind the Reds, the team was effectively out of pennant contention. Galan joined Russell,

Cavarretta, and Bryant as key club members lost for extensive stretches during 1940.

Against the league-leading Reds on August 7, Nicholson paced his team to a 10-inning, 5–3, victory. In the second, he clouted his 18th home run off Paul Derringer, a 380-foot bomb that landed in Crosley Field's right field bleachers. An inning later, he threw out Mike Dejan at the plate, trying to score from second on a base hit to right. In the ninth, Nicholson pulled off a rare unassisted double play. Running in at top speed to snag Harry Craft's fly, he continued on to first base, tagging the bag to double up Dejan, who apparently thought the ball was uncatchable, and was rounding second when it was caught.

After a 6–2 loss to the Pirates on August 9, the Cubs fell into fifth place. Nicholson poled a disputed seventh inning homer; Bucs manager Frankie Frisch unsuccessfully argued that the ball had curled around the Forbes Field foul pole in right, and was nothing but a long strike. In this game, player-manager Hartnett took over the catching duties, marking the first night game he'd caught in a long and distinguished career that would eventually land him in the Hall of Fame.

Working every angle to get the club to play with more consistency, Hartnett briefly benched Nicholson in mid–August, after the outfielder went zero for eight in a doubleheader loss at Cincinnati. The manager was also frustrated by Wrigley's unwillingness or inability to find him a first-rate shortstop; Dodgers rookie Pee Wee Reese was the man he coveted.

After he sat for several games, Hartnett brought Nicholson back gradually, with several unsuccessful pinch-hitting appearances. In a doubleheader split with the Giants, Bill pinch-hit a second-game, three-run homer into the left center field bleachers at Wrigley. He rode the pines again the next day in a loss to the Giants. Before that game, catcher Al Todd was benched for loafing during pregame practice. Todd told reporters he was tired from catching too many doubleheaders. Hartnett — who up to that time had caught more games than any catcher in history — was understandably not sympathetic.

Phil Wrigley bestowed the dreaded "vote of confidence" upon his manager as August wound down, announcing his intention to rehire Gabby for the 1941 campaign. The next day, Dizzy Dean was recalled from Tulsa. On the last day of the month, the Cubs purchased two players from the PCL's Los Angeles Angels: outfielder Lou Novikoff and second baseman Lou Stringer. As Wrigley owned both franchises, he essentially purchased the players from himself.

Novikoff was built along the lines of former Cubs outfielder Hack Wilson; short and stocky, with tiny (size five and a half) feet. He was popularly known among fans as the "Mad Russian." In 1940, Novikoff feasted on PCL pitching. At the time of his purchase, he was pounding the ball at a .356 clip, with 33 home runs and 142 RBIs. Both Novikoff and Stringer would report to Catalina Island for spring training in 1941, along with pitcher Paul Erickson, who had also been purchased from Tulsa.

While the season drew to a climax, the inconsistent Cubs fell into sixth place, four games under .500. Before a Labor Day crowd of 26,120 at Wrigley, they split a doubleheader with the Pirates, to end a five-game losing streak. Nicholson's three-run homer in the nightcap was his 21st round tripper of the season.

The Cubs lost 11 of 13 games after Hartnett was given Wrigley's vote of confidence, and Edward Burns of the *Trib* wrote on September 8: "Veteran baseball men who have seen the Cubs recently frankly say they never before have seen such an outfit bearing the Wrigley banner."

Corpulent Burns was none too popular with Cubs players. The highlight of his journalistic career may have come in the mid–'30s, at spring training on Catalina. During a barroom brawl he took a punch — intended for a fellow sportswriter named Jimmy Corcoran — in his ample midsection. The assailant was the Cubs' broadcaster, Ronald "Dutch" Reagan.

Dean made a splash in his return to the mound on September 11, throwing a two-hit, 3–2 victory over the Dodgers in the second game of a doubleheader. The Cubs took the first game, as well, behind the pitching of Passeau and the slugging of Nicholson, who hit his 23rd four-bagger.

But Dizzy's fortunes took a nosedive on September 22. He was pounded by the Cards in an 8–1 loss, and his days with the club were essentially over. He would pitch one inning in 1941 before the team gave him his unconditional release.

A last-gasp effort to attain fourth place (below which the team had not finished since 1925) went for naught on September 27, in an 11–1 loss to the Cards. Nicholson's single and Russell's double were the only hits the Cubs could muster on the day.

The North Siders ended the year in fifth, four games below .500 and 25½ games behind eventual world champs Cincinnati. For the season, Nicholson batted .297, with 25 home runs and 98 RBIs. He was second in the league in slugging to Johnny Mize (.636 to .534), and his home run total was also second only to Mize. These accomplishments earned him sixth place in the balloting for major league Rookie of the Year (an award for which he was technically still eligible, despite his major league experience in 1936 and 1939), behind winner Lou Boudreau, Cleveland shortstop. Cubs teammate and pitcher Vern Olsen was fourth in the voting.

A final piece of business awaited the Cubs before the season officially ended: the one-sided City Series with the White Sox. The 23rd version was held coincident with the World Series. Just before the City Series began Irving Vaughan, who had been highly critical of the Cubs' play during the regular season, speculated about 1941's prospects:

> Some of the [Cubs] looked so feeble during the season that it is a cinch a few of them will be traded. Just who'll take 'em, we don't know, but maybe the club's front office can figure it out.

No one was surprised when the Sox won the series for the sixth straight time, in six games. Nicholson performed adequately, however, batting .280 in 25 at-bats, with a double, and a homer. His five RBIs led all players for the series. He committed an embarrassing gaffe in game one, when his 375-foot smash to the outfield wall netted him only a single, after he failed to touch first base and had to retrace his footsteps.

Each White Sox player received a $634.00 check for winning the post-season clash; Bill returned to Chestertown with a $422.00 loser's share. He also earned his $1,000.00 bonus, the incentive offered by management for becoming a regular on the team.

8

The Last Prewar Season

Phil Wrigley's "vote of confidence" notwithstanding, Gabby Hartnett was fired one month after the 1940 season ended. The axe was wielded by new general manager Jim Gallagher, a 36-year-old former Chicago newspaperman whom many believed had no business running a big league ballclub. As his new manager, Gallagher selected Jimmie Wilson, a former catcher who'd piloted a miserable Phillies team several years before.

The new general manager was a Notre Dame alum, a large man with bushy eyebrows, protruding ears, and a thin mustache. His experience with baseball was limited to writing about it. Branch Rickey, the general manager of the Dodgers, called him "nothing more than a glorified office boy."

In fairness to Gallagher, the team he inherited had steadily declined in quality after the '38 National League championship squad. Wrigley's reluctance to fund player development through a minor league system surely did not help matters.

At Wrigley's direction, Gallagher employed a penurious approach to negotiating player contracts. In early February, 1941, Nicholson sent his proposed season contract back unsigned, unsatisfied with its terms. He explained to reporters that he wanted to talk personally with Gallagher, but didn't anticipate any problems. Nicholson's perennial contract hassles with Gallagher in subsequent years would become a more reliable harbinger of spring than the blooming of forsythia.

Bill described the relationship between the two: "He hated me. Jim Gallagher didn't like me at all.... Every time they mentioned my name, you know, they give me a big hand and every time they mentioned Gallagher, not very often, they booed. And I didn't try to show him up, but he and I didn't get along, contract-wise. He didn't want to give me any money."

Nicholson occasionally complained to Gallagher about the white hitter's backdrop at Wrigley Field. Other players did, too — like Billy Herman — but without success. After listening to Bill express his concerns on one occasion, Gallagher replied, "It's all in your head."

By February 18, 13 Cubs remained unsigned, including Nicholson, Stan Hack, Billy Herman, Bill Lee, Phil Cavarretta, and Hank Leiber. Gallagher shipped contract holdout Zeke Bonura to the Minneapolis Millers of the American Association, a maneuver calculated to let unsigned Cubs know that everyone was expendable. The general manager then publicly rebuked Bill Lee, who had written to the Associated Press from his home in Louisiana, complaining about Gallagher's treatment of Bonura.

The train carrying the Cubs west towards Catalina Island for spring training was scheduled to depart Chicago on February 23. As the date drew near, Gallagher warned the holdouts that if they signed their contracts after the scheduled departure, financial responsibility for transportation to California would be theirs.

Nicholson — heftier than ever at 217 pounds — and Cavarretta met with Gallagher at his Wrigley Field office on February 22. After being treated to lunch by the general manager, both signed their contracts, undoubtedly for less than they thought they were worth. The two Cubs stalwarts were aboard the Santa Fe Scout when it departed Chicago the next evening, on its three-day journey to Los Angeles. During the trip, they were able to relax and talk baseball with new manager Wilson and his coaches Charlie Grimm and Dick Spalding.

Gradually, most of the unsigned vets caved in and ended their holdouts; Russell and Hack signed on February 26, but Lee and Leiber stuck to their guns. The exhibition season commenced on March 15, with a 4–2 loss to the Athletics before 2,000 fans at L.A. Wrigley; Nicholson clubbed a home run. Dubbed the "Two Lous" by reporters, PCL newcomers Stringer and Novikoff played well in the field, and the latter made a spectacular diving catch.

Three days later, against the A's in Anaheim, Bill launched one over the 394-foot wall in right field, the first homer hit into that section of the three-year-old park. Novikoff made two more circus catches in left, each time taking an extra-base hit away from second baseman "Crash" Davis, the inspiration for the eponymous Kevin Costner character in the 1988 baseball movie classic, *Bull Durham*.

The Cubs were playing impressively. Over a six-game period, in 50 innings of exhibition play, they amassed 106 hits and scored 76 runs. When the team broke camp and headed back east they continued their torrid performance, until hitting a five-game losing skid. But in Tucson on April 3, the "two Bills," Nicholson and Herman, homered in the first spring triumph over the A's. The White Sox were defeated two days later in Phoenix by a 16–6 count; Herman had three homers, Nicholson two. Then, Nicholson hit two more in another victory over the Sox. Journeying to Amarillo on April 9, in a 15–11 slugfest with the Sox, the victorious Cubs hit five homers, three by Herman and one each by Nicholson and Novikoff.

A reconstructed infield awaited the team at Wrigley Field in Chicago, where 6,967 chilled patrons saw a 2–1 exhibition victory over the Sox on April 12. The Cubs broke out new caps, with an elliptical "C" on the front, and new windbreakers, which came in handy on this brisk afternoon. Most of the fans sat in the sun-dappled bleachers rather than the frigid grandstand. They watched Sox hurler Eddie Smith plunk Nicholson with a pitch while the bases were loaded in the eighth inning, to send home the winning run.

Soon, Bill Lee ended his holdout, reportedly signing for $10,000, plus performance incentives that might earn him more at season's end. Lee demanded $15,000 early in the negotiations, while Gallagher proposed a $12,500 compromise. Once Lee rejected the counterproposal, Gallagher took it off the table and the humiliated pitcher eventually paid the piper, agreeing to $2,500 less than he could have had a month before. Leiber was now the only holdout.

Opening Day was April 15 at home, and 17,008 came out to see the newest edition of the Cubs defeat Pittsburgh, 7–4. The game was off to an ominous start when leadoff hitter Frankie Gustine hit a line drive off pitcher Claude Passeau's shin. The crowd was silent as Andy Lotshaw attended to what many feared was a broken leg. Passeau stayed in the game, though, to see Nicholson's three-run homer sail into the right center field bleachers in the third. Despite rookie shortstop Stringer's four errors, the team hung on to win. Three other rookies started the game for the home team: first baseman Eddie Waitkus, left fielder Novikoff, and catcher Clyde McCullough.

Bill hit his second round-tripper of the young season on April 18, in a 6–4 triumph over St. Louis at Sportsman's Park, as pitcher Charley Root won his 194th career game. A third Nicholson homer came in an 11–10 victory over St. Louis, in which Stringer committed three more errors. By April 24, however, the North Siders settled into a pattern that would become all-too-familiar in 1941: long stretches of spotty pitching and anemic hitting that caused Jimmie Wilson to juggle his lineup virtually on a daily basis.

Chicago sportswriters were amused to hear Cubs hitters complaining that the new white uniforms sported by peanut and popcorn vendors, working in the center field bleachers, made it difficult to see pitched balls, a variation on the theme that had been advanced by Chicago hitters for years.

"I can't see white on white," Nicholson said several years later. "Put an egg in a white cup, and I'd probably eat the cup. Give the ball a white background, and I'll swing for the background." Gallagher, naturally, scoffed at the players' complaints, and again reminded Nicholson and his teammates that it was all in their heads.

Rookie outfielder Novikoff had earned a spot on Jimmie Wilson's bench by the end of April. He accomplished that feat by batting only .154 and exhibiting some truly abominable fielding. The "Mad Russian" caught the ball adequately and, at times, brilliantly in spring training when balls were hit in front of him. The problem was his abject terror of colliding with the brick wall in back of him at Wrigley Field. This was evident on April 27, in an 8–5 loss to the Cards, during which Nicholson hit his third home run, in the first inning off Mort Cooper.

A catchable fly off the bat of Johnny Mize turned into a double when Novikoff retreated tentatively and then made a lame stab at the ball, now 10 feet to his rear. Edward Burns, writing in the next day's *Trib*, was blunt:

> [Novikoff was benched] after an awkward fielding maneuver which has become painfully familiar to Cub followers in the brief time he has been a Cub... [He] revealed his horror of brick, concrete and tin when those materials are used in the construction of outfield barriers.

Bill Nicholson rarely had a bad word to say about anyone. But, years later, he couldn't contain himself when it came to the "Mad Russian."

"Oh, God, he was the worst outfielder I ever saw," he declaimed. "Some of the sportswriters kept tabs on him. And they said he let in more runs than he hit in.... And I never seen him drive in a tough run, which is a bad thing to say about anybody, but he seemed to have that trait."

In late June, Novikoff was banished to Milwaukee of the American Association, though he returned to Cubs livery later in the year, after hitting .370 for the Brewers, in 90 games.

Newly-signed Hank Leiber rejoined the team on April 29, as the Cubs lost their fourth straight and fell into sixth place, a position from which they would only occasionally emerge during the course of the season. Bill socked a two-run homer in the 11-inning loss to the Boston Bees.

A week later, Cubs fans were stunned to hear of Gallagher's first major trade, sending long-time star Billy Herman, a holdover from the '38 N.L. championship team, to the much-despised Dodgers, in return for infielder Johnny Hudson, outfielder Charlie Gilbert, and $65,000 in cash. Herman had the last laugh when the Dodgers captured the 1941 N.L. flag, before losing to the Yankees in the World Series. There was still a lot of baseball left in the 31-year-old infielder, and he had several more productive seasons before his retirement and eventual election to the Hall of Fame. On the other hand,

Hudson's career lasted another 78 games, while Gilbert played a total of 121 games with the Cubs, before he was traded to the Phillies.

Although Nicholson was hitting homers and driving in runs, he still struggled occasionally against lefthanded pitching. After singling against Giants southpaw Carl Hubbell on May 6 at the Polo Grounds, Nicholson was two for 19 against lefthanders for the season. His manager was not fazed:

> He's a good ball player. In fact, I would say he will be a great ball player. He's better than a .300 hitter and one of these years he will come up with one of those big seasons.... The idea got around that Nicholson couldn't hit lefthanded pitching. So they had him in and out of the lineup ... [and] he never got settled. Southpaws still give him trouble but some of his best hits ... have been against lefties.

Although hitting only .244, Bill's 23 RBIs led the league on May 13. John Kieran of the *New York Times* wrote a week later that "Nicholson's batting average is mediocre, but he belongs with Rudy York, Flash Gordon, Mel Ott and Dolf Camilli, the boys who hit when hits mean runs."

As Wilson incessantly revamped his lineup, Nicholson was dropped from the fourth to the fifth slot, in favor of Leiber. Chicago sportswriters continued to dismiss the protestations of Cub regulars about the white shirts in center field. After a 2–1 loss to the Giants, Edward Burns cracked, "The Cubs were quite punchless, doubtless because of six fans in the center field bleachers who had on white, or nearly white, shirts."

In late May, the team took three straight from Brooklyn. En route to a 9–1 victory on the 20th, Nicholson robbed former teammate Billy Herman of a sure triple by making what Ed Burns described as "the most spectacular diving catch imaginable" in the fourth inning. After hauling in Joe Medwick's fly ball for the next out, however, Bill lost a drive hit by Cookie Lavagetto into the blinding sun, suddenly ducking away at the last instant to avoid being conked on the head with the ball. The Dodgers' only run scored as a consequence.

The next day, Bill banged a grand-slam homer into Wrigley's right field bleachers off lefthander Frank Hoerst, in a 7–3 defeat of the Phillies. Five weeks into the season, Nicholson had eight home runs and 32 RBIs, despite a still-tepid .257 average. The fourth-place Cubs now trailed league-leading St. Louis by six and one-half games.

In the ninth inning of a 6–5 loss at St. Louis a week later, Bill injured his left heel while landing awkwardly on first base. When the team arrived in Pittsburgh, he was taken from the train to St. Francis Hospital for examination. Although x-rays revealed no fracture, the foot was badly bruised, and Nicholson did not play in the next two contests.

He returned for the first game of a twin bill at Shibe Park against the Phillies, skying a bases-loaded double off the right field scoreboard in the fifth. The heel was still sore, however, and Wilson removed him in the first inning of the next day's game. Bill spent several sessions with Andy Lotshaw, alternately soaking his foot in scalding water, then icing it, before returning to action in a June 6 loss to the Dodgers.

Chicago pulled to within one game of third-place New York on June 10, as Bill drove a fifth-inning pitch over the double-decked right field stands at the Polo Grounds with two on, in an 11–0 whitewashing of the Giants. The *Times'* Kieran was prompted to opine a week later: "Burly Bill Nicholson ... with a mediocre batting average, is easily the best hitter in the National League from one point of view. He drives runs over in flocks." As those words were written, the Cubs outfielder had posted an unusual statistic: he had more RBIs than hits for the season. One sportswriter thought this to be a telling indicator: "[I]t means that he must make nearly every one of his hits count."

Indeed, Nicholson always prided himself on his ability to hit with runners on base. He told *Chicago Daily News* sportswriter John Carmichael: "It should be easier to hit with men on base, especially in a tight game. In such a spot, a pitcher has to be careful; often, he gets too cautious. He has a tendency, from pressure, to get behind a hitter and then has to come in with a pitch you like."

Cubs batters' "imaginary" difficulties seeing pitched balls at Wrigley were underscored on June 24, when Leiber was beaned by Cliff Melton, during a 3–1 loss to the Giants. Although able to walk off the field with assistance, he was transported to Illinois Masonic Hospital, and diagnosed with a concussion. Hank had been struck with a pitch four years before by Bob Feller, in the same spot, at the base of his skull behind the left ear. Unfortunately, Melton's pitch effectively ended Leiber's career, and the 31 year old was out of baseball after 1942.

Pitchers at Wrigley Field rarely threw at batters intentionally; they didn't need to. Displaying a humanitarian spirit uncommon in the game of that era, opposing pitchers were actually fearful of hurting batters. Nicholson recounted: "I got thrown at quite a lot, but I don't remember getting thrown at in Cubs park, because those pitchers knew you couldn't see good up there. They had the advantage over us."

Phil Wrigley finally agreed to block off the lower sections of the center field bleachers early in July, and paint the seats brown. The action was taken, said the *Trib,* "purely as a psychological sop to the floundering athletes, rather than thru [sic] an acknowledgment of an actual optical hazard." *The Sporting News* jocularly reported that "[m]en of science had advised that of all colors that might be soothing and sharpening to ball players' eyes, seal brown unquestionably was the most soothing of all."

On July 3, with the new hitter's background, the Cubs beat the Cards, 2–1, although each team managed only five hits. Then, on a cloudless Independence Day, 39,423 squeezed into Wrigley and watched the Cubs sweep a doubleheader from St. Louis. Nicholson poked his 15th homer in the first game, which was halted at 4:00 P.M., briefly, so those in attendance could listen to President Roosevelt's address to the nation. From his home in Hyde Park, New York, the president warned isolationists:

> It is indeed a fallacy, based on no logic, for any American to suggest that the rule of force can defeat human freedom in all the other parts of the world and allow it to survive in the United States alone.

Dizzy Dean left the Cubs for St. Louis to start a radio announcing career with station KMOX. Pundits calculated that, based on his contract, Dean earned $10,000 for pitching one bad inning on April 25. To Nicholson's delight, however, Dean was replaced on the coaching staff by a familiar face — Kiki Cuyler, the manager at Chattanooga who had worked so assiduously with him on his hitting style several years before. It didn't take long for Cuyler to spot a flaw in Nicholson's hitting approach.

Favoring his injured left heel, the slugger wasn't evenly distributing his weight as he swung. After watching him hit, Cuyler told Bill: "You have a face just like a feller named Nicholson I used to know in Chattanooga. Otherwise, though, you bear little resemblance to the Nicholson I knew."

"You're trying to hit off balance," he continued. "You don't go after that bad high one as much as you used to, but you're worse off trying to hit off that front foot."

A further bit of good news in this otherwise gloomy season was the selection of four Cubs to the N.L. All Star team: pitcher Passeau, third baseman Hack, and outfielders Leiber and Nicholson. Pitcher Vern Olsen was later substituted for the injured Leiber, who'd now missed two All-Star games because of medical maladies.

Ted Williams hit a two-run homer in the bottom of the ninth off Passeau to win the game for the American League, 7–5, before more than 50,000, at Detroit's Briggs Stadium. Bill started in right field and batted fifth. In his only plate appearance he struck out, looking at a Bob Feller curveball in the top of the second, before being replaced by Bob Elliott in the bottom of the fourth. Although they were in different leagues, Nicholson faced Feller frequently throughout the years in exhibition games.

"I did fairly well off him," Bill recalled. "His curve bothered me more than his speed. I could hit his speed pretty good. I got base hits off him, but his curve gave me a little trouble. Gave a lot of them trouble. I remember my roommate, he was supposed to be one of the best curveball hitters in the National League — Stan Hack — and I saw him strike out three times in one game with that good curve of his. He really was a hard thrower and that curveball of his snapped just like a crack of a whip. It really broke."

The N.L. entered the ninth inning with a lead, but squandered it. Nicholson described the play that ultimately cost his team the game: "...[W]e had that one won.... Billy Herman, he was playing second base, and we had them beat, 5–4, and there was one out in the ninth inning, and I think it was two men on, and DiMaggio hit a sharp hit ball to Billy Herman. And Billy turned, he thought he was throwing to the first baseman, and he was throwing to the coach up the line. I think he had the same suit or something, and he mistook it and so that made two on, and so who comes up behind DiMaggio but Ted Williams.... Passeau pitched to Ted Williams and he hit it on top of the roof, and they won it, 7–5."

When regular season play resumed, Nicholson slumped badly at the plate. He was one for nine in a three game series with Brooklyn. In one of the games, righthander Kirby Higbe fanned Bill his first two times at bat. He swung and missed at every pitch, without so much as a foul tip. His third time up, he whiffed again, this time looking at a third strike.

In the bottom of the ninth with no score, Brooklyn player/manager Durocher pinch-hit for Higbe. The bases were loaded with Dodgers and there was one out. The contest then ended in dramatic fashion: on a one ball and no strikes count, Durocher laid down a perfect suicide squeeze bunt to score Medwick from third. As the Ebbets Field faithful celebrated in raucous delight, frustrated Cubs hurler Vern Olsen heaved the ball over the stadium roof.

Charley Root won his 198th career game on July 16, over Philadelphia, as Nicholson emerged from his hitting funk with a single, double, and two RBIs. Root helped the cause by clouting a home run of his own.

Bill smacked his 17th homer, off Carl Hubbell of the Giants three days later, and an eighth-inning grand slam on July 29, as the Cubs went on a tear, winning 10 out of 12. Hubbell was one of those rare lefthanders against whom Bill usually enjoyed success. His specialty pitch, the screwball, broke in on lefthanded batters. Consequently, Nicholson usually saw a steady diet of curveballs from the Giants' ace, and he had no trouble hitting them.

True to form, Chicago then dropped five straight, before beating the Cardinals, 6–2, at Sportsman's Park, behind Olsen's four-hitter. Nicholson's two bases-loaded singles produced four runs. By the time Bill homered for the 21st time in a loss to the Cards on August 11, the North Siders had dropped 10 of 12. A zero for 24 hitting drought prompted Jimmie Wilson to bench Nicholson against the Reds on August 17.

In Gallagher's continued purge of veteran Cubs, Larry French and Augie Galan, key members of the '38 N.L. champs, were claimed off waivers by the Dodgers on August 19, and they joined Herman and several other former Cubs players now earning a living wearing Dodger blue. French won 15 games for the '42 Dodgers before enlisting in the Navy. As a naval officer, he participated in the D-Day invasion at Normandy, and remained in his country's service until retirement, in 1969. Galan appeared in two more All-Star games for Brooklyn, and played with distinction until his retirement after the 1949 season.

Responding to criticism, Gallagher offered an *apologia* for the dismal season: "Wilson and I inherited a club which had gone pretty much to seed. It usually takes years to rebuild such a team...."

In the waning days of the campaign, the sixth-place North Siders swept a doubleheader from the Dodgers at Wrigley, trimming Brooklyn's lead over the Cards to one and a half games. In a reunion of sorts, Nicholson singled off Larry French in the ninth inning of the first game to clinch the win.

In the second contest, "Hot Potato" Hamlin struck Nicholson out three times. In his fourth at-bat, this time against old nemesis Johnny Allen, Bill walloped his 25th home run to provide the winning score, in a 5–3 triumph.

The Cubs' 7–3 win at Sportsman's Park on September 20 dashed Cardinal hopes of catching Brooklyn in the N.L. pennant chase. Tied at three in the top of the ninth, pinch-hitter Bob Scheffing hit a first-pitch grand-slam homer into the left field bleachers to plate the winning runs. Bill's 26th — and final — circuit clout came in the fifth.

Following a season-ending loss to the Cards on September 28, Cubs players prepared for the 25th City Series against their rivals from the South Side. They were again no match for their American League counterparts. The Sox, who finished third in the A.L., swept in four games. Nicholson did not have a single hit, until the 6–0 finale at Comiskey Park.

The team's sixth-place finish, 30 games behind the Dodgers, was its lowest in 16 years, and season's attendance (545,159) declined. Whether coincidental or not, the midseason center field bleacher experiment seemed to have been a success for Cubs hitters, however. When the bleachers were cordoned off for the July 3 game, the team's home record was 15-21; after that time, 23-18. The batting averages of D'Allesandro, Sturgeon, Stringer, Hack, Cavarretta, and McCullough were all higher after July 3 than before. Nicholson's batting average rose from a pre–July 3 .236 to a more respectable .274 thereafter, although his early season heel injury surely plagued him more than he acknowledged.

Despite his power numbers — 26 homers (third in the N.L.) and 98 RBIs (fifth), Nicholson's season-long average plummeted to .254 and his 91 strikeouts (third most in the league) would be the highest season total of his career. He was fifth in the league in walks, with 82, and his fielding improved to .971, just below the league average for right fielders. His overall performance earned him a 16th place finish in the voting for the league's Most Valuable Player, won by Brooklyn's Dolf Camilli.

Bill and Nancy were blessed with the birth of their second boy, Albert Kane Nicholson, on November 7. With fellow Eastern Shoreman Jimmie Foxx, Bill was feted at a turkey and ham banquet at the Easton Fire House, sponsored by the Eastern Shore Sports Writers' Association on November 18. Home Run Baker, Coach Kibler, Jake Flowers, and about 300 others attended the affair.

Nineteen days later, the Japanese bombed Pearl Harbor, Hawaii, and America emerged from its isolation to enter the second world war. Major league baseball would never be the same.

9

Baseball, As Usual

While British-held Singapore surrendered to the Japanese, and the "Battling Bastards of Bataan" girded for their final fight with the enemy in the Philippines, the business of baseball went on pretty much as usual. Three weeks after Pearl Harbor, baseball commissioner Kenesaw Mountain Landis wrote a letter to President Roosevelt, seeking guidance as to how the game should operate during the war — if at all. In mid-January, 1942, Roosevelt replied:

> I honestly feel that it would be best for the country to keep baseball going. There will be fewer people unemployed and everybody will work longer hours and harder than ever before. And that means that they ought to have a chance for recreation and for taking their minds off their work even more than before.

The president, in what came to be known as the "Green Light Letter," also expressed his desire that major league teams play more night games, to accommodate defense workers employed during the daytime hours.

Seizing upon FDR's sentiment, Gallagher announced that night games could even be played at Wrigley Field. In fact, he said, the Cubs had been preparing for just such an eventuality at the end of 1941, but halted work on the project after the events of December 7. In the end, no lights were erected, and the club donated to the federal government 165 tons of steel, 35,000 feet of copper wire, and other equipment it had acquired for the work.

Though some questioned the notion of young men playing a child's game for pay, while others were dying overseas, the public embraced the idea of continuing the major league schedule. *The Sporting News* polled its readers on whether the game ought to continue. One soldier responded: "Baseball is part of the American way of life. Remove it, and you remove something from the lives of American citizens, soldiers, and sailors."

By late January, 1942, only 29 players from major league rosters had enlisted, 18 from the National League. Among established stars, Hank Greenberg, Bob Feller, Cecil Travis, and Ted Williams left to join the fight. Seven

Washington Senators joined up; no Cubs player did so until the end of the month, when rookie pitcher Walter Lanfranconi enlisted in the navy. The 1941 National League Most Valuable Player, Brooklyn's Dolf Camilli, had five children, and was not going anywhere.

League owners decided to permit 14 home night games to be played by each team, except Washington, which was allowed 21. An overture by the Cubs to use Comiskey Park for their night games was rebuffed by White Sox brass, meaning that all home Cubs games for 1942 would be played during the daytime.

The main contingent of Catalina-bound Cubs players was slated to leave Chicago's Northwestern Station by train at 6:15 P.M., on February 18. A slimmed-down Bill Nicholson was the first Cub to arrive at the Wrigley Field offices, two days before departure. A winter of chopping wood and working on the farm had whittled him to 207 chiseled pounds. He'd laid off the bread and butter, which he suspected was the cause of his excessive 1941 *avoirdupois* and diminished batting average.

The comfortable Union Pacific Streamliner on which 22 players, manager Wilson, and coaches Spalding and Cuyler were to travel had all the modern conveniences, including its own barber. Just prior to departure, Cubs radio announcer Bob Elson broadcast interviews of the players at the station. Once the long journey began, Nicholson was snapped by a newspaper photographer writing a letter to Nancy and the kids back home in Chestertown.

The Cubs caravan arrived on the morning of February 20, in Los Angeles. Most of the players were clothed in fedoras and topcoats, and many flashed Winston Churchill's now-popular "V" sign to the welcoming crowd. Nicholson smoked a cigar.

With wartime baseball revenues certain to dwindle, Phil Wrigley's marching orders to his general manager had not changed: hold the line on player salaries. When the train pulled out of Chicago, Billy Myers, Rip Russell, and rookie Harry "Peanuts" Lowrey remained unsigned. Gallagher barred them from training camp, warning: "I have given them my best figures and I don't care whether they sign at the figures I have dictated or not."

Myers remained at his home in Pennsylvania, and never played major league baseball again. Lowrey, a native Californian and PCL veteran, soon came to terms with the team, grumbling: "I'm on a major league roster, but you'd never know it from the salary offered." Russell also caved in, giving up his job as an extra in the Lou Gehrig movie being filmed in Los Angeles, which starred Gary Cooper. Nicholson had been selected by readers of *The Sporting News*, the previous October, as a candidate for Gehrig's role, along with 18 others, including Hank Greenberg, Jimmie Foxx, and Babe Ruth, before Cooper was chosen.

What with wartime travel restrictions, steamer service between the mainland and Catalina was suspended. Instead, the players boarded two water taxis for a three-hour trip to the island. After several days of workouts, there were only minor injuries to report, including blisters on the hands of Hack and Nicholson. Pitcher Paul Erickson broke his nose when hit by a ball. The club took its first formal batting practice on February 25, as each of the 21 pitchers threw in five minute shifts.

Gallagher predicted that the Reds and Dodgers would be the teams to beat in the National League for 1942, but that the Cubs would be competitive with both teams, unless military call-ups intervened. Andy Lotshaw concurred, informing one reporter:

> We are going to have the best pitching staff in the league and if we can only get some hitting we'll whip 'em all. Of course, we didn't have our first hitting practice until today, but I have listened to some of the rookies in the clubhouse tell how they can bust the old apple. I didn't learn their names, but if they are telling the truth about their hitting, our troubles are over.

It turned out they were not telling the truth, and the Cubs' offensive woes continued during 1942.

Jimmie Wilson established 10 spring training rules which he posted prominently in the clubhouse:

1. don't cut loose before you are in shape
2. be yourself—don't try to copy other players
3. no bowling—the contrast in weight with a baseball is too great
4. pitchers field and fielders bat during pepper games
5. no poker or betting on horses—no mention of horses in the clubhouse or on the field
6. no smoking or sitting around the ball field
7. curfew at midnight
8. no fooling or wrestling in the clubhouse
9. no throwing ice water in the showers
10. rise at 7:30 every morning

Excitement was high on February 24, when unfounded rumors of a Japanese submarine attack on the mainland spread through camp. Catalina was a little calmer four days later, when newsreel crews came out to film the team in training. For several hours, they recorded the North Siders going through their paces, so that hometown fans could see Chicago's National League team preparing for the upcoming season.

After all the hoopla, the Cubs were relieved to begin intrasquad play in early March. A new game format was announced. Rather than the traditional

"Regulars" v. "Yannigans" rivalry, catchers Clyde McCullough and Bob Scheffing selected two teams, the "Nightowls" and the "Grumpies." Nicholson was a Nightowl. Each player paid $1.00 into a pool, with the victors in the series collecting the fund. In the first game, the Nightowls won, 17–9, after scoring ten runs in the third inning. When each team won two games and the pot rose to $42.00, Wilson rearranged the squads, fearful that the rivalry was getting out of hand.

Bill hit a three-run homer and two-run single on March 9 in the penultimate intrasquad game, and the next day he added another home run and two singles. Gallows humor prevailed during the finale when the players were informed by newsmen that it was the ninth anniversary of the last southern California earthquake.

After the game, the Cubs packed up their equipment, which was shipped to Los Angeles by barge. The team departed the island by water taxi on March 12 at 8:30 A.M., clearing the submarine nets and the wartime immigration barge before reaching the mainland. By 1:00 P.M., the North Siders were securely ensconced at the Biltmore Hotel in L.A.

The first spring exhibition game, on Friday, March 13, resulted in a 13–3 defeat of the crosstown White Sox. Wilson's club then lost seven consecutive games, including three to the Sox. In the seventh defeat, Nicholson blasted a two-run homer in the sixth, but earned a scolding from the *Trib* for his outfielding:

> One of the intermittent lapses to which Bill Nicholson is addicted aided the Sox to get their first inning run.... Wally Moses flied to right and should have been retired, but the ball popped out of Nicholson's hands in Nick Altrock [the noted baseball comedian] fashion.

To stem the losing tide, Wilson summoned Novikoff, Dallesandro, and Cy Block from Kiki Cuyler's undefeated "B" team, and the result was a 10–4 defeat of the Pirates. Left fielder Novikoff knocked a first-inning grand slam, after Nicholson was intentionally walked by pitcher Rip Sewell, purveyor of the high, arcing lob he called the "eephus" pitch.

Righthanded rookie pitcher Ed Hanyzewski, discovered by Jimmie Wilson the previous year during an exhibition game appearance against the Cubs in South Bend, Indiana, surrendered one hit in five innings but lost, 4–3, to Connie Mack's A's on March 25. The lone safety came off the bat of Dee Miles — traded for Nicholson in 1939 — who was then picked off first base. Bill had three hits in four appearances, including a triple, and batted in two runs. As the Cubs ended their stay in Los Angeles on March 31, the A's were defeated, 15–4. For the game, Nicholson had seven RBIs, off two singles and (for the fourth consecutive game) a homer.

A story appeared in local newspapers that the Dodgers were trading pitcher Whitlow Wyatt and outfielder Ducky Medwick to the Cubs, for Passeau and either Nicholson or Novikoff. Gallagher indignantly proclaimed that Brooklyn was tampering with his club by floating the trade rumor. Dan Daniel, writing in *The Sporting News*, and unimpressed with the current Chicago lineup, dismissed Gallagher's protestations and asserted that the Cubs *needed* tampering. Calling their vested uniforms "nutty," he added:

> You go in the clubhouse and put on one of them fruitcake suits ... the Cubs do not amount to much until they stop looking like Bloomer Girls or them wooden ball players you see years ago in fronta [sic] cigar stores.

The Chicagoans traveled east by train, beginning their tour with a 17-inning, 7–7 tie with the Sox in Tucson. The game ended when the umpire declared that he had run out of baseballs, after four hours of play. A couple days later, Nicholson's seventh-inning, two-run homer over the left field wall contributed to an 8–7 trimming of the Sox. Tensions were running high over the approaching regular season, however. Catcher McCullough and Novikoff, who was not in the lineup, had what the papers called a "verbal flareup" on the bench, and were ready to settle their differences via fisticuffs before coach Dick Spalding intervened.

The North Siders traveled on to Albuquerque, and then were rained out in Tucumcari, New Mexico, where Bill and others played cards on the train to while away the hours, while another group shot pool in the local billiards parlor. Following a game in Tulsa, the Cubs faced the White Sox in Fort Dodge, Iowa. Trailing, 14–13, in the bottom of the ninth, the National Leaguers scored three runs and won after Charlie Gilbert and Nicholson doubled, and Babe Dahlgren — who'd replaced Lou Gehrig at first base back in 1939 — homered.

As the start of the regular season approached, Shirley Povich of the *Washington Post* wrote of Nicholson effusively in his daily column, "This Morning":

> Clark Griffith is rueing the day he sold outfielder Bill Nicholson to the Chicago Cubs.... Nicholson, who has blossomed as a home run hitter with the Cubs, would fit very nicely into the punchless Washington outfield this season. Joe Engel, Chattanooga president, persuaded Griffith to sell Nicholson to the Cubs two years ago [saying,] "Nicholson is ... so deaf he can't hear the other outfielders telling him to take a ball or lay off it.... He's going to have a bad accident out there." "I never wanted to sell Nicholson," said Griffith, "but Engel advised me to take the money so I made the deal. I wish I had him back now. I don't care how deaf he is. You don't make base hits with your ears."

By this time, opposing teams had developed a shift to employ against the pull-hitting Nicholson. Similar to the strategy used by American League clubs when Ted Williams batted, the shortstop realigned himself to the right of second base; the second baseman played back about 15 feet onto the grass; and the first baseman played on the right field foul line. This formation was to discourage Nicholson from hitting the ball to the right side, and dare him to hit it to the left.

When first greeted with the stratagem, Bill went to Wilson. "Jimmie, I'm going to try to do some hitting to left field," he explained. "I want to poke that outside ball to left field once in a while."

"Poke it to left field and you get only a single, maybe a double once in a while," Wilson responded. "Don't do it. You'd be screwy. The fans pay to see you hit home runs and so does the front office. Stick to hitting over the wall." Taking Wilson's advice to heart, Nicholson tried to hit the ball to the right, or not at all.

The Cubs traveled by streamliner train to St. Louis for the opener against the Cards, arriving in the evening on April 13. The pitching matchup of Claude Passeau v. Mort Cooper attracted only 13,821 customers. Traditional red, white, and blue bunting decorated the stands at Sportsman's Park, and a brass band played before the game. It looked like any other Opening Day, except for one thing: the North Siders' road uniforms for 1942 were a departure from the customary gray flannels. They were powder blue, and they drew good-natured ribbing from opposing players. By the end of the year, the Cubs complained that they felt like hot dogs, sporting unconventional baseball suits while wallowing near the bottom of the standings. On this day, though, the Cubs were victors, 5–4.

The next day fortunes were reversed, as St. Louis took a 4–2 decision. The Chicagoans managed only four hits. Nicholson whiffed three times, and Dallesandro and Gilbert left the game with injuries. To add insult to those injuries, Jimmie Wilson was ejected by the umpires for poor comportment on this frustrating afternoon. After losing again the next day, the North Siders were glad to return to the Windy City for their home opener against the Reds on April 17.

Pregame ceremonies began at 12:30 P.M., as 480 Marines and sailors marched onto Wrigley Field. The Leathernecks conducted a bayonet drill, and Bob Strong's Orchestra entertained, along with the 40-piece Navy Pier Band. Only 10,149 came out, though, to see Big Bill Lee beat Reds ace Johnny Vander Meer, 3–2. Nicholson had a double in four trips.

While Novikoff became the darling of Chicago fans, owing to his early season offensive prowess, Bill struggled at the plate, showing a .200 average, no homers, and one RBI, after 39 at-bats. On April 26 against the Reds, he struck out, grounded into a rare double play, struck out again, and reached on a fielder's choice, stranding a total of four base runners, before singling in the tenth.

A day afterwards, he appeared to have broken out of his slump, in a 9–5 loss at Cincinnati's Crosley Field. Nicholson batted in all five of the Cubs' runs with a single and two triples. Reds outfielder Ival Goodman had to make a diving catch of a line drive off Bill's bat, with two runners on, to preserve the Reds' victory.

Nicholson always hit better on the road than in his home park. The wind was a problem, in the early season, and so were the white shirts in center field. He explained to a journalist: "When you got in a slump in Chicago, you just couldn't get out of it, because you couldn't get your timing back. That was big trouble." When the journalist asked, "How would you get out of it, then?," Bill's succinct response was: "Go on the road."

He continued to be hot-and-cold at the plate throughout early May. As the only lefty in Wilson's lineup against the Giants on May 2, he went three for four in a 1–0 loss at Wrigley. In the sixth, he made a spectacular catch of a wicked line drive off the bat of former teammate Babe Barna, in deep right field. But two days later, in an exhibition game against Lieutenant Mickey Cochrane's Great Lakes Naval Training Center team, he was hitless in two at-bats. Eight thousand seamen and Commissioner Landis watched the Cubs win, 6–3, in a contest that was broadcast back to Chicago by Bob Elson on WGN.

Throughout the course of the war, the Cubs and other teams increasingly filled their open dates with games against service teams, at the military bases. The players didn't seem to mind. For many, it made them feel like they were part of the war effort. Nicholson and the other players often felt embarrassed about not being in the service, although some were not fit, according to military standards. As more soldiers traveled on the trains throughout the war, Don Johnson said, "GIs would come up and ask why you weren't in the service—some jocularly, others not."

As the season progressed, the war was never far away. Almost daily, there were grim reminders of events overseas: crippled veterans being wheeled onto the field before games; war bond drives; more benefit games. Before the May 12 matchup against the Braves in Boston, the national anthem was followed by an announcement informing spectators to seek shelter under the grandstand of Braves Field in the event of an enemy attack. Nicholson hit his second home run, off Lou Tost, in a Cubs victory.

Bill always seemed to play well against manager Casey Stengel's Braves. In his first 40 times at bat against Boston during the '42 campaign, he pounded 19 hits: seven singles, five doubles, three triples, and four home runs.

The next year, before a Cubs-Braves game, Stengel walked over to Jimmie Wilson and pointed to Nicholson, warming up in right. "Take that guy out of there," Casey ordered.

Wilson looked at his counterpart with a puzzled expression. Stengel continued to implore. "Take him out and I'll let you play two men in his place, and I'll agree to use only eight men against your ten. Just take him out."

Regardless of Cub fortunes, which were not currently bright, the rivalry with the Dodgers continued to produce exciting baseball. In 1942, unfortunately, the Cubs were usually on the wrong end of the score. Durocher's men took a doubleheader from Chicago on May 17 — 8–2 and 4–3 — before a bellowing Ebbets Field mob of 37,901. Nicholson homered in the first contest. Between games, organist Gladys Gooding played "Three Blind Mice" as the plate umpire Bill Stewart and his two colleagues took the field, to their visible consternation and the crowd's delight.

While Brooklynites screamed and threw paper during the second game, beanballs began to fly. According to Durocher, the Cubs' bench yelled to their pitcher Johnny Schmitz: "Take the button off his cap," when Billy Herman stepped to the plate. The former Cubs second baseman soon found himself on the seat of his pants. Dodgers' rookie hurler Les Webber, watching from the dugout, was heard to proclaim: "I don't care who he is, but the first Cub up in this inning is going down." Len Merullo was the target of Webber's first pitch. It was nothing personal. As Durocher explained, in justification: "If you can't take it, go out and get a broom and go to work."

In the ninth, with the tying run on base and Nicholson at bat, Durocher strolled out to the pitcher's mound. Webber told his manager: "Don't worry about Nicholson, boss. I'll bust one down on the handle for him, and he may hit me, but you can be sure he will not hit one out of the park to beat us." True to his word, he retired the Cubs' slugger, and Brooklyn went on to the 4–3 triumph. Gladys Gooding apologized to Stewart after the game.

The next day, Cubs pitcher Vallie Eaves, the Oklahoma Indian who played briefly for Connie Mack on the 1935 A's, was sent home from Brooklyn because he showed up drunk before a 4–1 Dodgers victory, in which Nicholson fanned three times.

After a day on the bench during the Dodgers series finale, a 5–1 drubbing, Bill returned to action against the Giants in a 6–3 loss, at the Polo Grounds. Before the game, Nicholson and Giants player-manager Mel Ott swapped bats. "We did this just about this time last summer and right away I got started on my best hit streak of the year," Bill explained after the game. His first time up, he broke Ott's bat while swinging at a Bob Carpenter fastball; Ott then hit a two-run shot off Passeau, with Bill's Louisville Slugger, in the bottom of the inning. Using his own bat, Nicholson singled in the seventh, and homered over the right field roof in the ninth.

Nicholson's arm continued to draw notice, even if his bat was sometimes inconsistent. A record 1942 Wrigley Field crowd of 34,185 was treated to an example of his throwing ability in a 3–0 loss to the Cardinals on May 31, which ended a modest four-game Cubs winning streak. In the eighth inning, Stan Musial tried to score from first base on a double by Whitey Kurowski. Chasing down the ball in right, Nicholson fielded it cleanly and fired a strike to catcher Clyde McCullough, who tagged Musial out. The Cardinal star sprained his ankle on the play, and had to be carried off the field by his teammates. The next day's *Trib* contained a photo of Musial's slide, under the headline, "A Cardinals Speed Boy Pays for His Daring." When he retired from baseball in 1953, Nicholson tabbed Musial as "the finest player I ever saw."

The next day, 10,000 soldiers were in attendance at Camp Grant, Illinois, to cheer the post team past the Cubs, 4–3. Nicholson singled twice in four at-bats in the losing effort. Before the game, he and his teammates posed for pictures with former Cubs batboy Vince Garrity, now known as Private Garrity, U.S. Army. Seeing Vince in uniform brought the war even closer to the Cubs players.

Important baseball news came later in the day, with the announcement that the punchless Cubs had purchased the contract of Jimmie Foxx from the Boston Red Sox. Passed up by the other seven American League clubs at the $7,500 waiver price, Chicago shelled out $10,000 to acquire the aging slugger. Gallagher told the press: "We need a wallop and Foxx looks like a good bet to supply it. Sure, we know he's 34 and past his peak, but he's still dangerous." Wilson projected Foxx as the replacement for slumping Rip Russell at first base. Somebody forgot to tell Russell, though; he homered in each of the next three games.

Truth be told, there were sound reasons that other American League teams passed up the chance to acquire Foxx. The great "Double X" was now, unfortunately, a has-been. He was bothered by nagging injuries, and he drank too much. Although he would resurface with the Phillies in 1945 to hit .268 in 224 at bats, his storied career was essentially over.

"I saw him quite a bit," Bill told the *Queen Anne's Record-Observer* in 1987. "We stayed at the same hotel about ten blocks from Wrigley Field. We ate dinner together sometimes. He was very easy to be with, a heck of a nice fellow."

It was upsetting to Nicholson to see his former idol fade. "I know one thing: he was drinking too hard. That was his big problem. But I didn't see anything except that he was going down fast. Maybe it was affecting his eyes or something. He could still, once in a while, hit one just like a shot out of the park. He still had plenty of power."

Wilson benched second baseman Stringer, and moved Russell to second, to accommodate Foxx at first base. After a 2–0 loss to the Dodgers, the slumping Nicholson (seven hits in his last 34 at bats) was dropped to fifth in the batting order in favor of Foxx.

Jimmie was suffering from sore ribs, however, and when he pulled a leg muscle in a win over the Phillies a couple days later, he was removed from the game and saw limited duty thereafter.

The first night contest in the history of Ebbets Field ended in a 6–0 Cubs victory on June 15. Nicholson hit a double and drove home two runs; Foxx tripled, and Novikoff chipped in with three hits.

A unique wartime doubleheader took place on June 29 in Cincinnati. In the first game, a mixed team of Reds and Cubs played against, and lost to, the Great Lakes Naval Training Station team, composed mostly of major leaguers who were in the nation's service. The starting Reds/Cubs team, as selected by Cincinnati fans, included Cavarretta in center, Nicholson in right, and Hack at third.

The second game, a regular season contest between the Reds and Cubs, resulted in a defeat for the Chicagoans. The games raised $36,000 for the Army-Navy Relief Fund, but Nicholson was hitless for the day.

By July 2, Bill, who had been passed over for the All-Star game, raised his average to a solid .283, to accompany seven home runs and 39 RBIs. Foxx, after a month in a Cubs uniform, was struggling at .182, with only one homer.

Leo Durocher and his Dodgers paid a visit to Wrigley Field in mid–July. In the third of four games, the long-simmering feud between the teams erupted in a beanball war. It began after Novikoff and Foxx belted back-to-back home runs in the bottom of the fourth. With his team holding a 5–2 lead, and Nicholson at bat, Brooklyn manager Durocher called time, and strolled out to the mound to talk to his pitcher, Kirby Higbe.

After the manager departed, Higbe's first pitch was thrown behind Nicholson's back. Jimmie Wilson, coaching third base, immediately ducked into the Cubs dugout and sent hard-throwing Paul Erickson to the bullpen to warm up. When Chicago pitcher Hiram Bithorn, from Puerto Rico, and his Cuban catcher Chico Hernandez took the field in the top of the fifth, Durocher and the Brooklyn bench jockeys let fly with their choicest invective, undoubtedly ethnic in nature. With two men on base, Bithorn dusted Higbe, but the ball got away from Hernandez and advanced the runners. As the name-calling became ceaseless, Wilson yanked both Bithorn and Hernandez, and put Paul Erickson on the mound, and Clyde McCullough behind the plate.

When the irate Bithorn headed for the showers, the heckling from the Brooklyn side became so intense that he turned and fired the ball at Durocher, sitting in the dugout. Brooklyn catcher Mickey Owen reached out and deflected the ball with his bare hand to protect his manager. Ed Burns wryly observed that Bithorn's "control had been bad during his entire performance, so he was unable to wing anybody in the Dodger cave." For his actions, N.L. president Ford Frick fined Bithorn $25.00. Wilson purportedly levied his own penalty against the Puerto Rican hurler, as well — for not hitting Durocher.

Not surprisingly, Erickson's first-pitch fastball knocked Ducky Medwick onto the seat of his pants. But the ball got by McCullough, and two runs scored. Brooklyn went on to win the game, 10–5. All was not forgotten, however.

Two games later, the Cubs dropped another 10–5 decision, before a Ladies' Day crowd of more than 20,000. As Erickson left the mound after the top half of the ninth, *he* got into it with Durocher and the Dodger bench jockeys, before umpire Lou Jorda stepped in to ensure order. In the defeat, Nicholson launched his ninth homer over the right field scoreboard, off Schoolboy Rowe, a shot estimated to have traveled about 425 feet.

Cubs infielder Len Merullo knew the anger and frustration players felt when competing against Durocher's Brooklyn team: "Leo Durocher was the most hated man in baseball. That's when you played against him. If you played for him, fine.... But when you played against him, you didn't like him.... He would get personal.... Even his own players didn't like it. But they knew what he was doing. And he got results. He got on Paul Erickson one day, and got on Hiram Bithorn one day, and they wound up throwing at him in the dugout! Throwing the ball at him! That's how mad he could get you."

Foxx's lack of production at bat soon resulted in his benching. Frustrated Jimmie Wilson inserted Novikoff into the cleanup spot, reasoning, "[T]hey all collapse when I put 'em in there, so it's only fair to let 'em take turns at becoming paralyzed."

The longest game of 1942 took place at Crosley Field on August 9. It took 18 innings for the Cubs to beat the Reds, 10–8, in the first game of a scheduled doubleheader. The second game was halted by darkness as the Reds won, 2–1. Nicholson was three for nine with two RBIs during the first game, and two for two with two doubles in the second. The games took seven hours and 11 minutes to play. Reds broadcaster Sam Baltes selected Bill for his 1942 "All Crosley Field Team" on his nightly show over WCPO radio. According to Baltes, Dolf Camilli, Giants pitcher Bill Lohrman, and Nicholson were "automatic, unquestioned selections" because of their performance against the home team during the year.

Bill continued his hitting tear, homering on August 14 and 15. The following day, in a doubleheader loss to Pittsburgh, he doubled, clouted another homer, and was hit by a pitch in four plate appearances in the first game. In the second, he belted homers his first two times at bat, then doubled and singled. He finished the day six for nine: three home runs, a double and two singles, to go with five runs scored and four RBIs.

When asked in later years to cite his greatest single individual performance, Nicholson recalled that doubleheader at Wrigley Field, although he remembered it a little differently. He recited the day's events to the *Pittsburgh Press'* Les Biederman, in 1953: "I had seven straight hits in a doubleheader and I can still remember the sequence: single, double, homer, homer, homer, double, and single. And yet the Pirates won both games!"

He maintained his streak the next day in another doubleheader with the Pirates. This time, the Cubs won both games. Homerless in the opening tilt, in the second game Nicholson drove the first pitch thrown to him high over the screen beyond the right field catwalk at Wrigley. It was his fifth homer in three days.

Although the North Siders were out of pennant contention, they did furnish their fans with skillful play on occasion. Thus on August 22, a muggy Saturday afternoon interrupted by rainstorms that caused the game to be delayed, the Cubs turned a rare triple play in the top of the 11th inning. With the game tied 4–4, the Reds' Lonnie Frey doubled and Bert Haas reached on an infield hit. Frey did not advance. Max Marshall squared to bunt, but popped the ball into the air. Catcher Clyde McCullough alertly grabbed it, and fired to Merullo covering second to double up Frey. Merullo threw on to first baseman Cavarretta, who forced Haas retreating to first.

Then, in the bottom of the inning, with one out, Nicholson — recently troubled by a sore back — parked a Junior Thompson offering over the right field bleachers onto Sheffield Avenue for a walk-off 5–4 victory.

To help the war effort, the Cubs sponsored Salvage Day on September 1. Game admission required only that fans bring scrap metal weighing at least two pounds. People came with baby carriages, sewing machines, and monkey wrenches. An estimated 10,000 pounds of junk was collected for the scrap metal campaign, and nearly 10,000 Cubs fans saw Passeau defeat the Giants, 10–5, aided by Bill's two-run homer off Hal Schumacher.

The season ended on September 27, after four consecutive losses ensured a sixth-place finish. The Cubs finished 18 games under .500, 38 games in back of pennant-winning St. Louis. Although Nicholson did not make the All-Star team for the first time in three years, he played well during the second half of the season. Statistically, he was second in the league in hits, third in total bases, second in triples, fourth in home runs, and eighth in RBIs.

The last post-season City Series lasted six games, with a predictable result: a White Sox victory. For the most part, the games were sparsely attended. Only 4,751 paid to see the opening-game loss to the White Sox at Wrigley. Ted Lyons — soon to join the United States Marine Corps — held the North Siders to three hits. The Cubs lost again the next day, 9–5, before another small crowd.

Nicholson went two for three in a 3–2 loss during game three, although the largest crowd yet — 20,819 — came out to Comiskey Park. It wasn't until the fourth game that the Cubs finally won, behind the pitching of Hi Bithorn, before a small home gathering. They followed their success the next day with a 2–1 victory at Comiskey in ten innings, before losing the finale, 4–1. It was the eighth straight city title for the White Sox. Nicholson finished the series with a mediocre .263 average and didn't drive in a run. His teammates fared no better; Cavarretta averaged .214, Hack .250, Dallesandro .143, and Novikoff .087.

The Cubs each took home a little more than $200.00 for their efforts in the series. There was no "wait 'til next year" for Nicholson and his teammates, however; the postseason City Series was never played again.

10

Coming Into His Own

The specter of the war being fought in Europe and the Pacific cast a shadow over every American institution as 1943 approached, and professional baseball was no exception. Scores of minor and semipro leagues shut down, short on manpower and money. Major league owners who blithely assumed it would continue to be "business as usual" were rudely awakened in December, 1942, at baseball's winter meetings. Joseph B. Eastman, director of the government's Office of Defense Transportation, urged major league clubs to conduct their spring training seasons closer to home, and forgo traditional sunny locales such as Florida, Texas, and California. "Mileage rationing" would ensure priority train travel to soldiers and supplies vital to the military effort.

After some initial squawking, Commissioner Landis whipped the owners in line, and by month's end most were actively seeking practice sites in closer proximity to their home cities. The start of spring training was pushed back by several weeks for all teams.

Cubs general manager Jim Gallagher considered Hot Springs, Arkansas, as a potential training site, but ultimately settled on French Lick, Indiana, 278 miles southeast of Chicago. Both the Cubs and White Sox agreed to train there, and lodge at the French Lick Springs Hotel, a health resort complete with bathing facilities and gaming casinos. Baseball diamonds were constructed for each team, near the golf course.

When the majority of the players arrived on March 22, rains and melting snow submerged the practice field. The Cubs practiced on the 14th fairway of the golf course, while Andy Lotshaw worked feverishly to ready the diamond.

There were other problems. Nine players, including Nicholson, Novikoff, and McCullough, were absent and holding out for more money. Gallagher, in a public relations euphemism, insisted on referring to the holdouts as "absentees." Jimmie Wilson told the press on March 25: "If Novikoff and McCullough don't want to play, that's all right. Both men were given raises and if they are not satisfied, let them stay where they are." Conspicuously absent from Wilson's remarks was any reference to his star slugger Nicholson, who arrived in camp on March 27, also unsigned. He and Nancy had just purchased and were renovating their first home, a red brick structure in the Federal style, at 103 Water Street in Chestertown.

There were now two children in the household, along with Nancy's mother, who helped to care for the boys, and Bill was hoping for a fatter paycheck. After all, Gallagher — denying talk of a Nicholson trade to Cincinnati in October, 1942 — told reporters he wouldn't trade Nicholson for any player in the league.

Having spent the winter working on the farm, and shooting ducks, geese and quail, Nicholson was reported to be in excellent physical condition. Once at French Lick, he was greeted warmly by teammates, issued a uniform, and assigned a room at the hotel. Bill worked out with the squad, and then reported to the dining room, where he spied Gallagher at an adjacent table. He called out a friendly greeting to the general manager, but was met with a stony silence. The grin on Bill's face vanished instantly.

Gallagher was furious, demanding to know who had permitted the unsigned player to work out with the team (it was Wilson). He grudgingly permitted Nicholson to practice that afternoon, but forbade him from returning until contract matters were resolved.

As Nicholson sat, his mates practiced. Catcher Al Todd was injured during a scrimmage; while pursuing a popup, he crashed into the water cooler and shattered a five-gallon bottle, sending shards of glass flying, and cutting himself in the process. A fragment hit and lacerated Chicago sportswriter Edgar Munzel, who promptly fainted. Several of his colleagues probably wished that they, too, were unconscious as they watched the 1943 Cubs sleepwalk through another dismal season.

Nicholson surrendered to Gallagher on March 29, and signed his contract for $13,000, $1,000 less than he'd sought. They settled their differences over a lunch, after which the normally tight-fisted general manager left an extravagant fifty cent tip. "We figure salary should be based on what a player has done and not what he thinks he can do," Gallagher explained.

Edward Burns of the *Trib* was, nevertheless, impressed with Nicholson's *chutzpah* for holding out as long as he did, remarking that the ballplayer displayed "good old eastern shore stubbornness to the extent never suspected of the mild and affable Maryland athlete."

On his first day back, Bill played in an intrasquad game. Several days later against the White Sox, with the count 3–2, he clubbed a grand-slam home run onto the 18th fairway of the golf course.

After 18 days of decent weather and double session workouts, Jimmie Wilson was enthusiastic about his club's performance. "This is the best training camp I've ever been in," he gushed. "The rest of them can have Florida, California, and the sunny southland. For me, I'll take French Lick." With a revamped lineup that included rookie Eddie Stanky at second, and six proven starting pitchers in Lon Warneke, Derringer, Lee, Passeau, Bithorn, and Hanyzewski, knowledgeable Cubs watchers (including even Edward Burns) anticipated a banner season.

Making their 1943 Wrigley Field regular season debut, the North Siders abandoned the sleeveless vests they had sported for the past several seasons and returned to more traditional and looser-fitting outfits. Burns applauded the change. Of Nicholson, he wrote: "He is a very modest man and often blushed furiously while exhibiting himself in those clingy crocheted numbers."

The 1943 major league season was affected by wartime restrictions in more ways than the elimination of excessive spring training travel. The schedule was streamlined so that there were fewer road trips. More benefit exhibition games against service teams were played. But the game was perhaps most affected by the modification of an essential article of equipment: the baseball.

For the 1943 season the A.G. Spalding Company, manufacturer of National League baseballs, decided to use a substitute product for war-rationed rubber. The result was a sphere with a horsehide cover and a core of granulated cork and balata, the rubber-like material commonly used in the manufacture of golf balls. The "balata ball" marked a virtual return to the "deadball" era. The spheres were so lifeless that, after a couple of months, the league opted to junk them, and use its remaining supply of 1942 balls. Even with this midseason infusion, the number of home runs hit during the 1943 season declined by more than 16 percent. In fact, only 11 major leaguers hit more than 20 home runs in a season during the years 1943–45.

Because the supply of 1942 balls was limited, they were not so readily discarded from play by umpires. Thus, on July 30, Cavarretta homered off the Dodgers' Johnny Allen; the ball was retrieved and put back in play. The next batter was Nicholson. Seven years before, as a nervous rookie, he'd whiffed in his first major league at-bat against Allen. This time, he drove Johnny's first offering over the right field wall and bleachers, into the street beyond: one ball, one pitcher, two pitches, two home runs. "So far as I know, the ball was still traveling when Durocher took me out of the game," said Allen later, of Bill's clout. It was the last pitch he threw for Brooklyn; he was soon traded to the crosstown Giants.

At the commencement of the regular season, Nicholson had been classified as 3A by the Selective Service Board; as the father of children born before September 15, 1942, he was not subject to be drafted by the military until the supply of unmarried men and married men without children was exhausted.

Now donning uniform number 43, which he would wear for the rest of his Cubs career, Nicholson led the team to an Opening Day victory over the Pirates at Wrigley, 6–3. He drove in two runs and had three hits in four trips. Cub fortunes headed steadily south thereafter.

Eleven games into the season, Pittsburgh's Rip Sewell was already the owner of three victories against the North Siders. With a doubleheader loss to the Pirates on May 2, the punchless Cubs had been shut out in four of 10 games. Edward Burns cracked:

> There are no white shirts in center field ... and the lads were dressed in their new baseball uniforms. Thus stripped of two of their long-time alibis, there was nothing for the fellows to do but admit they are cheese hitters.

National League president Ford Frick placed the stubborn Novikoff on baseball's ineligible list, on May 6. The "Mad Russian," a 47-day holdout, demanded a salary of $10,000, while Gallagher's top offer had been $6,000. Novikoff explained to the press that he was in a "war of nerves" with the general manager. Informed of Novikoff's remarks, Gallagher sneered, "That guy isn't half as stubborn as I am, buddy boy."

A nine-game losing streak ended in Boston on May 23, with a doubleheader victory over the Braves. In game one, Nicholson tripled off the left field fence and scored on Stanky's single. He also contributed two hits in the nightcap.

The day's biggest story, however, was the arrival of Novikoff by train from his home in California. The team was sorely in need of a righthanded-hitting outfielder, so Gallagher had adopted a more flexible negotiating stance. "Pants" Rowland, now working with the Cubs' Los Angeles Angels affiliate, had been enlisted to mediate the Mad Russian's contract dispute, and the parties eventually compromised at an annual paycheck of $8,500.

There was quite a commotion when the Santa Fe Chief, bearing the charismatic Novikoff, arrived at the Dearborn Street Station. Upon disembarking, he faced reporters and greeted cheering fans. Asked if he could help the last-place Cubs out of the cellar, Lou modestly quipped, "I'll try, but

10. Coming Into His Own

eight other fellows have to do something." In the next day's 4–2 loss to the Giants, he went hitless in four plate appearances.

By this time, Nicholson was batting .295, with 10 RBIs, but hadn't homered in 122 at-bats, the longest drought of his career. In fact, not one homer had been struck by the entire Cubs team. Danny Litwhiler of the Phillies led the league with four round-trippers, an unusually low total more than a month into the season.

As the 1943 balls were phased out, however, Nicholson began to hit the ball with more authority. His slugging began on May 30, in the first game of a doubleheader against the Braves at Wrigley Field. Al Javery, the Boston pitcher and winner of his four previous decisions, was the first victim. Nicholson bashed a pair of two-run homers, in the fourth and eighth innings, to end the Cubs' homerless streak, and help his teammates to a 5–1 win.

The next day, he hit two 1943 baseballs out of Wrigley against the Phillies in a doubleheader, with a single, double, and homer in the first contest. Forty-eight hours later, he hit his fifth homer in six games, this time in an 8–1 rout of the Dodgers.

Bill ascribed the sudden return of his home run power to a change in batting stance, and not the liveliness of the ball. "I was standing up too straight and keeping my arms close to my body. Now I am crouching and holding my arms out more," he explained.

Brooklyn manager Durocher, infuriated at the shellacking his squad received at the hands of the lowly Cubs, called a team meeting before the next day's game. It was so lengthy that the Dodgers missed half of their scheduled batting practice. Whatever Durocher told his players worked, as they pulverized Cub pitching, 18–5, scoring seven runs in the first off Derringer. Nicholson fanned three times, and grounded into a double play.

But the North Siders gained a measure of revenge a day later, knocking Brooklyn out of first place, on the strength of a 3–2 decision. The decisive play of the game was not evident from the box score, but exemplified Nicholson's all-around hustle and willingness to do whatever it took to win a ball game.

In the Cub fourth, with one out and Bill on first base, Novikoff grounded to short. Pee Wee Reese threw to Billy Herman at second, to force Nicholson. A strong throw to first by Herman would complete a double play and end the inning.

Bill slid hard into Herman, however, forcing his former teammate to hurry his throw to first. It sailed wide, Novikoff was safe, and the inning continued. Two runs scored thereafter, tilting the game in the Cubs' favor.

Wilson's men spent most of June in the N.L. cellar, jockeying with the

Pirates and Giants for seventh place. But just before the All-Star break, the Cubs went on the road and began to click, sweeping a doubleheader at Boston. Nicholson's eighth-inning homer in the nightcap provided the margin for the 5–4 victory. After losing a doubleheader to the Dodgers the next day — despite Nicholson's first-inning, first-game homer — they bounced back 24 hours later to win, behind the pitching of Passeau. In the first Chicago victory of the year at Ebbets Field, Nicholson ended the game with a spectacular catch of a line drive off the bat of Billy Herman. It marked the Chicagoans' seventh victory in their last 10 games. In what some were cynically calling the "Cellar Series," the Cubs then split a doubleheader with the last-place Giants. Nicholson's 400-foot, two-run blast in the seventh off Johnny Wittig clinched the 4–3 win.

Three Cubs were selected by vote of the N.L. managers for the All-Star game, to be played at Shibe Park: Passeau, Hack, and Nicholson. Thirty-three thousand fans descended on the field at Twenty First and Lehigh by car, bus, and the #54 trolley that rattled up Lehigh Avenue through North Philly. Eighty-six-year-old Michael Mack, Connie's older brother, was even spotted directing traffic in the street an hour before game time at 7:00 P.M. The fans were treated to a pregame show by Al Schacht.

The Nicholson family, including 350-pound Larny, drove up from Chestertown to witness the spectacle. The weather was so hot that sportswriters in the press box had stripped down to their undershirts to report the game. The game's start was delayed for 15 minutes, so that the British Broadcasting Company could short-wave the game to servicemen throughout the world. Broadcasters Mel Allen, Red Barber, and Bill Corum brought the action into living rooms across the United States on the CBS network, sponsored by the Gillette Safety Razor Company.

More than $100,000 was raised to benefit the fund established to provide servicemen with baseball equipment, as the host American League won, 5–3. Bill, batting cleanup behind the Cardinals' Stan Musial, was again hitless in two trips.

After the All-Star break, the North Siders picked up where they left off, clobbering the Reds, 8–0, behind Bill's home run and four RBIs. Wrapping up a road trip in which they won 13 of 19, Chicago took a doubleheader from the Reds on July 18, to take over fifth place. In the second game, with the bases full, Nicholson ripped a 3–0 fastball from Bucky Walters, to single in two runs. For the day, Bill had five hits, homered, and knocked in five runs.

The Cubs swept a three-game series from the Dodgers on July 30, winning the last game, 12–3. Nicholson hit his 12th homer (off Johnny Allen, again), doubled, singled, and walked. He added five RBIs to raise his league-leading total to 72. The sweep brought the North Siders to within six games of third place Brooklyn.

As usual, Cub prosperity did not last long. The club dropped 10 of the next 12 games, including four straight to the Braves. By August 14, they settled into seventh place, despite continued and prodigious offensive production from their all-star right fielder. In Brooklyn on August 19, Nicholson hit Curt Davis' first pitch over the Ebbets Field scoreboard, onto Bedford Avenue. Bill's 90 RBIs now led the majors, and his 18 home runs led the N.L.

In another defeat the following day, Durocher had to separate pitcher Whitlow Wyatt from umpire Tom Dunn, after Cavarretta walked on a pitch Wyatt thought should have been called a strike. Still flustered, Wyatt came inside with a fastball to the next batter, Nicholson. It was knocked out of the park, further incensing the Dodger hurler. In the bottom of the inning, unremitting Cubs bench jockeying finally caused Wyatt to leave the mound, and head towards Wilson in the visiting dugout. The scrappy manager met him halfway, but the ensuing melee was broken up. Brooklyn fans gave the hotheaded Wyatt a lusty booing when he came to bat later in the inning.

In 1955, when Wyatt was the Phillies' pitching coach, he was asked by a reporter to name the toughest batsman he faced during his career. Wyatt did not hesitate. "He was Bill Nicholson, and he took a mighty good cut. But he had my number. I don't believe I ever got him out," he said.

Nicholson hit another home run the following day, this time against the Giants at the Polo Grounds, a three-run clout in the first game of a Chicago doubleheader sweep. He was playing with some additional inspiration, having recently received a letter from a paratrooper overseas: "I've always admired your playing and I wonder if you'd be so kind as to send me a Cub cap," the soldier wrote. "I'd like to wear it going into battle." Nicholson, touched by the request, readily complied.

As the team wallowed near the N.L. basement, it was announced that the postseason City Series would not be played. The cancellation, Cubs officials said, was necessitated by Jim Gallagher's desire to see the World Series, to be played at the same time. In a nonbinding vote, a majority of the team nevertheless voted to participate in the annual affair; most of them were in need of the extra money they would earn by competing. Seven voted not to play, including Derringer, Passeau, Warneke, Hack, and Nicholson, who was selected for a touring team of all-stars headed for the South Pacific to entertain the troops.

Bill closed out the campaign with a bang, homering seven times in the last two weeks. In a doubleheader sweep of the pennant-winning Cardinals on September 19, he hit two round-trippers, two doubles, two singles, and drove in six more runs. Four days later, he hit two more homers off Schoolboy Rowe before only 1,177 fans at Wrigley, in an 8–7 victory over Philadelphia.

A day before the season's end, the War Department announced the cancellation of the South Pacific all-star tour, due to manpower and transportation problems. Bill would remain stateside during the off-season, assuming that his draft status did not change.

The season concluded with a doubleheader against the Braves at Chicago, and Nicholson went out with a bang. The teams split, as the Cubs helped Hi Bithorn to his 18th victory in the first game. Nicholson was three for three, scored four times, homered, and knocked in two. For the doubleheader, he reached base seven times in eight plate appearances.

Chicago wound up the 1943 campaign in fifth place, 30½ games behind St. Louis. For the first and only time in his career, Bill finished the season with a batting average exceeding .300—.309, to be exact. His 29 homers (more than the rest of the Cubs *combined*) led the N.L., and his 128 RBIs paced the majors. He was third in runs scored (95), fourth in hits (188), second in slugging percentage (.531), total bases (323), extra base hits (68) and strikeouts (86).

The Baseball Writers Association of America, however, selected St. Louis' Musial as the league's Most Valuable Player. His teammate Walker Cooper was second in the voting, Nicholson third. Many thought Nicholson was short-changed in the selection process because he played on a second-division ballclub.

Brooklyn's Johnny Cooney considered Bill the best player in either league. "Nicholson is the most determined player in the game," he added. "He may have had some faults when he was breaking in, but he has worked hard to cure them." Cubs teammate Paul Derringer agreed: "He's out there practicing fielding ground balls when the pitchers take their batting practice, long before the game starts."

"He's the greatest player in the league," Braves coach Bob Coleman posited. "Why, during the last week of the season, when most of the players were just playing out the string, Nicholson was holding private fielding and throwing practice to improve his play."

Bill viewed his year's accomplishments in characteristic fashion. He told a magazine writer years later: "Sure 128 [RBIs] was good, but it really wasn't anything. Hack Wilson had nearly 200 [actually 190] in 1930."

What was Bill Nicholson's contribution to the fortunes of the 1943 Cubs? Consider this: he drove in 20.25 percent of the team's runs, the sixth-best ratio in major league history. Babe Ruth's highest percentage was 20.18

percent, with the 1919 Boston Red Sox. Even Jim Gallagher was impressed. Reportedly, he saw to it that the club made up the difference between the amount Nicholson sought during his spring training holdout, and the contract upon which the parties settled. "We frequently make adjustments of that nature when a player deserves it," claimed the general manager. "He played great ball for us and we rewarded him accordingly."

Nicholson always felt slighted by the lack of attention he received in Kent County for his baseball accomplishments. After a year in the limelight, and with the overseas tour having been cancelled, Bill participated in the Baseball "Pheastival" in Huron, South Dakota, an annual gathering of major leaguers who played an exhibition game, and then spent several days hunting pheasant. He returned to Chestertown in late October, having been away since March, and bumped into a neighbor, who inquired: "Hey Bill, where have you been all summer?"

11
"Swish" and His Fans

To suggest that Bill Nicholson was popular with National League spectators, foreign and domestic, would be an understatement. Every city to which the Cubs traveled had its legion of fans eager to cheer or good-naturedly jeer him.

Nicholson was the strong, silent type, good-looking, and modest, besides. Former Cubs teammate Len Merullo remembered: "Bill had a great sense of humor, even though he was very quiet. He had a dry humor. Everybody loved him. He had those shiny white teeth and always had a smile on his face. He was about six feet tall, no more, and strong as a bull."

His popularity didn't start when he became a major leaguer; he was also lionized by the inhabitants of the minor league cities in which he played. Several weeks after his death, his stepdaughter Emily Joiner received a letter from a resident of Michigan named Robert Brown. He was 10 years old and living in Tennessee when Nicholson played for the Chattanooga Lookouts in 1939. He related:

> Once, following a game in which [Bill] caught the ball that ended the game, we kids swarmed onto the field as the players were running in. I was next to him, and he patted me on the head. That was a thrill I lived with for years. When he was hitting home runs for the Cubs, I would show my friends where "HE" had touched my head.

In retirement, and even after his death, scores of letters arrived at the Nicholson farm outside Chestertown, from Cubs fans who worshipped him when they were children. "My first real memories of Big League Baseball was listening to Bert Wilson [of radio station WIND] describing the Cubs games of 1943. I was 11 and living on a farm seventy miles west of beautiful Wrigley Field. It was pure joy when Bill hit a homer," wrote Al Benson.

"People's memories are short, but in the mid-forties Bill Nicholson was the best known ballplayer in Chicago. I was crushed when he was traded ... as far as a 14 year old can be," said Jim Revord.

11. "Swish" and His Fans

A safety patrol named Billy Stone, whose station was located near the right field bleachers at Wrigley Field, used to hoist himself up an ironwork grill outside the bleachers, onto the roof of a ticket office. From there, he could jump over a low fence and make his way into the bleachers, where he could watch his idol, Bill Nicholson.

In the mid-'40s, radio made Nicholson an icon in the Midwest, even for those not able to see him play in person. Cubs games were carried on several stations, including WGN, WCFL, WJJD, and WIND. P. Lorillard Company, a cigarette manufacturer, sponsored the popular WGN broadcasts by Dick Enroth and Jack Brickhouse, a shameless Cubs rooter who announced his last game in 1981. His famous excuse for Cubs futility was classic: "Any team can have a bad century!"

Nicholson later established relationships with many of his former fans via the mail, and invited several to visit him on the farm when they were in the Maryland area. One visitor expressed amazement that Bill was more interested in him and his family than in talking about long-ago baseball accomplishments.

Ladies especially loved the rugged outfielder. One tale has it that, during the '40s, a home run ball broke the window at a house on Sheffield Avenue, behind Wrigley's right field bleachers. The woman who lived in the home was told that Nicholson had hit the ball. As a Swish Nicholson fan, she decided to pay for the window herself. When she discovered some time later that another player had hit the home run ball, she marched directly to the Cubs offices and demanded damages, telling a club official: "You either replace my broken window, or I sue!"

There were many stories about the damage done by Nicholson home run balls, dating back to his minor league days. In Chattanooga, three small houses sat behind the right field wall. The occupants of the houses returned Nicholson's drives to management, in return for free admittance to the game. When Bill was sold to the Cubs, one of the residents told Wirt Gammon: "We are sorry Nicholson is leaving. He hits so many balls over here, we get to go in lots of games on them. No other player has ever hit many over here, so we won't go to many games, now."

Wirt Gammon asked the gentleman whether the home run shots had done any damage. "Oh, once he hit my sister on the leg," was the response. "She was sitting on the back steps. That's been three weeks ago and it's all right now. No, he hasn't broken any windows. He is considerate. Most of his drives clear these houses."

Another legend holds that a Philadelphian named Otto Gessner was sitting down to eat an apple pie in his house on Opal Street, beyond the Spite

Fence, when a Nicholson missile exited Connie Mack Stadium and struck his windowsill.

Roger Miller grew up outside of New York City and was a big Giants fan. He usually sat in the right field stands at the Polo Grounds, to root for his hero, Mel Ott. Miller remembers particularly one game in the mid–1940's. He was a teenager, and Nicholson and Ott were engaged in a race for the league home run crown.

During that era, defensive players leaving the field after the third out flipped their gloves in the air and left them on the field of play. After their team took its turn at bat, they would retrieve the gloves and resume their defensive positions. Ott, playing right field, left his glove there at inning's end. A mischievous Nicholson ran out to take his place in right, and spotted the glove. Knowing Miller and other spectators were looking on, he picked up the mitt, scooped up several handfuls of dirt and grass, and stuffed them in the glove's finger holes. The fans hooted and jeered Nicholson good-naturedly.

When the unsuspecting Ott ran out the next inning to take his place in the field, Giants partisans warned him not to put the glove on, but he didn't understand what they were yelling about, until he stuck his hand inside the leather. Bill, of course, was now safely ensconced in the visiting dugout, laughing at his friend and rival Ott.

Of course, Nicholson was, from time to time, on the receiving end of practical jokes perpetrated by his teammates. As an aging vet with the Phillies, he reported to the clubhouse at Clearwater, Florida for spring training in 1952. He entered the room to find his uniform nailed to the ceiling. His teammates howled in delight when the bewildered Nicholson had to look up to discover his pants and jersey.

As the oldest member of the Whiz Kids, the young Phillies called him "Papa Nick"; while visiting New York for a series against the Giants, they made him take them to Madison Square Garden to see the circus. Nicholson and teammate Eddie Waitkus thought it amusing that they had to wait until they were old-timers to be known as Whiz Kids.

In a major league career that spanned 1,677 contests, Nicholson was never ejected from a game by an umpire — although he probably should have been on May 17, 1949, playing with the Phillies against the Cardinals at Sportsman's Park. Remembering the game, Nicholson said: "I tried to [get thrown out] once, but I couldn't get the job done. [Alpha] Brazle was pitching when I was playing with the Phillies and he struck me out the first time up. The second time up, he got me two strikes and a couple balls, and he threw me a big curve ball and it was way, way inside and of course I knew it was inside because I had to hit it ... so I let it go, and 'course it kept rolling on, wound around the plate to the catcher, and he called me out. And I just said to [umpire Frank Dascoli], 'Sir, that ball was a foot inside when I had to hit at it.' Well, that was all I said that time."

"The third time I came up, situation got about the same, and he threw me that big curve ball, way inside, and he called me out again. So I said — I was hot, too, I guess — and I got him pretty bad, knowing that if you open your mouth real wide, he would throw you out. Well, I said a few things that I'd never said to him before, 'cause I always got along good with the umpires. Well, he still didn't throw me out."

"So the fourth time I came up.... We were behind 5–4 ... he threw that big curve ball again and he got it out over the plate, and I never hit one better." That home run tied the game, which was eventually won by the Phils in 12 innings.

His reputation was that of a gentleman, but one who would come to the aid of a teammate, in a heartbeat, if necessary. In 1946, when Merullo and the Dodgers' Dixie Walker tangled before a game at Ebbets Field, Brooklyn's finest were summoned to restore order. A bloodied Walker was receiving the worst of it, and soon Pee Wee Reese and Cavarretta were tussling, as well. Manager Charlie Grimm and Nicholson interceded to assist their teammates, and were themselves nearly arrested before the pugilistic activity ceased.

Omnipresent was the chaw of Beech-Nut tobacco in Nicholson's left jaw. He chewed only during the games, and never before or after. Beech-Nut was the most popular chew among ball players. Advertisements proclaimed that it was "dipped twice ... to hold that doubly delicious taste." *Trib* columnist Arch Ward remarked in 1942, half-jokingly, that Nicholson's biggest fear was the possibility the U.S. government would ration chewing tobacco, because he needed a pack-and-a-half a day, with an additional pack on dusty days. "Bill is said to be the champion 'freshener' among baseball chewers," Ward wrote.

Perhaps in response to Ward's remarks, fans in the Wrigley Field right field bleachers began to throw packages of Beech-Nut tobacco at him between innings. "I kept the whole team in tobacco," he claimed.

When Nicholson was with the Phillies, teammate Richie Ashburn was in a batting slump. Nicholson offered him Beech-Nut to shake him out of the doldrums. "I walked up to the plate, and I was gagging," Ashburn recalled. "I was trying not to swallow the juice and I was getting sick. But I got three hits that game and broke out of the slump."

Nicholson's other principal vice was the smoking of cigars, to the consternation of Phil Cavarretta, whose locker was situated next door. "He loved to smoke cigars after the game," Cavarretta remembered. "Nick and Stan Hack both smoked them."

During Nicholson's home run championship seasons of 1943 and 1944, he got a case of Wheaties for every dinger he hit. "They'd slide them down the backstop," related Merullo. "And after you hit your home run, the batboy would catch the Wheaties off the screen and hand it to the home run hitter. That box always went into my locker. I didn't have to hit home runs to eat!" According to Phil Cavarretta, the locker room at Wrigley Field was always stacked with boxes of Wheaties, for anyone to take. At the end of the season, Bill brought cases home to his friends in Chestertown, and donated the rest to the local hospital. He ate the cereal religiously, until later years, when he switched to oatmeal.

Nicholson was a principal participant in the endless poker games that occupied Charlie Grimm's Cubs when they had idle time, along with Merullo, Cavarretta, Lowrey and McCullough. They also shot craps, introducing young Gene Mauch to the game in 1948.

The fun-loving Nicholson would wrestle Merullo on the clubhouse floor, allowing the smaller player to "pin" him, before easily flipping him into the air as though he were a feather. Bill was also an expert at administering the "hot foot" to his teammates. On a road trip, in the lobby of the visiting team's hotel, he might get down on his hands and knees behind an unsuspecting Cub. Then, he would light a match to an accelerant such as a piece of newspaper, place it under the victim's shoe, and run away gleefully while the innocent recipient stamped his foot to put the fire out.

Although Bill did not drink to excess, he sometimes ran with "Monk" Meyer, a temperamental pitcher and teammate with both the Cubs and Phillies who imbibed with greater frequency than some of his teammates. Meyer always seemed to find trouble, with women, players, or managers.

Nicholson and Meyer were teammates at Philadelphia, from 1949–52. During a road trip to New York in 1950, a street "vendor" sold Monk a ring, alleged to be a two-carat diamond, for $50. When he arrived at the lobby of the team hotel, Meyer proudly displayed his new acquisition. Nicholson was skeptical. "Let me see that diamond," he said. "You don't mind if I scratch the floor with it, do you?"

Meyer handed it to Nicholson, who placed it on the floor and ground it with his shoe. To Monk's consternation, the "diamond" disintegrated. On the next trip to New York, however, Meyer got even; he located the dealer and, in the company of a policeman, managed to get his money back.

Nicholson was a man of many nicknames. "Nick," "Billy Nick," "The Maryland Broadback," "Muscles," "Burly Bill," and "Bad Bill" were only some of the monikers that appeared in the press during the course of his career. Of course, the most enduring was "Swish," or "Mr. Swish." The origin of that term is a matter of dispute.

Some claim Nicholson received the appellation because he struck out so often. It is true that Bill fanned with relative frequency: from 1941 through 1945, he finished second or third each year in National League strikeouts. In 1947, he led the league, with 83.

By the same token, his strikeout totals were extremely modest when viewed against the totals of players of this era. In 1941, for example, Nicholson posted the highest single season strikeout total of his career — 91, in 617 plate appearances. Roughly translated, this amounted to one strikeout for every 6.78 times at the plate. Brooklyn's Dolf Camilli led the league in strikeouts that year, with 115, in 641 plate appearances, or once every 5.57 trips to the plate.

Nicholson wearing sunglasses, 1940, Beech-Nut tobacco stains on his lower lip (*reproduced by permission from National Baseball Hall of Fame Library, Cooperstown, N.Y.*).

By comparison, in 2004, Adam Dunn of the Cincinnati Reds led the National League in strikeouts with 192 (a major league record), in 692 plate appearances. That amounted to a strikeout every 3.55 times up. Dunn struck out at a rate that makes Nicholson's numbers look quite tame. And they don't call him "Swish" Dunn.

Others claim the nickname "Swish" caught on because of the pure power generated by Nicholson's lefthanded swing. As Ed Athey, longtime Washington College baseball coach and athletic director said, "If he missed a pitch, you could hear his bat cutting the air."

Nicholson advanced at least two theories as to the origin of his nickname: "Every time I came to the plate, I would take a few practice swings to sort of measure the pitcher. After awhile, the fans just started yelling 'Swish' with each swing."

This account is consistent with a description provided by sportswriter Tim Cohane about a Cubs-Dodgers game in July, 1944: "The [Brooklyn] crowd of 11,738 ... got most of its evening fun out of roaring 'S-W-I-S-H' in unison every time Bad Bill Nicholson took one of his formidable preparatory swings."

Chicago Daily News sportswriter John Carmichael agreed:

> He'd step into the box, flex that cud of tobacco against his right [sic] cheek, level the bat once for size, and then ... Nick'd give the club a few practice swings. ... "Swish ... swish ... swish..." cried the alien fans, timing their resounding hisses with the rhythm of Nicholson's sweep against the empty air. He always claimed it never bothered him ... but the fans firmly believed they were tolling the knell for a feared and hated enemy.

In a radio interview for WBAL radio in 1994, however, Nicholson was more blunt. When asked by interviewer Dan Rodricks why he was called "Swish," he presented a simplistic theory: "I swung hard."

What seems to be undisputed is that the nickname began in Brooklyn, probably in 1942. Ebbets Field was a bandbox of a ballpark. The intimate atmosphere made the spectator feel as though he or she was a part of the action. Opposing players were never far from the fans, and always within earshot of an epithet or jeer. They had favorite opposing players who were the special object of their derision.

For instance, as he went into his smooth and rhythmic windup, the great Cincinnati pitcher Johnny Vander Meer would hear the Dodger faithful chant "one, two, three, four" in cadence. Dodgers radio announcer Red Barber thought that Brooklyn fans threw Nicholson "off balance by the tremendous 'swish' that rose from the stands every time he swung his bat."

Regardless of its origin, the nickname remained a source of pride throughout Nicholson's life. In later years, when signing autographs for fans, he always wrote his name as "Bill 'Swish' Nicholson."

Chicagoans did not usually call Nicholson "Swish." He was "Nick" or "Big Nick" to fans and teammates. Because there was thought to be some ill-will intended by New Yorkers who employed the "Swish" chant, Cubs fans were protective of their right fielder. Gentlemanly Mel Ott, perceived as a rival to Nicholson, was thus himself often the object of jeering and derision when he came to the Windy City, as a kind of reciprocal gesture.

After his death in 1996, Nicholson's stepdaughter Emily Joiner received many condolences from grieving fans. One was from a former Brooklyn resident named Patrick Hill, who said that Nicholson's good humor and tolerance in the face of Brooklyn hecklers was an example of good sportsmanship he would never forget. He sent along a poem about his experience as a young Dodgers fan in ecumenical Brooklyn, called "First Communion:"

11. "Swish" and His Fans

I made my first Communion
At Ebbets Field
When I joined
The chant of "Swish"

An orchestra
Of thirty thousand
Under the direction
Of Bill Nicholson.

"Suuuuhhh-wiish" we'd intone
When he'd move his bat slow
And "Swish-swish"
When he'd move it fast;
And with one loud "SWISH" would we respond
When he swung and missed the ball.

"Suuuuhhh-wiish," said the dads
And "Swish-swish" screeched their kids
And that one-armed man from Memphis;
While "SWISH" sang the Blacks
And "Swish-swish" joined the Jews
As did the nuns from East Canarsie.

"Suuuuhhh-wiish," "Suuuuhhh-wiish,"
"Swish-swish," "SWISH,"
"Suuuuhhh-wiish," "Suuuuhhh-wiish,"
"Swish-swish," "SWISH."

Oh, how did it start?
And why did it stop?
Where have you gone,
Bill Nicholson?

12

The Supreme Compliment

For his 1943 performance, Nicholson was named the right fielder on *The Sporting News'* major league All-Star team, which consisted of only 11 players. At 29, he was now one of the stars of the game, and should have been entitled to appropriate compensation by the team for whom he toiled. But he was weary of Jim Gallagher's tightfisted approach to contract negotiation and unsure of his military draft status after two years of war. Bill was led to believe that he would be conscripted if he reported to French Lick for spring training. For those reasons, on March 18, 1944, he announced that he was retiring from professional baseball. Few took him at his word, believing his declaration was nothing more than a ruse, designed to extract a few thousand dollars more from Phil Wrigley.

Recalling Nicholson's encounter with Gallagher in the hotel dining room at French Lick the year before, one newspaper wag suggested a script for Nicholson to use in current contract negotiations with the general manager:

> Now listen here, you. I went to French Lick last spring, advancing my own dough from Chestertown, Md. And what happens? You give me the brush and I gotta sign at 2 P.M. on an empty stomach, not being allowed to autograph a tab for lunch in the ... dining hall....

Ed Burns suggested in his weekly *Sporting News* column that team members disliked Gallagher so much that they wanted to see Nicholson "pull the hairs out of Smilin' Jim's famous mustache, a hair at a time—before ever mentioning salary." There was at least a grain of truth in Burns' theory, according to Phil Cavarretta, who knew Gallagher in his former life as a reporter for a Chicago newspaper. "He was nasty then, and nasty as a general manager, too," the former Cubs star remembered. "He would come into the clubhouse, yelling at the players, telling them they were not going to get raises if they didn't play better. The players didn't like him."

Those Cubs who had signed contracts reported to French Lick on March 20, and worked out in the horse training center. Fourteen members of the team were missing, including Passeau, Andy Pafko, Dallesandro, Nicholson, and Stan Hack, who had announced his retirement. News dispatches reported on March 22, however, that Nicholson had indeed signed a 1944 contract and was ready to report. As the days dragged on without his appearance, the press speculated that Bill's arrival was imminent. At the end of the month, though, he was still absent; now, the reports said that he was in Chestertown waiting to hear from his draft board.

Nicholson finally arrived in French Lick on April 5, but said he'd decide in a couple of days whether to retire. He explained to reporters: "My draft board in Chestertown said I would remain deferred if I stayed on the farm, but I would be put on 1-A as soon as I reported for baseball. My number would then be called in May, which means that if I passed the physical I would probably go in June. That's only about six months of baseball, and there's not much percentage in that."

Though Nicholson remained a popular figure in Chestertown, there was grumbling in the community about his draft status. Some questioned why it was that he was fit to play major league baseball, but not fit to serve his country. Kent Countians were fighting and dying overseas: Coach Kibler's son John Thomas Kibler, Jr., a former baseball player at Washington and Lee, would be killed later in 1944, after his plane was shot down in combat over Belgium. Eddie McMahan, a Chestertonian and acquaintance of Bill's who graduated in 1939 from Washington College and set several school track records, lost his life on Okinawa. A former teammate, Arthur Greims, Jr., a quarterback on the undefeated 1935 football team at Washington College, would die on November 27, during the Battle of the Bulge.

Nicholson's failure to serve in the military was something he did not like to talk about. There was some sense of guilt or shame about the subject that caused him to avoid the topic. In his defense, the number of men in their late 20s, with children, who served overseas during the war was relatively small. And it is ironic that, when Nicholson sought entry into the naval service many years before, he was summarily rejected.

Gallagher announced on April 6 that Nicholson had agreed to contract terms. Bill was looking for a raise to $17,500, but the Cubs offered $16,500, which would still make him the highest-paid player on the team. The Associated Press reported a day later that "Bill Nicholson ... still doesn't know which lettuce he wants — the kind he grows on his farm or the kind the Chicago Cubs are willing to unfold to keep him in baseball." The parties finally compromised at $17,000, and on April 8 Nicholson made his first exhibition game appearance, singling and hitting a sacrifice fly in a 10–3 loss to Cincinnati in Louisville.

The composition of the Spalding baseball had changed again, to a "buna-S core." It was the polar opposite of the balata ball of 1943. After early use, its liveliness caused the players to nickname it the "Rocket Ball." The Indians' Lou Boudreau observed, "If the cover was any tighter, it would be a golf ball."

After an abbreviated spring training, the Cubs returned to Chicago for a preseason City Series against the White Sox, who won two of three contests. Nicholson settled into his suite at the Sheridan Plaza Hotel, where he roomed with rookie shortstop Bill Schuster. In the last game, a 2–1 Cubs victory, he went three for five and drove in two runs with a double.

An Opening Day shutout over the Reds, in which Bill drove in two runs, was followed by 13 straight losses. In the second loss, the home opener against the Cardinals, Nicholson pursued a foul ball down the right field line and came face-to-face with Al Capone, watching the game from front row seats. The gangster, five years out of prison and suffering from syphilis, now spent most of his time in Florida. Capone, it should be noted, was adept with a baseball bat himself. He wielded one, with deadly effect, to eliminate John Scalisi and Albert Anselmi, who'd incurred his wrath for their role in the 1929 St. Valentine's Day Massacre on the North Side.

Jimmie Wilson, desperate to find some scoring punch, benched third baseman Tony York, who'd been batting third in the order. An overweight Jimmie Foxx, returning after a year's absence, was inserted in his place. After the losing streak had reached five games, rain forced postponement of the day's game in Pittsburgh. The cancellation was announced as the Cubs reached the locker room at Forbes Field, but Pirates manager Frankie Frisch offered to let the visitors use the field for practice. About half of the team opted to work out.

Nicholson and Foxx were the first to dress. They remained on the field for several hours, hitting, fielding, and running. Wilson gazed out at the two Eastern Shore farmers with admiration. "You can always tell the natural hustlers, when you give an order of that kind," said the manager. "Foxx and Nicholson have the spirit. You will note that some of the kid players elected to watch the others, although no player is in top condition yet."

In the first inning of the next day's game, Pirates leadoff hitter Frankie Gustine set himself in the batter's box and peered out at the beefy Foxx on third base. As if to test old "Double X," he bunted the first pitch down the third base line. A surprisingly nimble Foxx charged, and fielded the ball cleanly to throw Gustine out at first base. Later in the game, Jimmie doubled and even stole third base in the ninth inning.

12. The Supreme Compliment

But Foxx's deficiencies were embarrassingly revealed in a 4–2 loss in St. Louis on April 29, when he was caught napping on a bunt in the fifth, and dropped a fly ball that allowed the tying run to score.

Three days later, with the losing streak at nine and the team in last place, Wilson's resignation was requested and tendered. He soon accepted a coaching position with Cincinnati.

Hack Wilson volunteered to take the Cubs' vacant managerial post; Stan Hack was also said to be a candidate. Wrigley declined to hire a Hack, and, instead, chose to bring back another familiar face: Charlie Grimm, who managed the team from 1932 to 1938. Shortly after he was hired, "Jolly Cholly" waxed philosophical about the team's prospects:

> When a team gets into a slump such as this one, it can't be shaken off in a minute. Changing lineups continually doesn't help either. But this has to be done until something promising develops. Then the guys who draw the regular jobs will settle down and breathe easier. They'll also play better ball. We'll get along, don't worry about that.

It turned out that the Cubs were more relaxed and confident with Grimm than they'd been with Wilson. "Under Charlie we all enjoyed each other, had a lot of fun with each other," said Len Merullo. "When you played for Charlie Grimm, that's the type of ball club he had. He coached at third base, and he did his best to keep you loose. Some players, if you get in a rut, you beat yourself to death. You try all the harder, and you stop getting any base hits, and for me, it would affect my fielding. I was that type of ballplayer. I needed a guy like Charlie to snap me out of it."

When Grimm was hired, his streaky cleanup hitter Nicholson was batting .240, without a home run. Dour Irving Vaughan dubbed him, "Bill Nicholson, the so-called cleanup hitter." Nicholson had little use for Vaughan, whose acerbic commentaries were resented by many Cubs. Decades later, he still remembered Vaughan's jibe: "I hit fourth a good many years there, but you know when you were going bad I remember looking in the Chicago paper one morning, and I guess I had a bad day, and maybe popped up, maybe hit into a double play and struck out a couple of times. He ... never did have too much for me, you know.... He said 'the so-called fourth hitter did so and so,' and so that's the way it goes. You take your licks as well as your claps, too."

The first major decision Grimm made as manager was to appoint Phil Cavarretta team captain, to succeed the retired Hack. Chicago lost three games, before bouncing back with a victory over the Phillies, in which Bill belted his first round-tripper of the season and drove in two.

The North Siders were last in the league in hitting on May 21 at .226, and last in fielding with a .963 percentage. Their 34 errors led the league.

Passeau had a sore back, and the other pitchers were generally ineffective. Under Grimm's guiding hand, though, the team effected a gradual turnaround. They won six in a row and then a seventh, at Boston, when Bill drove his third homer of the season into the right field "jury box" at Braves Field, on a 3–2 pitch in the first inning.

At the end of May, on a road trip to New York, the Cubs lost four straight to the Giants. Nicholson and Mel Ott engaged in their annual bat swap. The Giants' slugger decided not to use Bill's, however — it was too heavy. "I'd have to get the batboy to help me carry it to the plate," he joked.

An encouraging development for the Chicagoans occurred on June 5, though, when Stan Hack announced that he was "unretiring," having found someone to manage his Oregon farm. Hack was Bill's fondest baseball friend. He envied the third baseman's ability to make consistent contact at the plate, which usually resulted in singles and doubles. For his part, Hack wished he had Nicholson's home run power. After the return of his cigar-smoking buddy, Bill's hitting continued its renascence, and by June 11 he was up to .272, with six homers, though Ott led the league with 14. When Jimmie Wilson returned to Wrigley Field in mid–June as a Reds coach and saw his former right fielder warming up, he remarked wistfully: "He looks tougher than ever when he's sitting on the other team's bench."

Despite some improvement, the Cubs languished in last place. On "War Fund Day," at Wrigley Field on June 28, players, sportswriters, and umpires paid for admission to the ballpark, just like the fans. Almost $16,000 was raised for various relief organizations, as the home team took two from archrival Brooklyn. Nicholson hit his first grand slam of the season in the inaugural contest, to help newly-acquired pitcher Bob Chipman end the Dodgers' five-game winning skein. Bill added another home run later in the game. A win the following day enabled the Cubs to sweep the series.

It was not until Independence Day that the North Siders finally climbed out of the N.L. cellar, however, with a doubleheader sweep of Boston that vaulted them into seventh place. The team announced that Jimmie Foxx was being dropped from the roster as a player, but would remain as a coach and bullpen catcher.

In a Sunday doubleheader at home against the Giants on July 9, an Ace Adams fastball bore in on Bill. Losing the pitch in the white-shirted background, he threw up both hands in an effort to protect his face. The ball struck his left thumb and forearm, then ricocheted off his forehead. The thumb was badly bruised, and even gripping the bat was painful, but he remained in the lineup.

It was a frightening moment that Nicholson never forgot. "I just couldn't see a thing up there. He reared back and looked like he threw a blank and I just saw it get by me like it was going to the catcher's glove, right over the middle of the plate. And he did it again and I just saw it go in the catcher's glove; I couldn't see a thing. So I said, 'Well, I'll lean a little more over that plate, maybe I can see a little bit. I might get a glimpse of it.' So I leaned over, and he came a little inside and hit me right between the horns."

A week later, the All-Star game was played at Forbes Field in Pittsburgh. Chicagoans Cavarretta, Don Johnson, and Nicholson were chosen to participate, by vote of the league's managers. Bill had the perfect excuse to take a few days off, to heal his hand, but the thought never crossed his mind. Columnist Red Smith later wrote of Nicholson's decision to play: "Some ballplayers consider the annual All Star game a great bore, seek excuses to avoid that extra day of work. Baseball was Bill's religion, and election to the All Star team was an honor to be treasured."

Bill took a day coach to Pittsburgh, and Nancy came out from Chestertown to meet him. She turned heads, as usual. Venerable Arch Ward, reporting from Forbes Field in his daily column, told readers that of all the wives, "none ... was prettier than Mrs. Nancy Nicholson...."

Nicholson spent the day in his hotel room, soaking the bad hand in a hot salt solution. As was customary for the All-Star game, the weather was steamy — 90 degrees at game time. Despite pregame predictions of a capacity crowd of 38,000, only 29,859 attended. Prospective fans seemed reluctant to stand in the heat waiting to buy tickets, and ticket scalpers took a beating. Most of the grandstands and bleachers were filled, though, and attendees included Hall of Famer Cy Young (who drove over from his Ohio farm), Commissioner Landis, Governor Edward A. Martin of Pennsylvania, and Cornelius D. Scully, mayor of Pittsburgh.

In the locker room before the game, N.L. manager Billy Southworth rallied his troops, who had been dominated by the A.L. in recent years. "They are ball players just like yourselves," he told them. "They have come up through the minors just as you have. Sure, there are some good ball players on the other side, but there are some very good ball players in this clubhouse. Don't forget that, and don't be under any tension. Just play your natural game and we can beat them."

Nicholson wasn't in the starting lineup, and sat anxiously on the top step of the dugout, a baseball bat in his hands, watching the early action. With one out in the bottom of the fifth, the N.L.'s Connie Ryan was on second base, with pitcher Ken Raffensberger due to bat. Southworth barked out Nicholson's name, and sent him in to pinch hit.

Bill grabbed another bat, and swung both of them high over his head to get loose, as he strode to the plate. Still hitless in All-Star competition, he dug in to face Red Sox sinker baller Tex Hughson, on the mound for the A.L. On the first pitch, he laced a bullet down the right field line for two bases, scattering players in the N.L. bullpen, and scoring Ryan to tie the game. Base coaches Freddie Fitzsimmons and Mike Gonzalez danced with joy in their respective boxes. The two-bagger started a rally that resulted in three more runs, and the National League went on to a 7–1 triumph. It was the worst defeat to date for the American League in the annual competition.

At game's end jubilant National Leaguers shouted and whistled in the damp Forbes Field locker room. Cardinals manager Billy Southworth told his team, "You were all good, every one of you." Then he turned to Nicholson and Pirates pitcher Rip Sewell: "You two were great." Southworth even planted an appreciative kiss on an embarrassed Nicholson's cheek.

Later, describing the come-from-behind victory, he told reporters: "I think Nicholson should get a lot of credit for it. That pinch double just started something the American League couldn't stop. They were really in there battling all the way, weren't they?"

The normally laid-back Nicholson was ebullient as he recounted the day's events. "Do you know what?," he asked a reporter. "That was the first hit I've ever made in an All-Star game. Brother, I really enjoyed it!"

Jim Gallagher was said to be so pleased with the performance of Nicholson and Cavarretta against American League competition that he was considering a challenge to the White Sox, in a revival of the moribund post-season City Series.

When the Cubs returned to action on July 13 against the Pirates at Wrigley, Grimm sat his star outfielder down, to give the hand a chance to heal. It was the first game Bill missed since 1942, ending his consecutive games streak at 348, the longest in the league among active players.

After the All-Star break, the Cubs continued to play uninspired baseball. Losing three of four games to the Braves in Boston, they dropped to sixth place. Saturday, July 22 found them in Harlem, for a four-game series against Mel Ott's fourth place Giants.

An unhappy Polo Grounds throng, numbering fewer than 8,000, let the home team have it, as the Giants gave up four unearned runs in a 6–3 loss. The fans were so unhappy with the Giants' defensive performance that they began to cheer sarcastically whenever a ball was fielded cleanly. Nicholson's eighth-inning home run, off the roof in right field, did nothing to raise their spirits.

Allied troops continued to fight their way across France; U.S. Marines battled their way across the Pacific; and New Yorkers awoke to a beautiful

12. The Supreme Compliment

Sunday, July 23. The temperature was forecast to be in the mid–80s, with low humidity. Baseball aficionados inclined to head for the ballpark had a *smorgasbord* from which to choose: the Dodgers were playing two games against the Pirates at Ebbetts Field, in Brooklyn; the Negro National League's New York Cubans faced off against the Philadelphia Stars in a doubleheader at Yankee Stadium, in Manhattan; the International League's Newark Bears played the Jersey City Giants at Ruppert Stadium in Newark; and the Cubs and Giants were set to play a twin bill at the Polo Grounds, beginning at 2:00 P.M. The 25,725 who attended the Giants-Cubs contest witnessed the tying or breaking of five major league records. It was a day Nicholson would never forget.

In the opener, the Cubs' Bob Chipman took the mound against the Giants' Bill Voiselle, a husky (6'4", 210 pound) righthander from tiny Ninety Six, South Carolina. Voiselle was Nicholson's "cousin," and Bill enjoyed big days at the plate when the South Carolinian took the mound for the opposition. The big pitcher made no pretense about his fear of the slugging Cubs outfielder, and acknowledged to an interviewer many years later: "Nicholson was a guy I always had trouble with. Boy, could he hit. And it wasn't like it is today with the live ball."

After a first inning walk, Nicholson hit three consecutive home runs, in the fourth, sixth, and eighth innings, respectively. "I hit two in a row off of Bill Voiselle," he remembered. "I could always hit him. Actually, I had five [sic] home runs, plus a single, in seven at-bats in that doubleheader. None of the homers was cheap, either. They were all line drives to right center. I was hot. When you're hot, you can hit anything."

In the 7–4 Cubs victory, Bill's last home run came off reliever Swede Hanson. He reached base every time he was up, scoring four runs and driving in the same number. The eighth-inning clout tied a modern major league record, held by Lou Gehrig and Jimmie Foxx: four home runs in four consecutive official at-bats, dating back to Nicholson's eighth-inning shot off none other than Johnny Allen the previous day.

In the second game, getting what he later called "the best ball to hit all day," Nicholson popped up straight over home plate for an out in his first time at bat, but singled in his second. The Cubs blew a third-inning, five-run lead, and the Giants led, 9–5, after six innings. In the top of the seventh, Bill's two-run, round-trip blast brought his team back to 9–7, but New York got a run back in the bottom of the frame. A wild eighth inning followed.

Stan Hack led off, against Giants reliever Ace Adams, with a walk. When Adams walked shortstop Bill Schuster, manager Ott removed him in favor of Ewald Pyle, who walked Cavarretta, to load the bases. Ott eyed Nicholson striding to the plate, called time, and trotted out to the mound from his position in right field, for at least the ninth time in the doubleheader.

Protecting a three-run lead with runners at every base, Ott knew one sure way to lose the game was to let Nicholson swing the bat. His message to Pyle and catcher Gus Mancuso was therefore short, and to the point: "He's killing us. Put him on."

Only two major league players had previously been accorded what has variously been called "The Treatment" and "The Supreme Compliment": being intentionally walked with the bases loaded. They were Hall of Famer Napoleon Lajoie in 1901, playing for the Philadelphia A's, and Del Bissonette, then a Brooklyn Dodger rookie, in 1928. On both occasions, the strategy worked, as the defensive team preserved a late-inning lead and went on to win the game.

No one was accorded this extraordinary deference after Nicholson until the San Francisco Giants' Barry Bonds in 1998, when the maneuver was employed successfully in the ninth inning of the Arizona Diamondbacks' 8–7 victory.

Nicholson's walk sent Hack home, and the score was now 10–8, Giants. Ott yanked Pyle, and brought Swede Hanson in to retire Ival Goodman. Hanson then hit Andy Pafko with an errant pitch, to drive in Schuster, and Cavarretta scored on an out by Don Johnson to tie the score, before the inning ended. The Giants scored two in the bottom of the eighth to regain the lead for good, however, as the Cubs were shut down by young Bob Barthelson in the ninth, to preserve the victory and vindicate Ott's unusual stratagem.

The hitting exhibition Nicholson conducted left fans and teammates awed. Cubs outfielder Andy Pafko couldn't believe his eyes: "I'll never forget it. Everybody talked about it." Writing in *The Sporting News*, Fred Lieb commented: "Maybe Bill can't tell the color of the paint on the outfield fences, or whether the ball comes to him in ivory, white or Larry MacPhail's old experiment of canary yellow, but, boy, how he can bash that horsehide over the fences!"

After the game, Ott lounged in a chair in the Giants' locker room, clad in his underwear, and talked with reporters. "They ought to make him play off somewhere by himself," he snorted. "There wasn't anything they pitched to him he didn't hit. He hit low fast balls, slow balls outside and curves inside. He measured Bill [Voiselle]'s change of pace and really put the bat on it, and him an anemic, too."

A curious scribe asked him, "What do you mean by 'anemic'?" Ott replied, "Well, that's what he tells you. His blood pressure is always down in his shoes and he's so tired all the time he can hardly stay on his feet. Now I'm only telling you what he says."

12. The Supreme Compliment

This gratuitous remark was telling. Nicholson was not a whiner. Ott was his friend, and if he confided to him that he was constantly fatigued, it suggests that diabetes may have begun its insidious course.

Ott was disgusted with the performance of his pitchers during the day. "I nearly lost my mind," he complained. "There's no excuse for that kind of pitching." Moments later, the team doctor entered the locker room brandishing a hypodermic needle, and injected Ott with vitamin B. While the manager continued to ramble for the reporters, the doctor examined Ott's left thigh, the site of a recent blow from a coach's fungo bat. "It's not too good," the doctor said. "Best thing you can do is go to bed and relax." The exasperated Ott replied, "You didn't think I was going out dancing, did you? Why, I was in my pajamas at eight o'clock last night!"

Forgotten in the celebration of Nicholson's performance was the great Ott's: a home run, triple, three singles, two walks, and seven RBIs for the day.

While Ott entertained his audience, Nicholson sat in the visiting team locker room, puffing on his customary cigar and accepting the congratulations of his teammates. When asked to explain his sudden power outburst, Nicholson told a reporter from the *New York Journal-American*: "I think the lively ball has helped me and then, too, I'm not cutting at so many bad ones. Gosh, I can't explain it. The Polo Grounds is good for a pull hitter and I'm one, that's all. It was just my day — or two days, rather."

The relationship between Ott and Nicholson remained cordial, despite their rivalry. Some Cubs fans nonetheless suggested that Ott had an additional motivation for issuing Nicholson the bases-loaded free pass: the two were engaged in a duel for the National League home run crown at the time. As further evidence that Ott was plotting against their hero, Nicholson supporters pointed to a July 7 doubleheader against Ott and his Giants at Wrigley. In the first game, in the top of the sixth, Ott homered to right. In the bottom of the inning, Bill hit a drive to the same field that was initially ruled a home run. Ott argued, successfully, to umpire Beans Reardon that the ball had caromed off the right field screen, turning what Cubs fans thought was a homer into a triple. The Wrigley faithful were so incensed they threw things from the stands, including a bottle that landed near Ott.

Suggestions that Ott was scheming against Nicholson turned out to be of little consequence. Although Nicholson and Ott each had 21 home runs at the end of July 23, Bill finished 1944 with a major league-leading 33, while Ott hit only five more for the rest of the season, to finish at 26.

Besides his four consecutive home runs, Nicholson's July 23 performance tied the major league record for most home runs in a doubleheader (four). His six home runs in a four-game span equaled another major league mark. The six hits Bill had for the day pushed his batting average above .300 for the first time in 1944. Two other records were set: most pitchers used by both clubs in a single game (14, in the nightcap), and most used by both clubs in a doubleheader — 19. Giants fans got their money's worth — five hours and eight minutes of record-setting baseball on a beautiful Sunday afternoon.

Reinvigorated by the feats of their slugging right fielder, the Cubs embarked on an 11-game winning streak that shot them into fourth place, the highest spot they had occupied in the standings this late in the year since 1939. When Grimm took over the managerial reins, the team was a lowly 1-10. At the time their winning streak ended, the team was 45-37 under the new skipper, and five games back of the third place Pirates.

Even when the streak ended on August 7, with a doubleheader loss to Pittsburgh, Nicholson continued to amaze. After a Cubs home loss to Brooklyn in 10 innings on August 10, the *New York Times'* Roscoe McGowan waxed poetic in describing Nicholson's 25th season homer, off Hal Gregg, "that sailed so far on the wings of the wind and Nicholson's power that it almost broke a window in a building across the street back of right field."

L.A. Times columnist Braven Dyer, who watched the same game, was no less impressed:

> Nicholson hits the ball on the nose ... In the eighth inning of Thursday's game he rifled one at Paul Waner so hard the Dodger right fielder couldn't hold it.... It went for an error but scored a run.... The Cub slugger adopts a crouching stance at the plate and apparently is death on pitches around his knees.... After he clouted his homer none of the Dodger chuckers ever game him one down there again.

The next day, the North Siders dropped their third straight to the Dodgers, 7–6, in 11 innings, despite Big Nick's efforts. The Cubs trailed in the bottom of the ninth, 5–5, with two outs. Nicholson, down to his last strike, drove Les Webber's next pitch over the right field wall, to send the game into extra innings. Now batting at a .303 clip for the season, he led the major leagues with 26 home runs and 82 RBIs.

A controversial Nicholson grand slam, down the right field line (his second of the year) beat the Braves in Boston on August 16, 11–3. The Braves argued that the ball was foul, but umpire Lou Jorda disagreed. Bill's offensive production dropped considerably thereafter. By August 24, he was mired in a three for 26 slump.

The following day, in a 2–0 loss to the Reds, he broke out with three hits, then clouted a solo home run (number 28 for the season), in a 10–7 defeat. By early September Bill's batting eye had returned and the team regained fourth place. Between games of a doubleheader against the Cardinals on the 15th, he was presented with a wristwatch for being voted by the fans as the most popular Cub.

Earl and Bertie drove up from Chestertown to see their son, and watch the Cubs beat the Phillies at Shibe Park on September 27, in 11 innings, 5–3. Bill's only hit was a single in the 11th that started the scoring rally.

The season ended on October 1, with a doubleheader split against Boston. For the year, Bill's batting average dipped slightly, to .287, but he led the majors in home runs (33), runs scored (116) and RBIs (122). He was second in slugging (.545); second in games played (156, counting suspended games); second in walks (93); and second in extra base hits (76). *The Sporting News* editorialized near the season's end, regarding Bill's Most Valuable Player chances: "[He] is a one man ball club, a prolific producer of drives out of the park, an incessant puncher with men on bases."

Bill journeyed again to South Dakota, on October 8, to participate in the diversion of pheasant hunting and an exhibition game with the Huron Armour Packers in the Baseball "Pheastival." Among other players, Paul Derringer, Jimmie Foxx, Paul Waner, Ival Goodman, Andy Pafko, and Dizzy Trout, coached by Kiki Cuyler, made the long trek. Proceeds from the game went towards the establishment of playgrounds in Huron.

Again, however, Nicholson was edged (this time by one vote) for the National League MVP award, by the pennant-winning Cardinals' shortstop Marty Marion. It was the third year in a row that a St. Louis player won the award. Marion's defensive prowess must have been given great weight by the voters; he hit .269 on the season, with 64 RBIs, and did not lead the league in a single offensive category.

One of the 24 baseball writers voting — rumored to be from Chicago — inexplicably left Nicholson off the ballot; had the scribe given him even a ninth place vote, Bill would have beaten Marion for the award.

When the results of the voting were announced on November 21, Nicholson reacted as could have been expected. "Marty probably deserved it. He's a hell of a shortstop," was all he could say. Of his own performance, Bill told writer Ross Forman nearly 50 years later: "I guess it was a fairly good year."

Dan Daniel of the *New York World Telegram* was bewildered. "In the face of numerous and varied high achievements, it is difficult to determine why the Cub outfielder has failed to get top billing in any baseball or general sports poll," he complained.

Most Valuable Player or not, at age 30 Swish Nicholson had the baseball world by the tail. As a four-time All-Star, and two-time home run and RBI champion, his most fervent hope now was to play in the World Series.

The wish was about to come true — that was the good news. The bad news was that 1944 marked the highwater mark in his individual career; never again would he approach the batting prowess he had displayed over the last five years.

13

The Year of the Billy Goat Curse

The president died, the world war ended, and the nuclear age dawned — all in the space of four months. Concentration camps were liberated; American soldiers returned from overseas. Though the achievement paled in comparison to the global events that made 1945 a watershed year, Chicagoans had additional reason to celebrate: the Cubs won the National League pennant for the first time since 1938.

What was it about this ball club that propelled them to a 98-win season, a 23-game improvement over 1944? The stewardship of Charlie Grimm was one reason; the mid-season acquisition of pitcher Hank Borowy from the Yankees was another. The team also had an uncanny ability to sweep doubleheaders, accomplishing the feat 20 times during the course of the campaign. The Cubs "owned" the Reds, as well, winning all 21 games the clubs played.

Cavarretta's league-leading .355 batting average, and the pitching of Hank Wyse (22-10) and Claude Passeau (17-9) didn't hurt, either. But in a year when their cleanup hitter's numbers fell off dramatically (Nicholson batted .243, with just 13 homers and 88 RBIs), the Cubs won the pennant for a very simple reason. Throughout the war years they lost fewer key players to the military than the other major contenders.

Chicagoans returned to the ballpark on the north side of town in droves. The team drew a record 1,036,386 to the friendly confines of Wrigley Field. The Cubs' smashing success on the field and at the gate wasn't foreseen at the beginning of the season.

Three key players were classified as 1-A, and ready to be drafted: Nicholson, infielder Don Johnson, and pitcher Paul Derringer. There were rumors of the enactment of "work or else" legislation in Congress, so that an eligible male would be required to work year-round in an "essential industry," or subject himself to conscription.

At the start of the year, Grimm sounded a note of optimism, telling members of the fourth estate that his team would be "plenty formidable when the bell rings.... Certainly, I'm optimistic over our 1945 chances — by wartime standards."

When spring training for pitchers and catchers got underway in French Lick on March 8, though, cold weather and floodwaters from the swollen Lost River necessitated indoor workouts at the hotel. Three practice pitching mounds had been built in the auditorium, and they were put to good use. A day later, Dom Dallesandro was inducted into the army and lost for the 1945 season.

The military draft had relentlessly depleted major league rosters during the course of the war. Of the 144 players who started the first game of 1941 for their respective teams, just 30 were left on big league rosters by the spring of 1945. Nicholson, Hack, Cavarretta, and Derringer were the only such Cubs remaining.

The draft, war plant manpower requirements, and travel restrictions limited the number of players available for spring training in 1945. By March 10, there were 12 players in the Cubs' camp. Four others were working out, with the parent club's permission, at the Los Angeles Angels training facility in California. Eighteen players were absent from either site, including Cavarretta, Hack, Pafko, and Passeau.

Nearly all major league teams were experiencing similar difficulties. Not until March 22, when War Manpower Commission chairman Paul McNutt granted major leaguers a right to return to baseball without penalty if they quit their defense jobs, did owners breathe a collective sigh of relief.

Bill was working at a war plant in Elkton, in nearby Cecil County, commuting from Chestertown. Starting in mid–March, when his shift ended, he motored to Wilmington, Delaware, the spring training locale for the Phillies, to work out with his National League rivals. He was photographed, taking his cuts in the batting cage, for an issue of *Life*. The picture accompanied a piece entitled, "The Phillies, Big Leagues Face a Tough Season With Players Too Old or Too Young," and featured the motley crew of players trying to catch on with the 1945 Philadelphia squad. Among those working out with Nicholson were several future "Whiz Kids," including catcher Andy Seminick and infielder Putsy Caballero, together with several shopworn vets, struggling to hang on for one more campaign, like Jimmie Foxx, Gus Mancuso, and Freddie Fitzsimmons.

"I am going to play ball again this year, but I may be late in reporting,"

Nicholson explained to reporters. "I am working in a war plant and won't leave my job until I have cleared up some problems.... I'm working out now to be in the best shape possible when I report."

After hearing of the War Manpower Commission's decision, Bill announced that he would report to the Cubs soon, thereby causing his reclassification to 1-A by the draft board. He kept himself in condition by exercising regularly, and informed Grimm by long distance telephone on April 2 that he was taking batting practice five times a week.

The Cubs had still not played a spring training game against a major league opponent by the end of March. Grimm was miffed that no one told him he would be sharing French Lick with the Reds, who were forced to relocate from their site at Indiana University. The North Siders were reduced to conducting workouts on a grassy knoll near the railroad depot.

Grimm read newspaper accounts of Nicholson's intrasquad game home run in Wilmington on April 8, but his star right fielder still did not report to French Lick, and the team departed spring training on April 11 without him. Grimm may not have known, but surely suspected, that Nicholson and Gallagher were again engaged in testy salary negotiations. In late '44, *The Sporting News* predicted an imminent tussle over the size of Bill's 1945 paycheck:

> Bill is not an avaricious soul, but he is fully mindful that if he is to keep his muscles strong and supple, he must have groceries, the best groceries. And it is no secret that the best victuals cost a pretty penny in Maryland, as elsewhere.

Having earned $18,000 for his 1944 efforts, Bill expected to be rewarded in 1945. He was mistaken. Of the contract negotiations with Gallagher, Nicholson recounted: "He cut me $3,000.00 after I led the league. I mean he sent me a contract, which threw fuel on the fire, for a $3,000.00 cut after I led the league for a second year, which was a good year, in '44. There were 33 home runs and 122 RBIs, and I was making 18 and then I had a lot of arguments about getting the 18 the year before.... I finally got 18, but I didn't get a raise."

Still upset over Gallagher's tactics, Bill was in no hurry to report to his team. He assured Grimm he would be in Chicago on April 17 for Opening Day against the Cardinals, and nothing more. President Roosevelt's death on April 12 suspended what was to be a four-game City Series with the Sox. The Cubs, *sans* Nicholson, won the first game 15–3; the remaining games were never played because of inclement weather.

Bill finally arrived in Chicago by train on April 14. Edward Burns of the *Trib* immediately revised his preseason prediction that the Cubs would finish fourth; he now prognosticated a pennant-winning season. Braven Dyer, of the *L.A. Times*, was more prescient, picking the Tigers to win in the American League, and the Cubs in the National, but only if Nicholson played the entire season.

When the 1945 campaign opened on April 17 at chilly Wrigley against St. Louis, pretty usherettes, clad in blue and gold uniforms, made their debut at the park. Rogers Hornsby and an estimated 15,000 youths from his baseball school, sponsored by the *Chicago Daily News*, were there. Bill picked up where he left off in 1944, hitting the season's inaugural home run, in his first at bat, off a fat pitch from Ted Wilks, in the second inning. Leading off, he watched two pitches go by before blasting a fastball against the screen in back of the bleachers in right center field — a drive of more than 400 feet. A relieved Grimm, coaching at third base, did a little dance, then whacked his slugger on the rear end as he trotted around third. In the ninth, with the score tied at two, Nicholson walked, stole second and slid across the plate with the winning run on Don Johnson's single to left.

Following a second-game loss to the Cardinals two days later, the Cubs journeyed to Pittsburgh for a four-game set against the Pirates. In the second contest, the North Siders eked out a 4–3 triumph, for Paul Derringer's second season victory. Bill's double in the seventh, off the right field screen at Forbes Field, scored Cavarretta with the winning run; his throw to the plate in the ninth inning, to toss out Bill Rodgers, preserved the victory.

A raucous doubleheader concluded the series the next day, as the Cubs took both games. In the home ninth of the nightcap, some of the 27,690 fans became dissatisfied with the performance of their Bucs, and began to pelt players, umpires, and even fellow spectators with seat cushions. Many stormed onto the field and engaged in fist fights. The game ended on Babe Dahlgren's fly ball to Nicholson in right, with cushions still flying.

Behind a six-game winning streak, Chicago was flying high atop the standings on April 28, though Nicholson was hitting only .240 and hadn't homered since Opening Day. This was no cause for alarm, however; he'd gotten off to slow starts in previous seasons and come on like gangbusters before long. Still, Associated Press baseball writer Joe Reichler cited the slumping Nicholson's performance in a wire service article detailing the batting woes of other stars, including Dixie Walker and Mel Ott.

After five straight losses, on May 7, Grimm decided to shake up his slumping lineup, removing Nicholson from his customary cleanup spot in favor of Cavarretta. The Cubs arrived a day later for a series in Philadelphia. With time on their hands before the game, some of the players participated in the V-E Day celebration that took place near the Liberty Bell. It was a chance for Billy and Albert, accompanied by Nancy, to visit their dad. The children talked "a blue streak, and mostly about the fine jail in Chestertown, Maryland, much to the distress of their mother," said an item in *The Sporting News*.

The Nicholson-Cavarretta switch did not help the struggling right fielder immediately; he had one hit in the next two contests. His ninth-inning homer at Boston on May 12, however, enabled the Cubs to edge the Braves, 13–12, for their second consecutive win. The team then commenced a six-game losing streak against the Braves, Giants, and Dodgers, dropping them into fifth place, eight-and-a-half games behind New York.

The North Siders turned the streak around with a Sunday doubleheader victory over Brooklyn at Ebbets Field, on May 20. The largest crowd at the tiny ballpark since 1942 — 36,176 — saw the Dodgers drop 4–2 and 4–1 decisions. In the third inning, as pitcher Curt Davis warmed up for the home team, Nicholson stood in the on-deck circle taking his practice swings. When he made his way to the plate, the customary cries of "Swish, Swish, Swish!," rose from the stands. He swatted the first pitch through a hole in the right field screen, for a home run.

In the second game, with "Swish!" again resounding through the ballpark, he doubled off the scoreboard, against Hal Gregg. Dissatisfied with what they perceived to have been the lack of quality umpiring throughout the day, the Brooklyn legions responded by pelting the field with paper, bottles, and orange peels.

The Cubs reached the .500 mark on May 23, when they beat the Phils, behind the pitching of Passeau. The victory must have been bittersweet for Nicholson, as he witnessed his idol Jimmie Foxx victimized by the ancient "hidden ball" trick in the sixth inning.

Trailing 4–3, Foxx singled for the visiting Phillies. A Vince DiMaggio single sent Foxx to second. Cubs shortstop Bill Schuster received the relay throw from left fielder Lowrey, but did not return the ball to the pitcher. When the next batter stepped up to the plate, Foxx took a lead off second and was promptly tagged out by Schuster.

Adding to the Phils' mortification, the batter flew out to Nicholson in right field. DiMaggio, apparently thinking there were two outs instead of one, was doubled off first base by Bill's throw to Cavarretta, taking the Phils completely out of the inning.

Nicholson raised his average to a season-high .293 on May 24, before his production fell off. On the morning of June 8, he passed his military pre-induction physical in Chicago. A wire service photo showed him being examined by a Navy doctor, and Cubs fans braced for the likelihood that the slugging outfielder would soon be donning another type of uniform. Nicholson said he would keep on playing until he heard from his draft board in Chestertown. A Chicago fan, fearful of Bill's imminent induction, had recently warned Arch Ward: "As Bill Nicholson goes, so go the Cubs."

But the '45 Cubs did not depend on Bill Nicholson's bat as earlier Chicago clubs had done. Cavarretta, Pafko, and Lowrey were knocking in the big runs now. Paradoxically, opposing pitchers were warier than ever of the big right fielder, fearful that he would break out of his slump against them. Indeed, on the afternoon of his military physical, when the Cubs beat the Reds, 7–3, to climb back into the fifth spot in the standings, Nicholson was intentionally walked three times.

From time to time, there would be flashes of the old Nicholson, and Cubs fans thought the slump was over. In the second game of a doubleheader win against the Reds, he hit a monstrous 400-foot three-run homer into Wrigley's center field bleachers, to put the team in front. He later doubled and scored, and was three for six on the day. Grimm's boys were now in fourth place, and trailed the league-leading Giants by only three games.

A week later, however, Bill went zero for eight in a doubleheader against the same Reds team. After a 4-for-43 stretch, his average declined to .255 at the end of June. Grimm continued to bat him third, but the skipper was running out of patience.

Despite his troubles, Nicholson neither grumbled nor cursed his bad luck. He remained congenial to all who approached him with suggestions, and made it a point to thank those who were concerned enough to offer their assistance. He had his own theory, which was shared by Grimm, as to the sudden fall-off in production: "I came to spring training in 1945 with a bad back, and because of the condition I developed a hitch in my swing. Even after the back got better, I still was hitching. It just seemed like I couldn't stop."

St. Louis' Johnny Hopp took a Ray Prim fastball in the head on June 24. He was carried unconscious from the field, and transported to Illinois Masonic Hospital with a concussion. Sightlines were as bad as they had ever been; the Cubs had long since ended their 1941 experiment, and resumed the sale of center field bleacher seats for the sake of financial expediency.

Mired in a horrendous slump, the capacity crowd booed Nicholson during the St. Louis series, as the Cubs dropped three out of four. But the team climbed into second with a doubleheader sweep at Boston on Independence Day. In the second game, Bill hit home runs seven and eight, including the game winner in the final inning off Bob Logan. When the Braves' Charley Workman struck out on a controversial call to end the game, emotional fans charged umpire George Barr, who had to be escorted from the field under police protection. One might have expected this type of behavior in rowdy Brooklyn, but not genteel Boston.

The Cubs traveled to Philadelphia for five games against the lowly Phils. Nancy drove over from Chestertown for the games. Bill got a crew hair cut, with Nancy's approval, hoping that a change of *coiffure* might inflate his .255 batting average. He was an ordinary six for 21 during the series, with four RBIs, but the Cubs swept the five games.

Riding the crest of a 10-game winning streak, the Cubs eased into first place on July 9 in the finale at Philadelphia. They added another victory, before losing the second game of a doubleheader to the Braves on July 12. Undaunted, they won five more games, then 17 of their next 23. At the halfway point of 1945, the team sported a 48–29 record, and led the second-place Cardinals by four games.

Although no major league All-Star game would be played because of wartime travel restrictions, *The Sporting News* again selected Bill to its team, despite his .258 average and minimal power production (8 home runs and 43 RBIs). On July 17, however, *Chicago Herald American* columnist Warren Brown, in his column "So They Tell Me," christened Nicholson "Ballast Bill," and claimed that the Cubs' first-half success was "accomplished ... with eight men. For all practical purposes, Nicholson has just been along for the ride in those first 77 games." Brown complained that too much time had been spent worrying about Nicholson, and not enough credit had been given to the other members of the team, "who have taken in all the slack, and have kept going at full speed ahead." He suggested that if the outfielder's name was anything other than Bill Nicholson, "Grimm would have benched him long since.... Certainly Charlie hasn't hesitated about sending in relief for any and all of his other precious charges when they drifted into what is known as a slump."

Privately, Nicholson must have been incensed over the treatment he received in the press, but his public *persona* remained unchanged. On occasions when he couldn't contribute with the bat, he let his glove do the talking. During a 5–0 blanking of the Dodgers at Wrigley on July 18, the day after Brown's column appeared, he made an extraordinary diving catch near the right field foul line to rob Eddie Basinski of a sure triple in the sixth inning.

A doubleheader against the Phillies at Wrigley on July 22 featured the appearance of a familiar face, at an unfamiliar position: Jimmie Foxx, on the pitcher's mound. He threw the last two innings of the first game, yielding no runs and only two infield singles. The Eastern Shoreman also struck out Nicholson and a slumping Cavarretta, in an 8–5 Cubs victory.

There were telling signs that this was no ordinary year for the Chicago team, however. In the second game, with the home team up, 3–1, and one out, a sure double play ball went through Merullo's legs at short. Ten runs went on to score in the inning and the Phils hung on, for an 11–6 win. After a day's rest, the North Siders shrugged off Merullo's gaffe, and won six straight. Through July 26, the Cubs led the league in hitting (.284), fielding percentage (.980), and victories (54).

The next day, Jim Gallagher pulled off the steal of the season, acquiring pitcher Hank Borowy from the Yankees, for the price of $97,000. Yanks general manager Larry McPhail apparently believed that Borowy, who thus far had 10 wins, had outlived his usefulness to the team. The Yankees originally were asking for a player in return, besides the cash, and Cavarretta, Pafko, Lowrey, and Nicholson were rumored to be among the candidates. A player exchange never came to pass, however.

Borowy, dubbed the "Pale Pole from New Jersey" by sportswriters, was a handsome but fragile righthander, who relied on pinpoint control to get hitters out. Manager Bill McKechnie of the Reds called him a "good seven inning pitcher." Hank was not even Gallagher's first choice among available Yankee hurlers. The Fordham University product proved to be the team's ace for the balance of the season, though, posting an 11-2 mark as a Cub, to go along with a 2.13 earned run average.

He started in the second game of a doubleheader at home, on July 29. When he popped out of the dugout to warm up, Borowy received a standing ovation from more than 43,000 fans in attendance. He then scattered seven hits in a 2–1 complete-game victory over the Reds, aided by Nicholson's ninth home run, a two-run shot, in the first inning.

August 1 was "Cookie Day" at Wrigley; fans brought 5,200 boxes of cookies and cakes to the ballpark, to be donated to Chicago's servicemen centers. In a 1–0 loss to Pittsburgh, Nicholson went hitless in four trips. The next day, Grimm decided to drop Bill from third to sixth in the batting order, hoping to relieve some of the pressure the right fielder was feeling in the middle of the lineup. Although the switch was modestly successful insofar as Nicholson's batting average was concerned (27 hits for his next 97 at bats), his homer and RBI totals were still stagnant.

Bill's leaping catch of Augie Galan's line drive to right, in the seventh inning, preserved a 4–3 victory over the Dodgers in Brooklyn, on August 17. When umpire Tom Dunn called Dixie Walker out at first base to end the game, hundreds of spectators rushed onto the field. A special policeman stopped one enraged fan who charged directly at Dunn. Outside the park, an irate woman ran up to a policeman. "Arrest that umpire — he just robbed the Dodgers!," she exclaimed.

During the Brooklyn series, Grimm chatted with respected sportswriter Arthur Daley of the *New York Times*. The subject was Nicholson, and Grimm was trying to explain why he was sticking by his right fielder, even in an off-year: "I just can't give up on the guy completely," Charley said. "He isn't hitting worth a lick, but his all-around play is better than ever. The one thing I can't get out of my mind is that Nick is liable to explode at any minute and win an important game for us."

Another New York sportswriter, Joe King of the *Daily News*, called Nicholson "the mystery man of the National League." New York Giants pitchers viewed Bill as an atomic bomb, according to King, "and when he'll explode nobody knows."

But the explosion never came. On August 28, Bill Nicholson was benched by Charlie Grimm, along with third baseman Stan Hack. Cavarretta replaced Bill in right field for a night game at Pittsburgh, and Heinz Becker took Cavarretta's spot at first base. The Cubs had dropped five straight games, in which they scored a grand total of eight runs, and Grimm needed to do something to shake up his moribund team. Their lead over the Cardinals had shrunk from 7½ to 2½ games in the space of a week. The *Trib*'s Edward Burns noted of Nicholson that, "it long has been apparent this season that he has lost his former fine sense of timing and other elements of slugging coordination." Few could argue with that proposition.

Although the Cubs won the August 28 game, Cavarretta was injured, and the next day Nicholson found himself back in the lineup, batting third against the Bucs. He doubled in four trips, in a 2–0 win. Restored to the starting nine, Bill homered on September 3, in a doubleheader sweep of the Reds, and several days later off his "cousin" Voiselle, blasted a 425-foot four-bagger into the teeth of the wind. By September 7, Jerry Liska of the Associated Press proclaimed: "Big Bill Nicholson has brushed off the kibitzers and personally packed the sock back into his terrible 'swish' to give the league-leading ... Cubs throbbing World Series fever."

Bill thought he'd found the formula again. "I just gave up on the 99 different stances everybody was trying to teach me," he explained. "I simply decided to go back to my old way of hitting — just standing up there and cutting at the ball." But days later there followed another dismal stretch at the plate, during which he had one hit in 21 at bats, though Grimm kept him in the lineup.

The team nursed its 2½ game lead over the Cardinals on September 11, with 19 contests left to play. After losses in three of their last five games, the Cubs faced the Braves at Wrigley that afternoon. Batting in the sixth slot, Nicholson powered a home run into the eighth row of the right field bleachers, off former teammate Big Bill Lee, to stake the North Siders to a 2–0 lead.

In the ninth inning, with the score tied at four, no outs, and runners at first and second, Nicholson took his practice cuts in the on-deck circle. Righthander Don Hendrickson, who struck Bill out in the seventh, was replaced by Braves' manager Del Bissonette; lefthander Bob Logan came on in relief. Then, the unthinkable happened. A startled Nicholson was called back from the on-deck circle in favor of a pinch-hitter, Frank Secory, who would hit .233 in 43 at bats for the year. Boos and catcalls rained down on Grimm, in the third base coaching box. Nicholson had socked a game-winning home run off Logan on July 4 to win the second game of a doubleheader, but Grimm wouldn't give him the chance this time.

Logan walked Secory to load the bases. One scratch single later, Cavarretta scored for the Cubs to win the game, and implicitly vindicate Grimm's decision to pinch-hit for Nicholson.

Though Grimm's strategy was successful, Chicago fans were shocked, and the heresy was discussed in newspapers throughout the land. Referring to Yankee pitcher Lefty Gomez' reputation as a weak hitter, one newspaper described the Secory for Nicholson substitution as: "Almost Like Gomez Batting for Ruth."

Being the ultimate team player, Nicholson wasn't fazed. In mid-September, in a 4–0 loss to Brooklyn at home, he recorded 10 putouts in right, two short of the major league record. In all, he handled 11 chances without error, tying the National League mark for right fielders.

Grimm's conversation with Arthur Daley a month earlier was called to mind in a game against the second-place Cardinals, on September 19. Clinging to a two-game lead with nine left to play, the Cubs were reeling from consecutive losses, one to this same St. Louis team. Smelling blood, 26,888 partisans packed Sportsman's Park, hoping to see the Redbirds pick up yet another game in the standings.

Nicholson sat on the bench against a nondescript lefthanded pitcher named George Dockins, owner of two straight victories over Chicago. Grimm packed his lineup with righthanded hitters, hoping to gain an edge, and even benched lefthanded third baseman Stan Hack, batting .322 for the season. With the score tied 1–1, the bases loaded, and no outs in the top of the tenth, St. Louis Manager Billy Southworth brought in righthander Ken Burkhart in relief of Dockins.

Burkhart was a journeyman whose pitching career ended in 1949, but who returned to the majors as a National League umpire from 1957 to 1973, to become part of one of the most controversial plays in World Series history.

During the Baltimore-Cincinnati series of 1970, Burkhart called the Reds' Bernie Carbo out at home plate, though replays showed clearly that Orioles catcher Elrod Hendricks had tagged Carbo with an empty glove. The baseball was in his other hand.

While Burkhart warmed up, Grimm sent Nicholson in to pinch-hit for Don Hughes. Bill slashed a single to right to drive in two, in an eventual 4–1 victory. The 10-inning win was the proverbial straw that broke St. Louis' back. Although they beat the Cubs the next day, the Cards never drew any closer in the pennant chase.

Chicago clinched the pennant on September 29, winning the first game of a doubleheader at Forbes Field in Pittsburgh, 4–3. After prevailing in the meaningless second game, 5–0, the Cubs carried Grimm on their shoulders into the locker room. The victory came on Grimm's 23rd wedding anniversary, and was Chicago's fifth N.L. title in the last 17 years, though the first since 1938.

The Detroit Tigers, buoyed by the return of several players from military service, won the American League pennant the next day, the last of the regular season. Based on the strength of their pitching staff, which included lefty Hal Newhouser and fireballing rookie Virgil Trucks, the Bengals were installed as the favorites to win the World Series, by most experts. The same teams met in 1935, when the Tigers won in six games. Cavarretta and Hack were the only remaining Cubs players from that era still on the team.

The 1945 opener was scheduled for October 3, at Detroit's Briggs Stadium. With the outcome of the American League race in doubt until the season's last day, the Cubs had not finalized travel and lodging arrangements. Because of a shortage of hotel rooms in the city, it was suggested that some members of the team could sleep in the state rooms of steamers anchored in the Detroit River. The players vehemently protested, so alternate accommodations were sought. Nicholson and several teammates found rooms at a cheesy hotel whose bed linens turned out to be lice-infested. From then on, the North Siders jokingly referred to each other as "The Yacht Club Boys."

The day before the first game, the Cubs took a 45-minute workout at Briggs Stadium, prematurely halted by a steady drizzle. Tiger players studied their rivals during batting practice, and saw Nicholson hit two batting practice pitches into the seats. A protective screen had been partially removed from the right field fence, which made it an even more attractive target for the lefthanded Nicholson.

Desperate to redeem himself for his subpar regular season performance, Bill told the press: "The only time I ever hit in this park was in the 1941 All Star game. A feller named Feller struck me out. I'll settle for one hit a game —

provided it comes at the right time." He pronounced himself fit, and claimed he felt better now than at any time during the season.

Fifty-four thousand, six hundred thirty-seven packed Briggs in frigid weather to watch the opener. During pregame ceremonies, Nicholson, Cavarretta, and Grimm shook hands with military veterans blinded during combat, and posed for a picture with the heroic servicemen.

Then, Newhouser took the mound for Detroit. In an effort to keep his hurler Hank Borowy warm, Andy Lotshaw wrapped several bricks in towels, then put them in boiling water. Borowy would sit on the heated bricks between innings to ward off the chill.

Despite Lotshaw's efforts, Borowy later complained: "I couldn't stay warm. For five innings, I just couldn't seem to get my arm loose." Although he gave up six hits, walked five, and hit one, the Tigers never scored.

The game was really over in the top of the first, when the Cubs scored four runs, featuring a two-run triple on a windblown fly off Nicholson's bat, misjudged by right fielder Roy Cullenbine. Bill added another RBI on a single in the seventh, and the Yacht Club Boys cruised, 9–0. Upon being removed from the game in the third inning, the frustrated Newhouser grabbed a bat and headed towards the Tigers clubhouse. Passing through a tunnel that led to the dressing room, "Prince Hal" espied a row of five light bulbs. He broke each one with the bat, before retiring to the showers.

The steam-heated visitors' dressing room contained a happy bunch of Cubs after the game. Coach Roy Johnson, who took a line drive off the shin in pregame practice, walked around the room congratulating the stars of the game, including Nicholson, continually chirping, "Nice work, buddy boy." Lotshaw scurried around the locker room — his dentures in his pocket — yelling, "Where are them bricks? Get me them bricks! I'll need them tomorrow!"

United Press correspondent Oscar Fraley thought Nicholson was finally back to 1943-44 form. "You have to watch Big Bill menace the pitcher with his oversized war club, threatening at any moment to belt the ball right back down the tosser's throat, to appreciate it," he enthused.

The weather moderated the next day, and the temperature was 15 degrees warmer for the Trucks v. Hank Wyse matchup. Most of the Cubs, including Nicholson, had faced Trucks during the regular season, when he pitched for the Great Lakes Naval Station team in exhibition games. In the locker room, Wyse discussed his strategy for pitching to Hank Greenberg, the slugging Detroit outfielder who had been shut down the day before by Borowy. "I think I know how to pitch to Hank," he said. "I watched every pitch Borowy threw yesterday and he knows those boys real well."

Superstitious Cubs Coach Red Smith saw to it that all Chicago players wore the same shirts and ties to the ballpark that had been worn the previous day. He even wanted Roy Johnson to take another fungo off the shin; not surprisingly, Johnson refused.

The second series game, however, belonged to Greenberg. In the first inning, he gunned down Stan Hack at the plate with a perfect throw from left to end a Cubs scoring threat. At bat — Wyse's prediction to the contrary — Greenberg mashed a 400-foot home run to left center in the fifth to plate three runs, and Detroit held on to win, 4–1. Bill's single brought home the sole Cubs run, and he made a sparkling play in right, pulling down a hard-hit line drive by Cullenbine, with the bases loaded in the seventh.

With the series knotted at a game apiece, Grimm chose 17-game winner Passeau to start the next day, October 5, against Stubby Overmire. The teams did not take batting practice before the game because of rain.

Passeau, the Mississippi nut farmer, was magnificent, allowing no runs, one hit, and only two baserunners, in one of the greatest pitching performances in World Series annals. The Cubs scored twice in the fourth, with the first run driven in by Nicholson's opposite-field bleeder over a drawn-in infield, scoring Lowrey. Cavarretta made a gorgeous diving stop, before throwing out Eddie Mayo at first in the home fourth, and the Tigers never threatened again.

Afterwards, Passeau conducted a post-mortem with the writers in the visitors' locker room. "The best things I had today were these outfielders making all those plays behind me. I had good control and took my time. I just got 'em out, one at a time," the Mississippian explained.

Grimm chimed in: "And our good friends over there — Mr. [Roy] Hughes and Mr. Nicholson. It was those two hits those guys got that won for us! Just a couple of cuties. Both of them put together wouldn't have hit the screen."

The Cubs boarded a train back to Chicago. It pulled into Union Station at 10:15 P.M., where loyal fans awaited. The balance of the series would be played on home turf, and the North Siders exuded the confidence one would expect from a team returning home with a two-to-one advantage in games. Even Edward Burns jumped on the bandwagon, telling his *Trib* readers: "It doesn't seem likely that the series will go the limit or even six games...."

Chicagoans waited all night for the chance to purchase 5,000 bleacher seats, and 2,500 standing-room-only spots. A queue, composed primarily of adult males, was at least 500 people long by 9:00 P.M., the day before the game. Most were clad in fedora hats, hands plunged into the pockets of their long overcoats to ward off the autumn chill. They were joined by women and children, some of whom earned money by charging $15 to hold a place in line for others.

Behind the right field wall, on Sheffield Avenue, lived a gentleman named Earl Marsh, out of work since June. He intended to cram 20 people into his bedroom — which overlooked the field — to watch the game, at $7.50 per person. Coffee was to be served, free of charge. Should the series go seven games, he stood to make $450.

A Greek immigrant and tavern owner named William Sianis purchased two tickets for the fourth game. One was for him, and the other was for a goat, covered with a blanket on which was pinned a sign that said, "We Got Detroit's Goat." Remarkably, Sianis brought the animal to other Cubs games during the season, apparently without incident.

On the day of the Wrigley opener, though, nearby fans complained about the goat and its unpleasant odor, and ushers were summonsed. They insisted on escorting Sianis and his goat from the ballpark. While he was being removed, Sianis reportedly raised his hands and proclaimed in a thick accent: "Cubs never gonna win anymore. There never gonna be another World Series played at Wrigley Field." Thus was born the "Billy Goat Curse." Beginning that day, the Cubs managed to lose three of the four home games, and ceded the championship to the Tigers. It is 62 years and counting since the franchise has returned to the World Series.

In the fateful fourth game, the Cubs took the field in brand new uniforms. Pitcher Ray Prim retired the first nine Tigers in order, before lightning struck. The fourth inning hadn't ended when the Bengals chased Prim and tallied four runs, their entire output for the game. The final score was 4–1, and Nicholson was hitless in four trips, against Detroit pitcher Dizzy Trout. To make matters worse, Bill committed the Cubs' first error of the series, when Roger Cramer's ground ball single got away from him in the fifth inning. After the game, in a silent Cubs clubhouse, Grimm rallied his troops: "Hang in there, gang! It's Borowy and more base hits tomorrow."

But the next day only brought more heartache. In front of a Sunday afternoon crowd of 43,463, Detroit hammered out an 8–4 victory behind Newhouser, who avenged his opening game defeat by besting Borowy. Nicholson singled, and drove in two runs.

When Borowy was removed by Grimm in the sixth inning, public address announcer Pat Pieper unwittingly confirmed the sense of impending doom settling over Wrigley Field when he paged an important city official: "Coroner A.L. Brodie, call your office!"

To their credit, the Cubs did not immediately require the coroner's assistance, rallying the next day to beat Detroit in 12 innings, 8–7, to set up the decisive seventh game. In the longest World Series game played to date — three hours, 28 minutes — Hank Greenberg was the figurative goat, when a base hit by Stan Hack bounced over his shoulder, allowing the winning run to score. Greenberg was upset that the official scorer charged him with an error on the play, and made his sentiments known. Four hours later, the scorer changed the ruling, and credited Hack with a double and an RBI.

Novelist Ward Just grew up in a suburb of Chicago and, as a 10 year old, attended game six with his father. In the ninth inning, with Pafko on second base and no one out, and Dizzy Trout pitching for the Tigers, Nicholson fanned. Just reminisced about the game and the Cubs' right fielder, 58 years later:

> I am certain that sometime in the late innings, Bill Nicholson took a mighty cut at a fastball and went down on strikes. My father and I were in the lower stands back of third base, prime seats, and when Nicholson took the long, haggard walk back to the dugout, everyone applauded because a man needed encouragement and there was always another day. He's Swish Nicholson, for God's sake, give him a hand.... Watch film of baseball games in those days and you're amused by the floppy uniforms, the trousers resembling pantaloons, the mitts ridiculously small, a child's mitt. But the uniforms did not look floppy then. And the athletes were sleek as greyhounds, except for Swish Nicholson, who was built like a stevedore....

The turning point of the series may have come in the sixth inning of that sixth game, when Cubs pitcher Passeau tore a finger nail on his pitching hand, fielding a smash off the bat of Jimmy Outlaw. Passeau was removed in the seventh because of the injury, and Borowy was pressed into service on short rest. After pitching four innings, the Pale Pole had nothing left in the tank for the seventh game.

Grimm nevertheless decided to start him in the finale, paying scant attention to the fact that he'd pitched in the fifth and sixth games. Five thousand seats went on sale the morning of the game, which were snapped up by fans who waited all night for the ticket office to open. Their cots and chairs lined Sheffield and Waveland Avenues outside the ballpark. Those who were unable to purchase tickets were upset. "That's a pretty dirty trick — the World Series happens here only once in seven years, and we can't see it," complained an unlucky fan.

Detroit scored five runs in the first, and the Cubs were finished. The final score was 9–3, as Grimm used six pitchers, including Passeau, in an effort to turn back the Motor City tide. Many of the players, including Nicholson, questioned their manager's wisdom in selecting his starting pitcher: "Borowy should never have started the seventh game," said Bill later. "They knew he needed his rest and he was a seven-inning pitcher when he was at his best.... Derringer, they could have used him. Because you knew Borowy wouldn't have a prayer. I thought they knew. I don't believe, just because he had a good year and won a couple of games.... That was bad managing, I think, and we all thought it at the time. He didn't have a prayer."

Some baseball writers called the 1945 World Series the worst in history. The *Chicago Herald American*'s Warren Brown, when asked who would win the series, said he didn't think either team was capable of doing so. After it was over, he likened the competition to "the fat men against the tall men at the office picnic":

> Fly balls were dropping besides fielders who made no effort to catch them. Players were tumbling going around the bases. The baseball was as far removed from previous major league standards as was possible without its perpetrators having themselves arrested for obtaining money under false pretenses.

One of the objects of Brown's derision, Detroit's Chuck Hostetler, a 42-year-old outfielder, tripped and fell between third and home, and was tagged out while he lay in the base path, costing his team an important run in the sixth game.

Afterwards, a friend was discussing the game with Chicago newspaperman Irv Kupcinet. Informed by the friend that he had taken his father to Wrigley Field to see the game, Kupcinet responded: "I know. I saw him fall between third and home."

Though not an artistic success, the 1945 fall classic was undeniably entertaining. It featured a one-hitter, an evicted billy goat, and a 12-inning nail-biter, before it was decided in the seventh game. The losing Cubs each pocketed $3,930.22 for their work during the series, while the Tiger players took home individual shares of $6,443.34.

Although he flopped at the plate in the four games played at Wrigley Field, Nicholson's eight RBIs for the series tied a major league record. He wasn't happy with his .208 World Series batting average, however, or his power production. "I should have knocked in 12 or 14. I never hit a home run — I just didn't have a jumpin' bat," he explained. An anonymous teammate told a reporter that Nicholson, who played well in the three Briggs Stadium contests, "tightened up" at Wrigley Field: "He was nice and loose at the plate in Detroit, but this field seems to do something to him." Bill mustered only two hits in 17 at-bats on his home grounds.

Tiger hitters, including second baseman Eddie Mayo, joined the chorus of complainants distracted by the hitter's background at Wrigley. Trying to shoehorn every possible fan into the ballpark, however, there was no way Cubs officials would block off the center field bleachers just to please the players, even in the World Series.

The year had been a strange and unpleasant one for Nicholson in many ways. He was benched for awhile, and lifted for a pinch hitter, though the possibility of such events would have evoked laughter a year before. He felt weak and sluggish at times.

"There was something the matter with me in '45," he later explained. "I played all year, but after the World Series which — if Passeau hadn't gotten hurt — we still could have won, I had a poor year. And I should've had a good year, 'cause I was just coming up all the time and improving and hitting home runs and stuff. Then, in '45, I didn't. And, of course, I don't know whether this is an excuse or not; I don't want it as an excuse but, anyhow, after the season, after the World Series, I knew that something was the matter because I had a lazy bat, a sluggish bat. I knew it was something, because I didn't have enough strength.

"So they sent me down to Illinois Masonic for a checkup, and they kept me in there a week. And they let me go, and I kept asking them what was my trouble and the doctor, he never told me anything. But the nurse told me. She said, 'I think you have a kidney infection'.... I didn't think any more about it. Well, in 1950, when I went down with diabetes with the Phillies, they said, 'When were you last in the hospital?' I thought, Illinois Masonic, 1945. So they sent out there for my records. And then they said, 'My God, you should have been watched, because you were showing sugar in 1945.'"

Cavarretta, whose locker was next to Nicholson's, also thought Nicholson was not the same player. According to him, Bill's complexion had taken on a yellowish hue, and he frequently looked tired.

Nicholson probably did not remain in the hospital for as long as he later remembered, for he was back in Huron, South Dakota for the Baseball "Pheastival" on October 14. Seven thousand saw the game, which was preceded by a mile-long parade. Fifteen hundred of the spectators were hunters, clad in red plaid shirts. Bill's team was managed by Paul Waner, and won the game at the state fairgrounds, 9–3. Old college rival Charlie Keller joined Bill, Cavarretta, Dizzy Trout, and others for the contest, and the hunting afterwards. Each player bagged his daily limit of eight pheasants before departing for home.

14

Benched

Call it "Jim Gallagher's Revenge." Surely, that's what the Cubs general manager sought in February, 1946, when Bill Nicholson's season contract was mailed to his home in Chestertown, more than a month later than usual.

In previous years, Gallagher's stingy salary offers did not reflect Nicholson's true value to the ball club. As a result, the big outfielder knew that, eventually, he would get the money he wanted or something close to it, if he just had the fortitude to keep staring until Gallagher blinked.

Now, though, the shoe was on the other foot. With his home run total dropping to 13, Nicholson's 1945 contribution, in management's estimation, had diminished enough to justify a substantial pay cut. Ed Burns knew what lay in store for Bill. He wrote in *The Sporting News*: "Some of those who have observed Gallagher's operations through the years said that James T. not only would give Nicholson a sickening carving, but that he would set a torture trap in the process."

When Bill received his 1946 contract, he was stunned. Although not surprised in the least by his proposed salary reduction, he said he "didn't expect to get whacked that hard." The outfielder told a reporter: "I hope to be able to get to talk by telephone with Gallagher tomorrow. Outside of the cut in salary, there are several other items I would like to discuss. I am not very happy over my batting work of last season, naturally, but I did not expect this kind of contract. Maybe the Cubs are figuring on trading me, or even releasing me. Naturally, I would like to know their plans because if the Cubs don't want me, I had better be looking around for another job." An Associated Press photographer arrived at the Nicholson family home in Chestertown and snapped Bill and Nancy, along with four-year-old Albert and the family's English Setter, poring over the contract. Even the dog looked unhappy.

Gallagher seemed to take great pleasure in reminding his players of their subservience. In 1948, Monk Meyer received a contract for the major league

Nancy, Bill, Albert, and a canine friend look none too happy after reviewing the Cubs' 1946 contract offer (*published with permission from Associated Press*).

minimum salary of $5,000.00. Based upon the pitcher's 1947 performance, Grimm promised he would help him get a raise. When Meyer told Gallagher of Grimm's pledge, the general manager's sarcastic response was: "Who's the boss, Grimm or me? You ought to be thankful to be in the big leagues!"

Nicholson's 1945 power decline was undeniable, but critics magnified his failures and diminished several statistical successes. Opposing pitchers were still wary of him. He was walked 92 times, fourth-best in the league. He reached base six times after being hit by pitches, fourth in the N.L. He fielded almost flawlessly, with three errors in 315 chances, for a .990 percentage. Bill Nicholson, however, was not paid to walk, or even to catch the ball. He was supposed to supply the power for the Cubs lineup, and in 1945 he failed to do that.

Meanwhile, with the team ready to return to Catalina Island, their prewar spring stomping grounds, Grimm talked up Chicago's prospects. "I'm optimistic over our chances to repeat this season," he asserted. "We have a good, fundamentally strong club aided by returning servicemen." On the subject of his slumping right fielder, he cautioned: "Big Nick will have to fight for his job. We've got a lot of players, professional players if you will, this year."

Ignoring Grimm's warning, Bill remained at home, determined to sit out the season, if necessary. He was sure he would regain his batting eye, and had stayed in shape in the offseason by working outdoors, hunting, and fishing. After returning his unsigned contract to the Cubs, it came back to him several days later. One of Gallagher's assistants wrote on it: "Gallagher is on vacation." Nicholson sent it back to Chicago right away, still unsigned.

While the early arrivals at Catalina worked out, pitcher Paul Erickson shagged fly balls in practice. After making several nice catches he joked, "I guess Bill Nicholson will sign up in a hurry when he reads about this."

Most of the squad reported by February 25. Because the channel steamer service from the mainland had not yet been restored, a "Flying Tiger" freight plane dropped the players off on the island's mountaintop airstrip. Nicholson's negotiations continued back east, with Jack Doyle, as Gallagher had gone ahead to Catalina. Not until early March did the parties agree to terms. Although the final figure was not released, it was widely reported that most of the proposed paycut was restored to induce Bill to sign.

Nicholson arrived by plane on March 4. According to an account later provided to author Rich Westcott, Bill's teammates were more than a little surprised to see him. Nicholson told Westcott:

> My top salary in baseball was $18,000.00. So one year after winning the home run title, I wanted a raise. Instead, they offered me a cut of $3,000.00. I held out all spring. Finally, I decided to fly to Catalina Island, where the Cubs trained, and meet with them. I went to get on a plane, but they wouldn't let me on because it was full. So I had to get the next plane. When I got to camp, the players gave me a big welcome. It seems the plane I was originally supposed to get had crashed and everybody was killed. They thought I was on that plane, too. They were really surprised when I showed up.

14. Benched

The defending N.L. champions were a confident bunch in training. Hack, Cavarretta, Wyse, Mickey Livingston, pitcher Les Fleming, and Nicholson spent their leisure time hunting wild boar on the island, and bagged 10 during their short stay. There was cautious optimism in camp that Bill would return to his pre–1945 batting form, reinforced when he doubled and scored three runs in his first intrasquad game. Grimm usually batted him in the third slot during scrimmages. In the exhibition game opener against the St. Louis Browns on March 15, he powered a two-run homer in the first inning off Bob Muncrief, at L.A. Wrigley. Several players, including Nicholson, were sent by the team for an eye examination in Pasadena on March 18; Nicholson and Heinz Becker were determined to be color blind, but otherwise had normal eyesight. Cavarretta and Hack were also pronounced optically fit for the upcoming season.

But the recurrence of a back injury, with which he had struggled during 1945, sidelined Nicholson, and 6'2", 200-pound rookie Marvin "Twitch" Rickert took his place in right field against the Browns, on March 22. Bill played with the "B" team, and went three for five with a double in a defeat of the Los Angeles Angels, before rejoining the starters on March 26. Evidencing the depths into which some baseball writers thought his career had plunged, a newspaper headline the next day blared: "Cubs Win One 3–2, Even With Bill Nicholson; He Pops Up Three Times Against Angels."

Grimm stuck by the right fielder, telling the *L.A. Times*:

> I'm sure he's going to come along all right. Right now, he's bothered by a lame back which is holding him back. Nick's been our home run leader the last six years, even tho [sic] he fell off to 13 last season where his average before had been around 25. He's a great outfielder and it'll help us plenty if he gets going again this summer.

As the North Siders barnstormed their way back to Wrigley Field, however, Grimm sounded a warning. In dusty Del Rio, Texas, the Cubs prepared to face off against the Browns. Between gusts of wind that blew grit into the eyes of the players and spectators, Grimm worried out loud to reporters, regarding the pennant prospects of the other N.L. teams, especially the Cardinals and Giants, and admonished:

> The improvement of the other teams means that we must improve to win and that is something that must come from Bill Nicholson's bat. As you know, Nicholson batted .243 last season, but we couldn't get by again with that because of the tougher competition. Bill may work out his own problem, whatever it is, but it may take time.

As spring training drew to a close, Nicholson's chance of retaining his starting spot in right field was evaporating. In early April, he was batting only

Nicholson trains at Catalina Island with "Dim Dom" Dallesandro and Lenny Merullo (*courtesy Emily Joiner*).

.163. Rickert, who performed well early, began to fade, but Dom Dallesandro had returned from the military to give Grimm another option. In a seven-game spring City Series against the White Sox, Bill saw virtually no action. Gallagher denied rumors that the team was trying to trade him.

When the season opened in Cincinnati on April 16, Rickert started in right in a 4–3 win; Nicholson appeared as a pinch hitter, unsuccessfully. He regained a starting spot, however, when center fielder Andy Pafko went down with an injury two days later. Chicago swept the three-game series, and was riding high for its home opener against St. Louis on April 20.

Television station WBKB announced its intention to broadcast the contest to the Chicago fans unable to come to the ballpark. The medium was in its infancy, however, and electrical interference ultimately prevented the airing of the game. Still, the Cubs held their National League pennant-raising ceremony before a crowd of nearly 41,000. Bill's old minor league teammate Harry Brecheen beat Borowy, 2–0, while Nicholson sat, and new right fielder Rickert went hitless.

Starting the next day in a loss to the Cards, Bill singled in a run in the fifth, but misplayed a fly ball three innings later, leading to two St. Louis tallies that were the margin of victory. After producing only two hits in 14 at bats, he returned to his spot on the bench on April 25. In a defensive rotation that was utilized for much of the season, Cavarretta went to right field, Waitkus to first, and Rickert to center, filling in for the oft-injured Pafko.

Gallagher was again denying reports that Nicholson was on the auction block. "Nicholson in a slump is a better ball player than a lot of players I can think of," he insisted.

Inevitably, Chicago "boo birds" vocalized their discontent with Nicholson's lack of production. His loyal fans were stung by the criticism, and wrote letters to the newspapers complaining about the treatment being accorded number 43 by Grimm and hostile fans. One letter writer complained: "I've watched a lot of unusual happenings on the diamond, but I never thought I'd live to see the day when Bob Scheffing would pinch hit for Bill Nicholson."

Curtis McKinney of Chattanooga wrote the *Trib* to complain about the booing, and asserted, "I happen to know Bill personally and I assure Cubs fans that if they'll get behind him, he'll help your club a lot." Doubtless such sentiments were of solace to Bill, but they didn't help his batting average, which hovered under .200 through mid–May.

"They never should boo him in Chicago," Braves outfielder Tommy Holmes said. "The outfielders still back up when he comes to the plate and even when he isn't hitting, he's one of the best right fielders in the game. He can do everything that a great outfielder should do defensively."

Against Bill Voiselle and the Giants on May 3, he drove in the only run of a 1–0 victory with a fourth-inning single. After a doubleheader split with Boston in late May, during which he homered in the first game, Bill brought his average up to .204. He hit a homer in a 19–3 blowout of the Giants on May 18, and followed that performance with another round-tripper in the first game of a doubleheader the next day at Boston's Braves Field. Jimmy Britt, the Braves broadcaster who was calling the game, employed his trademark line in describing Bill's clout: "There it goes — right out of the park! That's one ball we'll never see again!"

After the second game, Britt headed for his car, parked on Gaffney Street, in back of right field. He found his five-day-old Ford Coupe's front window had been smashed. Nicholson's home run ball lay on the front seat.

His Boston performance earned Bill a start against the Dodgers at Ebbets Field on May 22, in what would turn out to be another Cubs-Dodgers imbroglio. It began with a conflagration at second base, when Merullo slid into fiery Eddie Stanky. The two tangled briefly before another Dodger player jumped in and punched Merullo in the eye. Merullo and Stanky were ejected from the game, which the Cubs lost, 2–1, in 13 innings.

Having learned that Pee Wee Reese was the player who'd clocked him, Merullo approached the Brooklyn shortstop the next day during batting practice. After saying his piece, Merullo started to walk away. Reese yelled something back to Merullo, and the two went nose-to-nose for a moment, before the Dodgers' Dixie Walker clocked Lenny with a sucker punch behind his ear. Walker fled, but was pursued and tackled by Merullo, who bloodied him and knocked out his tooth. The Cubs lost the game, 2–1, in 11 innings. A substantial police presence on the field and in the dugouts was required to maintain order during the contest. Nicholson did nothing offensively to help the cause, going hitless in seven at-bats during the two contests.

At May's end, Eddie Waitkus returned to the lineup from injury, and Bill was yanked from the starting nine once more. That was his status on Saturday, June 1, when thieves broke into the team's locker room at Wrigley, and made off with cleats, gloves, jackets, sunglasses, caps, and three bats that belonged to Nicholson. The police were called in to investigate. "Maybe the [thieves] did me a favor," Bill remarked good-naturedly. "I wasn't doing any good with [the bats] and maybe some new timber will help me change my luck."

The next day, he was called on to pinch hit in the first game of a doubleheader split with the Braves. Using a brand new Louisville Slugger, he homered over the right field wall, although the team lost, 6–3. Nicholson sat in the dugout for the second game. And when he resumed his hitting slump, a local wiseacre wrote to the *Trib*, "Wonder how Bill Nicholson ever discovered his bats were missing?"

In early June, the third-place Cubs were not getting the pitching and timely hitting they had come to expect in 1945. Borowy was battling inconsistency, Passeau injury. Bill's two-run pinch single with the bases loaded in the ninth inning gave his team a 6–5 victory over the Pirates at Forbes Field on June 27, but his batting average was dismal. Waitkus led the team with a .317 percentage on June 30, while Nicholson had sunk to .198, with only three home runs and 12 RBIs. Rickert's power numbers were not much better, but at least he was hitting .280.

Grimm did what he could to work Nicholson into the lineup. After hitting two doubles the previous day, Bill started both games of a doubleheader at Shibe Park against the Phillies on July 28. He went four for eight. In the first game, he hit a three-run homer off Hugh Mulcahy, doubled, and then singled, to drive in a total of six runs. In the second game, he doubled off the 331-foot right field wall.

14. Benched

He got two more hits off the Giants at the Polo Grounds, followed by a solo home run into the upper right field stands, in an 8–1 triumph on the last day of July. The game marked the return of Passeau, who'd been out for 10 days with a back injury and sustained five straight losses before that. Six-foot nine-inch lefthander Johnny Gee started the game on the mound for the Giants. In a comical effort to accustom Cubs batters to Gee's southpaw offerings, tiny Dom Dallesandro (height: five feet, five inches) pitched pregame batting practice to his teammates.

With 10 hits in his last six games, Bill was pounding the ball at a .345 clip. Then, he went cold again. Still, he raised his average to .227 by August 3. Poised to make a stretch run at the end of August, the Cubs ran off seven straight victories. Then, a series of devastating injuries beset the team. Hack, McCullough, and Waitkus sustained broken fingers. Don Johnson broke his hand. Passeau's back problem flared. Nicholson injured his hip sliding into base, and developed bursitis in his right shoulder. Even coach Roy Johnson got hurt; his jaw was fractured when a line drive hit him while pitching batting practice.

Nicholson's first-pitch, pinch-hit homer off Brooklyn's Hal Gregg provided the decisive runs in a 4–3 win at Wrigley, on August 28. Tempering the elation of the victory, Pafko broke his arm while colliding with the center field wall and was lost for the season. It being a Cubs-Dodgers game, there was — of course — the obligatory extracurricular entertainment. Durocher invited several heckling Cubs fans onto the field late in the game, just in case they wanted to engage him pugilistically. Order was soon restored by Chicago's finest.

After August 29, the North Siders played sub–.500 baseball in their remaining 31 games and fell out of pennant contention. St. Louis and Brooklyn were left to fight it out for the N.L. flag. The Cubs still had some say as to whom the pennant winner would be, with eight games scheduled against the Cardinals and four against the Dodgers, at season's end.

Before the largest Sunday Ebbets Field crowd of the season, on September 15, the Cubs split a doubleheader, winning, 4–3, and losing, 2–0. Nicholson tripled off the top of the right field wall in the opener, but his error in the nightcap led to a Brooklyn run. That game was called after five innings, because of an invasion of aphids. Thousands of spectators were slapping themselves and their neighbors in the stands with scorecards and newspapers, trying to shoo the pesky bugs away.

Eventually, the insects made their way onto the field. As Dodger hurler Kirby Higbe took the mound for his warmups in the top of the sixth, he started slapping at himself with his glove, and other players followed suit. Noting the lateness of the hour, the umpires huddled in deference to the intrusive insects and — amid some criticism from the visiting team — called the game a Dodgers victory.

A day later, the Cubs took care of the home team, 10–7. The score was tied at five in the top of the seventh, and rookie Paul Minner was on the mound for Brooklyn. "I was scared to death," Minner remembered. "I walked the first batter, gave up a bunt single, walked the third...."

Now, Nicholson strode to the dish, with the sacks full. The right-handed rookie worked carefully, throwing three pitches out of the strike zone. Nicholson laid off each one. Down in the count, 3–0, Minner threw two strikes, each of which Nicholson took. With the count full, the next pitch was a fastball, and Nicholson timed it perfectly. He powered the ball over the right field scoreboard, onto adjacent Bedford Avenue, for a grand-slam home run. Afterwards, Durocher consoled his young pitcher. "Well, kid, you can't win 'em all," was the manager's blunt assessment.

Brooklyn now trailed St. Louis by two games, but bounced back the next day to defeat the Cubs, 4–2. Batting in his old cleanup spot, Nicholson was hitless.

The Cubs lost two out of three to St. Louis, in late September. In the middle game, a Chicago victory, Nicholson tripled in the sixth off Howard Pollett; in the eighth, he made a tough, one-handed running catch of a drive off the bat of Enos Slaughter, before 42,324 Wrigley patrons.

On the morrow, though, Slaughter returned the favor, making a great play on a ball Bill hit off the right field wall, preventing a Cub baserunner from scoring, and preserving St. Louis' 1–0 victory.

The Cards and Dodgers were dead even on September 27. Two days later, on the last day of the regular season, Brooklyn bested Boston, 4–0, as the Cubs played the Cardinals at Sportsman's Park. After their game, Dodgers fans lingered in the outfield at Ebbets Field, watching the scoreboard for news from St. Louis. A great roar went up when the 8–3 final score, in favor of Chicago, was posted. With identical records, the Cards and Dodgers would engage in a best-of-three game playoff, for the N.L. pennant. But there would be no Dodger flag this year. St. Louis won the first two games, to win the flag, and then vanquished the Boston Red Sox in the World Series.

At the end of the season, Nicholson submitted to yet another physical examination. "My shoulders have been aching for most of the last two months," he complained. "I'd like to find out the cause of the trouble." Again, doctors found nothing amiss. Indeed, Bill had shown signs of regaining his old form during September, raising his final season batting average to .220, when it had hovered around .200 for much of the year. In pinch-hitting appearances, he batted at a hefty .353 clip for the season.

He entertained thoughts of playing winter ball in Puerto Rico. The president of the San Juan team, a friend of Hi Bithorn, had extended an invitation to play for his team. Ultimately, however, Bill declined the offer. He needed to rest.

It was now undeniable that the big right fielder was on the trading block. The Cubs were still looking for a shortstop, and they had a surplus of major league caliber catchers, along with their right fielder, who had market value. Cincinnati's Eddie Miller, the Giants' Buddy Kerr, and St. Louis' Marty Marion were all mentioned as possibilities in a one-for-one swap.

Bill sensed the end was coming. Although he enjoyed Chicago and its fans, he hated Wrigley Field, its wind, and visibility problems. He confided to teammates that he hoped to be traded and get a fresh start in another city.

Gallagher was firm about what it would take to pry Nicholson out of the North Side. He told the press: "The Cubs would not consider a deal for Nicholson unless a shortstop were involved, and the Giants have that shortstop in Buddy Kerr." Giants manager Mel Ott bristled at the suggestion of parting with his star infielder, but Bill Rigney was floated as an alternative. Probably because the Cubs would not also throw a pitcher into the deal, the trade didn't occur. Bill Nicholson was going to remain in Chicago, at least for the immediate future.

15

The Cubs in Decline

Nineteen forty-seven marked the beginning of the Cubs' precipitous fall from contention in the National League. Not until 1967 would the franchise again rise as high as third in the standings. Phil Wrigley's election to economize on minor league player development finally came home to roost. The North Siders, for 20 years, were to remain a second division club.

Grimm's squad, upset by its disheartening third-place finish in 1946, was itching to go by early February. For the first time in six years, there were no contract holdouts. Nicholson agreed to a $15,000 pact early in the year. With all players signed, Grimm headed to Catalina Island several weeks ahead of his charges, for a personal vacation. Pitchers and catchers were set to report in mid–February, veterans a week later.

Grimm thought Chicago had no chance to return to the World Series if Nicholson's hitting slump continued. In spring training, he wanted the right fielder to get as many repetitions at bat as possible. To that end, when Grimm divided the club into two squads for batting practice, Nicholson hit with both groups.

When the players arrived by train from Chicago, they included Bill's minor league teammate Ace Parker, now a professional football star, destined to be cut by the Cubs before the regular season began. At Catalina, Waitkus, Merullo, Cavarretta, Dallesandro, and others renewed acquaintances at the country club patio on February 23, over a fried chicken dinner, in gorgeous 85-degree weather. The Cubs never wanted for food during their Catalina stay. Wrigley ordered 1,700 tons of prime beef to be shipped to the island for the team's consumption.

Informed of the new batting practice arrangement, Nicholson was delighted, acknowledging that he needed as much practice as he could get. Once workouts began, Grimm announced that Bill would play every inning of every spring game, including intrasquad and exhibition games. "Nick will be in there from start to finish every day we play, even if we get tangled in an 18-inning overtime game," the skipper told reporters. "After the last exhibition game in Wrigley Field on April 13, we'll put together all those Nicholson innings and if they spell 's-l-u-g-g-e-r,' as I hope and think they will, then Nick will be in right field when the Cubs open against the Pittsburgh Pirates on April 15."

Half of the scheduled exhibition games were against minor league competition, providing a fine opportunity for Nicholson to regain his hitting stroke. At the suggestion of well-meaning fans and teammates, he'd tried everything last year: letting his toe nails grow; shaving under his arms; sporting a crew cut. One fan even ran onto the field before a game to give Bill a batting lesson.

When the first intrasquad game between the Regulars and Yannigans took place on March 4, Nicholson was the star of the show, blasting two consecutive home runs off Borowy. With exhibition games set to begin in four days, Grimm was encouraged. But in a 6–3 loss to the White Sox that marked the beginning of the exhibition season, Bill's bat was quiet, and he made a costly error in the field, when a base hit rolled under his glove and went all the way to the wall. After another loss to the Sox in which Bill doubled in four trips, the Cubs bested the minor league Los Angeles Angels, behind a 350-foot Nicholson clout to right center field.

The Cleveland Indians came to L.A. Wrigley on March 15 for an exhibition showdown with their midwest cousins. The legendary baseball clown Max Patkin — heir to the throne of Al Schacht — and sidekick Johnny Price entertained more than 5,000 fans during the game. In the fifth, with the Indians leading, 5–1, Pafko's grand slam tied the score. The next batter, Nicholson, drove a solo shot over the right field screen, to give the Cubs a lead they did not relinquish. The final score was 7–5.

Because Indians ace Bob Feller was slated to pitch, 23,550 crammed into Wrigley the next day. Hundreds bought standing-room-only tickets, and the contest was delayed by half an hour to accommodate the record crowd. In an uncharacteristically rough performance, "Rapid Robert" was bombed by the Cubs, surrendering five runs in as many innings. Pafko had another homer, a three-run poke, and Nicholson had two hits and two RBIs. Displaying his dangerous pickoff move, Feller did nab two Cubs base runners who had strayed too far off second base. Nicholson told a reporter that Feller's fastball was fading, and he was now relying more on his curveball.

Besides his inconsistent hitting, Bill was facing another crisis. His once-wavy hair was beginning to thin noticeably. Teammates learned that, in an effort to replenish the follicles, he paid former Cubs pitcher Jake Mooty $18.00

for a bottle of "hair restorer." Despite religious use of the product, Bill was disappointed with the results, and discontinued its use amid good-natured needling from teammates.

After a four-for-five performance, including a double and home run, against the Oakland Oaks, Bill pulled a muscle in his right leg, and finally missed some playing time. He pinch hit a home run against the Indians, though, on March 26 — the third consecutive game in which he'd homered.

The leg began to mend, but was aggravated on April 6 in Fort Worth, running out a ground ball, when he accelerated to avoid a double play. Grimm decided to send Bill back to Chicago ahead of the team for reevaluation and treatment. He checked into Illinois Masonic Hospital on April 8. After being examined by team physician Ladislaus Braun, Nicholson insisted, "[T]here's nothing wrong with me that a few home runs and heat won't cure...." Now at a svelte 200 pounds, and having averaged .345 with five home runs in exhibition games, he insisted he would be ready for Opening Day. Dr. Braun seemed to agree: "He has nothing more than a pulled muscle in his right leg, which should be taken care of by a little rest and heat."

Word of Nicholson's resurgence was making its way through the major league grapevine. One day in spring training, the Cardinals were lounging in their St. Petersburg clubhouse before beginning the day's workouts. St. Louis pitcher George "Red" Munger lay on a rubbing table, reading the sports section of a newspaper, before he suddenly let it drop. "Did you see this?," he called to no one in particular. "Bill Nicholson is hitting the ball hard again for the Cubs. Talk about bad news! That guy scares me to death. You can almost see the sawdust running out of the bat handle."

Back in Chicago early in April, Nicholson insisted on playing in an exhibition against the White Sox at Wrigley, before 16,000 fans, in the 32-degree weather. He was greeted with a thunderous ovation, managed to get two hits, and did not reaggravate his injury, as the Cubs won, 5–3. Of the seven exhibition games the two Chicago teams played during the spring, the Cubs uncharacteristically took four.

When the season opened on April 15, however, the storyline changed a bit. The Pirates came to town and took a 1-0 decision, despite Borowy's five-hitter. Hank Greenberg, now playing for the Pirates, knocked in the only run of the game, and Nicholson — batting fifth in the order — was without a hit in four trips.

After dropping the first three games of the young season, the North Siders rebounded with three wins, lost a ten-inning game to the Reds, then won 11 of their next 14. In a 7–4 victory over the Cardinals at Sportsman's Park, Bill was plunked with a pitch in the first inning, while the bases were loaded, to send in the team's first run. He also belted two homers, and drove in six. The initial homer was a grand slam off Howard Pollett in the fifth; the second a leadoff shot in the seventh off Fred Schmidt that landed on the right field pavilion roof.

The season's maiden series against the Dodgers began on April 29 at Ebbets Field, with a 10–6 defeat. Brooklyn was now the early N.L. leader, and winners of six straight. The next day, however, fortunes were reversed. A crowd of more than 20,000, including 4,500 high school boys and girls, attended the game, which was knotted at 1–1 in the top of the ninth.

The school children were enjoying themselves, boisterously chanting "Swish!" whenever Nicholson batted, and were especially delighted when he struck out in the seventh on a lusty cut at Ralph Branca's pitch.

With two outs and a runner on, the high schoolers were into their "Swish" chant again, until Branca's next offering met Nicholson's bat. Roscoe McGowan of the *New York Times* described the ensuing scene:

> The fans watched with bated [sic] breath as the ball sailed high and far toward the right field screen and then went on into Bedford Avenue just inside the foul pole. They had been pulling for it to go foul, but as Nick trotted around the bases ... they cheered the old slugger.

The horsehide bounced among cars in the parking lot about 400 feet from home plate. Though he was hitting only .182 after 13 games, Bill still had three homers and eleven batted in to lead the team in both categories.

Brooklyn exacted retribution the following day, 5–2. Nicholson had a tough outing at the plate: Dixie Walker made a running one-handed grab of his eighth-inning drive right in front of the Ebbets Field scoreboard, and another drive to right field hit the screen next to the foul pole, and bounced back onto the field, turning a potential home run into a double.

The Cubs were atop the standings in mid–May. Nicholson reinjured his chronically sore back, but was in the lineup on May 18 for Dodgers rookie Jackie Robinson's first visit to Wrigley Field. Robinson's Chicago debut was much anticipated, especially in the city's black community, but also by Cubs players. Some of them were not too keen to play against a black player, including Claude Passeau, who promised to throw at the rookie.

In early May, testimonials and dinners in the black community were planned to honor the Dodger infielder, to the consternation of Brooklyn club president Branch Rickey. "He needs rest, and he needs time to eat his meals," Rickey scolded. Jackie was exhausted from all of the attention lavished upon him. Rickey thought there were "too many well-wishers and entirely too many trying to cash in on Robinson's popularity, too many trying to exploit him. It would be best for all these people to let Robinson alone."

Cubs employees and Chicago police were uneasy about the possibility of violence during the two-game series. The *Chicago Defender*, widely circulated in the black community, warned in its May 3 edition:

> Wrigley Field officials will not tolerate any whiskey bottle toters nor those who carry pints in their hip pockets. Those who haven't washed their filthy mouths out with soap and salt better stay as far away from Addison and Clark as the stockyards at 47th and Ashland.

A special squad of 10 black police officers from the South Side attended the contest, as a precaution. Before the game, thousands of black citizens poured out of the elevated trains, or alighted from crowded automobiles, and entered Wrigley Field. Most were dressed in their Sunday finery.

The largest paid crowd in the park's history — 46,572 — witnessed a 4–2 Brooklyn win, and the fifth straight Chicago loss. Nicholson's most important contribution was defensive in nature; a flashy catch in the fourth, that robbed Bruce Edwards of an extra base hit. Robinson struck out twice, but was well-received by the home crowd. Many black spectators wept openly at the sight of their hero. A Cubs official described the congregation as "the most orderly large crowd in the history of Wrigley Field," and added that "the Negro fans behaved better than our average Sunday fans...."

Dixie Walker was not as well-received as his rookie teammate. North Side fans had not forgotten Walker's sucker punch at Lenny Merullo the previous year, and razzed him during the game whenever presented with the opportunity to do so. Walker, a Georgian, had been a ringleader of the group of disgruntled Dodgers who did not want to play with Robinson because of his color. Thus there was some justice to the treatment Walker received at the hands of both white and black Wrigley Field patrons. At his request, he was traded to Pittsburgh at the end of the season.

On the 20th, the Cubs edged the Phils, 3–2, in 11 innings, on a windy, 40-degree day. Bill led off the ninth inning with his second successive leadoff double, and scored the tying run, going three for five on the day. Lonnie Frey's single in the bottom of the 11th, with the bases filled, drove in the winning run.

Even though he was averaging only .208, Nicholson's clutch hitting had accounted for four of the team's 17 wins. Some Cubs fans, nonetheless, remained cynical about Bill's performance. During a game in mid–May against the Giants at Wrigley, a big red balloon sailed from the grandstand into right field. New York outfielder Willard Marshall tried to pick it up, but booted it instead. A fan was heard to say, "That's the difference between the Giants and Cubs. They got a right fielder that can't field a balloon and we got one that can't hit a balloon!"

15. The Cubs in Decline

After spending a good portion of the month atop the N.L. standings, the Cubs dropped out of first on May 28, after a loss to the Pirates. Nicholson was down to a pitiful .198 at the plate; then, he went on a rampage. He homered on May 30, and was four for eight in a doubleheader with Pittsburgh. The next day, he homered off future Phillies teammate Blix Donnelly, in a 7–1 victory.

An emaciated Babe Ruth, afflicted with throat cancer, watched the Cubs-Giants game at the Polo Grounds, on June 3. More than 30,000 cheered his appearance. Clad in a tan coat and cap, the Babe sat next to the Giants' dugout, looking decidedly different from the rakish character with whom Nicholson had posed for newspaper photos in 1940.

The game The Babe saw was a comedy of errors for Chicago, in an 8–3 loss. First, Stan Hack injured his ankle in the third, and was carried off the field on a stretcher. In the fifth, a base hit off Johnny Mize's booming bat struck Bill in the mouth, and he was forced to repair to the Cubs' dugout for treatment before returning to the field. In the eighth, a foul popup struck Waitkus on the top of the head, and he fell head over heels into the box seats. Catcher Clyde McCullough managed to drop a fly popup in front of the plate, while the bases were loaded with two outs, scoring two Giant runs and prolonging the inning.

The next day, though, the Cubs returned to a first place tie with the Giants, after a 6–0 whitewashing of the New Yorkers. It was the first time the Giants had been shut out all season. In the sixth, Nicholson crushed a two-run shot into the right field stands off Gene Thompson. But with his average still hovering around .200, Grimm benched Nicholson on June 10, before a loss to Boston. Dallesandro had been hitting well, going six for eight in a doubleheader sweep, and so for the next week and a half Nicholson saw only pinch-hitting duty.

With Cavarretta sidelined by injury, Bill was pressed into service on June 22 against the Braves. It didn't hurt that Bill Voiselle happened to be the starting pitcher. In an 8–7 loss that wasn't decided until the bottom of the 11th, Bill singled, tripled, and homered, scored three times and knocked in two. He crashed into the wall at Wrigley spearing a drive in a victory over the Pirates on June 28, breaking his sunglasses and suffering a nasty cut over his right eye in the process.

Shuffled around in the batting order in early July, Bill was hitting in the number three spot on July 5, when his sixth-inning double knocked in two runs to help Doyle Lade beat the Pirates, 4–3. A nine-game Cubs losing streak followed, broken on July 15 in a win at Boston. Nicholson hit home run number 12 into the right field jury box at Braves Field, off Johnny Sain.

Bill discussed his inconsistency at the plate with a United Press correspondent, after a two-game series against the Giants at the Polo Grounds. "I've been trying everything I know to bring my batting average over .200, but most of the days I just can't seem to buy a base hit," he said. "I tried changing my stance, swinging early, and a lot of other things, but I haven't had much success at all."

The writer asked Nicholson to identify the pitcher with whom he had the most difficulty. "They're all tough, especially when you're not hitting," was his reply. "But if I was pinned down to name one pitcher who gives me the most trouble, I guess it would have to be Dave Koslo of the Giants. I never have any luck hitting against him."

One presumably well-intentioned fan wrote to Bill: "I know what's the matter with you.... You should hit right-handed like you throw and eat." Bill was almost tempted to follow this advice.

In late July, a prankster phoned the sports desks at several Chicago newspapers to report that Nicholson, Waitkus, and $100,000 were being shipped to the Reds, in exchange for lanky pitcher Ewell Blackwell. The accounts found their way into print. Embarrassed members of the city media later acknowledged their alacrity in reporting the story.

Despite his struggles at the plate, Nicholson was still popular with fans throughout the country. *Sport* magazine even ran a story about the Chicago right fielder in its August issue. *Trib* readers saw the following promo for the article in late July:

> "Pitcher's Poison"— that's what they call Chicago's Bill Nicholson. He squeezes a bat so hard you can almost see the sawdust run out the handle. What's behind his strange hitting power? Why do pitchers fear his batting power even when his average is low? Find out in your big August Sport now on sale at your newsdealers.

Billy Stone bought the magazine, cut out the color photograph of Nicholson that accompanied the article, had Nicholson autograph it, and then carefully mounted it on cardboard. He covered his treasure in plastic, and stored it in a cigar box, along with a complete set of 1948 Bowman baseball cards, for posterity. Alas, when he went away to the University of Michigan in the mid–'50s, his mother threw the box away.

For the fourth time in history, the Cubs passed the million mark in home attendance, on August 5, in an 8–2 loss to the Cardinals. Bill homered in the second off Harry Brecheen, for a 1–0 Chicago lead that lasted only until the fourth inning. He also fanned twice.

Ewell Blackwell — the subject of trade rumors only months before — and the Reds came to Wrigley on August 8, to play four games. Blackwell's parents journeyed from their home in Bonita, California, to see their son pitch a professional game for the first time. Nicholson spoiled their afternoon.

Blackwell had pitched around Big Nick throughout the game, walking him three times with runners on. Bill singled and reached on an error, as well. But when he came up in the bottom of the 11th, with the score tied and one out, he connected squarely with Blackwell's third pitch, sending it into the right field bleachers, for a walk-off Chicago win. Nicholson remembered the day well: "I had a single, home run, and should have had a double, but they gave [center fielder] Bert Haas an error. We also had a triple play in that game when Merullo caught a liner by Babe Young."

Eight days later against the Reds at Crosley Field, Bill hit two homers in a losing effort, as Cincy scored twice in the ninth to edge the Cubs, 7–6.

August 28 was Charlie Grimm's 49th birthday. The team was in Brooklyn to face the first-place Dodgers. Twelve thousand American Legionnaires were part of a crowd of 22,375 who saw the homestanding team prevail, 6–2. Both Chicago runs were solo Nicholson homers, and he hit the ball hard every time up. In the ninth, Bill drove a ball into Bedford Avenue that was foul by a few feet, before grounding out to Jackie Robinson.

The sun was setting on "Smiling Stan" Hack's illustrious Cubs career, which dated back to 1932. In recognition of what appeared to be his impending retirement from the game, the Cubs held "Stan Hack Day" at Wrigley on August 30. In a pregame ceremony, Hack was showered with gifts from players, fans, and local businesses. Among the bounty was a $3,500 gray Cadillac sedan, a deep freeze, and a $1,000 television set. Hack graciously told the fans it was the happiest day of his life. Nicholson hit a home run for his buddy in the sixth, but Pittsburgh prevailed, 13–6.

The Cubs were mathematically eliminated from pennant contention after a September 3 loss to the Cardinals, but Bill hit six home runs in the last three weeks of the season. There were two against Pittsburgh on September 6 in a Chicago loss, one of which came off Rip Sewell's famous "eephus" pitch. On the 17th, the Giants' Dave Koslo — Nicholson's toughest opposing hurler — was the victim. Two days later, St. Louis' Alpha Brazle — with whose offerings Bill always struggled — surrendered a seventh-inning shot. Johnny Vander Meer of the Reds was on the receiving end on September 23.

In the season finale, at home against the Cardinals on September 28, the mayor of Lockport, Illinois, watched the game after landing by helicopter on the field. A second-inning Nicholson homer, off Ken Burkhart, supplied all the offense needed in a 3–0 win. Bill also snagged a twisting drive off the bat of Erv Dusek, a few feet from the right field wall, in the seventh, to help winning pitcher Johnny Schmitz.

In the fourth inning, Bill walked and went to third on a wild pitch. Sliding into base, he scraped his ankle and tore his cleats. He left the game for emergency repairs, and Borowy was inserted as a "courtesy" runner. Hank scored on a subsequent base hit by Ray Mack.

When the Cardinals came to bat in the top of the fifth, Nicholson re-entered the game in right field, as was permissible under then-prevailing rules. The courtesy runner rule was utilized on only two subsequent occasions in the major leagues, in 1949, before it was abrogated.

The season concluded with Chicago in sixth place, 25 games behind the Dodgers, and 16 games under .500. Nicholson's individual performance was a mixed bag. He had regained a semblance of his home run hitting prowess, finishing seventh in the league with 26. His on-base and slugging percentage ranked him 10th in the league, but he led the N.L. with 87 strikeouts. Based on a productive September (34 hits in his last 36 games, including six doubles, seven homers and 17 RBIs), he managed to boost his batting average, but only to .244.

In the field, he handled 291 chances, with only three errors, and his .990 fielding percentage led National League outfielders. With his career in seeming decline, Nicholson was particularly pleased with the defensive aspect of his game. In later years, he told an interviewer: "I was always pretty proud of my fielding ability. I could catch the ball pretty well, and except for the times I had a sore arm, which I would get occasionally, I could throw the ball pretty well."

At the winter baseball meetings in New York City in mid–December, Jim Gallagher insisted the Cubs were not in the market for new talent. "There'll be no deals, so don't worry about anything but the Christmas rush at busy intersections," he joked to reporters. Cubs followers knew, however, that the team still coveted a quality shortstop. Billy Cox of Brooklyn was a possibility, with Waitkus or Cavarretta as the *quid pro quo*. Nicholson was shopped around, with no takers except the Pirates, who offered $40,000 in a straight player-for-cash deal. Gallagher declined.

A franchise-saving shortstop did not materialize in Chicago until the arrival of Ernie Banks, in 1953. In the meantime, the 1948 team turned into one of the worst in Chicago history. It was also the last Cubs team for which Bill Nicholson would play.

16

Farewell to the Windy City

Before the end of April, 1948, the current edition of the Cubs was headed nowhere, fast. When September arrived, Chicago's National League franchise was dead last, 25½ games behind the pennant-winning Boston Braves. It had been nearly 25 years since the Cubs occupied the cellar at season's end. When, a day after the end of the season, Jim Gallagher traded Bill Nicholson straight up for the Phillies' Harry "The Hat" Walker, the slugging right fielder left a sinking ship behind.

Nineteen forty-eight was to be a "rebuilding" year. With inexperienced players at second and short, outfielder Andy Pafko on third base, and a stripped-down pitching staff, the Cubs were doomed from the start. Pitchers Johnny Schmitz and Monk Meyer won 18 and 10 games, respectively, but no other pitcher won as many as five. Pafko, Cavarretta, Nicholson, and Waitkus were the only threats offensively. Not much could have been expected of Charlie Grimm's boys, and not much was produced.

Although Nicholson had been in a three-year batting funk, he was still a feared hitter. Cubs scout Jigger Statz reminded baseball fans that Bill couldn't be judged solely by his batting average. "Bill is a guy who is apt to hit that long ball any time he walks to the plate," he said. "He must be pitched to carefully, and he'll draw many walks as a result."

Gallagher actually raised Bill's salary by $1,000, to $16,000, in early February. For the first time in recent memory, the main contingent of Cubs regulars did not travel together from Chicago to spring training. Instead, Nicholson and several teammates boarded a westbound Santa Fe Chief from the Dearborn Street Station, with veteran members of the White Sox, on February 27. Sadly, Catalina was permanently abandoned as a training site. Today, city hall and a fire station sit where Nicholson and his fellow outfielders used to roam, and children play on a soccer field in the area between home plate and first base.

When drills began in early March, at L. A. Wrigley, Grimm announced that Nicholson would bat second in the order, ahead of Pafko and Cavarretta. The manager abandoned this experiment before very long.

Despite several off-years, Nicholson was sought that spring by another N.L. team, the Phillies. Philadelphia Manager Ben Chapman — notorious for the viciousness he exhibited towards Jackie Robinson the previous season — made no secret of the fact that he wanted the Cubs' right fielder.

"I have six shortstops who are better than any one the Cubs have, and they can have any one of mine except Eddie Miller or Granville Hamner for Nicholson," he said early in March. "They need a shortstop and I need an outfielder so I'm hoping we can get together on the deal." When the Phils finally acquired Nicholson seven months later, however, Chapman had been fired.

Within a week of reporting to spring training, Bill injured his right heel. Then he hurt his shoulder, several weeks later. What was initially thought to be a separation turned out to be a sprain, fortunately. He also developed soreness in his chest, which was diagnosed as an "arthritic condition," further affecting his conditioning.

He hit a solo home run in Phoenix on March 29, in an 11–6 loss to the White Sox, the sixth straight Cubs loss during the exhibition season. "I think I'm going to hit a lot more like that," Bill told reporters. "I really believe I'm back again after hitting the way I did in my real good years."

Three days later, the North Siders were in Juarez, Mexico, to face the St. Louis Browns in a contest won by Chicago, 5–0, and Bill hit a pinch double. The last time Bill played in Mexico, he was a promising 22 year old, struggling to prove himself with Connie Mack's Philadelphia Athletics. Now, as a 33-year-old veteran, he was trying to regain the form that made him such a potent offensive weapon in the years before 1945.

Late in 1947, he had a teammate film him, with a motion picture camera, during plate appearances. "That's how I found out what I've been doing wrong these last few years," he said. He called his problem, "The Big Rock."

"In getting ready to hit ... I was rocking way back," Bill explained. "By the time I rocked back and then tried to get my bat through, the ball was on top of me. I was swinging late on everything.... Lots of times the ball was getting past me before I could bring the bat through."

While the Cubs played their way back to Chicago, Nicholson was limited mainly to pinch-hitting duties. On Opening Day in Pittsburgh, he batted sixth and went two for three with a double, as the Pirates' Rip Sewell bested Monk Meyer, 3–2. The Cubs triumphed the next day, 6–3. In the second inning, Nicholson powered his first home run, down the right field line.

Despite two fine hitting performances, the *Trib's* Arch Ward remained skeptical. Speaking of Nicholson in his April 23rd "In the Wake of the News" column, he told readers: "The management still has confidence in him. If we had the same kind of optimism, we'd be looking over the form charts for something that might beat the Calumet farm entry in the Kentucky Derby."

Nicholson answered the cynics by homering in a 6–2 triumph over the Cardinals a day later, with a gargantuan smash. Alpha Brazle was the fourth-inning victim, which the right fielder thought was an accomplishment. "I always had trouble with Max Lanier and Alpha Brazle when they were with the Cardinals," said Bill. "We used to go into St. Louis, and they would throw four straight lefthanders against us. One was Howie Pollett. I liked to hit against him. And once in a while, I'd get one against Harry Brecheen. But I could never hit Lanier or Brazle."

Bill's home run shot passed just inches to the right of the center field scoreboard before landing on Sheffield Avenue, where it struck a building and then rebounded onto a southbound automobile. Although no player has ever hit the scoreboard on a fly, this was as close as anyone ever came to doing so. More than a decade later, Roberto Clemente of the Pirates nearly accomplished the feat, but missed wide left. Before Opening Day at Wrigley, in April, 1951, the legendary golfer Sam Snead, who was in the city for treatment of his ailing wrist, tried to hit the 27-foot structure with a golf ball. First, from home plate, he hit it with a four-iron. Then, using a two-iron and no tee, he drove one over the scoreboard. Cincinnati manager Luke Sewell was not impressed, rhetorically asking, "Yeah, but can he hit a curve ball?"

The Cubs settled into eighth place on April 30, and did not emerge from the second division for the rest of the campaign, occasionally rising as high as sixth in the standings. There were three four-game losing streaks, two five-game losing streaks, one seven-game losing streak, and one ten-game losing streak during the course of the season.

Nicholson's average was .301 on May 22, with three homers and 10 RBIs, before he cooled. By the time June rolled around, he was slumping, and then benched on June 2 in favor of Phil Cavarretta. Complaining of a sore back, he entered Illinois Masonic Hospital on June 5 for a checkup. After being given a clean bill of health, Bill returned to the lineup on June 8, knocking in the only run off the Braves' Vern Bickford in an 11–1 rout.

Though the North Siders were playing poorly, they did enjoy some success against archrival Brooklyn. The visiting Chicagoans beat Brooklyn for the fifth time in seven tries on June 20, 5–2. Pafko, about whom trade rumors were swirling, went five for five. In the eighth, with Pafko on first, Bill hit a Harry Taylor fastball atop the loudspeaker, next to the Bulova clock on the right field scoreboard at Ebbets Field. He also doubled in the ninth inning.

Umpire Dusty Boggess fractured his collarbone, after being hit by a foul tip, and was transported to the hospital. As he departed, Ebbets Field organist Gladys Gooding segued into a rendition of the popular hit, "You Always Hurt the One You Love."

Phillies rookie pitcher Robin Roberts pitched the second game of a doubleheader against the Cubs at Shibe Park on Sunday, June 27. Growing up in Springfield, Illinois, he was an ardent Cubs fan. His favorite player was Bill Nicholson. He'd even gotten Bill's autograph, as a kid. When they became teammates, Roberts was reluctant to tell him that fact, because he didn't want to make his hero feel old. In a game shortened to eight innings because of the Sunday curfew, the Phils beat Chicago, 7–4, though Roberts surrendered two hits to his boyhood hero. The next year, to Roberts' delight, they were teammates.

"I certainly was not disappointed when I got to know Nick personally," Roberts said. "I remember in 1953 Nick was on third base in the eighth inning of a game against the Braves in which I happened to be going after my 100th career win. Our batter hit a fly ball to right field deep enough to score Nick easily, but Nick slid into home even though there was no throw. When he came into the dugout, I asked, 'Nick, why did you slide home?' He said, 'That's as far as I have to go.' That was a great crack, but the truth is that Bill Nicholson was one of those ballplayers that played hard all the time, no matter what the score or the circumstances. He practiced hard and he played hard."

Back in the lineup again, Nicholson maintained an average in the respectable .270 range throughout July, but trailed team leader Pafko in both homers and RBIs. Cardinals pitcher Red Munger—who'd been so terrified of Bill, during spring training in 1947—started against the Cubs at Sportsman's Park on July 6. With two out and two strikes on Nicholson in the first inning, he threw a pitch that Munger and catcher Bill Baker thought was strike three. Plate umpire Butch Henline disagreed, though, and called it a ball.

Munger and Baker were incredulous. "Go ahead and squawk," Henline said. "Squawk as hard as you want, but don't make it too long. I missed that one. But don't show me up, or I'll have to put you out of the game. Now, if you strike Nicholson out, you'll make it easier for yourself, and me too."

Bill doubled on the next pitch, leading to a five-run inning. With the Cubs ahead, 10–8, after eight innings, the game was called so that the North Siders could make their train connection back to Chicago. Later in the year, Henline became the first umpire to eject Jackie Robinson from a game.

The Pirates' Elmer Riddle had beaten the Cubs four times, before a July 9 matchup at Wrigley against young Cubs hurler Ralph Hamner. Nicholson's sixth-inning home run into the bleachers, with Pafko aboard, provided the two runs needed to end Riddle's streak, 2–1. The next day, he hit a three-run homer (number 12 for the year) as the Cubs beat Pittsburgh, 4–2.

In late July, wallowing in the N.L. cellar, the North Siders dropped a doubleheader at Wrigley against the Dodgers, before more than 40,000 fans. Mirroring the fans' discontent, Edward Burns expressed his displeasure with Phil Wrigley's obsessive attention to ballpark amenities, but indifference to the quality of his team: "It is difficult sometimes for an innocent bystander who doesn't eat hot dogs, sweats too much after a bottle of beer, and who already has a baseball cap, to see anything thrilling in one Cub flop after another."

The season's highlight for Nicholson was the clubbing of his 200th career home run on July 25, at home against New York. He achieved this milestone with one out in the seventh inning, driving Alex Konikowski's first pitch off the top row of Wrigley's right field bleachers. Nicholson was the twelfth player in National League history to reach the 200 homer plateau, although scores have accomplished the feat since then. Besides his offensive contribution, Bill made a fine catch near the 368-foot sign in right field, to end a Giants scoring threat in the eighth, and help preserve a 6–3 Cubs victory.

For the Giants, outfielder Bobby Thomson also belted a round-tripper. Young Thomson's star was ascending as Nicholson's descended. He remembered the powerful right fielder, almost 50 years later: "Nicholson was a guy I appreciated as a young player. Swish was so strong, and he had a swing that was always interesting to watch when he got hold of one. I can still see that big 'swish' of his."

Andy Pafko continued to lead the way at the plate for Chicago. In early August he was batting .331, to go with 19 homers and 72 RBIs. Nicholson had three fewer home runs, and 54 RBIs, but had dipped to .258. With the Cubs out of the pennant race, there was not a lot to play for except pride, a commodity Nicholson possessed in abundance.

The North Siders played at Brooklyn on August 4. In the first inning, Jackie Robinson's steal of home precipitated a ten-minute argument with the plate umpire that resulted in pitcher Monk Meyer's ejection from the game. Behind Bill's two-run double in the fifth, and solo home run in the seventh, the game was knotted at 4–4 in the top of the ninth. With the bases loaded, and Rex Barney on the mound, Nicholson struck a drive that left the ballpark, foul by inches. The next pitch was a curveball that he looked at for strike three, and the final out. The Dodgers then won the game, 5–4, in the bottom of the ninth.

Sensing the end of his Chicago Cubs career was at hand, the Bill Nicholson Fan Club held a day in their hero's honor on August 21, before a game against Cincinnati. Members occupied 80 box seats, and presented Bill with a beautiful trophy. He didn't play, however, in the 2–0 Reds victory.

On the hottest day of the season, in humid 90-degree weather, Nicholson faced his nemesis Dave Koslo at Wrigley on August 24. He hit his 17th homer into the right field bleachers in the sixth inning, and had two other hits. His teammates left 14 runners stranded in scoring position, though, and the Giants won, 7–4.

When the Dodgers came to Chicago for the last time of the season on August 31, they were riding the crest of a seven-game winning streak, in first place. Hank Borowy was unimpressed, and threw a one-hit, 3–0, shutout (aided by two Nicholson hits) in the first game of a doubleheader, before a

The old slugger connecting at Wrigley Field, 1948, in his final season as a Cub. Roy Campanella is the Dodgers' catcher. The swing depicted in this photo was used by sculptor Ken Herlihy as a model for the statue in Chestertown (*courtesy Emily Joiner*).

crowd of 47,171. An additional 20,000 were turned away. Many in the crowd were black citizens who had come only to root for the player affectionately referred to by them as "Jackie." They left disappointed, after Brooklyn dropped the second game, with Robinson hitless for the day.

Knowing how much the fans longed for Robinson's success, Borowy was almost apologetic after the game, telling reporters: "I hated to upset the applecart for the Dodgers, but I had to think of myself and my family." Another Chicago win, two days later, cut Brooklyn's lead to two percentage points in the standings, ahead of the Boston Braves.

In the season's waning days, Wrigley placed an advertisement in local papers, admitting that "this season's rebuilding has been a flop," but promising, "If one system doesn't work, we will try another."

Nicholson's last appearance in a Cubs uniform was on September 29, at home, in a loss to the Reds. He batted fifth, had one hit, and drove in the only Cubs run. He did not play in a three-game road trip to St. Louis, as young Clarence Maddern took over in right field.

A day after the last game of this miserable season, Bill Nicholson was unceremoniously shipped to the Philadelphia Phillies for Walker, brother of the much-despised (by Cubs fans, at least) Dixie. Harry led the N.L. in hitting in 1947, but appeared in only 111 games for the Phils in 1948 due to injury. He went on to play 42 games for the Cubs in 1949, before being traded to the Reds.

News of the Nicholson-for-Walker exchange was greeted with outrage from Bill's loyal Windy City fans, who thought he was the fall guy for a franchise interested only in the bottom line, and oblivious to the results on the field. As one fan wrote to Arch Ward earlier in the season, "No wonder Bill Nicholson can't hit. His shoulders are sagging from carrying the Cubs for several years."

In truth, Nicholson was relieved to leave Wrigley. Although he loved the city and its fans, he was disenchanted with management and the press. The field was never his favorite. He wrote to a fan in 1984: "The fans were absolutely the greatest in the world, but I didn't enjoy playing in Wrigley Field because it was so hard to see the ball, and it was sometimes so cold and windy. I'd rather play in any other park than Wrigley Field. I hit many, many balls that would've been home runs that were stopped by the wind and became just big outs. But the worst thing was all the white shirts in the center field bleachers. Sometimes, you just couldn't see. It was really dangerous."

Former Cubs infielder Billy Jurges, soon to become manager of the Boston Red Sox, was happy for his former teammate. He told sportswriter Dan Daniel, "Nick still is a great hitter and will prove it now that he has got away from Wrigley Field, which was a mental hazard for Bill."

Less than a week after the Nicholson-Walker deal, the Phillies purchased Monk Meyer, and then traded pitchers Dutch Leonard and Walt Dubiel to the Cubs for Hank Borowy and Eddie Waitkus. Thus, four players who finished 1948 with the lowly Cubs would now be teammates for a young Phillies team, of whom big things were expected. In 44 at bats at Shibe Park in '48, Nicholson hit a respectable .273, with three doubles and two triples among his 12 hits. He'd not hit a home run, however. "I just can't seem to get the range," he explained. "Maybe when I play there every day I'll get the rhythm."

With the geographical proximity of Philadelphia to Chestertown, Bill could not have been happier. He would be closer to Nancy and the boys, who were growing up fast and missed their father during the long season.

For the Cubs fans he left behind, however, a void was created that was never filled. His many admirers remained loyal, greeting Nicholson with homemade signs from the stands when he returned to Chicago with his new team the next year. As one forlorn Swish admirer wrote at year's end, "Although I'm a Cub fan, I try not to become too partial. My favorite player, for instance, is on the Phillies: Bill Nicholson."

As if to begin a new chapter, Bill homered twice at the fifth annual Baseball "Pheastival," in a 13–13 tie against the Pacific Coast League All Stars on October 17. Greeting him at the plate after each of his clouts was his team's cleanup hitter, Joe DiMaggio, but the game attracted only 2,000 fans, in 48-degree weather.

Still not done with baseball for the year, Nicholson then embarked on a barnstorming tour with his former teammate Phil Cavarretta's team. He traveled throughout the midwest with Enos Slaughter, Joe Page, and Johnny Lindell of the Yankees through late October, playing ball against local nines, before returning to the Eastern Shore.

17

The City of Brotherly Love

The weather was unseasonably cold, with temperatures in the high 40s, at Clearwater's Athletic Field in early March, 1949. This was the Philadelphia Phillies' third spring training at the Florida site, which had been transformed from a recreational park to a big-league facility. A 34-game exhibition slate awaited the team, to be capped by a three-game City Series with the A's, April 15–17 at Shibe Park, the stadium now shared by Philadelphia's two ball teams.

The 44 players in the major league camp were directed by Manager Eddie Sawyer, an honors graduate of Ithaca College, and the holder of an advanced degree from Cornell University. Sawyer employed a hands-off managerial style, in contrast to his predecessor, fiery Ben Chapman, whom he had succeeded midway through the 1948 season. Under Sawyer, the players played the game, and the manager interfered only when absolutely necessary. There were few pregame meetings to discuss opposing hitters, and Sawyer's catchers called all the pitches, without his interference. This manager, however, was no slouch. As befit his educational achievements, he was a man of great intellect, who possessed a memory so keen that he was able to recite the play-by-play of games that had been contested a decade before.

Over the winter, Philadelphia owner Bob Carpenter bolstered his youthful team with the addition of the four Cub veterans. They complemented the core of youngsters who would comprise 1950's "Whiz Kids:" outfielders Richie Ashburn (age 22) and Del Ennis (23); shortstop Granny Hamner (21); and pitchers Curt Simmons (19) and Robin Roberts (22). Fourteen players who would make the 1949 roster were under 25. Early in the spring, Carpenter sounded a cautionary note: "We're still a year or perhaps two away. But by 1950 or 1951, we're going to be the ones to beat." His prediction was very close to the mark.

Nicholson signed his contract early; he would earn $15,000 for the upcoming year. Sawyer was pleased to have the veteran in camp, and encouraged the younger players to emulate him. "Every day he'd go to the outfield while we pitchers and utility players took early batting practice," recalled Roberts. "He didn't just shag balls, but reacted to everything as if it was a game condition, running down every hit and playing the carom off the fence and throwing to second or third as if he had a runner to catch. That's how he prepared. What a man to know and be around!"

Ashburn and Putsy Caballero considered Nicholson to be the leader of the team. Caballero said: "We listened to whatever he told us. We had to — he was so big, if you didn't listen you were afraid he would beat the hell out of you."

The Phils were a close-knit group. After workouts, the players often sat together in front of the clubhouse just beyond the third-base line, drinking Coca-Cola from the large refrigerated chest on the porch, talking to reporters. The camaraderie extended to non–players, as well. Monk Meyer could be seen cutting the hair of *Inquirer* beat writer Stan Baumgartner, and owner Carpenter might be found in the bullpen giving instruction to one of his young pitchers. Hank Borowy, who did not leave Chicago on the best of terms, promised Joe Reichler: "This is a fighting bunch that is going to be tough to beat." In fact, the team had been christened "The Fightin' Phils," and a large sign with that nickname hung over the clubhouse entrance.

Swish begins a new career with the Phillies in Clearwater, Florida, in the winter of 1949 (*courtesy Emily Joiner*).

Meyer was just glad to be gone from Chicago. He had been in the doghouse since his ejection from the game against Brooklyn in which Jackie Robinson stole home, the previous August. Charlie Grimm later called Monk a "bad actor" and a "redneck," and Meyer thought he had been treated shabbily. He told reporters at Clearwater: "This is a good club to be with. Everybody makes you feel at home. I feel I'm going to have a good year. Especially against Grimm's Cubs."

Nicholson found the new training facilities to his liking. He knew club personnel from his spring training stint with the Phillies in Wilmington in 1945, as well as players like Putsy Caballero, Andy Seminick, and Granny Hamner. The right-field fence at Athletic Field was only about 280 feet from the plate, although a high screen extended upwards above it. In an early exhibition game, Bill homered against the Reds, over the screen in the sixth, to break a 1–1 tie, and help Meyer win, 2–1.

Six days later, the Boston Red Sox came to Clearwater. Carpenter had blanketed the city with ads promoting the game and the appearance of Red Sox stars like Ted Williams, Bobby Doerr, and Dominic DiMaggio. When the Sox arrived, however, they brought only a "B" team, *sans* the big stars, except for third baseman Johnny Pesky. Approximately 1,700 fans who had paid to see the game were understandably upset.

The irate Carpenter confronted Boston manager Joe McCarthy on the Red Sox bench. "Why didn't you let us know you weren't bringing the men?," he demanded. McCarthy responded flippantly, "Why didn't you telephone us and ask?"

"I can understand why they call you a push-button manager!" Carpenter shot back before McCarthy shooed him out of the dugout. The Philadelphia owner offered a full refund to any fan who felt aggrieved, and about 25 took him up on the offer. Those who remained saw the home team win, 9–7, behind Nicholson's two-run four-bagger in the fifth.

Bill and Granny Hamner each had two-run homers in a 7–3 win over new manager Casey Stengel's Yankees at Clearwater a week later. It must have seemed to Stengel that wherever he managed, he could not escape Bill and his booming bat. His four-bagger came off Bob Porterfield, in the third. The next day, against the Senators in Orlando, he homered off Walt Masterson in the sixth, with Del Ennis aboard, to break a 2–2 tie, in a 7–4 Philadelphia triumph.

Nicholson was gone, but not forgotten, in Chicago. The newspapers there continued to receive correspondence from Nicholson fans suggesting what it was going to be like when the Cubs faced their former star. "Irving of Evanston" wrote Arch Ward and wanted to know, "Are the Bill Nicholson fans going to cheer or boo when Bill comes to Wrigley Field next summer and wins a couple of ball games for the Phillies by knocking the ball out of the park?" Alfred Link of Chicago predicted: "Bill Nicholson? He'll come back here with the Phillies and bust a lot of windows across the street from right field." June Kosko told the *Trib*: "I was always partial to Bill Nicholson and I liked Hank Borowy ... and the young fans in this neighborhood set up a howl when they were traded."

The Phils headed north, with stops for games in Alabama, Georgia, and Tennessee, after departing Florida early in April. The final exhibition game was held in Baltimore, against the International League's Orioles, at Baltimore Stadium. Bill hit a monstrous triple in the eighth, and the Phils won handily.

Philadelphia fans anxiously awaited the return of the team to the city, believing that — for the first time in more than 30 years — their Phillies might finally be a legitimate pennant contender. It was the lowly A's, however, who captured the spring City Series, two games to one. Nicholson had only one hit in 11 trips.

Pennant-raising day at Boston's Braves Field took place on April 18. The defending N.L. champs hosted Philadelphia on a raw, windy Opening Day. Only 9,195 showed up, as the governor of Massachusetts threw out the ceremonial first pitch, before the Phils' 4–0 shutout. Hitting fifth in the Philadelphia order, Nicholson had one hit in three tries. His first inning walk forced in the only run the club would need. The Braves' Johnny Sain took the loss; lefthander Ken Heintzelman got the win for the visitors.

After losing their next three to Boston, the Phillies returned home to face Brooklyn. Two days before the game, the team staged an open house at the Philadelphia Arena. The players came in uniform to meet and greet their fans, at 6:00 P.M. Ballpark fare was served, and entertainment was provided by Max Patkin, among others. There were even expensive door prizes.

The field at Shibe Park had been renovated for the 1949 season, at a cost of $300,000. The North Philly ballpark was also spruced up, to make it more fan-friendly. A state-of-the art "annunciator" had been purchased. Installed on the upper deck beyond third base, it flashed the number of the player at bat, the ball and strike count, outs, and rulings on hits and errors. Shibe Park had its own version of Ebbets Field's Gladys Gooding, in electric organist Dot Langdon. As part of her *repertoire,* after every Robin Roberts victory, she played, "When the Red, Red Robin Comes Bob, Bob, Bobbin' Along."

As the Phils took the field for the home opener, the crowd was large and enthusiastic, despite an 8–6 loss to the Dodgers. The clubs split a Sunday doubleheader the next day, before 33,748, in a cold, swirling wind. Following a 7–4 victory in the first game, the Phils had the tying run on third base, with one out in the home seventh of the nightcap. At the plate was Swish Nicholson. Boisterous Philadelphia partisans made so much noise that reporters covering the game from the press box could hear neither the clicking of the telegraphs, nor the keys of their own typewriters. To the crowd's delight, Nicholson struck a single to right, knocking in two runs. Unfortunately, Waitkus was thrown out trying to steal home, to end the inning. The Philadelphians frittered away the lead, and ultimately lost, 6–5.

Early in the season, Nicholson was tepid at the plate, batting only .211 on April 28, with one homer and five RBIs. On the last of the month, however, in a 12–4 win at Ebbets Field, he had a three-run homer to help winning pitcher Borowy. A five-game winning streak followed, enabling the club to even its record at 8–8, on May 4. Frustrated by his inconsistent batting, Bill was hitless against the Pirates on May 7, and was held out of the first game of a doubleheader at Shibe against the Reds the next day.

During that game, Sawyer employed five shortstops. Hamner, who started, was injured in the second inning. Caballero took over for him, but was lifted in the ninth for a pinch hitter. Second baseman Buddy Blattner succeeded Caballero, but collided with Ennis in the 11th inning, and had to be removed from the game. Sawyer then brought in third-string catcher Ken Silvestri to play second base, and moved second baseman Eddie Miller to shortstop. He alternated the two between those positions, depending upon whether the batter was right or lefthanded. The Reds finally scored seven unanswered runs in the top of the 12th to win, 14–7.

After the game, anxious to get back in a hitting groove, Nicholson confided in his friend Waitkus. "Every time I go to the plate, I have a half dozen thoughts go through my mind, and I end up popping the ball up," he complained. Waitkus responded: "You're not paid to think. You're paid to hit the ball."

With Waitkus' advice fresh in his mind, Bill started the second game. He went three for four, with a home run and five RBIs, in an 8–1 walkover, which ended after six innings because of a Sunday curfew. Feeling relaxed again, in the next 14 games, he pounded the ball at a .351 clip, with three homers. On May 17, his sixth round tripper — off Alpha Brazle, no less — tied the score in the eighth inning, and the Phils edged the Cardinals in 12, 5–4.

A scheduled visit to Chicago for a three-game series was ruined by rain. Only one game was played in the much-anticipated return of the four former Cubs, on May 21. Swish's fans turned out to welcome their hero back home. One of them was Billy Stone, now a safety patrol at Lemoyne Grammar School. Before the game, he went to a nearby dime store and bought a pair of cufflinks, and somehow wrangled a pouch of Beech-Nut chewing tobacco from Fishman's Market. While the players warmed up, he managed to get Nicholson's attention, and threw him the tobacco and cufflinks. Nicholson took the offering, looked up at the youngster in the stands, and smiled.

Although he was hitless in three at bats, the Phils came out on top, 5–1, behind the pitching of Borowy.

A Nicholson four-bagger off the Giants' Larry Jansen, just inside the right field foul pole, led to a come-from-behind victory at Shibe at the end of May. The next day, the team dropped a doubleheader to New York, however, 4–2, in 15 innings, and 3–0, in a seven-inning contest shortened by the curfew. In retrospect, the first game was a pivotal moment in Nicholson's 1949 season. After going two for four, he tore a muscle under his right arm while making a throw from right field in the ninth inning. "It felt as if someone drove a sword through my side," Bill told reporters afterward. He was forced to leave the game, and Bobby Thomson's two-run homer broke a 2–2 deadlock in the bottom of the 15th to win it for the Giants.

At the time of his injury, Nicholson had raised his average for the year to .282, with seven homers and 23 RBIs. He missed the next 15 games, as Stan Hollmig and Jack Mayo shared right field duties. During his absence, the Phils won 10 of 15.

When Nicholson returned to the lineup on June 11, he went through a horrific five-week stretch during which he managed only one hit in 33 at bats. His slump was in its infancy when the fifth-place Phils returned to Chicago for four games, beginning June 14. The Windy City was Philadelphia's first stop on a scheduled 15-game trip that would also take them to St. Louis, Pittsburgh, and Cincinnati before they returned home.

The club arrived by train from Philadelphia on June 13, and lodged at the Edgewater Beach Hotel, five minutes from Wrigley Field. The next day, on an overcast Tuesday afternoon, they whipped the home town club, 9–2, behind the pitching of Monk Meyer. It was the first game managed by the Cubs' new skipper, Frankie Frisch, who'd just relieved the beleaguered Charlie Grimm. Bill was hitless, but his roommate Waitkus had a single and scored two runs. The blond first baseman was averaging .306, and National League fans had thus far made him the leading vote-getter, at his position, for the All-Star team. Sitting among the Wrigley Field crowd that day was a 19-year-old Chicago "Baseball Annie" named Ruth Ann Steinhagen. She was a six-foot tall beauty who had an unrequited crush on Waitkus, and profound psychiatric issues.

At the conclusion of the game, Nicholson, Waitkus, Meyer, and his *fiancee* went out for dinner and drinks. Nicholson and Waitkus took a separate cab back to the hotel, arriving about 11:15 P.M. They had a doubleheader to play the next day. A bellhop informed Waitkus that there was a note for him at the front desk. While Nicholson searched for Meyer, Waitkus read the note, inviting him to a room on the 12th floor of the hotel, to meet with a

17. The City of Brotherly Love

Former Cubs at Phillies training camp, 1949. Left to right are "Monk" Meyer, Hank Borowy, Nicholson, and Eddie Waitkus. Less than four months later, Waitkus was shot by a crazed fan, and nearly lost his life (*courtesy Emily Joiner*).

woman identifying herself as Ruth Burns. After discussing the note with Nicholson, Waitkus called Burns' room and arranged to meet her there.

When he arrived around 11:30 P.M., the door was opened by an attractive young lady. She asked him to sit down, and they had a brief conversation. The woman then said to Waitkus, "I have a surprise for you." She went to a closet and pulled out a .22 caliber rifle. "For two years you've been bothering me, and now you're going to die," she pronounced, before she shot him, just below the heart. The assailant—Ruth Ann Steinhagen—then called police, calmly telling them, "There's a man shot in my room."

Waitkus was transported to Illinois Masonic Hospital, near death. The bullet had torn through his chest, penetrating his right lung, before lodging near his spine. Steinhagen told police: "I'm really not sorry. I'm sorry Eddie has to suffer so. I'm sorry it had to be him. But I had to shoot somebody." Her hotel reservations at the Edgewater had been made about one month before, she said, and volunteered that she brought a paring knife with the idea of stabbing Waitkus, and then using the firearm on herself. Police later discovered that her bedroom was a veritable shrine to Waitkus, cluttered with souvenirs and memorabilia.

Not until Nicholson heard the wail of sirens did he discover his roommate's fate. Several Phils, including Nicholson and Meyer, wanted to keep a bedside vigil at the hospital, but were sent home by doctors. Said Bill of Waitkus: "He's one of the sweetest guys I ever knew. I never got such a shock in my life. He's not the kind of man who goes around getting in trouble. I've been in baseball 15 years and never roomed with a finer guy."

Though numbed by the events, the Phils managed to win both games of the next day's twin bill, with Dick Sisler taking over at first base. An exhausted Nicholson played the first game without a hit, and sat the second.

The team made it a clean sweep the following day. With two outs and two on in the ninth, Sawyer let relief pitcher Jim Konstanty bat. His single drove Nicholson in with the deciding tally, in a 4–3 victory.

After four operations, Waitkus survived and played for several more seasons. He was never the same player, however. Addictions to cigarettes and alcohol undoubtedly contributed to his premature death in 1972, from esophageal cancer. He was 53 years old. Steinhagen, incompetent to stand trial, spent nearly three years in a state mental facility before being released. She was never prosecuted. The Waitkus incident was the inspiration for Bernard Malamud's 1952 novel, *The Natural*, about a promising ballplayer named Roy Hobbs, who is shot by a deranged woman in a hotel room.

Malamud is said to have been present at a game at Ebbets Field on Memorial Day, 1946, when Boston's 'Bama Rowell hit a double off the scoreboard, which struck the large Bulova clock, shattering several light bulbs. Shards of glass descended upon Dodger right fielder Dixie Walker. At the time of Rowell's blow, the clock read 4:25 P.M. It stopped exactly one hour later. That event inspired a scene in the movie version of *The Natural*, when Roy Hobbs' home run strikes a light tower at the fictional "Knights' Field," raining broken glass onto the field.

Waitkus spent more than a month in the hospital. When he returned to Philadelphia on July 17, looking thin and drawn, in excess of 500 fans waited in the rain to welcome him, at Philadelphia International Airport. Surgically implanted was a tube, exiting his back, to siphon off fluid buildup. The first baseman told the multitude what it wanted to hear. "I'm rarin' to go," he gamely announced, and added that he'd return to action before the end of the season.

A five-game losing streak in late July evened Philadelphia's record at 47–47, before a doubleheader sweep of the Cubs on July 30 at Wrigley Field. In game one, marking the team's first visit to the Windy City since the Waitkus shooting, Bill clubbed his eighth homer, to seal the 4–3 victory. The next day, the Phils extended their streak to three wins, with a 5–4 decision, in 10 innings. After another round-tripper at Crosley Field in a loss against the Reds on August 1, Bill had homered in every National League park except Pittsburgh's Forbes Field, although he only had nine for the season.

After the Chicago sweep, the Phils reverted to losing ways, dropping 10 of 14, including five in a row. In the first game of a doubleheader on August 4, Meyer was shellacked, and could not make it out of the first inning. When Sawyer came out to the mound to remove him, Monk threw a temper tantrum and slammed the ball down. Reaching the dugout, he kicked a bucket, and fell over grimacing in pain. Taken to the hospital for x-rays, he was told there was a break and doctors casted his foot.

Several days later, still hobbled by the cast, he sidled up to Nicholson in the dugout. Meyer told Bill that his foot was really not feeling too badly. Knowing that Meyer had previously broken his ankle, Bill told him to have the foot checked again and told him, "Your old break probably showed up on the x-ray." Nicholson was right. Within days, Meyer had resumed his place in the starting rotation, and went 9–3 for the rest of the season.

In mid–August, Sawyer was distressed at his team's performance on and off the field. They were not playing with the requisite intensity, and the normally hands-off manager called a clubhouse meeting before a series in Brooklyn, on August 16. Regulars were threatened with the loss of their starting positions if performance didn't improve on the field. A team curfew was imposed, and the players' wives were barred from traveling with the team. Believing that the Phillies were eating too much and had gotten fat and lazy, Sawyer began a new system to discourage overeating. Team trainer Frank Wiechec would dole out $6.00 per diem for meal money, supplanting the old procedure whereby the players would simply sign a hotel food bill after their sumptuous repasts.

"There has to be a boss and discipline in every business," the Philadelphia skipper explained. "This is particularly true of youngsters who have been babied for the past 10 or 15 years. Ever since the C[ivilian] C[onservation] C[orps] camps they have been spoiled. Then came the war. Many youngsters who never got any farther than in some camp 50 miles from home were carried around on plush cushions and babied until they thought the world owed them a soft living."

Sawyer's diatribe had the desired effect. The Phils won 20 of their next 28 contests, vaulting into third place. The streak began with a three-game sweep of Brooklyn. The first game, a 2–1 decision, went 12 innings. Although Nicholson was hitless, his two-out catch in the seventh, on a drive off the bat of Billy Cox, saved the game for Philadelphia.

Back home at Shibe Park three days later, the Phils treated Waitkus, with a day in his honor. Despite his optimistic promise, he would not return to action during the 1949 season. Appearing terribly frail, the first baseman was presented with a brand new automobile, television, luggage, golf clubs, and other gifts from the team, sponsors and fans. Perhaps the most touching present was one of his first baseman's gloves, which team members had appropriated from his locker, after the shooting. It had been bronzed, and mounted on a velvet-covered plaque, along with two silver baseballs. Signatures of players, coaches, and others associated with the Phillies team were etched on a silver plate fastened to the trophy.

Buoyed by their inspirational teammate as he continued his recovery, the Phils went out and drubbed the Giants (now managed by Leo Durocher), 7–1, to extend their winning streak to four.

The Phils played perhaps their most unusual game of the season on August 21. In the nightcap of a doubleheader at home, trailing 4–2 in the top of the ninth, center fielder Ashburn dove for a drive hit by the Giants' Joe Lafata. Although it appeared that he'd made the catch, the umpire ruled Ashburn had trapped the ball. An argument resulted, with several Phillies players and Sawyer pleading their case. Soon, the fans began to express their displeasure by throwing fruit, papers, and other material onto the field. Although alcohol was not sold at Shibe Park, several smuggled beer bottles were tossed, one hitting an umpire on the bounce. Some of the fans in the upper deck began to bombard those in the lower seats with these dangerous missiles. Outfielders Ashburn, Ennis, and Nicholson soon retreated to the relative safety of the infield.

Order was briefly restored, but when the plate umpire was struck by a tomato, and a base umpire by another bottle, the game was forfeited to the Giants. Thereafter, soft drinks were dispensed only by the cup at Shibe Park, and no bottles were ever sold there again.

Nicholson's home run in the seventh inning, at home against the Braves on September 3, tied the score in a game the Phils went on to win, 6–3. On the last day of the season, at Shibe Park, Burt Shotton's Dodgers clinched the pennant with a 10-inning, 9–7 victory. It was the first of three consecutive years in which the Dodgers would need to beat the Phils on the last day of the season to win the N.L. crown.

Philadelphia finished third, with a season's record of 81 wins and 73 losses, a 15-game improvement over 1948. The win total represented the most victories by a Phillies team since 1917. Nicholson finished the year at .234, with 40 RBIs, in 299 at bats. His 11 homers marked the last time he would reach double figures in that category.

Transplanted Chicago pitchers Borowy and Meyer chipped in with 17 and 12 victories, respectively. Factoring in Heintzelman's 17 wins, and Roberts' 15, and with young Curt Simmons coming into his own, Philadelphia starting pitching appeared to be set for 1950.

After watching the Brooklyn players celebrate their title on the field at Shibe Park, Sawyer addressed his team in the locker room, as they packed to head home for the winter. "Come back next year ready to win," he told them. "We are going to win it all next year."

18

The Whiz Kids

Sometime before Thanksgiving, 1949, Nicholson joined Eddie Waitkus, already in Clearwater, to begin training for the upcoming season. Waitkus had come to Florida earlier in the month, to rehabilitate with trainer Frank Wiechec. The workouts were grueling for Waitkus, but he was in fine shape by the time the rest of his teammates arrived in late February. Of the early weeks with Wiechec in Clearwater, Waitkus said: "It's impossible for anyone to realize the torture I went through the first month I arrived here. Every movement was an agony in itself. I had to teach my muscles to respond to my bidding practically one by one. It was purely stubbornness that prevented me from throwing in the sponge."

Bill was in Clearwater with Waitkus because he wanted to make sure he was ready for the grind of the regular season. He'd been troubled by sore legs and an aching back in '49. Late in the season, he even submitted to treatment by an osteopath. Now he would be facing challenges from Johnny Blatnik, Stan Hollmig, Eddie Mayo, and Ed Sanicki, all of whom were angling for the starting right fielder job.

Wiechec was the antithesis of Andy Lotshaw. He held an advanced degree from Temple University, and spent four years as a physical therapy instructor at the Mayo Clinic in Minnesota. He was one of the first trainers who sought to prevent injury, rather than merely treat it. When trauma occurred to his players, ice and diathermy were likely to be the modes of treatment, not Coca-Cola, wintergreen, or other magic potions.

Nicholson frequently suffered from a sore throwing arm, dating back to his days with the Cubs. "Well, I might have thrown a little too hard early, or something," he recalled. "'Course, we had Andy Lotshaw out there. And Andy was a good old fellow, but he couldn't do much, as far as knowing what was the matter with the arm. He'd rub a little Coca-Cola on it and say, 'It's going to be alright.' But Wiechec, he said I knotted up back there on my back, and he would rub that out and then I got so I could throw very accurately and very good."

Monk Meyer joined Waitkus and Nicholson in Clearwater, several weeks before the rest of the team arrived. "Eddie, Russ, and Bill were a trio, always together," said Meyer's former wife Mary Meyer Oswalt. "They had such a good time together, even that winter when Eddie was trying to get back in shape after the shooting."

Consistent with the approach adopted in mid-1949, Sawyer ran a spartan training camp. No wives, families, or automobiles were permitted. The players lived at the team hotel, about a mile from the Athletic Field. They walked to and from practice sessions. In seeming defiance of Sawyer's edict, however, pitcher Jim Konstanty brought his family to Clearwater. They stayed at another hotel. Soon, other players followed suit. In this early challenge to his managerial autonomy, Sawyer diplomatically backed off. He denied that families had ever been barred, claiming that he only meant for all players to live in the team hotel.

Sawyer thought the old blue and white Phillies uniforms were bad *karma*, associated with the losing teams of earlier years. For the regular season of 1950, therefore, the Fightin' Phils would be clad in red-trimmed unis, and red caps; the color blue disappeared completely. The white "P" on the front of the scarlet caps appeared in a different script, and there was a white button on the top. At home, the Phils would wear pinstripes, like the Yankees, only red instead of blue.

Bob Carpenter was clearly pleased with the new direction of his club, and the man at the helm, Eddie Sawyer. "Maybe it's better that your manager was not a big league star," he told the *Washington Post*'s Shirley Povich. "Then, he can get a clear viewpoint about what they ought to do, in his own image. Too many managers who were stars think of ball players in terms of what they would do themselves, and don't have the patience that is required of a manager." The Phils had drawn 840,000 fans in 1949, and "almost made money," according to Carpenter. He was excited for the new season.

In early exhibition action, Sawyer's club routed the Kansas City Blues of the American Association, 13–2, on March 16, pounding out 15 hits, including four-baggers from Mike Goliat, Waitkus, Ennis, and Nicholson.

Bill homered again in a 13–8 victory over the Senators at Clearwater on March 27, for his second consecutive pinch-hit round-tripper. Three days later against the same team, Big Nick blasted another ball out of the park in the third inning, and the Phils won their fourth straight, 10–3. In the fifth, however, he was picked off first base by Mickey Grasso. In his attempt to avoid the tag, he sprained an ankle.

It was the first of several injuries with which Bill would be afflicted during the 1950 campaign. When the season opened, he was hobbled with a strained Achilles tendon, then saw limited action before being placed on the disabled list on May 17, where he languished for nearly a month. Despite his injury, one observer noted: "Bill looks better at the plate than I have ever seen him. He is hitting high balls fiercely to right field, something that he never did before."

The club headed west in early May for an extended road trip, and the first stop was Chicago. The Phils were again staying at the Edgewater Beach Hotel. A jittery Waitkus, literally returning to the scene of the crime, confided to his roommate Nicholson, "I just hope I get through this series alive." To rid Waitkus of his fears, Nicholson and Meyer dragged him to all their old Chicago haunts in the evenings, as their team split the two-game series.

After the western swing in early May, during which the club won seven of nine, the Phils returned to 30th Street Station in Philadelphia by train, in the company of the Boston Braves, also returning home on the Capitol Limited. Now in first place by half a game, the Philadelphia players were met by several hundred cheering fans. As they alighted from two special Pullman cars, supporters called out words of encouragement to the players, elbowing their way through the throng. One shouted to Sawyer: "Hey there, Eddie. Keep 'em going! Let's win a pennant!" The biggest applause was reserved for Robin Roberts, who won a 3–2 decision the previous night in Pittsburgh; Dick Sisler, now playing left field, who was the hitting star of several contests; and Waitkus.

When Bill finally returned to the team on June 18, Philadelphia was in third place, two and a half games behind league-leading St. Louis, and one and a half games behind the Dodgers. On that day, the Phils swept a doubleheader from Cincinnati at Shibe Park, coming from behind in both games. Pinch-hitting for Curt Simmons in the ninth inning of the first game, Bill's single drove in the winning run. In the second game, however, he grounded into a rare double play, batting for Stan Lopata in the sixth.

Philadelphia held a one-half game lead over the Cardinals entering play on July 2, with the Dodgers one and a half out. The Phils and Brooklyn were scheduled to play a doubleheader at Shibe Park. In the first game, the score was deadlocked at 4–4 in the bottom of the eighth, with Ralph Branca on the hill. The Dodgers hurler, a native New Yorker with a penchant for surrendering home runs, had already thrown 14 "gopher balls" on the season. Monk Meyer was scheduled to hit, but with one out and one on, it was number 12, Bill Nicholson, heading for the plate.

The crowd of 35,118 was nearly 2,000 over capacity. They screamed with anticipation at the sight of the old slugger, taking his practice swings, with the familiar cud of tobacco in his left jaw. He slammed Branca's inside fastball high over the right field scoreboard, just as he had done in April, 1948, as a Cub. The blow resulted in the fourth straight defeat for Brooklyn, 6–4.

Nicholson's 1950 heroics against the Dodgers were not yet complete. Six days later, this time at Ebbets Field, the two teams squared off again. Now, the Phils were in a first-place tie with the Cardinals, while the Dodgers had dropped to fourth, four games back.

Robin Roberts started on the mound for Philadelphia. He surrendered only three hits — one of which was a first-inning leadoff homer by Billy Cox — before being relieved by Konstanty. In the top of the ninth, the score was 1–1 when Willie Jones doubled high off the right field wall. After Sisler popped to Reese for the second out, Andy Seminick was walked intentionally. Second baseman Mike Goliat was due to bat against Dodgers hurler Don Newcombe, when Sawyer went to his bench, and sent up lefthanded swatter Swish Nicholson.

The Dodgers called time to confer on the mound, strategizing over the best way to pitch the aging veteran. Before the Brooklyn crowd even had a chance to start the "Swish" chant, Newcombe's first offering was met with a resounding crack from Nicholson's bat. The ball was skied towards the outfield wall. Right fielder Carl Furillo retreated as far as he could go, and stood helplessly at the base of the scoreboard, watching the horsehide disappear into the Brooklyn sky and out of the park for a three-run homer. Robin Roberts wondered afterwards exactly what it was that the Dodgers discussed on the mound. Nicholson's two pinch-hit home runs within six days, and the resultant victories over Brooklyn, were manifested in the Phils' two-game margin over the Dodgers in the standings at season's end.

In the front end of a doubleheader split with Pittsburgh at Forbes Field on July 19, Bill hit what may have been the shortest triple in big league history. The score was 1–1 in the 11th inning, with one out, when Nicholson lofted a dizzying popup directly over home plate. Bucs catcher Clyde McCullough and third baseman Danny O'Connell pursued the ball. Just as McCullough gloved it, he collided with O'Connell. The ball dropped to the ground, three feet in front of the plate, and bounced off the catcher. By the time it was retrieved, the alert Nicholson had motored into third base. Putsy Caballero was inserted as a pinch runner, and he scored on Granny Hamner's home run, to provide the decisive runs in the 3–2 contest.

The Phillies held a comfortable five-game lead entering play on August 12, "Kid's Day" at Shibe Park. The game against Leo Durocher's New York Giants drew 23,741, including thousands of children. The players, regrettably, set a poor example for the young fans who came to the game.

Primarily responsible for the unfortunate events of the day was Nicholson's former teammate Eddie Stanky, now playing second base for the Giants. The bandy-legged native of Philadelphia played the game the way Durocher liked to play it — aggressively. Stanky wasn't nicknamed "The Brat" for nothing; he, like Durocher, would do just about anything to win.

Phils catcher Andy Seminick had played well against Durocher's Giants, a fact of which Durocher was very much aware. On August 11, Stanky — probably with Durocher's prodding — adopted a tactic designed to disrupt Seminick when he was batting. "The Brat" stood in Andy's line of vision before the pitch was delivered, waving his arms, and jumping up and down.

Before the next day's game, Sawyer complained to the umpires about Stanky's conduct. There was no rule specifically prohibiting this shenanigan, so the umpires placed a telephone call to N.L. president Ford Frick; they were unable to reach him. Durocher agreed to instruct Stanky to desist from his jumping jacks until a ruling from Frick could be obtained.

When Seminick came to bat in the second, Stanky waved his arms before pitcher Sheldon Jones delivered the pitch, but made a show of standing still just before the ball was thrown. Seminick, fuming, drew a base on balls, and advanced to second on a wild pitch. When Mike Goliat singled, Seminick — a brawny sort who was a meatcutter in the off-season — headed for third and tore into Giants third baseman Hank Thompson, knocking him unconscious with a forearm shiver to the jaw. The woozy fielder was removed from the game, and Durocher called off all bets.

Seminick came to bat again in the fourth, and Stanky resumed his calisthenics as the pitch was thrown. The Phils' catcher swung, flinging the bat into the field. Second-base umpire Lon Warneke, the former Cubs pitcher, immediately ejected Stanky — but not Seminick — from the game. Naturally, Durocher raced onto the field, demanding to know the reason for Stanky's ejection. Lon claimed Stanky's actions were "conduct detrimental to baseball," and made a farce of the game. Durocher finally returned to the dugout and the game resumed.

Bill Rigney took Stanky's place, but later wished he hadn't. After Seminick walked again, Goliat hit a grounder to shortstop Alvin Dark. As Dark tossed to Rigney on second base for the inning-ending force out, Seminick charged. He bumped Rigney, who jumped on top of the sliding catcher. Describing Rigney's reaction, pitcher Robin Roberts recalled: "That was a big mistake on his part. Andy, on the bottom, grabbed Bill by his shirt with his left hand and just started popping him with his right. Rigney was still on top and bouncing up like a rag doll every time Andy would hit him."

After 10 minutes of on-field bedlam, the police finally restored order.

Rigney and Seminick were invited by the umpires to repair to their respective clubhouses for the balance of the contest, won by the Phils, 5–4, in 11 innings.

When the game ended, Sawyer derided Stanky's actions as "strictly bush league stuff." Durocher was indignant, and defended his player: "Smart ball players have been pulling stuff like that for all the 25 years I've been in baseball and it's perfectly legal as far as I'm concerned."

As the season wore on, Nicholson began to experience heaviness and fatigue unlike any he'd previously known. There were other symptoms, too. He was losing too much weight. "I'd develop a terrific thirst and hunger," he said. "I'd drink water and keep on eating, but was always thirsty and hungry." Fearful of being diagnosed with cancer or some other serious affliction, Nicholson did not seek medical advice.

Waitkus, too, was wearing down. He told the *Bulletin*'s Frank Yeutter: "What an ordeal the last six weeks [of the season] was! I'd get up in the morning just as tired and jittery as when I went to bed. I roomed with Bill Nicholson, and I knew he was a sick man. He kept losing weight all the time. Between worrying about the team and not being able to get to sleep myself, then seeing Nick get worse, I was in a horrible mental state."

Returning on the train from a road swing, Nicholson sat in a dining car with Philadelphia sportswriter Stan Baumgartner as dinner was served. He looked at the steak on the plate in front of him, and then turned to Baumgartner. "You'll have to excuse me," Nicholson said. "I'm dizzy. I just can't eat." Baumgartner thought nothing of the incident at the time, but realized its significance several weeks later.

At the end of August, Philadelphia held a comfortable six-game lead over second-place Brooklyn. September was dismal, however; the Whiz Kids went 13–16. Their problems began when Durocher's Giants swept a Shibe Park doubleheader, blanking the Phils twice, 2–0, and 9–0. In the first game, Bill dropped Monte Irvin's easy fly ball in the top of seventh for a two-base error that led to a Dodger run.

Two days later, Brooklyn came to town for another doubleheader. Before the first game, Nicholson stood in the outfield with Roberts, shagging fly balls. Eyeing his haggard teammate, Roberts said, "Bill, you don't look too good."

"I don't feel too good," was Nicholson's reply. "I've lost about 15 pounds." Roberts suggested that Nicholson talk to Wiechec.

Brooklyn, who started the day 7½ games back, swept the twi-night twinbill, 2–0, and 3–2. The good news for the Dodgers was that they were now only three games back in the loss column; the bad news was that catcher Roy

Campanella fractured his thumb in the second game, on a foul tip off the bat of Willie Jones, and was lost for the season. Pinch-hitting for Konstanty, Bill popped up weakly to end the second game. He could barely drag himself back to the dugout.

At Wiechec's insistence, Bill was taken to Jefferson Hospital in Philadelphia, to discover the cause of his problems. After tests, he learned that he was, and had for some time been, a diabetic. His condition would require him to sit out the rest of the year. Doctors also intimated that his athletic career was over.

"This thing got me so bad I thought I was going to die or something," he said several weeks later. "I lost 17 pounds and felt weaker than a baby. In the last game I played against the Giants on Labor Day, I couldn't bring my bat around. All my coordination was gone."

In some ways, the diagnosis must have been a relief. Before the discovery of the disease, Bill had begun to doubt himself and his baseball ability. "Then I got thinking that maybe I was yellow — that I was starting to crack up in the close ball games," he acknowledged. "But I just couldn't believe that, for I always got my biggest kick out of playing in tight games."

Although never a heavy drinker, Nicholson harkened back to his days with Charlie Grimm's 1945 Cubs. There were always a couple of tubs of beer on ice for the players after the game. In the warm weather, especially, Bill would consume a bottle or two before leaving the clubhouse at the end of a game. Doctors were now telling him that drinking alcohol was contraindicated for a diabetic. "One of the worst things I could've done, I guess," he said ruefully.

In Nicholson's absence, the Phils continued their swoon. The season came down to the final game, on October 1, against Brooklyn at Ebbets Field. Holding a one-game lead, a Phillies loss would mean a three-game playoff with the Dodgers. A Philadelphia victory would clinch the team's first pennant in 35 years. Dick Sisler's 10th-inning, three-run homer carried the Phils to a 4–1 victory, and the team's second-ever N.L. title. This time, it was the Phillies celebrating on Ebbets Field, the reverse of 1949, when Brooklyn clinched in the season-ending game at Shibe Park.

Happy for his teammates, but disappointed at his fate, Nicholson refused to concede that the season was over, much less his career. After being hospitalized for three weeks, he was released in time to work out for several days, before the World Series against the Yankees. The day before the opening game, he told the writers: "I feel wonderful now. I'm still taking my insulin once a day, but maybe my diet will take care of it soon. I lost 17 pounds, but I've got ten of 'em back."

Nicholson shared his teammate's enthusiasm. "I got a feeling we're going to beat those Yankees in the World Series," he predicted. "We have the same spirit the Cardinals used to have, and you know how far that carried them. It could do the same for us."

Despite playing three close games, the Phils were swept in four straight by the Bronx Bombers, who were in the second year of a five-season World Series winning streak. Nicholson could only watch, however. Doctors would not clear him to play; a nurse even accompanied him to the first game. Worried about his baseball future, he told reporters he did not intend to retire from the game, and would even consider playing Triple A ball, if necessary.

Later, he expressed ambivalence about his late-season misfortune: "I might have helped a little, had I kept my strength. God knows we didn't hit a lick against the Yankees. Everybody stopped hitting weeks before. I was a pretty good late-season hitter, even in my good years. But it was not a great blow to me to be out of it. I wasn't happy, but I accepted what happened. I would have been a liability."

During the 1950 season, Nicholson appeared in 41 games, and had only 66 plate appearances. His average was .224, with three home runs — two of which won crucial games against the Dodgers — and 10 RBIs, the lowest numbers of his career to date. At nearly 36 years of age, Swish Nicholson was clearly in the twilight of his baseball career. What effect diabetes would have on his diminishing skills remained to be seen.

19

The Giants Win the Pennant

For the remaining three years of his major league tenure, Bill Nicholson kept himself in excellent physical condition. He had no choice if he was to have any chance at playing with his accustomed level of proficiency. Though he injected himself with insulin twice a day, he always brought a candy bar to the ballpark. If his insulin injection caused him to feel tired or sluggish, eating the candy raised his blood sugar and made him feel better.

Bill maintained a daily diet of 3,000 calories, and ate throughout the day. During day games, when he was not able to eat a midday meal, he had to be especially careful. "On a hot day, I run a lot and I break out in a cold sweat," he told a reporter. "Then I have to have something sweet right away. Usually I bring a candy bar to the bench for such emergencies, but sometimes another player will see the candy and eat it before I can get to it. Then, I take a lump of sugar."

Bill received his 1951 contract in January at the Chestertown post office; he signed and sent it back within minutes. Attired in a fancy outfit, featuring a bow tie, and covered by a snazzy topcoat and fedora, he told an inquiring reporter that he'd licked his diabetes, and had never felt better. He was delighted that, despite his month long absence from the team the previous season, his pay had not been cut.

Nicholson reported to spring training in the best shape of his life. Hearkening back to the recovery made by teammate Waitkus the year before, he said: "If I do half as well as Eddie, I'll be a mighty happy ballplayer. After all, the doctors told me in August I'd never play again, but here I am."

Sawyer thought his team's '51 prospects were excellent. Before the previous year's championship season, he picked his club to finish no higher than third. Now he said: "We're the champs — we're the ones they'll have to beat. And don't forget our club should be a lot better because of another year of experience." A preseason United Press International dispatch suggested that

Nicholson might break into the starting lineup, "since he is fast, has a good arm and acts like he isn't close to his 35 years."

Baumgartner wrote in *The Sporting News*:

> Nicholson's return to top form has been one of the spectacular developments in Florida. The big fellow has been playing better than he ever did. His hitting has been splendid. In the final game against Washington, he drove two home runs over the 350 foot right field fence like bullets. And he is the best all-around outfielder on the club.

The Phils headed north before the start of the season, and stopped in Jacksonville, to play an exhibition against the Dodgers at City Park. Wherever the Brooklyn team played, a loyal cadre of black fans materialized to cheer on Robinson, Campanella, Newcombe, & Co. A record 7,973 fans — probably two thirds of whom were black — saw a thrilling 10-inning affair that culminated in a 5–4 Brooklyn win. The Dodgers were winning with two out in the visiting ninth when Nicholson hit Jim Romano's pitch over the right field wall, to drive in Del Ennis.

After a 5–2 Opening Day conquest of the Dodgers, Brooklyn returned the favor the next day behind Preacher Roe, 4–3. Two days later, before the home opener against Boston, the Phils raised the N.L. pennant over Shibe Park, for the first time in 35 years. But the Braves took two close games, before Philadelphia won the final game of the series, 6–5. Trailing, 5–4, in the bottom of the ninth, Bill pinch hit for pitcher Bubba Church, and doubled off Johnny Sain. Waitkus also doubled to tie the score, and Willie Jones had a bases-loaded single to score Waitkus. The team then ran off four more wins, to equal its longest such skein for the season.

Appearing mostly in pinch-hitting roles, Nicholson doubled off Red Munger of the Cardinals on May 5 at home, during an 11-inning loss, as St. Louis regained the league lead. Against the same team 10 days later in Sportsman's Park, Nicholson pinch hit for Mike Goliat in the ninth with the bases loaded. His single scored two runs, in a 5–4 victory.

At the close of play on May 31, the Phils were stuck in seventh place, seven games below .500, after a 4–3 loss at Ebbets Field to the first-place Dodgers. The game was highlighted by an eighth-inning fight between Monk Meyer and Jackie Robinson.

With Robinson dancing off third base, batter Carl Furillo missed the ball on a suicide squeeze attempt. Robinson ended up in a rundown, but somehow managed to elude frantic Phillies fielders. Meyer, covering the plate, dropped Willie Jones' throw. As Robinson attempted to score, Meyer threw a football block on him. Jackie finally broke free, after which words were exchanged. Both players promised to settle the matter under the stands after the game, but nothing more came of the incident. The two would become teammates on the Dodgers in 1953.

Returning to the Windy City in mid–June, before a Ladies' Day crowd at Wrigley, Bill hit his first season homer and doubled, in an 11–3 Phillies rout. He homered again a week later against the Pirates, as Philadelphia swept a three-game series at Forbes Field, to draw within a game of .500.

A two-run Nicholson homer in the top of the ninth, off reliever Frank Smith, broke a 2–2 tie, and the Reds were defeated, 4–2, in the second game of a Crosley Field doubleheader on June 24, to salvage a split for the day.

Not until late July, however, were the Philadelphians able to surpass the .500 mark. On July 27, in the midst of a four-game winning streak, the team returned to Wrigley Field, and shut out the Cubs, 2–0. The game was interrupted twice by rain. Bill had two doubles and scored the first run, to lift the Phils within one percentage point of third place.

Losing, 5–1, to the Reds at Crosley Field in the eighth inning, Nicholson's pinch-hit double to left off Ken Raffensberger scored two, and ignited a rally that resulted in a 7–5 Phils win, on August 2. The team won seven of its next nine games, before running into the streaking Giants. Philadelphia then dropped eight games in a row in mid–August — six of them to New York — as Durocher's charges closed the gap with league-leading Brooklyn.

Eleven-year-old Billy Nicholson, Jr. was in the stands, watching his dad, as the Giants won their seventh in a row, and the Phils lost their sixth in the streak. Bill tripled as a pinch hitter in the fourth, with the bases loaded. He remained in the game, and homered in the ninth. Giants scout Hans Lobert sat in the press box watching the game. After Nicholson's homer against the "Williams Shift," Lobert joked: "I know what's wrong with that shift. It ain't high enough."

The Philadelphia losing streak ended on August 21 in a doubleheader sweep of the Cubs at Shibe Park. With the bases loaded and the game tied, 2–2, in the ninth, Paul Minner walked Nicholson to force in the winning run.

The Cubs were shut out the next day, 4–0, by Robin Roberts, who won his 17th game. Batting cleanup against his old mates, Bill went three-for-four, with an RBI single in the first, and a triple in the sixth. It evened the Phils' record at 60-60, and marked the last time the team reached .500 for the season.

Nicholson went on a mini-home run spree in late August and early September. He drove the first pitch he saw over the right field wall, facing Herm Wehmeier of the Reds, on August 27. He hit home run number six one week later, over the right field roof at the Polo Grounds, to help Robin Roberts to his 18th victory, and then a solo smash into Bedford Avenue two days later off Ralph Branca, in a 5–2 loss at Brooklyn. Indeed, the *New York Times'* beat writer Roscoe McGowen was still referring in print to the aging Phillie as "Bad Bill" Nicholson, while Philadelphia prepared to play six of their final eight games against the Dodgers.

After two straight losses to Philadelphia, the Dodgers maintained a precarious three-game lead over the Giants on September 22. Following a 4–3 Phils win a week later, Brooklyn found itself in a tie atop the standings, with Durocher's Giants. As 18,000 Shibe Park patrons booed, Nicholson was intentionally passed in the ninth by Carl Erskine, with the score knotted at three. Willie Jones then laced a single to knock in the winning run.

Although Sawyer's Phils were seven games below .500, in fifth place, and out of the pennant chase, they exerted considerable influence over the outcome of the 1951 N.L. title hunt. In the season closer at Shibe Park, the Dodgers needed a win to force a playoff with the Giants. Almost 32,000 — many of them Brooklynites — crowded the old Philadelphia ballpark on September 30 to witness the contest. Trailing at one point, 6–1, Brooklyn battled back to tie the game and eventually win it, 9–8, in 14 innings, on a Jackie Robinson home run.

All baseball fans know what happened next — the Giants won the pennant on October 3, after Bobby Thomson's famous home run off the Dodgers' Branca. Many forget, however, a controversial call in the September 30 game made by umpire Lon Warneke, Nicholson's former Cubs teammate.

In the home 12th, Eddie Waitkus hit a two-out line shot on which the potential winning run would have scored. Robinson dove to his right and seemed to trap the ball in his glove; Warneke, however, saw it differently, and called Waitkus out. Robin Roberts, the runner on third base, to this day insists that the ball was trapped. "I couldn't believe the call. But it seemed like nobody argued or anything," he said. Were it not for Warneke's call, the Phils would have prevailed in the game, and there would have been no need for the famous playoff series that immortalized Thomson.

Thus ended a disappointing year for the Philadelphia club. They finished fifth, 23½ games behind New York. Attendance fell by nearly 280,000. Pitcher Curt Simmons was lost to the military, and several regulars had subpar years. Ashburn did lead the league in hitting at .344, and Roberts won 21 games, but there were few other bright spots. Nicholson's playing time more than doubled from 1950, and he had eight homers and 30 RBIs in only 170 at bats.

Bill signed on to play with Danny Litwhiler's All-Stars, who included Carl Furillo, Danny Murtaugh, and Nellie Fox, before returning to Chestertown. They played a series of games in Pennsylvania against local teams, through late October.

After the season, Sawyer expressed his disenchantment with several members of the Phillies, in no uncertain terms. "All that World Series money went to their heads in '51. They thought they'd win games just by showing up," he said. In particular, he was upset with Eddie Waitkus, with whom he had fallen out late in the season. "Waitkus isn't strong enough to party at night they way he does and be ready for games the next day," the manager complained.

When Waitkus heard of Sawyer's comments, it soured the relationship between the two. "It really ended their friendship, because Eddie figured Sawyer wanted him off the team," Nicholson explained years later. "Heck, most of us struggled that year, and quite frankly, most of us partied too much, but Sawyer chose to single out Eddie."

Del Ennis and Dick Sisler were also singled out for criticism, and Sawyer said, "Ennis is definitely on the trade list." Nicholson received no such condemnation from his manager. "Bill Nicholson made a remarkable comeback and I was pleased with him," Sawyer crowed. He sported a .306 mark as a pinch hitter for the season, good for 12th in the league.

In November, Bill was the best man at Waitkus' wedding, in Albany, New York, along with more than 150 guests, who packed St. Patrick's Church. Although not present for the ceremony, Sawyer weighed in on the event, opining that "[m]arried life should make [Waitkus] more content, take away the tension. And he has a splendid wife who has his welfare first in her mind."

20

Shakeup on the Phillies

Nineteen fifty-two began with some cheery news for Bill. In early February, he learned of his election to the all-time Cubs team, by the Chicago chapter of the Baseball Writers of America. The voting panel included several of his former nemeses, including Irving Vaughan, Edward Burns, and Warren Brown, so this was no small feat. Seven outfielders were named, including Hack Wilson, Kiki Cuyler, and Riggs Stephenson.

It was a disgruntled group of Phillies, however, who arrived in Clearwater in February. Owner Bob Carpenter slashed salaries across the board after the mediocre 1951 campaign. The players were again discouraged from bringing their wives and families to camp, and recreational activities like golf were *verboten*. Sawyer had a run-in with pitcher Steve Ridzik, and fined Willie "Puddin'head" Jones $200. He refused to disclose the infraction Jones had committed, telling the press, "If Jones wishes to give you the details, it is up to him." Puddin'head's response soon followed: "I haven't a darn thing to say about it — see Sawyer." In the end, the manager's martial discipline with his players would prove to be his undoing.

In the early spring training games at Clearwater, Sawyer tried several right fielders, including Tommy Brown, Jack Mayo, and Mel Clark. As the Phils barnstormed north to Philadelphia, they stopped on April 9 in Lynchburg, Virginia, to play the Cardinals; Bill homered in the loss.

On Opening Day at the Polo Grounds, under the lights, Nicholson started in right field and batted fifth. He had one of only four team hits, in a 5–3 loss to the defending N.L. champion Giants. But Sawyer played the aging veteran sparingly. Bill had a pinch-hit, two-run homer against the Reds on May 4, and a squib, bases-loaded single in the bottom of the ninth that enabled the Phils to beat the Cardinals, 2–1, in mid–June.

A week later, with the club in sixth place, seven games below .500, Sawyer was relieved of his duties. The Whiz Kids manager's last game, ironically, was a 6–0 whitewashing of the Giants. His dismissal came as no surprise to the team. The tight-lipped Sawyer was not particularly friendly with many of the players, and they had come to resent his confrontational style. Steve O'Neill, who managed the 1945 Tigers team that defeated the Cubs in the World Series, assumed the helm.

In retrospect, Bill thought Sawyer was a good, but not great manager. "Eddie Sawyer didn't have a hell of a lot to operate with," he explained. "He didn't have too good a bench. Sawyer did a good job. I think he got a lot out of his ball club."

Overall, the managerial change had a positive effect on the Phils, who went 59–32 the rest of the way, to finish in fourth place, 9½ games behind the pennant-winning Dodgers.

Although Bill hit only six home runs during the season, he made most of them count. In the second game of a doubleheader at Ebbets Field on July 2, he pinch hit for Monk Meyer in the eighth inning. His two-run circuit clout provided the team's only runs, in a 2–1 conquest. He had four pinch-hitting appearances for the year against the Dodgers, and homered in two of them, just as he had in 1950. He even played the spoiler against Durocher's Giants, who were still battling to catch Brooklyn on September 21. A three-run shot off Jim Hearn, over the Spite Fence in the fourth inning, was pivotal in the 6–2 Phils victory.

Two weeks before the end of the season, and uncertain of his baseball future, Nicholson approached O'Neill. "Steve, what have you planned for me next year? Am I going to be with the club?" he asked.

O'Neill's response was heartening to the aging outfielder. "What do you mean — are you going to be with the club?," O'Neill shot back. "You're the best pinch hitter I have. Do you know where there is a better one?" Bill walked away on a cloud, grateful to learn of his inclusion in the Phils' 1953 plans.

During the final series of the season, at the Polo Grounds, Nicholson stroked an RBI single and his fifth season homer (off the upper right field deck), in a 7–3 win. The next day, Robin Roberts won his 28th game — the most in the N.L. since 1935. Nicholson was two for five, with two RBIs. Batting cleanup, he homered, along with Willie Jones. Roberts, Nicholson, and Jones mugged for photographers after the game, as the pitcher held up Curt Simmons' uniform — number 28 — for the camera.

Although Nicholson's six home runs and 19 RBIs for the year seem meager in comparison to his halcyon years in the early '40s, they project to impressive totals over the course of a full season. Using his 608 official at-bats in 1943 as a model, the 1952 totals project 41 home runs and 131 RBIs for a full season. Nicholson's 233 career home runs placed him fourth among active major league players, behind only Johnny Mize (355); Ted Williams (324), and Ralph Kiner (294).

Time was running out, though, and Nicholson knew it. He would be 38 years old before 1952 ended. Only a handful of major league players of his vintage were still active at year's end. In 1953, the Cubs' venerable Dutch Leonard and Alpha Brazle of the Cardinals were the only N.L. players older than the Eastern Shore outfielder.

CBS radio broadcast a program called "Comeback," on November 14. A nationwide audience heard Red Barber narrate a story about Nicholson's recovery from his 1950 diabetic attack. Bill also recorded a message in aid of the American Diabetes Association's detection drive.

In late January, 1953, Steve O'Neill announced that Nicholson would be given a shot as the starting right fielder, if his health did not fail. The Phillies manager was impressed by the fact that the hustling outfielder, despite his health problems, kept himself in top physical condition. By early March, O'Neill suggested that Nicholson was the presumptive starter, but if he faltered Johnny Wyrostek or Mel Clark would be given a chance to win the job.

In the offseason, Monk Meyer had been unloaded to the Dodgers for first baseman Earl Torgeson, who was expected to supplant Waitkus at first base. Carpenter's shortsighted decision to play "bonus baby" Ted Kazanski at shortstop resulted in Granny Hamner's move to second base. A freakish lawnmower accident to pitcher Curt Simmons cost him a month of the season, and the '53 Phils ended the year tied for third, 22 games in back of the Dodgers who lost — again — to the Yankees in the World Series.

In May, Nicholson began to play regularly. In his first five games, he was 10 for 16, including three doubles, a triple, and two homers, bringing his average to more than .500 for the year. Stan Baumgartner remarked: "He is hitting balls he hasn't touched in five years. The first time he went to bat against Pittsburgh as a pinch hitter this season, he hit a high pitch for two bases. He hasn't touched such a pitch successfully for five seasons."

Bill explained: "Until this year I was so weak at bat that I fell away from the plate when I swung, so that I would get more leverage on the ball. This caused me to strike out a lot. This season, I can stand up to the dish and swish the bat without any trouble. Maybe my eyes are clearer, too ... I do know that I feel much better...." But as the season progressed, Bill's body simply could not withstand the rigors of daily games. "My nerves went down; I started shaking on that plate," he acknowledged. "Yeah, I wasn't right." He appeared in only 38 games, batting .210 in a mere 62 at bats, the lowest average of his career. There were a few highlights: playing in place of slumping

Del Ennis, he singled, doubled, and tripled against Pittsburgh on May 27, to help his team end a five-game losing streak, in the first game of a doubleheader. In the second game, he hit his first home run of the year, and ended the day six for nine.

A two-run clout in the first inning helped the club to a 12–3 defeat of the Giants, on May 29. It was Nicholson's final major league homer.

He discussed, with *Pittsburgh Press* columnist Les Biederman, the medical regimen to which he adhered daily during the 1953 campaign. "Yes, I still take my two shots of insulin every morning. Shoot myself with the needle either in the legs, arms or shoulders. One shot is the regular type, the quick acting. The other is protein zinc, slow acting. The regular insulin takes care of breakfast and the protein takes care of the remainder of the day."

In early September, Nicholson told a reporter that he expected to be unconditionally released at season's end. "It had to come some time," Bill said wistfully. "The diabetes robbed me of my strength. I can't maintain proper chemical balance between the sugar content in my bloodstream and the insulin I have to use. So what's the use of kidding myself? I'll be 38 [sic] in December. I know that I'm finished."

Even when Nicholson managed to get on base, he was usually removed for a pinch runner. "The Phillies used Putsy Caballero to run for me," he recounted. "He was a kid and a pretty good base runner. I was no speedster, but I had pretty good legs. One day we were loosening up in the outfield and I said I thought I could outrun Putsy for 10 bucks. He took me up on it— and I won by a couple of strides. But there's a difference between running the bases and running straightaway."

Still, Nicholson had second thoughts about his decision. "Sure, I hate to leave baseball," he explained. "Maybe some other team may want me, but I doubt it. Maybe I'd manage in the minors if I was offered that chance. But, on the other hand, I have a farm on the Eastern Shore and enough money to live comfortably. I've been happy in baseball. My record isn't the best in the majors, but I won't have to apologize for it. You never think of this day when you first break in. But it has to come."

The end came on September 19, in a 5–4 loss to pennant-winning Brooklyn at Ebbets Field, the diamond where Nicholson often shone so brightly, and where enemy fans first dubbed him "Swish." How ironic was it that he would pinch hit in the ninth inning for Robin Roberts, whose hero growing up outside Chicago was Swish Nicholson, and that the opposing pitcher was his good friend Monk Meyer? And if Nicholson couldn't hit a home run, perhaps it was fitting that he struck out—giving Dodgers fans an emphatic and final "swishhh." He did not appear in the team's last seven games.

He returned home, where Nancy had been supervising the remodeling and renovation of the 125 acre farm in Broad Neck, near Langford Bay, which they had recently purchased. To a local newspaper, however, Bill denied the retirement reports, in early October. "Quit? Not I," he said. "The story of my 'retirement' was the result of the case of a reporter [the *Philadelphia Evening Bulletin*'s Frank Yeutter] having nothing else to write about.... I told [him] I'd probably get my release at the end of the season. The next thing I knew, I was 'retiring,' an independently wealthy man, to my 'country estate.' That's for the birds. I've got to work for a living, and baseball is the only job I've ever had...." While acknowledging that he could no longer be an everyday player, he insisted he could be a utility player and pinch hitter, or even manage or coach.

His initial protestations to the contrary, Nicholson announced his official retirement at a luncheon given in his honor at the Vesper Club, in downtown Philadelphia, on October 29. He was quitting, he said, because, "I have run out of gas as a player," but added that he would enjoy remaining in the game in some capacity. There was talk of his managing the International League's Syracuse Chiefs, or the Eastern League's Schenectady Blue Jays. Club owner Bob Carpenter wanted Bill to remain with the organization in some capacity, and hoped to find a spot for him. "He's been a great player, a fine person to know, and a fine man to have around young players," he said. The *Salisbury* (Md.) *Times* reported in its December 2, 1953, edition that an unnamed source in the Phillies front office expected Bill to assume a position with the team by mid–January, 1954.

In the end, however, Bill retired to his farm on Broad Neck. "I can only eke out a living there, so I'll have to go to work some place," he quipped.

When pressed by a reporter, he named an all-star team of players with and against whom he had competed. The catchers were Gabby Hartnett and Roy Campanella, and the pitchers were Robin Roberts and Carl Hubbell. At first was Johnny Mize; at second, Billy Herman. Nicholson named Marty Marion as the shortstop and Stan Hack at third base. The outfield was composed of Stan Musial ("the finest player I ever saw"), Paul Waner, and Duke Snider, "even though I've seen Ashburn make some great catches."

He railed against the bonus system then in vogue, whereby major league teams signed inexperienced youngsters — like Ted Kazanski — for large sums of money. "It affects the morale of the older men on the team," he complained. "No matter how much they fight against it, they can't help saying to themselves, 'That untried kid got more than I have been able to save in my whole career.'

"But," he mused, "I suppose that is the only way the big leagues can get first-class material in today's highly competitive market."

21

Is There Life After Baseball?

The life of a professional ballplayer requires long absences from one's home and family. It is an unavoidable incident of athletic stardom that, while the player is away earning his living, household matters become the domain of the spouse. This sometimes leads to estrangement between husband and wife.

In Bill Nicholson's case, his wife Nancy and two children took a back seat to his professional obligations. When a family crisis arose, he was usually unavailable. Even the offseason frequently saw him away from home, on hunting trips with teammates or friends, at locations as far-flung as South Dakota, or barnstorming with other major league players in post-season tournaments throughout the northeast. Mackey Dutton, a longtime family friend and frequent baby-sitter for the boys, knew that Bill "was crazy about Nancy. But he was gone all the time." Even when he was home, he was not particularly talkative. Inevitably, his absence created fissures in the marital relationship that were never repaired.

When Bill returned to Chestertown after the 1953 season, he shuffled in and out of a number of jobs, besides that of gentleman farmer. He sold real estate with W. Clark Grieb during 1953 and 1954, and became a race track inspector for several years thereafter. He drove over to Delaware Park horse racing track with several faculty members from Washington College during the summer months, and enjoyed entertaining them on the trip with baseball stories.

He still had the itch to get back into baseball, though, in some capacity. Joe Engel invited him to join the Lookouts in a playing capacity for 1955, but Nicholson concluded that the Tennessee heat was too severe for his diabetic condition. He was a regular on the "rubber chicken" circuit, speaking to various service organizations and youth groups, and attended the occasional testimonial dinner, including one for Home Run Baker, in 1955. When Baker was inducted into the Maryland Sports Hall of Fame in July of that year, at Memorial Stadium in Baltimore, Nicholson greeted Connie Mack for the last time. The Tall Tactician died seven months later, aged 93.

Over the years, Nancy developed a network of friends with whom she associated during the baseball season. These included Louisa Carpenter, Eugenia Bankhead, and her more famous sister, the noted screen actress Tallulah.

Louisa d'Andelot Carpenter was the daughter of R.M. Carpenter, a vice-president and director of the E.I. du Pont de Nemours & Company, and the heiress to a fortune. She was the niece of Pierre S. du Pont, chairman of the board of the du Pont Company. As a young girl riding in New York horse shows, Louisa became a protégée of Tallulah Bankhead. Later, she was an accomplished fox hunter, fisherwoman, and aviatrix. Her brother Robert purchased the Phillies in 1947.

In the '30s and '40s, Louisa owned a mansion in Rehoboth Beach, Delaware, where she regularly entertained Hollywood celebrities, including Bankhead. In a day when such things were not discussed, it was an open secret that Louisa, although married to a prominent businessman, was bisexual. She came to Kent County after World War II, and purchased several large estates. During this period she befriended Nancy Nicholson.

Louisa became an integral part of the Kent County community, and was widely respected for her civic contributions and charitable work. In the early '60s, she was the catalyst for the construction of Washington Park, a housing development for low-income residents of the county. She gave generously to the improvement of Kent-Queen Anne's Hospital, and donated land upon which to build a summer camp for crippled children. Elmer Horsey, her accountant and later mayor of Chestertown, described her as "one of the finest people I've ever known. She believed in helping the unfortunate."

Because of her financial generosity, she was generally well-regarded in Kent, although her relationship with Nancy was a subject of local gossip. Some suggested they were lovers. Others, including Horsey, scoffed at that notion.

Eugenia Bankhead was a prominent, and somewhat eccentric, socialite who was married three times to Morton Hoyt, son of the Solicitor General during the administration of President William Howard Taft. The first Bankhead-Hoyt marriage was annulled, and the second and third ended in divorce.

Several years after the last divorce, Hoyt was erroneously reported to be dying in Nice, France. Eugenia set out for France with the intention of marrying Hoyt again. She arrived to great fanfare, in the company of her pet monkey, who sat on her shoulder, eating peanuts, and tossing the shells at newspaper reporters. When Eugenia arrived at Hoyt's bedside, however, he refused to see her.

In the company of Louisa and Eugenia, Nancy became a jet-setter, who journeyed to Europe and Asia. Sometimes she took the boys with her, to Bill's consternation. She even removed them from school for a year, while they traveled on the continent. Although the boys idolized their father, his distance and unavailability during baseball season did not make for a close relationship as years passed.

Nancy's male liaisons were numerous. She made no pretense about her sexual activity, and frequently walked naked around the backyard of the Florida home she maintained in later years. Teenaged friends of Billy and Albert always enjoyed visits to the Nicholson home in Chestertown during the summer, when Nancy could be seen parading around in her scanty swimsuits.

Harrison Vickers remembers Nancy making the rounds of local gatherings, sometimes in Louisa's company. When she arrived, dressed to the nines, "heads turned. She was a big, sexy woman," said Vickers. Louisa, by contrast, frequently dressed like a man, and the two made for an odd couple.

In the early 1960s, Louisa built a bowling alley in Queen Anne's County, and installed Bill as the manager. In an effort to publicize the fledgling enterprise, she conducted zany promotions, even bringing a chimpanzee to drum up customers. But Bill was uncomfortable running a business, and lasted only a couple of years on the job. He preferred farming and hunting, which he carried on throughout the '50s and early '60s, and from which always he derived a sense of satisfaction.

By 1964, Nicholson concluded that he was happiest on his farm. There, he planted grains, trained hunting dogs, and maintained the blinds and decoys for the wing hunters he hosted annually. The happiest time of year was when the first Canadian geese came rolling back, to winter on the Shore. Alan Joiner, who lived with Nicholson in the last years of his life, remembered how desperately he wanted to be the first to tell the old ballplayer that the geese had finally arrived. It seemed that every year, when he'd tell of hearing the first geese, the still-competitive Nicholson would retort, "I heard them yesterday."

Once, Bill was in the Kent-Queen Anne's Hospital, suffering from a diabetic attack, and had been laid up for several days. When Alan came to visit him, with news of the first geese, Nicholson one-upped him again. "I been hearing them for a week," he growled.

Besides hunting, Bill also grew produce for the family's consumption, cultivated his fruit orchards, and planted trees along the lane leading to the farm house, some of which were descendants of the lindens at Fancy Farm. When in good health, he made a daily drive into Chestertown to purchase as many as five daily newspapers — from Baltimore, Washington, Wilmington, Philadelphia, and New York — and read the sports pages thoroughly.

Bill's brother Albert acquired Fancy Farm in 1951. During his ownership, it became primarily a grain farm. Upon Albert's death in 1982, his widow Sue placed the farm under easement to the Maryland Environmental Trust, to assure its continued use for agricultural purposes.

Nicholson was a familiar sight in downtown Chestertown, in his pickup truck, usually with a couple of dogs in the cab. His beloved standard poodles — Peaches and Cha-Cha — would sit next to him when he drove. If headed into town, he would typically stop at Stam's drug store on High Street, to pick up his medical supplies, and greet well-wishers.

As Bill donned his winter hat — featuring long ear flaps — during one frosty winter day, Alan Joiner followed him down a long lane, from the farm to the main road. Through the rear window of the truck cab, he could see Nicholson, Peaches, and Cha-Cha, sitting abreast on the front seat. From the back, they looked like three people. When the truck reached the road, the old ballplayer looked left, then right, then left again before making his turn. The dogs' heads turned with his, in unison.

Bill told Margaret Fallaw that he could have pursued a career other than farming, like many retired ballplayers had done. "A lot of fellows do now ... half a dozen, maybe, have been doctors, or something else. I guess I could have done the same thing, but maybe they didn't have the interest in the country that I did. So I did what I like to do, and maybe that wasn't the right thing to do but I enjoyed it. So I guess being happy is worth a hell of a lot more than being extremely rich and not happy."

In later years, "Mr. Bill downplayed the baseball part of his life," according to Emily Joiner. "The farm was his life." He always told interviewers, inquiring about his post-baseball life, that he was a farmer who hunted and fished, although he complained that his old fishing holes were now polluted.

Nicholson was inducted into Maryland's athletic hall of fame, called the "Shrine of Immortals," on August 26, 1966, at Baltimore's Memorial Stadium, preceding an Orioles–Red Sox game. His portrait, swinging a bat for the 1949 Phillies, was presented at the ceremony. There, more than a decade after his major league career ended, he still exhibited the modesty that characterized his career, when he remarked: "I wonder if I'm good enough. I feel like I'm sneaking in the back door."

Bill had invested cautiously in the stock market, and received a small pension from Major League Baseball. He was able to afford a private school education for the boys at McDonough School in Baltimore. After a stint in the military, Billy attended the University of Maryland. Then there was a year of law school, and marriage to Margo, before he decided to become a stockbroker.

By the late '60s, life with Nancy had become problematic for her husband. Her sexual proclivities were well-known in Kent County, and must have been embarrassing to him. Attendance at glamorous parties, and dalliances with persons of both sexes, had become too much for her husband to bear. After 29 years of marriage, Bill and Nancy divorced in 1967.

They maintained a friendship, however, and Bill continued to associate with Nancy's friends, including Tallulah and Eugenia Bankhead. When Tallulah passed away, two days after Bill's 54th birthday in 1968, he was a pallbearer at her funeral, at Old St. Paul's.

At the gravesite, guns of local hunters could be heard firing in the distance, and "the unending flybies of geese raised a cacophony that all but drowned out the last repetition of the Lord's Prayer," according to a news report of the ceremony.

After the divorce, Bill began to spend more time with Diana Hudson Curlett, with whom he had played bridge throughout the years, and who was a widowed mother of six children, five of whom were girls. The Hudson farm backed up to the Nicholsons', and Diana first saw Bill Nicholson as a youth, riding on his horse through the fields. She told her daughters that he was "the most handsome man she had ever seen on the back of a horse." When Bill became an eligible bachelor again, she baked him a pie, and they began to see each other more frequently. They married in a quiet ceremony on December 2, 1970.

Diana was a devoted wife, and the social antithesis of Nancy. Bill and his new spouse were homebodies, who took great enjoyment in their bridge-playing, participating every year in the tournament they organized at the Chester River Yacht and Country Club. They hosted wing-hunters in season, and Diana would rise early to fix breakfast for the hungry shooters.

Nicholson regularly responded to fan letters, requests for autographs and pictures. "We never knew he was so famous," stepdaughter Emily Joiner remarked. He spoke very little about his former career. "It was hard to get him to talk," said her husband, Alan. "People would be frustrated."

Emily knew how difficult it was for this virile ex–baseball player to inherit a family with five girls, four of whom were still living in the home. "He was living quietly by himself, and then suddenly you're living with five women," she said. But he came to enjoy the female companionship, and the Curlett girls loved to be around him. Emily remembered a softball game in front of the farm house. The girls had to coax him into playing, but he finally agreed. When it was his turn to bat, Nicholson hit the ball so hard that he literally knocked the cover off it, and so far that the innards were never found.

He maintained his dry humor. The first time that the Curlett children had dinner at the farmhouse, they watched Nicholson's Chesapeake Bay retriever, Brandy, lick the plates clean at the end of the meal. Bill then put the plates back in the cupboard, and told the astonished children, "This is how we do dishes down here in Broad Neck!" The dogs had the run of the house and yard. Bill even kept the doors of his truck open, because the animals loved to sleep inside the vehicle.

No longer much of a church-goer, he resisted efforts by Emily to attend Sunday services at Old St. Paul's. Knowing the cemetery there would be his final resting place, he would jokingly decline her invitation, explaining, "I'm going to be at St. Paul's a good long time."

Albert Nicholson bore a strong resemblance to his famous father, broad of build and handsome. He, too, attended the University of Maryland, married a young lady named Margo, fathered two children, and trained as a stockbroker. But while residing in Florida, he had an affair with a woman who suffered from a serious drug problem. After a time, he deserted his wife and family to live with her. Following an arrest in Florida for drug possession, he returned to Maryland in 1974, intending to go back to Florida for his trial in October.

Out of money, Albert declined his father's offer of financial assistance, and decided to hitchhike to Florida in early October. When he did not arrive timely, his family became concerned. His disappearance baffled Bill and Nancy, and they were worried. Not until weeks later did they learn the tragic news: Albert had been struck by a vehicle on an interstate in North Carolina, on October 3. Someone stole the wallet from his lifeless body, and it lay in the morgue unidentified. Not until a check, payable to him, was discovered in Albert's shoe was a connection made. The woman on whose account the check was drawn was contacted in Chestertown, and she provided his family's address. It was left to Billy to fly to North Carolina and identify his brother's body. The remains were returned to Maryland and, eventually, interred in a plot purchased by Nancy at Old St. Paul's.

Albert's death was the first in a series of family losses from which Bill never fully recovered. Less than a year later, when an invitation was extended from the Phillies to participate in the Whiz Kids' 25th anniversary Old-Timers Game in Philadelphia, Bill was not interested. Though he followed the sport on the radio and television, he had not seen a professional game in person since 1966, upon his induction into the Shrine of the Immortals.

Billy and Margo thought participating in a reunion with his former teammates would be a tonic for Bill's flagging spirits. They were met with resistance, however. "I don't want to go. Everyone will be too old," Nicholson insisted. But, finally, he was persuaded to attend.

Diana, Billy, and Margo drove Bill to Philadelphia's Bellevue–Stratford Hotel, where the Whiz Kids would be housed for the reunion weekend. When they pulled up in front of the hotel, there were scores of fans waiting, calling his name. "He was joyous," Margo Bailey remembered. "It transformed him. His shoulders came back; he said it was the best weekend of his life."

The former Whiz Kids laughed, caught up on old times, participated in an abbreviated game at Veterans Stadium — against the likes of Andy Pafko, Bobby Thomson, and Enos Slaughter, among others — and played cards. Nicholson left with a baseball autographed by his former teammates, which he treasured for the rest of his days, as well as a painting depicting him in his Phillies uniform. Larry Shenk, the Phillies' publicity director, wrote Bill after the weekend: "I'd heard a lot about the unity on the 1950 club and following

The 1950 Whiz Kids celebrate their 25th reunion at Veterans' Stadium. Nicholson is #12, at the upper left, standing next to Robin Roberts. Former manager Eddie Sawyer, in glasses, has his arms folded in the middle of the second row (*courtesy Emily Joiner*).

that weekend, I witnessed the closeness of the group first-hand. It was something to experience. I also learned you guys don't sleep very much."

Bill never saw a big-league game again, except on television. He seldom heard from former Cubs teammates, after Stan Hack's passing in 1979, and had only occasional calls from former Phillies players. But he followed the sport religiously, with special attention to his former Chicago team, and the nearby Orioles. WBAL radio, which broadcast Baltimore's games, was nearly always on during the spring and summer months at the farmhouse. Though he rooted for the Orioles, he was always a National League man when it came to the All-Star games or the World Series. When the Cubs finally installed lights at Wrigley Field in 1988, Bill told a fan: "I knew it had to come, but I was hoping the Cubs could stay unique by staying without the lights. That's my opinion, and everybody has a right to theirs."

Nancy Nicholson continued her high-profile lifestyle after the divorce, though she married again, this time to a wealthy New Orleans businessman named John Latrobe. She maintained homes in New Orleans and Fort Lauderdale. Little more than a year after Albert's death, however, Nancy perished in an airplane crash, 300 yards short of the runway at Easton, Maryland, Municipal Airport, along with Louisa Carpenter and their pilot.

The $800,000 Mitsubishi turboprop in which they traveled, owned by Louisa, was returning from Fort Lauderdale to the Eastern Shore on February 11, 1976. Chauffeur William Smith, who was to drive Louisa and Nancy back to Chestertown upon the plane's arrival, watched in horror as the twin-engine plane made its runway approach and then suddenly spiraled, wing over wing, into a field adjacent to a nearby trailer court. The pilot, a former military aviator, had been employed by Louisa for ten years.

Nancy was buried alongside the remains of her son, at Old St. Paul's. Pallbearers included her husband John Latrobe, Elmer Horsey, and former Baltimore Colts linebacker Steve Stonebreaker.

Bill was inducted into the inaugural class of the Washington College Athletic Hall of Fame in October, 1981, along with 11 others, including Jake Flowers and Coach Kibler. But his health continued its steady decline.

When Diana died of lung cancer, in 1990, he seemed overwhelmed. Preparing meals, and attending to his daily insulin routine, became too difficult for him. The Joiners decided to move into the farmhouse, and he was delighted to have them. There is no way he could have survived without their assistance.

"He took care of his diet. He still had a strong body," Emily emphasized. "But he had circulatory issues with his feet, occasional losses of consciousness and persistent bladder problems." He continued to inject insulin twice a day, but the blood test kits frequently confused him. Over his later years, the rescue squad was summoned to the farm dozens of times. Alan recalls a blackout Bill sustained in the middle of the night, which came on without aura. When he came downstairs the next morning, "he looked like he'd been beaten up."

The insulin shock into which he sometimes descended Bill called "getting shaky." He usually stocked two or three half-gallons of orange juice in the refrigerator, which he would drink when that shaky feeling came on.

Billy's marriage to Margo ended in divorce. He, too, was a diabetic, and was drinking too much. A stint as the town manager of Chestertown ended in 1983, but he found similar employment in St. Michaels, in nearby Talbot County. He met, and then married, a local girl named Pamela Yerkes McCauley. In the summer of 1985, while honeymooning in Martinique with his new bride, Billy had a seizure and bled severely from his nose. Returning to Maryland to be examined by doctors, he received a grim diagnosis: nasopharyngeal cancer. Eight weeks of radiation treatment followed, during which Billy remained on the job in St. Michaels. He fought valiantly against the disease for six years, before succumbing on June 24, 1991. The words "Never Quit" were inscribed on his tombstone at Old St. Pauls. Having now lost both of his wives and children, Bill's grief was compounded by a feeling of guilt over the rocky relationship he and his eldest son had endured.

Over his final years, Nicholson's old fans still wrote and occasionally visited him on the farm. Chicagoan Jim Revord saw him twice. "He was a very unassuming humble person and was more interested in finding out information about ... my wife, son, and myself, as I tried to get him to talk more about himself," Revord recalls.

Another fan spoke to him by telephone, volunteering that he had a photo of the '42 Cubs, but couldn't name all the players. Always accommodating, Bill told him to mail the photo, and he'd identify them.

He went to a Woolworth's in Dover, Delaware, and had hundreds of post card pictures made to send to fans who wanted an autograph. But requests to appear at autograph shows, where he could have made money signing his name, were not his cup of tea. He disliked the idea of charging a fee to his fans. "I guess it's alright, but seems like it's greedy to me," he said. And, besides, by the late '80s his bladder trouble had become virtually unmanageable in a public setting. "It comes on you and then you have to go to the bathroom or you don't make it, almost," he confessed.

Frequently, he sat in the big country kitchen of the farm house, his dogs by his side, replying to his correspondence. Only a couple of plaques and photographs, scattered throughout the house, attested to the fact that he'd once been a major league star. He was flattered by the attention he got, and took particular pleasure in showing visitors a scrapbook sent to him by a female admirer, who had compiled it during Bill's glory days in Chicago.

He held strong opinions about the state of the game. After expansion began in the early 1960's, he thought there were too many teams. "The talent is spread too thin," he said. "And they're not schooled in the minors, especially on cutoff plays. Artificial turf is rough on outfielders. Some balls bounce higher than a two-story building." He was intrigued, though, by the introduction of the designated hitter. "It would have prolonged my career," he suggested.

Nearly 400 people packed the dining hall at Washington College on November 17, 1991, in tribute to Billy Nick, and to raise money for the statue that would stand in his honor. Former major leaguers Robin Roberts, Andy Pafko, Eddie Sawyer, Curt Simmons, Dallas Green, and "Spook" Jacobs, among others, traveled from their homes to greet their friend on "Bill Nicholson Day." There were local dignitaries, Kent Countians, and the president of Washington College, all anxious to recognize the accomplishments of the former baseball star.

"I wouldn't have missed this function for all the world," Pafko said. "I'll always be grateful to Bill for his help when I came up as a rookie in 1943. He's a wonderful individual and I'm proud to say I'm his friend and teammate."

Bill had been discharged from the hospital earlier in the day, suffering from pneumonia, and looked ghastly. He was pale, and his cheeks were sunken. His illness and subsequent weight loss caused the cardigan sweater he wore to hang off his frail body. He looked nothing like the handsome young slugger whose image appeared in the photographs that had been blown up and displayed in the hall. His disease had taken both a physical and emotional toll. Depressed at a recent hospitalization, he told a caregiver that he had become a burden, and wasn't much good for anything.

But on the evening of the testimonial dinner, he temporarily forgot his troubles. This was an evening to celebrate, to reminisce and laugh at baseball stories enhanced by the passage of time, and the age of those relating them. Curt Simmons claimed to still bear scars from pepper games he'd played years before with Nicholson. Dallas Green remembered playing against Bill in an exhibition game, while the young pitcher was attending the University of Delaware. After the aging slugger belted a homer off Green's curveball, the Delaware coach said, "I told you to throw him fastballs." Next time up, Green threw Nicholson a fastball, and Bill hit another homer. The exasperated pitcher turned to his coach and yelled, "He hit yours further than he hit mine!"

Former Whiz Kids manager Sawyer even got in a dig at Jim Gallagher, describing him as a former newspaperman who "didn't know whether the ball was blown up, sewn up, or stuffed." Robin Roberts said there were three ballplayers past whom he could not throw a fastball: Yogi Berra, Smokey Burgess, and Bill Nicholson.

John Steadman, the venerable sports columnist for the *Sun*, described Nicholson as a "hero who didn't have clay feet," and concluded a moving oration by turning to Bill and saying, "You represent the finest quality that's within the human spirit." Others spoke eloquently of Nicholson's work ethic on the baseball diamond, and yearned for the day when contemporary players would share the same virtue.

The master of ceremonies, long-time Eastern Shore sports *aficionado* Hurtt Deringer, paid tribute to a teenage boy from Elizabethtown, Pennsylvania, who spurred renewed interest in Nicholson and his career. While visiting Kent County, the youngster's meeting with the old star received widespread publicity. Interest in the retired ballplayer's career was revived, providing the impetus for construction of the statue, at a cost of $35,000, funded by donations from friends and admirers. It was the first time a Maryland athlete was honored by such a tribute. Since that time, statues dedicated to other Maryland major league icons have been erected, including Babe Ruth, Jimmie Foxx, and Cal Ripken, Jr.

The dedication ceremony was held on a beautiful Saturday, October 3, 1992, before hundreds of fans and admirers. Louis Goldstein, Bill's former college teammate and now the state comptroller, drove over from Annapolis. Nicholson arrived about a half-hour before the unveiling, to greet well-wishers and sign autographs. The statue was unveiled at 4:00 P.M. by Mrs. Robert Downes of Wilmington, who had been instrumental in the project, and provided substantial financial assistance for it. The sculptor, Kenneth Herlihy, modeled the figure from a photograph taken of Nicholson in a home game against the Dodgers, during the 1948 season. The inscription below the statue reads: "This statue of a baseball great is placed as a tribute to the man, as an inspiration to the nations' youth, and as a reminder that sport is important to the American dream."

Even up to the year before his death, Nicholson remained a fixture in the Kent community, and was often called upon to throw out the ceremonial first pitch during opening day ceremonies for local youth baseball organizations.

The rescue squad made one last trip to the farmhouse on Broad Neck on a cold and snowy March 8, 1996. Bill was transported to Kent-Queen Anne's Hospital in Chestertown, where he died of a heart attack later that day, less than three months after the death of his younger brother, Larny.

Nicholson at the statue dedication in Chestertown, October 3, 1992 (*courtesy Emily Joiner*).

Richie Ashburn, Nicholson's former Phillies teammate and now a Philadelphia sportscaster, said upon hearing of his death: "He was one of the great gentlemen of the game. I was 22 when he joined us. He was everybody's role model. He was at the end of his career, but he still had an unbelievable work ethic. In pregame practice, he played every ball hit his way like the game was on the line. He was a handsome brute. All the women loved him."

Robin Roberts worshipped Nicholson as a boy, growing up in Springfield, Illinois. "He was one of my first heroes," Robin explained, "and I was fortunate that he came over with the Phillies when I was playing with them, so I was able to play with my hero."

Philadelphia Inquirer beat writer Allen Lewis thought "the fact that he was a wartime ballplayer when he did his best work hurt his reputation. He would have been better known had it not been wartime."

Old nemesis Jim Gallagher, reached at his home in Virginia, was informed of the sad news by a reporter. "Don't tell me he died," the former

Swish signs an autograph for a young fan at the dedication ceremony (*courtesy Emily Joiner*).

general manager said. "I can't keep up with things anymore. He sure could whack the ball."

The Joiners received letters and reminiscences from throughout the country. Cards, poems, and tributes poured in from fans and former teammates. The staff at Stam's drug store sent a card that said, simply: "Mr. Bill will be missed."

Reverend William L. Graham presided at funeral services at Old St. Paul's on March 12. Louis Goldstein eulogized Bill at the memorial service. "Bill did have God and the love of his fellow men and women within him all his life," Goldstein said. "He came from a wonderful family. They took me in when I arrived in Chestertown. I was from the western shore — regarded here as land on which God's eyes never looked and on which human feet never trod. I knew his parents and his brothers, and they were good people — like Bill was."

Goldstein concluded:

> Yesterday is history, today is an experience and tomorrow is a gift of life and all that goes with it. Bill Nicholson lived life to the fullest. He made the most of his gifts and he made life more joyous for everyone who knew him. May God love and bless him real good.

Nicholson was interred in a family plot, next to his brothers. The gravesite was surrounded by tall cedars and oaks, looking out over the millpond. Two hundred people attended the graveside service in clear, cold weather, with patchy snow still on the ground. The epitaph on his simple monument reads: "Nicholson, William Beck, Sr. — 'Swish' — December 11, 1914–March 8, 1996 — Major League Baseball Player 1936–1953."

Emily Joiner, who so lovingly cared for "Mr. Bill" during the last years of his life, inherited the farm, and the house that sits on it. Bill's modest estate was comprised of his house, personal effects, and farmland. After payment of his debts, his furniture, guns, decoys and memorabilia, and a small amount invested in mutual funds, were divided and given to his grandchildren.

Among the more interesting items he had retained over the years were Louisville Slugger bats, including one used by Eddie Waitkus; uniforms; gloves; cleats; a 1938 team photo of the Williamsport Grays; a Phillies warm-up jacket; and a bronze bust, created as a model for the statue on Cross Street.

Epilogue

Beneath the pinnacle of baseball superstardom there exists a substrate, consisting of players whose accomplishments fall just short of the statistical benchmarks that typically merit Hall of Fame consideration. Some had careers shortened by illness or injury. Others simply did not exhibit sustained proficiency at their craft for the requisite period of time. The remainder habitually played for losing teams, or against inferior competition. To some extent, Swish Nicholson meets all those criteria.

He retired from baseball at the nadir of his career, after diabetes made playing the game he loved too arduous a task. His greatest years, 1940 to 1944, included two seasons against competition diluted by the exodus of players to the military. Though he played on the 1945 Cubs, who lost in seven games to the Tigers in the World Series, he had a comparatively poor regular season, and never fulfilled the promise suggested by his performance during the previous five and a half years. Indeed, his detractors point to Nicholson's success during the war era, and gradual decline thereafter, as proof that his accomplishments were tainted. They argue that his statistics were inflated, having been compiled against pitchers who would have been minor leaguers, were it not for the outbreak of world war. The proponents of those arguments ignore at least three salient facts.

First, Nicholson excelled against prewar competition in 1939, 1940, and 1941, and was selected to the National League All-Star team in the latter two years. As New York sportswriter Joe King said in July, 1944, Nicholson was "a genuine prewar thumper." His batting average before the war was .278; from 1942–45 it was .284. He homered one time for every 22.2 at bats before 1942; during the war years, he homered once every 26.9 at bats.

Second, after Pearl Harbor and the outbreak of hostilities, not all major leaguers were immediately pressed into military service; 1942 big league rosters weren't radically different from the previous year's, and so the competition was essentially unchanged from 1941.

Third, there were many prewar major league stars not serving in the military (or inducted towards the end of the conflict) who did not approach the level of run production Nicholson sustained between 1942 and 1945. Players like Rudy York, Mel Ott, Joe Medwick, Stan Musial, and Vince DiMaggio, to name only a few, did not dominate the World War II game like Nicholson did.

"They never gave me any credit for that during the war years, but there were still ... a lot of good ballplayers and damn few weak pitchers," Nicholson maintained, in his own defense.

Baseball historian David Jordan has suggested that many of the war era players who served in the military were of average skill, anyway, and were replaced by players only marginally inferior, if at all. Because there were only 16 major league teams, comprised of about 400 players, the minor league system in December, 1941, was of comparatively higher quality than is the case today.

What's more, it's likely that Nicholson was diabetic during the last years of the war. He complained to Mel Ott about his chronic run-down condition as early as 1944, and checked into Illinois Masonic Hospital after the 1945 season because he felt so poorly. While the "Whiz Kids" prepared to play the Yankees in the 1950 World Series, he was in the hospital recovering from a diabetic attack that caused him to lose nearly 20 pounds. Reviewing medical records from 1945, doctors at Jefferson Hospital in Philadelphia concluded that his disease had probably been present and undiagnosed for at least five years.

David Finoli, in his 1992 book *For the Good of the Country*, compiled statistics for major league baseball players of the World War II era. During those years, Nicholson ranked fourth in total hits, third in slugging percentage (behind Musial and Ott), first in total bases, first in runs scored, and first in RBIs. Based upon his analysis, Finoli concluded that Nicholson was the most valuable player in the major leagues during the war era, ahead of Ott (ninth most valuable) and Musial (tenth).

Respected baseball analyst Bill James ranked the 100 best players in major league history, at each position, in 2001. The best right fielder, in his view, was Babe Ruth, followed by Hank Aaron, Frank Robinson, Mel Ott, and Pete Rose. Dixie Walker is 30th; Kiki Cuyler, 39th. Bobby Thomson is ranked 59th, and Nicholson is a quite respectable 65th.

Responding to the war-time competition issue, James offered:

> Nicholson is entitled to more respect than he has received.... Yes, a lot of the good pitchers were not there, but on the other hand, the balata ball used during the war was not easy to drive.... Also, Nicholson's complaint about Wrigley

being a tough place to hit at that time is solid.... Putting these things together, I think Nicholson's war-time numbers are essentially legit.

Achieving his greatest success with the Cubs, Nicholson is still among the club's all-time leaders in games played (16th, with 1,349); doubles (15th, with 245); home runs (seventh, with 205); and RBIs (11th, with 833). In an era when the word "steroid" hadn't been invented, he led the Chicagoans in home runs for eight straight years, a club record later broken by Sammy Sosa. His eight career grand slams with the Cubs were exceeded only by Hall of Famer Ernie Banks. At the time of his retirement, Nicholson's 235 home runs ranked him 25th all-time among major league sluggers. It was thus no surprise when Vine Line, the official newspaper of the Cubs, selected Nicholson as an outfielder on its "All-Ivy" team in 1991. He joined 27 others Cubs greats, featuring 14 Hall of Famers and an outfield comprising Hack Wilson, Andy Pafko, Billy Williams, Kiki Cuyler, Riggs Stephenson, Andre Dawson, and Hank Sauer.

Nicholson was deceptively fast afoot. In 1952, at age 37, he was timed in 3.7 seconds from the batter's box to first base, 19th best in the National League. As hard as he struck the ball, he retired as one of the toughest men to double up in the history of the game, hitting into a double play only once every 90.7 at-bats.

Former teammate Putsy Caballero thought Bill's reputation suffered because of having played the majority of his baseball days in Chicago. "Nicholson spent the best years of his career in the Midwest with the Cubs," Caballero explained. "Back in those days, the coverage of ballplayers was heavily geared toward the east. The Yankees, for instance, might have 20 writers traveling along with their club, while the Cubs would be lucky to have six. Same with the rest of the east ballclubs — they always got more attention than the west."

Caballero considered Nicholson to be "one of the all-time greats. He wasn't exactly a Ted Williams or a Joe DiMaggio, but as an all-around player he was just one cut below those guys."

John Steadman, veteran Baltimore sportswriter, named his all-time Maryland baseball team in 1994, comprised of those who were born in the state. The battery was pitcher Lefty Grove and catcher Babe Phelps. The infield was comprised of first baseman Jimmie Foxx; second baseman and Negro League immortal Judy Johnson; third baseman Home Run Baker; and shortstop Cal Ripken, Jr. In the outfield were Babe Ruth in left; Al Kaline in center — and Bill Nicholson, in right.

Big Nick will never be enshrined in Cooperstown; in his first year of eligibility for the Hall, he received a grand total of one vote. He never received another. His meteoric rise and puzzling decline place him among the pantheon of players like Pete Reiser and "Smokey Joe" Wood, who — because of injury or illness — never lived up to their early billing. Even on his beloved Eastern Shore, Nicholson would probably be at the bottom of a list of homegrown greats: Foxx, Baker, and — of more recent vintage — Harold Baines, from St. Michaels.

How good he would have been, had he remained healthy, will never be known. What he accomplished in his brief run at the top was, however, pretty heady stuff for a farmer from Chestertown. There, Swish Nicholson will always be remembered, with affection, and there's a statue to prove it.

Appendix: Bill Nicholson's Regular Season Career Statistics and World Series Record

Year	Club	League	G	AB	R	H	2B	3B	HR	RBI	BA	FA
1936	Phila.	A.L.	11	12	2	0	0	0	0	0	.000	1.000
1936	Okla.City	Tex.	14	48	4	8	1	0	0	5	.167	.952
1937	W'msport	NY-P	10	23	5	5	1	0	1	9	.217	1.000
1937	P'mouth	Pied.	121	468	79	145	26	7	20	92	.310	.954
1938	W'msport	East.	137	511	96	154	26	17	22§	96	.301	.958
1939	Chatt'ga*	South.	105	383	82	128	29	8	23§	85	.334	.951
1939	Chicago	N.L.	58	220	37	65	12	5	5	38	.295	.955
1940	Chicago**	N.L.	135	491	78	146	27	7	25	98	.297	.951
1941	Chicago**	N.L.	147	532	74	135	26	1	26	98	.254	.971
1942	Chicago	N.L.	152	588	83	173	22	11	21	78	.294	.988
1943	Chicago**	N.L.	154	608	95	188	30	9	29§	128§	.309	.978
1944	Chicago**	N.L.	156	582	116	167	35	8	33§	122§	.287	.978
1945	Chicago	N.L.	151	559	82	136	28	4	13	88	.243	.990
1946	Chicago	N.L.	105	296	36	65	13	2	8	41	.220	.973
1947	Chicago	N.L.	148	487	69	119	28	1	26	75	.244	.990§
1948	Chicago†	N.L.	143	494	68	129	24	5	19	67	.261	.980
1949	Phila.	N.L.	98	299	42	70	8	3	11	40	.234	.995
1950	Phila.	N.L.	41	58	3	13	2	1	3	10	.224	.952
1951	Phila.	N.L.	85	170	23	41	9	2	8	30	.241	.981
1952	Phila.	N.L.	55	88	17	24	3	0	6	19	.273	.982
1953	Phila.	N.L.	38	62	12	13	5	1	2	16	.210	.977
M.L.	TOTALS	16 YRS	1677	5546	837	1484	272	60	235	948	.268	.979

*Sold to Chicago Cubs for $35,000.00, June 25, 1939
†Traded to Philadelphia Phillies for Harry Walker, October 4, 1948
§Led League
**Selected to National League All-Star team

World Series Record

Year	Club	League	G	AB	R	H	2B	3B	HR	RBI	BA	FA
1945	Chicago	N.L.	7	28	1	6	1	1	0	8*	.214	.900

*Tied major league record

Chapter Notes

Most of the material used in this book is from primary sources — newspapers, magazines, school records, public documents, videotapes, and interviews. Virtually all of the research was done by the author. Some of the source material was obtained from clippings in Nicholson's file at the National Baseball Library in Cooperstown, New York, which may be undated, or from a newspaper not readily identifiable. Any material derived from those sources is duly noted, with an explanation. Newspaper and magazine page numbers, where available and contained in the endnotes, represent the first page of the article cited.

The Marge Fallaw, Dan Rodricks, and Norman Macht interviews were transcribed from cassette tapes, to which the author listened, and have been punctuated for clarity.

Day-to-day accounts of baseball seasons, including statistics, were gleaned principally from the pages of the *Chicago Tribune, New York Times, Philadelphia Inquirer, Washington Post,* and *The Sporting News.*

Chapter 1

3 — "As late as ... 'another forgotten ballplayer.'" *Chicago Sun Times,* May 6, 1990, page 20.

6 — "A three story ... kitchen/servants' quarters." *Washington Post,* October 13, 1955, page 37.

6 — "Family lore holds ... refute the claim." Interview with Emily Joiner, December 12, 2004.

6 — "'I was born ... a few generations.'" Interview with Margaret Fallaw, May 12, 1984.

7 — "As a boy ... he occasionally drove." *Ibid.*

8 — "Nicholson remembered: 'We ... all the boys.'" *Ibid.*

8 — "One of the ... delight local children." *The Enterprise,* December 17, 1930.

8 — "Each of the ... and fruit trees." E-mail from Emily Joiner, July 13, 2005.

9 — "A prodigious fruit ... with the Cubs." *Chicago Tribune,* April 27, 1942, page 19.

9 — "Describing the family's ... 'horses and mules.'" Fallaw interview.

9 — "'We had a ... a big operation.'" *Ibid.*

9 — "In his youth ... could tote three." *Chicago Tribune,* April 18, 1942, page 19.

10 — "Bill had scant ... 'be second base!'" Fallaw interview.

10 — "'Back when I ... Cardinals] in 1926.'" *Queen Anne's Record-Observer,* October 28, 1987.

10 — "It was not ... other transportation available." Emily Joiner interview.

10 — "A local newspaper ... 'gun–like throwing arm.'" *The Enterprise,* March 19, 1930.

11 — "Though the Chestertonians ... county high schools." *Ibid.*, April 30, 1930.
11 — "Chestertown then bested ... the next week." *Ibid.*, December 10, 1930.
11 — "The match was ... a state championship." *Ibid.*, December 17, 1930, page 10.
11 — "With only a ... the winning shot." *Ibid.*, January 28, 1930.
12 — "Five days later ... in center field." *Ibid.*, June 24, 1930.
12 — "'He was my ... in the minors.'" — Westcott, *Diamond Greats*, page 244.
12 — "Nicholson did have ... the World Series." Interview with Norman Macht, August 11, 1989.
12 — "She remembered her ... 'the special one.'" — Interview with Miriam Hoffecker, December 12, 2004.
13 — "On Saturday nights ... the latest dances." *Ibid.*
14 — "'We got a ... in Kent County.'" Fallaw interview.
14 — "An editorial in ... 'and delayed justice.'" *The Enterprise*, December 9, 1931.
14 — "In 1920, when ... on as employees." United States Census, 1920 and 1930.
15 — "The Chestertown Athletics ... students from Garnet." *Baltimore Afro-American*, September 20, 1930, page 14.
15 — "A black outfielder ... into the pocket." *The Enterprise*, August 12, 1931.
15 — "A year before ... were really good." — *Chicago Cubs Quarterly*, June-July, 1993, page 124.
15 — "'Robinson was playing ... "rinky-dinks" in.'" Fallaw interview.
15 — "When hard times ... an excellent soup." *Ibid.*
16 — "The Nicholsons always ... and 'Cha-Cha.'" Emily Joiner interview.
16 — "By the time ... his adult size." Fallaw interview

Chapter 2

17 — "After Senators owner ... of Kibler's edict." Minor League Baseball.com, Team #8, Salisbury Indians.
17 — "'Yes it is ... the national pastime.'" Mowbray, *The Eastern Shore Baseball League*, page 43.
18 — "He neither smoked, ... athletes not to?'" Interview with Jane Bristoll, February 2, 2007.
18 — "Once a week ... for their children." Interview with Harrison Vickers, April 7, 2006.
18 — "'In football we ... a suitable sacrifice.'" Thompson, *Washington: The College at Chester*, page 218.
19 — "One former player ... 'think of Napolean.'" E-mail from Ed Athey, December 8, 2005.
20 — "Daily workouts were ... identify them, instead." E-mail from Ed Athey, December 7, 2005.
20 — "A stern taskmaster ... to his coaching." *Ibid.*
20 — "Recalling his football ... 'devil they were.'" *Washington College Alumni News*, Spring, 1987.
20 — "*The Enterprise* said ... 'lack is experience." *The Enterprise*, September 23, 1931.
21 — "The tiny Washington ... opening day patsies,..." Interview with Hurtt Deringer, December 30, 2004.
21 — "A preview of ... 'showing of 1930.'" *Washington Post*, September 26, 1931, page 13.
21 — "Sportswriter Bob Considine ... 'of the visitors.'" *Ibid.*, September 27, 1931, page M15.
21 — "A reporter for ... 'yard for yard....'" *The Enterprise*, September 30, 1931.
21 — "In an account ... 'desire, and more.'" *Washington Evening Star*, September 29, 1931.
22 — "Harrison Vickers, a ... must be mistaken." Vickers interview.
23 — "The *Washington Elm* ... 'next year's foes.'" *Washington Elm*, November 14, 1931.
23 — "Later he would ... 'couple of days.'" Fallaw interview.
23 — "Years after his ... their hitting skills." *The Sporting News*, April 17, 1941, page 4.
24 — "The local press ... 'class diamond prospects.'" *The Enterprise*, June 11, 1930.
24 — "The team's rabid ... the other teams." *Ibid.*, July 20, 1932, page 6.
25 — "Of young outfielder ... to a career." *Ibid.*
25 — "'One time, we ... in one year.'" Fallaw interview.
25 — "A verbose *Washington* ... 'the final whistle.'" *Washington Post*, September 25, 1932, page 13.
26 — "Echoing the *Post* ... 'avalanche of touchdowns.'" Beale, *Kings of American Football*, page 120.
26 — "But the *Diamondback*, ... 'the massacre stoically.'" *Diamondback*, September 26, 1932.
26 — "Said the *Elm* ... 'real plunging back....'" *Washington Elm*, October 8, 1932, page 1
26 — "One, Ellery Ward, ... 'to be great.'" *Sports Heritage*, July, 1987, page 7.
26 — "The next day's ... 'were off-side.'" *Washington Post*, October 9, 1932, page 18.
27 — "'A *Baltimore Sun* ... of the afternoon.'" *Baltimore Sun*, October 16, 1932.
27 — "The *Sun* reporter ... 'of the game.'" *Ibid.*, October 30, 1932.
27 — "The Shore gridders ... before game time." Interview with Charlie Berry, December 31, 2004.
28 — "Ticket takers were ... on the sidelines." *The Enterprise*, November 9, 1932.
29 — "After the 8–0 ... 'line practically unaided.'" *Washington Elm*, December 3, 1932.

29—"*The Enterprise* was ... 'hard to stop.'" *The Enterprise*, November 30, 1932, page 6.
29—"Nicholson always downplayed ... 'I got there.'" Fallaw interview.
29—"A special representative ... alcohol and tobacco." *Washington Elm*, March 11, 1933.
30—"'No one can ... alcohol or nicotine.'" *Anaconda Standard*, November 9, 1913, page 33.
30—"In the early ... long hard drives." *Washington Elm*, March 25, 1933, page 3.
30—"With the school ... League's Baltimore Orioles." Berry interview.
30—"Accustomed to making ... hand-me-downs." E-mail from Ed Athey, November 25, 2005.
31—"On a sultry ... University of Maryland." Berry interview.
31—"After the major ... first eight games." *Washington Post*, May 24, 1933, page 15.
32—"Shortstop Berry watched ... 'hit to me.'" Berry interview.
32—"Bill spent the ... 'a lot more.'" Fallaw interview.
32—"Whether Bill wanted ... 'was in Maryland.'" Campbell, *Famous American Athletes of Today*, page 240.
33—"In retirement, however, ... 'interested or not.'" Fallaw interview.
33—"The president wore ... chief executive's presence." Vickers interview.
33—"As basketball season ... 'ability and willingness.'" *Washington Elm*, January 13, 1934.
34—"The school yearbook ... 'not so successful.'" *Pegasus*, 1934.
34—"Physicals for the ... on June 7." *Washington Post*, June 8, 1934, page 6.
34—"After routine optical ... 'recommend your rejection.'" Campbell, *Famous American Athletes of Today*, page 249.

Chapter 3

35—"The local nine ... on the team." *The Transcript*, August 18, 1934.
35—"The Maroons held ... 'a "side injury."'" *Washington Post*, October 6, 1934.
35—"Occasionally, Gallaudet fielded ... 'of a bitch.'" Berry interview.
36—"A student correspondent ... ploughed Hopkins under." *Washington Elm*, October 27, 1934, page 2.
36—"The next week ... a gaudy 3–0." *Pegasus*, 1935.
38—"A student sportswriter ... 'score of 9–3.'" *Diamondback*, April 8, 1935.
38—"Days later, the ... 'an entire season.'" *Washington Post*, April 16, 1935, page 17.
38—"'Bill Nicholson seems ... the local squad.'" *Washington Elm*, May 4, 1935.
38—"Louis Goldstein, a ... 'make the run.'" *Washington College Magazine*, Summer, 1996, page 6.
39—"That contest was ... their return trip." *Washington Post*, May 12, 1935, page SP3.
39—"His team attracted ... by Hobart Tignor." Berry interview.
39—"As recently as ... 'have lost interest.'" *Galveston Daily News*, July 21, 1929, page 19.
39—"'I should have ... ideal for me....'" *Washington College Alumni News*, Spring, 1987, page 11.
40—"College teammate Charlie ... during the war." Berry interview.
40—"Margo Bailey, who ... always on display." Interview with Margo Bailey, December 28, 2004.
40—"H. Hurtt Deringer, ... 'quite a person.'" Deringer interview.
40—"His portrayal was ... 'in the men.'" Interview with Betty Beck Welton, February 21, 2005.
41—"After scoring the ... to defeat, 33–12." *Washington Elm*, November 2, 1935.
43—"Beneath his photo ... 'a good student.'" *Pegasus*, 1936.

Chapter 4

44—"As recorded in ... 'assigned a locker.'" *Philadelphia Inquirer*, June 11, 1936, page 21.
45—"Some players enjoyed ... nearly-empty stadium." Kuklick, *To Every Thing a Season*, page 73.
45—"Once, he went ... he calmly replied." en.wikipedia.org/wiki/Connie_Mack(baseball)
45—"'[In 1936] I ... like they did.'" Fallaw interview.
45—"The *Inquirer*'s James ... for the afternoon." *Philadelphia Inquirer*, June 14, 1936, page S1.
46—"'Mr. Mack should ... nerves took over.'" *Sports Collectors Digest*, January 9, 2000.
47—"Naktenis, from Duke ... 'hill by 1936.'" Interview with Pete Naktenis, October 24, 2006.
47—"Despite the fact ... 'of Nicholson's presence.'" *The Enterprise*, June 17, 1936, page 1.
47—"'I would like...' told a reporter." *Daily Oklahoman*, July 19, 1936.
48—"The correspondent for ... 'at the plate....'" *Ibid.*, July 27, 1936.
48—"'He hasn't been ... a good cut.'" *Ibid.*, July 29, 1936, page 11.
49—"Soon, Nicholson's spirited ... 'what really counts.'" *Ibid.*, July 31, 1936, page 15.
49—"Bus Ham, the ... 'strong and true.'" *Daily Oklahoman*, July 29, 1936, page 11.
49—"Bill stopped off ... the artificial illumination." *The Enterprise*, August 5, 1936, page 2.
49—"John Drebinger of ... 'mind would dictate.'" *New York Times*, August 16, 1936, page S1.

50—"'I'd sit on ... third great team.'" Fallaw interview.
50—"From Mack, Nicholson ... all of 'em." Interview with Norman Macht, August 11, 1989.
50—"Jess Hill, who ... 'and the Yankees....'" *Washington Post*, December 21, 1937, page 19.
50—"Bill Werber, who ... 'or my way?'" Interview with Bill Werber, January 23, 2007.
51—"The veterans, including ... and baseball gear." *Ibid.*
51—"The A's went ... could even begin." NEA Services dispatch, March 23, 1937.
51—"The *Elm* reported ... 'seen him work.'" *Washington Elm*, February 27, 1937, page 1.
52—"Sports columnist Red ... 'of the squad.'" *New York Herald Tribune*, October 31, 1953.
52—"Sixty years later, ... being in camp." Werber interview.
52—"'Nobody went to ... morning,' recalled Nicholson." Fallaw interview.
52—"'We rooted for ... bulls,' Werber said." Werber interview.
54—"Werber had the ... *'despacio, por favor!'*" Werber interview.
54—"Upon hearing of ... old man's reply." *New York Herald Tribune*, October 31, 1953.

Chapter 5

55—"A sportswriter for ... 'and defensive skill.'" *Gazette and Bulletin*, April 20, 1937, page 9.
56—"With a record ... according to Bill." Fallaw interview.
57—"After the game, ... 'major league slugger.'" *Norfolk Virginian-Pilot*, May 14, 1937.
58—"'Sometimes we'd play ... sleeping all night.'" Fallaw interview.
58—"'The third one ... base,' he recounted." *The Sporting News*, April 22, 1953.
58—"'[W]hen we were ... shack,' Nicholson recalled." Fallaw interview.
59—"The *Virginian-Pilot* ... 'scored four runs.'" *Norfolk Virginian-Pilot*, August 1, 1937.
59—"Schacht, who was ... the Red Sox." Boston, *1939*, page 191.
60—"Of the local ... 'ready this year.'" *Norfolk Virginian-Pilot*, August 13, 1937.
60—"A newspaper account ... 'his circuit clout.'" *Ibid.*, August 18, 1937.
61—"When the Grays ... or hell-raiser.'" Interview with Randy Gumpert, December 31, 2004.
61—"Though his team ... game against Albany." *Grit*, June 19, 1938.
62—"Reporting on a ... 'in center field.'" *Ibid.*, June 12, 1938.
62—"A local columnist, ... 'worth a trial.'" *Ibid.*, August 7, 1938.
63—"'That was my ... college in mathematics.'" Macht interview.

63—"He later told ... 'you have him.'" *Chattanooga Daily Times*, May 4, 1939.
64—"'People used to ... we just clicked.'" www.baseballpilgrimages.com/engelstadium
64—"'Nicholson is not ... a close play!'" *Chattanooga Daily Times*, April 2, 1939.
64—"[O]ne of the...' converted Gammon asserted." *Ibid.*, April 13, 1939.
65—"With war clouds ... 'in the nose!'" *Ibid.*, April 17, 1939.
65—"Before the home ... 'Watch our smoke!'" *Ibid.*, April 18, 1939.
65—"I'll take $50,000.00 ... built for him.'" *Ibid.*, July 24, 1939.
65—"'You stayed at ... to the hotel.'" Fallaw interview.
66—"On the occasion ... 'fell an ox.'" *Chattanooga Daily Times*, May 6, 1939.
67—"Yet another scoring ... 'him loud applause.'" *Ibid.*, May 27, 1939.
68—"But Dodgers general ... 'a great hitter.'" *New York Herald Tribune*, August 16, 1944.
68—"At a Shriners ... 'before the other.'" *Chattanooga Daily Times*, June 23, 1939.
69—"The Brooklyn general ... 'ahead of him.'" *New York Herald Tribune*, August 16, 1944.
69—"In the second ... 'him,' Wrigley commanded." *New York Times*, March 27, 1943, page 17.
69—"'Kiki Cuyler phoned ... we bought him.'" Associated Press dispatch, July 8, 1939.
69—"Bill laconically recounted ... 'the Chicago Cubs.'" Fallaw interview.
69—"'I should have...' declined Engel's invitation" *Chattanooga Daily Times*, June 26, 1939.
70—"He pointed out ... 'show me something?'" *Ibid.*, July 8, 1939.
70—"He is the ... league,' Richards insisted." *Ibid.*, July 7, 1939.
70—"That hurts my ... of baseball here.'" *Ibid.*, June 26, 1939.
70—"Before Bill's last ... the minor leagues.'" *Ibid.*, July 23, 1939.
71—"Nicholson was touched ... nice to me!'" *Ibid.*, July 26, 1939.
71—"A local sportswriter ... of the park.'" *Ibid.*, July 30, 1939, page 9.

Chapter 6

72—"'I feel I...' French told reporters." *Chicago Tribune*, August 1, 1939, page 21.
74—"They tell me ... major league stuff.'" NEA Service dispatch, August 8, 1939.
74—"'One time I ... interested in it.'" Macht interview.
74—"Former Cubs infielder ... met Mr. Wrigley.'" Golenbock, *Wrigleyville*, page 284.
74—"I have only ... game this season.'" Associated Press dispatch, July 8, 1939.

74 — "Moments before the ... expression of discontent." *New York Times*, August 2, 1939, page 27.
75 — "The next day, ... 'of the afternoon.'" *Chicago Tribune*, August 2, 1939, page 23.
75 — "The *Trib* reporter ... 'behind the foliage.'" *Ibid.*, August 5, 1939, page 11.
75 — "Collisions with the ... 'off that wall.'" Fallaw interview.
75 — "Yeah, one year ... going to be.'" *Ibid.*

Chapter 7

80 — "Veteran PCL scribe ... the '40 Cubs." *Los Angeles Times*, March 24, 1940, page A14.
80 — "In his tell-all ... 'against the fence.'" Durocher, *Nice Guys Finish Last*, page 188.
80 — "In July, 1945 ... 'a big beast.'" Associated Press dispatch, July 11, 1945.
81 — "'Durocher always appealed...' been the best." Macht interview.
82 — "He credited Cubs ... 'away from me.'" *Chicago Tribune*, April 9, 1940, page 19.
82 — "According to former ... the injured area." Vitti, *The Cubs on Catalina*, page 218.
82 — "His wife told ... rejoin the team." *Chicago Tribune*, April 12, 1940, page 25.
82 — "A disgusted Wrigley ... 'side-show attraction.'" Vitti, *The Cubs on Catalina*, page 136.
83 — "A perplexed Hartnett ... 'find another starter.'" *Chicago Tribune*, May 12, 1940, page 19.
83 — "Nicholson was still ... 'as left fielders.'" *Ibid.*, May 14, 1940, page 21.
84 — "'When it got ... that way today.'" Nicholson letter to Bill Mortell, December 10, 1984.
84 — "'One day, he ... have killed me.'" Macht interview.
84 — "Phil Cavarretta recalled ... 'still there today.'" Interview with Phil Cavarretta, January 5, 2007.
84 — "'Chicago was a ... hitters,' he said." Theodore, *Baseball's Natural*, page 39.
85 — "Stewart said: I've ... in center field." *The Sporting News*, April 21, 1948, page 15.
87 — "*Trib* correspondent Edward ... 'to the occasion.'" *Chicago Tribune*, July 20, 1940, page 15.
87 — "'They lowered the ... 'Knock him down!'" Macht interview.
88 — "Remembering this unique ... 'seen it since.'" Fallaw interview.
91 — "Just before the ... 'figure it out.'" *Chicago Tribune*, September 29, 1940, page B5.

Chapter 8

92 — "Branch Rickey, the ... 'glorified office boy.'" http://www.historicbaseball.com
92 — "Bill described the ... 'me any money.'" Macht interview.

93 — "After listening to ... 'in your head.'" *Ibid.*
94 — "'I can't see ... for the background.'" *New York Journal-American*, July 25, 1944, page 14.
95 — "Edward Burns, writing ... 'of outfield barriers.'" *Chicago Tribune*, April 28, 1941, page 19.
95 — "'Oh, God, he ... have that trait.'" Macht interview.
96 — "His manager was ... 'been against lefties.'" *Washington Post*, June 11, 1941, page 20.
96 — "John Kieran, of ... 'hits mean runs.'" *New York Times*, May 20, 1941, page 32.
96 — "After a 2-1 ... 'nearly white, shirts.'" *Chicago Tribune*, May 16, 1941, page 25.
97 — "The *Times*' Kieran ... 'over in flocks.'" *New York Times*, June 17, 1941, page 25.
97 — "One sportswriter thought ... 'his hits count.'" Newspaper clipping in National Baseball Library, by Will Wedge, June 10, 1941.
97 — "He told *Chicago* ... 'pitch you like.'" *Sport*, August, 1947, page 50.
97 — "Nicholson recounted: 'I ... advantage over us.'" Fallaw interview.
97 — "The action was ... 'actual optical hazard.'" *Chicago Tribune*, July 3, 1941, page 19.
97 — "*The Sporting News* ... 'soothing of all.'" *The Sporting News*, March 19, 1942, page 3.
98 — "From his home ... 'United States alone.'" *Chicago Tribune*, July 5, 1941, page 2.
98 — "'I did fairly ... It really broke.'" Fallaw interview.
99 — "Nicholson described the ... 'won it, 7-5.'" *Ibid.*
100 — "Responding to criticism, ... 'such a team....'" *Chicago Tribune*, August 27, 1941.

Chapter 9

102 — "In mid-January, ... the daytime hours." *Washington Post*, January 17, 1942, page 18.
103 — "He'd laid off ... diminished batting average." *Id*, March 19, 1942, page 3.
103 — "Gallagher barred them ... 'dictated or not.'" *Los Angeles Times*, February 19, 1942, page 14.
103 — "Lowrey, a native ... 'the salary offered.'" *Ibid.*, February 21, 1942, page 12.
104 — "Andy Lotshaw concurred ... 'troubles are over.'" *Chicago Tribune*, February 27, 1942, page 26.
104 — "Jimmie Wilson established ... 7:30 every morning." *Ibid.*, February 23, 1942, page 25.
105 — "In the seventh ... 'baseball comedian] fashion.'" *Ibid.*, March 23, 1942, page 17.
106 — "Dan Daniel, writing ... '[sic] cigar stores.'" *The Sporting News*, April 2, 1942, page 4.

106—"Catcher McCullough and ... Dick Spalding intervened." *Chicago Tribune,* April 4, 1942, page 19.
106—"As the start ... 'with you ears.'" *Washington Post,* April 7, 1942, page 19.
107—"When first greeted ... 'over the wall.'" *The Sporting News,* August 17, 1949, page 14.
108—"He explained to ... 'on the road.'" Macht interview.
108—"Nicholson and the ... 'jocularly, others not.'" *Ft. Worth Star-Telegram,* March 12, 1995, page 7.
109—"The next year ... 'take him out.'" Gilbert, *They Also Served,* page 105.
109—"According to Durocher ... 'to beat us.'" *The Sporting News,* June 4, 1942, page 5.
109—"We did this ... after the game." *Ibid.,* May 28, 1942.
110—"When he retired ... 'I ever saw.'" *Philadelphia Evening Bulletin,* October 30, 1953.
110—"Gallagher told the ... 'he's still dangerous.'" *Chicago Tribune,* June 2, 1942, page 25.
110—"'I saw him ... a nice fellow.'" *Queen Anne's Record-Observer,* November 11, 1987.
110—"'I know one ... plenty of power.'" Macht interview.
112—"Ed Burns wryly ... 'the Dodger cave.'" *Chicago Tribune,* July 16, 1942, page 19.
112—"Cubs infielder Len ... 'could get you.'" Golenbock, *Wrigleyville,* page 299.
112—"Frustrated Jimmie Wilson ... 'at becoming paralyzed.'" *New York Times,* August 2, 1942, page S1.
112—"Reds' broadcaster Sam ... during the year." *The Sporting News,* August 13, 1942, page 18.
113—"He recited the ... 'won both games!'" *Pittsburgh Press,* May 29, 1953.

Chapter 10

116—"Jimmie Wilson told ... 'where they are.'" *New York Times,* March 26, 1943, page 22.
116—"After all, Gallagher ... in the league." *The Sporting News,* October 22, 1942, page 13.
116—"They settled their ... 'do,' Gallagher explained." Associated Press dispatch, March 30, 1943.
116—"Edward Burns of ... 'affable Maryland athlete.'" *Chicago Tribune,* March 30, 1943, page 19.
117—"'This is the ... take French Lick.'" *Ibid.,* April 12, 1943.
117—"Of Nicholson, he ... 'clingy crocheted numbers.'" *Ibid.,* March 28, 1943, page A2.
117—"'So far as...' of Bill's clout." *The Sporting News,* August 12, 1943, page 13.
118—"Edward Burns cracked ... 'are cheese hitters.'" *Chicago Tribune,* May 3, 1943, page 25.
118—"Informed of Novikoff's ... 'am, buddy boy.'" *Washington Post,* May 7, 1943, page 16.
118—"Asked if he ... 'to do something.'" *Ibid.,* May 24, 1943, page 21.
119—"I was standing ... 'more,' he explained." *The Sporting News,* June 10, 1943, page 10.
121—"In 1955, when ... 'out,' he said." *Ibid.,* April 6, 1955, page 4.
121—"He was playing ... 'going into battle.'" *Ibid.,* September 9, 1943, page 4.
122—"Brooklyn's Johnny Cooney ... 'the game starts.'" Gilbert, *They Also Served,* page 104.
122—"'He's the greatest ... improve his play.'" *The Sporting News,* October 21, 1943, page 2.
122—"He told a ... 190] in 1930.'" *Chicago Cubs Quarterly,* June-July, 1993, page 124.
123—"'We frequently make ... rewarded him accordingly.'" *The Sporting News,* October 21, 1943, page 15.
123—"He returned to ... 'been all summer?'" Roberts, *My Life in Baseball,* page 49.

Chapter 11

124—"Former Cubs teammate ... 'as a bull.'" Golenbock, *Wrigleyville,* page 297.
124—"'People's memories are...' said Jim Revord." E-mail from Jim Revord, July 8, 2005.
125—"A safety patrol ... idol, Bill Nicholson." Interview with Bill Stone, January 15, 2007.
125—"One visitor expressed ... long-ago baseball accomplishments." E-mail from Jim Revord, July 8, 2005, E-mail from Jim Revord, July 8, 2005.
125—"The woman who ... 'or I'll sue!'" *New York Times,* September 21, 1945, page 24.
125—"When Bill was ... 'clear these houses.'" *Chattanooga Daily Times,* July 30, 1939.
125—"Another legend holds ... struck his windowsill." Kuklick, *To Every Thing a Season,* page 109.
126—"Roger Miller grew ... and rival Ott." Interview with Roger Miller, November, 2005.
126—"Remembering the game, ... 'hit one better.'" Macht interview.
127—"*Trib* columnist Arch ... 'chewers,' Ward wrote." *Chicago Tribune,* March 14, 1942, page 19.
127—"Perhaps in response ... 'tobacco,' he claimed." *Washington College Alumni News,* Spring, 1987, page 11.
127—"When Nicholson was ... 'of the slump.'" *The Sporting News,* June 27, 1983, page 9.
127—"Nicholson's other principal ... 'both smoked them.'" Interview with Phil Cavarretta, January 5, 2007.
128—"'They'd slide them ... runs to eat!'" Golenbock, *Wrigleyville,* page 295.

Notes — Chapters 12, 13

128 — "At the end ... switched to oatmeal." Emily Joiner interview.
128 — "On a road ... the fire out." Cavarretta interview.
128 — "During a road ... his money back." Roberts, *My Life in Baseball*, page 112.
129 — "As Ed Athey ... 'cutting the air.'" *Washington College Magazine*, Summer, 1996, page 14.
129 — "Nicholson advanced at ... 'with each swing.'" Westcott, *Diamond Greats*, page 241.
130 — "This account is ... 'formidable preparatory swings.'" *New York World Telegram & Sun*, July 27, 1944.
130 — "*Chicago Daily News* ... 'and hated enemy.'" *Sport*, August, 1947, page 50.
130 — "Dodgers radio announcer ... 'swung the bat.'" *New York Times*, October 3, 1943, page SM10.

Chapter 12

132 — "Recalling Nicholson's encounter ... 'the ... dining hall.'" *The Sporting News*, September 9, 1943, page 8.
132 — "Ed Burns suggested ... 'ever mentioning salary.'" *Ibid*.
132 — "There was at ... 'didn't like him.'" Cavarretta interview.
133 — "He explained to ... 'percentage in that.'" *Washington Post*, April 6, 1944, page 12.
134 — "After early use, ... 'a golf ball.'" *Time*, April 10, 1944.
134 — "'You can always ... top condition yet.'" *Chicago Tribune*, April 26, 1944, page 27.
135 — "Shortly after he ... worry about that.'" *Ibid.*, May 10, 1944, page 25.
135 — "'Under Charlie we ... out of it.'" Golenbock, *Wrigleyville*, page 295.
135 — "Dour Irving Vaughan ... 'so-called cleanup hitter.'" *Chicago Tribune*, May 11, 1944, page 25.
135 — "Decades later, he ... 'your claps, too.'" Fallaw interview.
136 — "'I'd have to ... plate,' he joked." *The Sporting News*, June 15, 1944, page 10.
136 — "When Jimmie Wilson ... 'other team's bench.'" *Chicago Tribune*, June 21, 1944, page 21.
136 — "It was a ... 'between the horns.'" Fallaw interview.
137 — "Columnist Red Smith ... 'to be treasured.'" *New York Herald Tribune*, October 31, 1953.
137 — "Venerable Arch Ward, ... 'Mrs. Nancy Nicholson....'" *Chicago Tribune*, July 11, 1944, page 19.
137 — "'They are ball ... can beat them.'" *The Sporting News*, July 20, 1944, page 6.
137 — "Nicholson wasn't in ... to the plate." Campbell, *Great American Athletes of Today*, page 237.

138 — "Cardinals' manager Billy ... 'way, weren't they?'" *New York Times*, July 11, 1944, page 14.
138 — "'Do you know ... 'really enjoyed it.'" *The Sporting News*, July 13, 1944.
139 — "The big pitcher ... 'the live ball.'" Westcott, *Masters of the Diamond*, page 152.
139 — "'I hit two ... can hit anything.'" Westcott, *Diamond Greats*, page 244.
139 — "In the second ... in his second." Fallaw interview.
140 — "His message to ... 'Put him on.'" *Chicago Tribune*, March 17, 1996, section 3, page 14.
140 — "Cubs outfielder Andy ... 'talked about it.'" *Chicago Tribune*, March 17, 1996, section 3, page 14.
140 — "Writing in *The* ... 'over the fences!'" *The Sporting News*, July 27, 1944, page 17.
140 — "'They ought to ... o'clock last night!'" Newspaper clipping from National Baseball Library, "Nick's Blood Pressure Low, RBI Mark High," by Lester Rice, July 24, 1944.
141 — "When asked to ... 'two days, rather.'" *New York Journal-American*, July 25, 1944.
142 — "After a Cubs ... 'of right field.'" *New York Times*, August 11, 1944, page 10.
142 — "*L.A. Times* columnist ... 'down there again.'" *Los Angeles Times*, August 13, 1944, page A5.
143 — "*The Sporting News* ... 'men on bases.'" *The Sporting News*, September 14, 1944, page 10.
143 — "'Marty probably deserved...' he could say." *Chicago Tribune*, March 17, 1996.
143 — "Of his own ... 'fairly good year.'" *Chicago Cubs Quarterly*, June-July, 1993, page 124.
143 — "Dan Daniel of ... 'poll,' he complained." *New York World Telegram & Sun*, December 9, 1944.

Chapter 13

146 — "At the start ... 'by wartime standards.'" *Washington Post*, March 17, 1945, page 8.
146 — "Bill was working ... National League rivals." *New York Times*, March 21, 1945, page 28.
146 — "He was photographed ... and Freddie Fitzsimmons." *Life*, April 23, 1945.
146 — "'I am going ... when I report.'" *The Sporting News*, March 22, 1945, page 17.
147 — "Of the contract ... 'get a raise.'" Macht interview.
148 — "It was a ... '*The Sporting News*.'" *The Sporting News*, May 24, 1945, page 10.
150 — "A Chicago fan ... 'go the Cubs.'" *Chicago Tribune*, June 6, 1945, page 23.
150 — "He had his ... 'I couldn't stop.'" *New York World Telegram & Sun*, July 18, 1947.
151 — "Nancy drove over ... 255 batting average." *Chicago Tribune*, July 24, 1945, page 15.

152 — "Manager Bill McKechnie ... 'seven inning pitcher.'" *Ibid.*, August 10, 1945, page 19.
152 — "Outside the park ... 'Dodgers!,' she exclaimed." *New York Times*, August 18, 1945, page 14.
153 — "During the Brooklyn ... 'game for us.'" *Ibid.*, September 21, 1945, page 24.
153 — "Another New York ... 'explode nobody knows.'" Gilbert, *They Also Served*, page 227.
153 — "The *Trib*'s Edward ... 'of slugging coordination.'" *Chicago Tribune*, August 28, 1945, page 17.
153 — "'I just gave ... at the ball.'" Associated Press dispatch, September 7, 1945.
154 — "Referring to Yankee ... 'Batting for Ruth.'" Gilbert, *They Also Served*, page 228.
155 — "Desperate to redeem ... during the season." *New York Times*, October 4, 1945, page 19.
156 — "Despite Lotshaw's efforts ... Tigers never scored." *Ibid.*, page 18.
156 — "Coach Roy Johnson ... 'need them tomorrow!'" *Chicago Tribune*, October 4, 1945, page 29.
156 — "'I think I ... boys real well.'" *Washington Post*, October 5, 1945, page 14.
157 — "Afterwards, Passeau conducted ... 'hit the screen.'" *Chicago Tribune*, October 6, 1945, page 21.
157 — "Even Edward Burns ... 'even six games....'" *Ibid.*, page 19.
158 — "Behind the right ... to make $450.00." *Washington Post*, October 8, 1945, page 11.
158 — "A Greek immigrant ... from the ballpark." *Chicago Tribune*, October 6, 1945, page A1.
158 — "After the game ... 'base hits tomorrow.'" *New York Times*, October 7, 1945, page S1.
158 — "When Borowy was ... 'call your office!'" *Washington Post*, October 8, 1945, page 11.
159 — "Novelist Ward just ... 'like a stevedore,....'" *Ibid.*, October 15, 2003, section 5, page 1.
159 — "'That's a pretty ... an unlucky fan.'" *Ibid.*, October 11, 1945.
159 — "Many of the ... 'have a prayer.'" Macht interview.
160 — "Afterward, a friend ... 'third and home.'" Gilbert, *They Also Served*, page 256.
160 — "An anonymous teammate ... 'something to him.'" *Chicago Tribune*, October 9, 1945.
161 — "'There was something ... sugar in 1945.'" Fallaw interview

Chapter 14

162 — "Ed Burns knew ... 'in the process.'" *The Sporting News*, February 21, 1946, page 12.
162 — "Although not surprised ... 'whacked that hard.'" Associated Press dispatch, March 3, 1946.
162 — "The outfielder told ... 'for another job.'" *Chicago Tribune*, February 14, 1946, page 29.
163 — "When Meyer told ... 'the big leagues!'" *Ibid.*, March 2, 1949.
164 — "'I'm optimistic over ... will, this year.'" *Washington Post*, February 16, 1946, page 8.
164 — "After making several ... 'reads about this.'" Vitti, *The Cubs on Catalina*, page 63.
164 — "According to an ... 'I showed up.'" Westcott, *Diamond Greats*, page 244.
165 — "Grimm stuck by ... 'again this summer.'" *Los Angeles Times*, March 28, 1946, page A6.
165 — "In dusty Del ... 'may take time.'" *Chicago Tribune*, April 4, 1946, page 29.
167 — "'Nicholson in a ... of,' he insisted." *The Sporting News*, April 25, 1946, page 20.
167 — "One letter writer ... 'for Bill Nicholson.'" *Chicago Tribune*, April 26, 1946.
167 — "Curtis McKinney, of ... 'club a lot.'" *Ibid.*, June 9, 1946, page A5.
167 — "Jimmy Britt, the ... the front seat." *The Sporting News*, July 10, 1946, page 18.
168 — "'Maybe the [thieves] ... change my luck.'" *New York Times*, June 3, 1946, page 36.
168 — "And when he ... 'bats were missing?'" *Chicago Tribune*, June 24, 1946.
170 — "The score was ... manager's blunt assessment." *Chicago Sun–Times*, May 15, 2005.
170 — "My shoulders have ... 'of the trouble.'" *The Sporting News*, October 9, 1946, page 22.
171 — "Gallagher was firm ... 'in Buddy Kerr.'" *New York Times*, December 3, 1946, page 45.

Chapter 15

172 — "Nick will be ... 'on April 15.'" *Chicago Tribune*, March 1, 1947, page 19.
174 — "After being examined ... 'heat won't cure....'" *Ibid.*, April 9, 1947, page 33.
174 — "Dr. Braun seemed ... 'rest and heat.'" *Ibid.*
174 — "One day in ... 'the bat handle.'" *Sport*, August, 1947, page 50.
175 — "Roscoe McGowan of ... 'the old slugger.'" *New York Times*, May 1, 1947.
175 — "'He needs rest ... meals,' Rickey scolded." *Chicago Defender*, May 3, 1947.
175 — "Jackie was exhausted ... 'let Robinson alone.'" *Ibid.*
176 — "A Cubs official ... average Sunday fans....'" *Ibid.*, May 24, 1947.
176 — "A fan was ... hit a balloon!'" *Chicago Tribune*, May 25, 1947, page A4.
178 — "'I've been trying ... hitting against him.'" *New York World Telegram & Sun*, July 18, 1947.
178 — "One presumably well-intentioned ... 'throw and eat.'" *Sport*, August, 1947, page 50.

178—"Despite his struggles ... 'at your newsdealers.'" *Chicago Tribune*, July 28, 1947, page 30.
178—"Billy Stone bought ... the box away." Stone interview.
179—"Nicholson remembered the ... 'by Babe Young.'" *Washington Post*, August 9, 1947.
180—"In later years, ... 'ball pretty well.'" *Sports Heritage*, July/August, 1987, page 6.
180—"'There'll be no...' joked to reporters." *Chicago Tribune*, December 11, 1947, page 57.

Chapter 16

181—"'Bill is a ... as a result.'" *Long Beach Press Telegram*, March 8, 1948.
182—"'I have six ... on the deal.'" *Washington Post*, March 5, 1948, page 10.
182—"'I think I'm ... real good years.'" *The Sporting News*, April 14, 1948, page 16.
182—"'That's how I ... the bat through.'" *Ibid*.
183—"'I always had ... Lanier or Brazle.'" Westcott, *Diamond Greats*, page 245.
184—"'I certainly was ... he played hard.'" Roberts, *My Life in Baseball*, page 48.
184—"Cardinals pitcher Red ... 'and me too.'" *The Sporting News*, July 21, 1948, page 20.
185—"Mirroring the fans ... 'flop after another.'" *Chicago Tribune*, July 22, 1948, page B1.
185—"He remembered the ... 'sswwishh of his.'" Interview with Bobby Thomson, November 30, 2005.
187—"Knowing how much ... 'and my family.'" *New York Times*, September 1, 1948, page 28.
187—"In the season's ... 'will try another.'" *The Sporting News*, September 8, 1948, page 8.
187—"As one fan ... 'for several years.'" *Chicago Tribune*, August 3, 1948, page B1.
187—"He wrote to ... 'was really dangerous.'" Nicholson letter to Bill Mortell, December 10, 1984.
188—"'I just can't ... get the rhythm.'" *The Sporting News*, March 2, 1949.
188—"As one forlorn ... 'Phillies: Bill Nicholson.'" *Chicago Tribune*, December 31, 1948, page A1.

Chapter 17

189—"Early in the ... 'ones to beat.'" *Chicago Tribune*, March 18, 1949, page B3.
190—"'Every day he'd ... and be around!'" *Baltimore Sun*, October 8, 1995.
190—"Ashburn and Putsy ... 'out of you.'" *Sports Heritage*, July/August, 1987, page 6.
190—"Hank Borowy, who ... the clubhouse entrance." *Washington Post*, March 19, 1949, page 15.
190—"He told reporters ... 'against Grimm's Cubs.'" *Chicago Tribune*, March 2, 1949.

191—"The irate Carpenter ... in the fifth." *Washington Post*, March 23, 1949, page 17.
191—"'Irving of Evanston ... of the park?'" *Chicago Tribune*, January 11, 1949, page B1.
191—"Alfred Link of ... they were traded.'" *Ibid.*, March 22, 1949, page B3.
193—"After the game ... 'hit the ball.'" Theodore, *Baseball's Natural*, page 40.
193—"One of them ... stands, and smiled." Stone interview.
194—"It felt as ... told reporters afterward." *Chicago Tribune*, May 31, 1949.
195—"The woman then ... souvenirs and memorabilia." *Chicago Tribune*, June 15–16, 1949, page 1 in each edition.
196—"Said Bill of ... 'a finer guy.'" Theodore, *Baseball's Natural*, page 12.
196—"'I'm rarin' to...' of the season." *Chicago Tribune*, July 18, 1949.
197—"Several days later ... 'on the x-ray.'" Roberts, *My Life in Baseball*, page 57.
197—"'There has to ... a soft living.'" *The Sporting News*, August 31, 1949, page 7.
199—"'Come back next ... all next year.'" Roberts, *My Life in Baseball*, page 64

Chapter 18

200—"Of the early ... 'in the sponge.'" *Chicago Tribune*, March 4, 1950, page A3.
200—"'Well, I might ... and very good.'" Macht interview.
201—"'Eddie, Russ and ... after the shooting.'" Theodore, *Baseball's Natural*, page 57.
201—"'Maybe it's better...' the new season." *Washington Post*, March 14, 1950, page 14.
202—"Despite his injury ... 'never did before.'" *The Sporting News*, March 29, 1950, page 11.
202—"A jittery Waitkus ... 'this series alive.'" Theodore, *Baseball's Natural*, page 72.
202—"One shouted to ... contests; and Waitkus." *Ibid*.
204—"Naturally, Durocher raced ... of the game." *New York Times*, August 13, 1950, page S1.
204—"Describing Rigney's reaction ... 'would hit him.'" Roberts, *My Life in Baseball*, page 76.
205—"When the game ... 'as I'm concerned.'" *New York Times*, August 13, 1950, page S1.
205—"'I'd develop a ... thirsty and hungry.'" *Pittsburgh Press*, May 29, 1953.
205—"He told the ... 'horrible mental state.'" Theodore, *Baseball's Natural*, page 75.
205—"Returning on the ... several weeks later." *The Sporting News*, January 7, 1953, page 33.
205—"Before the first ... talk to Wiechec." Roberts, *My Life in Baseball*, page 79.
206—"'This thing got ... in tight games.'" United Press dispatch, March 28, 1951.

206 — "'One of the...' he said ruefully." Macht interview.
206 — "The day before ... 'of 'em back.'" *New York Times*, October 4, 1950, page 50.
207 — "Nicholson shared his ... 'same for us.'" Associated Press, October 5, 1950.
207 — "Later, he expressed ... 'been a liability.'" *Wilmington News Journal*, October 18, 1980, page A3.

Chapter 19

208 — "'On a hot ... lump of sugar.'" *Pittsburgh Press*, May 29, 1953.
208 — "Hearkening back to ... 'here I am.'" United Press dispatch, March 28, 1951.
208 — "Now he said: ... 'year of experience.'" *Ibid.*, April 4, 1951.
208 — "A preseason United ... 'his 35 years.'" *Ibid.*
209 — "Baumgartner wrote in ... 'on the club.'" *The Sporting News*, April 11, 1951, page 10.
210 — "Giants scout Hans ... 'ain't high enough.'" *Ibid.*, August 17, 1951, page 17.
211 — "Robin Roberts, 'the ... anything,' he said." Roberts, *My Life in Baseball*, page 105.
212 — "'All that World ... the manager complained.'" Theodore, *Baseball's Natural*, page 86.
212 — "When Waitkus heard ... 'single out Eddie.'" *Ibid.*
212 — "Del Ennis and ... 'him,' Sawyer crowed." *The Sporting News*, November 7, 1951, page 8.
212 — "In November, Bill ... 'in her mind.'" Theodore, *Baseball's Natural*, page 95.

Chapter 20

213 — "Sawyer had a ... 'it — see Sawyer.'" *The Sporting News*, March 26, 1952, page 18; April 2, 1952, page 8.
214 — "In retrospect, Bill ... 'his ball club.'" Macht interview.
214 — "Two weeks before ... Phils' 1953 plans." *The Sporting News*, October 8, 1952, page 22.
215 — "CBS radio broadcast ... Association's detection drive." *Ibid.*, November 19, 1952, page 26.
215 — "Stan Baumgartner remarked: ... 'feel much better....'" *Ibid.*, June 10, 1953, page 11.
215 — "But as the ... 'I wasn't right.'" Macht interview.
216 — "He discussed, with ... 'of the day.'" *Pittsburgh Press*, May 29, 1953.
216 — "In early September, ... 'that I'm finished.'" *Philadelphia Evening Bulletin*, September 9, 1953.
216 — "Still, Nicholson had ... 'has to come.'" *Philadelphia Evening Bulletin*, September 9, 1953.
217 — "He returned home, ... manage or coach." *Kent County News*, October 2, 1953, page 5.
217 — "'He's been a ... players,' he said." *Philadelphia Evening Bulletin*, October 30, 1953.
217 — "The *Salisbury* (Md.) ... by mid–January, 1954." *Salisbury Times*, December 2, 1953, page 14.
217 — "When pressed by ... 'some great catches.'" *Philadelphia Inquirer*, October 30, 1953.
217 — "He railed against ... 'highly competitive market.'" *Ibid.*

Chapter 21

218 — "Mackey Dutton, a ... 'all the time.'" Interview with Mackey Dutton, January 3, 2005.
219 — "'In the '30s' ... businessman, was bisexual." www.camprehoboth.com/issue06_28_02/camp_memories.htm
219 — "Elmer Horsey, her ... 'helping the unfortunate.'" Interview with Elmer Horsey, May, 2006.
219 — "Eugenia Bankhead was ... to see her." *Washington Post*, August 22, 1949, page B2.
220 — "In the company ... on the continent." Deringer interview.
220 — "Harrison Vickers remembers ... an odd couple." Vickers interview.
220 — "In the early ... on the job." Elmer Horsey interview.
220 — "Alan Joiner, who ... 'week,' he growled." Interview with Alan Joiner, January 7, 2007.
221 — "As Bill donned ... his, in unison." Alan Joiner interview.
221 — "Bill told Margaret ... 'and not happy.'" Fallaw interview.
222 — "At the gravesite, ... of the ceremony." *Washington Post*, December 15, 1968, page D20.
223 — "Nicholson regularly responded ... 'good long time.'" Emily and Alan Joiner interview.
223 — "Less than a ... 'of his life.'" Interview with Margo Bailey.
224 — "Larry Shenk, the ... 'sleep very much.'" Letter to Bill Nicholson from Larry Shenk, August 25, 1975.
225 — "Bill never saw ... at the farmhouse." Emily Joiner interview.
225 — "When the Cubs ... 'right to theirs.'" Letter from Bill Nicholson to Jim Revord, August 21, 1988.
225 — "When Diana died ... feeling came on." Emily Joiner interview.
226 — "He met, and ... Old St. Pauls." Interview with Pamela Soutter.
226 — "Over his final ... 'himself,' Revord recalls." E-mail from Jim Revord, July 8, 2005.
226 — "He went to ... 'almost,' he confessed." Macht interview.

226 — "Frequently, he sat ... days in Chicago." Emily Joiner interview.

227 — "He held strong ... 'career,' he suggested." *Chicago Sun-Times,* August 2, 1987, page 95.

227 — "Bill had been ... received widespread publicity." Videotape of November 17, 1991, testimonial dinner.

229 — "Richie Ashburn, Nicholson's ... 'women loved him.'" *Chicago Tribune,* March 17, 1996, section 3, page 14.

229 — "Robin Roberts worshipped ... 'not been wartime.'" *Philadelphia Inquirer,* March 11, 1996.

229 — "Old nemesis Jim ... 'whacked the ball.'" *Chicago Tribune,* March 17, 1996, section 3 page 14.

231 — "Emily Joiner, who ... on Cross Street." Kent County probate records.

Epilogue

234 — "'They never gave ... his own defense." Phalen, *Our Chicago Cubs,* page 27.

234 — "Baseball historian David ... the case today." Jordan, *A Fresh Look at Wartime Baseball.*

234 — "David Finoli, in ... and Musial (tenth)." Finoli, *For the Good of the Country,* page 45.

234 — "Respected baseball analyst ... 'are essentially legit.'" James, *The New Bill James Historical Baseball Abstract,* page 830.

235 — "Former teammate Putsy ... 'below those guys.'" *Sports Heritage,* July/August, 1987, page 6.

235 — "John Steadman, veteran ... Nicholson, in right." *Baltimore Sun,* July 17, 1994.

Bibliography

Newspapers

Anaconda (Montana) *Standard*, November 9, 1913
Baltimore Afro-American, 1914–1932
Baltimore Sun, 1932–1936, October 8, 1995
Chattanooga Daily Times, April–September, 1939
Chicago American, October 10, 1964
Chicago Defender, April–September, 1947
Chicago Tribune, 1939–2003
Chicago Herald-American, 1945
Chicago Sun Times, 1945
Daily Oklahoman (Oklahoma City), July–August, 1936
Diamondback (University of Maryland), 1931–1936
Galveston (Texas) *Daily News*, July 21, 1929
Gazette and Bulletin (Williamsport, Pa.), 1937
Grit (Williamsport, Pa.), 1938
Kent (County) *News*, 1914–1996
Long Beach (California) *Press Telegram*, March 8, 1948
Los Angeles Times, 1939–1953
New York Herald Tribune, August 16, 1944; October 31, 1953
New York Times, 1931–1996
New York World-Telegram, July 18, 1947
Norfolk Virginian-Pilot, April–September, 1937
Philadelphia Evening Bulletin, September 9, 1953; October 30, 1953
Philadelphia Inquirer, 1936–1996
Phillies Report, January 16, 1992
Pittsburgh Press, May 29, 1953
Queen Anne's (Maryland) *Record-Observer*, November 11, 1987
Salisbury (Maryland) *Times*, December 2, 1953
The Sporting News, 1936–1996
The Enterprise (Chestertown, Md.), 1932
The Transcript (Chestertown, Md.), 1934
Washington College Alumni News, Spring, 1987
Washington College Elm, September, 1931–June, 1936
Washington Evening Star, 1931–1936
Washington Post, 1932–1996

Washington Times, January 15, 2007
Wilmington (Delaware) *News-Journal,* October 18, 1980

Magazine Articles

Carmichael, John C., "Old Swish Can Still Swat," *Sport,* August, 1947
Chicago Cubs Quarterly, June–July, 1993
Day, Robert, "Pitching: A Writer's Guide to the Baseball Greats," *Washington College Magazine,* Summer, 1996
"Fun for All," *Time,* April 10, 1944
Gilden, Jack, "Me and Swish," *Chesapeake Life,* October, 2005
Gilden, Jack, "Right Place at the Wrong Time," *Sports Heritage,* July/August, 1987
Landskroener, Marcia C., "Hog Lard, Turpentine & Mustard: Telling Tales of Old Kent," *Washington College Magazine,* Winter, 1987
Mayer, Bob, "'Swish' Nicholson," *The National Pastime,* Volume 15, 1995
Spalding Official Baseball Guide, 1939
Sports Collectors Digest, January 9, 2000
"The Phillies, Big Leagues Face a Tough Season with Players Too Old or Too Young," *Life,* April 23, 1945

Books

Boston, Talmage. *1939, Baseball's Tipping Point.* Albany, TX: Bright Sky Press, 2005.
Brown, Warren. *The Chicago Cubs.* New York: G.P. Putnam's Sons, 1946.
Campbell, Gordon. *Famous American Athletes of Today.* Ninth Series Volume. Boston: L.C. Page, 1945.
Durocher, Leo, with Ed Linn. *Nice Guys Finish Last.* New York: Simon & Schuster, 1975.
Finoli, David. *For the Good of the Country.* Jefferson, NC: McFarland, 1992.
Gentile, Derek. *The Complete Chicago Cubs: The Total Encyclopedia of the Team.* New York: Black Dog & Leventhal, 2002.
Gilbert, Bill. *They Also Served; Baseball and the Home Front, 1941–1945.* New York: Crown, 1992.
Golenbock, Peter. *Wrigleyville.* New York: St. Martin's Griffin, 1996.
Horsey, Joan, and R. Jerry Keiser. *Kent County.* Charleston, SC: Arcadia, 2005.
James, Bill. *The New Bill James Historical Baseball Abstract.* New York: Free Press, 2003.
Jordan, David M. "A Fresh Look at Wartime Baseball." Society for American Baseball Research paper presented in 1991.
Kahn, Roger. *The Boys of Summer.* New York: Harper and Row, 1972.
Keiser, R. Jerry, et al. *Chestertown and Kent County.* Charleston, SC: Arcadia, 2005.
Kuklick, Bruce. *To Every Thing a Season.* Princeton, NJ: Princeton University Press, 1991.
Lewis, Allen. *The Philadelphia Phillies: A Pictorial History.* Virginia Beach, VA: JCP 1981.
Millikin, Mark R. *Jimmie Foxx: The Pride of Sudlersville.* Lanham, MD: Scarecrow, 1998.
Okrent, Daniel, and Harris Lewine, eds. *The Ultimate Baseball Book.* Boston: Houghton Mifflin, 1981.
Phalen, Rick. *Our Chicago Cubs.* South Bend, IN: Diamond Communications, 1992.
Roberts, Robin. *My Life in Baseball.* Chicago: Triumph Books, 2003.
Skipper, John C. *The Cubs Win the Pennant.* Jefferson, NC: McFarland, 2004.
Theodore, John. *Baseball's Natural: The Story of Eddie Waitkus.* Carbondale: Southern Illinois University Press, 2002.
Thompson, William L., et al. *Washington: The College at Chester.* Chestertown, MD: The Literary House Press, 2000.
Vitti, Jim. *The Cubs on Catalina.* Darien, CT: Settefrati Press, 2003.

Ward, Geoffrey C. *Baseball: An Illustrated History.* New York: Alfred A. Knopf, 1994.
Westcott, Rich. *Diamond Greats.* London: Meckler Books, 1988.
____. *Masters of the Diamond.* Jefferson, NC: McFarland, 1994.
Yeutter, Frank. *Jim Konstanty.* New York: A.S. Barnes, 1951.

Interviews

Bailey, Margo (telephone)
Berry, Charles (telephone)
Bristoll, Jane (telephone)
Cavarretta, Phil (telephone)
Deringer, H. Hurtt
Dutton, Mackey (telephone)
Gumpert, Randy (telephone)
Hoffecker, Miriam Ford
Horsey, Elmer
Horsey, Joan
Joiner, Alan
Joiner, Emily
McDonnell, Maje (telephone)
Miller, Roger
Naktenis, Pete (telephone)
Nicholson, Bill, by Margaret Fallaw
Nicholson, Bill, by Norman Macht
Nicholson, Bill, by Dan Roderick
Rasin, George (telephone)
Skipp, Stefan (telephone)
Stone, Bill (telephone)
Soutter, Pamela (telephone)
Thomson, Bobby (telephone)
Vickers, Harrison
Welton, Betty Beck (telephone)
Werber, Bill (telephone)

Correspondence

Athey, Ed
Deane, Bill
Deringer, H. Hurtt
Friedrich, Marty
Gumpert, Randy
Joiner, Emily
Mortell, Bill
O'Neill, Buck
Pafko, Andy
Pedersen, Jeannine
Revord, Jim
Roberts, Robin
Wysart, Paul

Miscellaneous

Associated Press, NEA Services, and United Press dispatches
Census Records, United States, 1910–1930
Probate Records, Kent County Courthouse
Transcript of Academic Records, Washington College, 1931–1936
Videotape, Testimonial Dinner for Bill Nicholson, November 17, 1991
Washington College *Pegasus,* 1932–1938

Websites

www.baseball-almanac.com
www.baseballyarn.com
www.camprehoboth.com
www.gluckman.com
www.minorleaguebaseball.com
www.retrosheet.org
www.springtrainingmagazine.com

Index

Aaron, Hank 234
Adams, Ace 136, 139
Allen, Johnny 46, 100, 117, 118, 120, 139
Allen, Mel 120
Altrock, Nick 105
Anselmi, Albert 134
Ashburn, Richie 127, 189, 190, 198, 211, 217, 229
Athey, Ed 20, 129
Auker, Eldon 47

Bailey, Margo 40, 222, 224, 226
Baines, Harold 236
Baker, Bill 184
Baker, Frank "Home Run" 17, 30, 57, 101, 218, 235, 236
Baltes, Sam 112, 113
Baltimore American 29
Baltimore Evening Sun 41
Baltimore Sun 27, 228
Bankhead, Eugenia 219, 220, 222
Bankhead, Tallulah 219, 222
Banks, Ernie 180, 235
Barber, Red 120, 130, 215
Barlick, Al 58
Barna, Babe 29, 61, 63, 68, 70, 108
Barney, Rex 185
Barr, George 151
Barry, Jack 29
Bartell, Dick 78
Barthelson, Bob 140
Basinski, Eddie 151
Baumgartner, Stan 190, 205, 209, 215
Beck, Alverta Brice 7
Beck, James Thomas 7
Becker, Heinz 153, 165
Bender, "Chief" 68
Benjamin, Stan 64, 68
Benson, Al 124
Berra, Yogi 228
Berry, Charlie 31, 32, 39, 40, 41, 42
Betterton Beach 13, 14

Bickford, Vern 183
Biederman, Les 113, 216
"Billy Goat Curse" 158
Bissonette, Del 140, 154
Bithorn, Hiram 59, 111, 112, 114, 117, 122, 171
Blackburne, Lena 51
Blackwell, Ewell 178, 179
Blatnik, Johnny 200
Blattner, Buddy 193
Block, Cy 105
Bloodworth, Jimmy 71
Bloom, David 70
Boggess, Dusty 184
Bonds, Barry 2, 140
Bonura, Zeke 93
Borowy, Hank 145, 152, 156, 158, 159, 168, 173, 174, 180, 186, 187, 188, 190, 192, 195, 199
Boudreau, Lou 90, 134
Branca, Ralph 175, 202, 203, 211
Branch, Norman 59
Braun, Ladislaus 174
Braves Field 108, 136, 167, 177, 192
Brazle, Alpha 70, 126, 179, 183, 193, 215
Brecheen, Harry 57, 59, 60, 166, 178, 183
Brickhouse, Jack 125
Bridges, Tommy 50
Briggs Stadium 98, 155, 156, 160
Britt, Jimmy 167
Brodie, A.L. 158
Brown, Robert 124
Brown, Tommy 213
Brown, Warren 151, 160, 213
Bryant, Clay 78, 83, 89
Bull Durham 93
Burgess, Smokey 228
Burkhart, Ken 154, 155, 179
Burns, Edward 87, 90, 95, 96, 112, 116, 117, 118, 132, 147, 153, 157, 162, 185, 213
Byrd, Harry C. "Curley" 21, 25, 26, 43
Byrd, Harry Clifton, Jr. 12

Index

Caballero, Putsy 146, 190, 191, 193, 203, 216, 235
Cambria, Joe 68
Camelli, Hank 57, 64
Camilli, Dolf 96, 101, 103, 113, 129
Campanella, Roy 186, 206, 209, 217
Capone, Al 134
Carbo, Bernie 155
Carey, J. Warren "Moxie" 22, 31, 39
Carmichael, John 97, 130
Carpenter, Bob (owner) 189, 191, 201, 213, 215, 217, 219
Carpenter, Bob (player) 109
Carpenter, Louisa d'Andelot 219, 220, 225
Carpenter, R.M. 219
Casey, Hugh 86, 87
Catalina Island, spring training 78, 79, 88, 90, 93, 103, 104, 164, 172, 181
Cavarretta, Phil 78, 83, 84, 89, 93, 100, 111, 113, 114, 117, 121, 127, 128, 132, 135, 137, 138, 139, 140, 145, 146, 148, 149, 150, 151, 152, 153, 154, 155, 156, 157, 161, 165, 167, 172, 177, 180, 181, 182, 183, 188
Chapman, Ben 182, 189
Chattanooga Daily Times 64, 65, 66
Chesapeake Bay League 24, 25, 30
Chestertown High School 10, 11, 16, 22, 37
Chicago Defender 176
Chicago Daily News 97, 130, 148
Chicago Herald American 151, 160
Chicago Tribune 72, 75, 83, 87, 90, 95, 97, 105, 110, 116, 127, 147, 157, 167, 168, 178, 183
Chipman, Bob 136, 139
Church, Bubba 209
Churchill, Winston 103
Clark, Mel 213, 215
Clearwater, Florida, spring training 126, 189, 190, 191, 200, 201, 213
Clemente, Roberto 2, 183
Clunk, J. Roy 56
Cochrane, Mickey 39, 108
Cohane, Tim 130
Cohen, Abe 8
Coleman, Bob 122
Collins, Eddie 29
Comiskey Park 77, 82, 100, 103, 114
Connie Mack Stadium *see* Shibe Park
Considine, Bob 21
Cooney, Johnny 122
Cooper, Gary 13, 103
Cooper, Mort 95, 107
Cooper, Walker 122
Corcoran, Jimmy 90
Corum, Bill 120
Costner, Kevin 93
Cotille, Tony 62
Cox, Billy 180, 197, 203
Craft, Harry 89
Cramer, Roger 158

Crosley Field 83, 89, 108, 112, 179, 197, 210
Crowley, "Boots" 58
Cullenbine, Roy 48, 156, 157
Curlett, Diana Hudson 222, 225
Cuyler, Kiki 64, 67, 68, 69, 82, 98, 103, 105, 143, 213, 234, 235

Dahlgren, Babe 66, 106, 148
Daily Oklahoman 48, 49
Daley, Arthur 153, 154
Dallesandro, Dom 79, 80, 82, 83, 100, 105, 107, 114, 133, 146, 166, 169, 172, 177
Daniel, Dan 106, 143, 187
Dark, Alvin 204
Dascoli, Frank 127
Davis, "Crash" 29, 93
Davis, Curt 121, 149
Davis, George 14
Dawson, Andre 235
Dean, "Chubby" 29
Dean, Dizzy 47, 63, 72, 73, 74, 75, 78, 81, 82, 83, 89, 90, 98
DeBerry, Hank 68
Dejan, Mike 89
Deringer, H. Hurtt 40, 228
Deringer, W.D. 24
Derringer, Paul 89, 117, 119, 121, 122, 143, 145, 146, 148, 159
Diamondback 26, 38
Dickey, Bill 49
DiMaggio, Dominic 191
DiMaggio, Joe 49, 87, 99, 188, 235
DiMaggio, Vince 149, 234
Dockins, George 154
Doerr, Bobby 191
Donnelly, Blix 177
Donovan, Lefty 59
Dorsey, Tommy 79
Downes, Mrs. Robert 228
Doyle, Jack 68, 69, 164
Drebinger, John 49
Dubiel, Walt 188
Dumschott, "Dutch" 33
Dunn, Adam 129
Dunn, Tom 87, 121, 152
du Pont, Pierre S. 219
Durocher, Leo 80, 81, 87, 99, 109, 111, 112, 118, 119, 121, 169, 170, 198, 203, 204, 205, 210, 211, 214
Dusek, Erv 179
Dutton, Mackey 218
Dwyer, Ellis 36
Dyer, Braven 142, 148
Dykes, Jimmie 29, 81

Easterling, Paul "Pound 'Em" 48
Eastern League 61
Eastern Shore League 17
Eastman, Joseph B. 115
Eaves, Vallie 39, 109
Ebbets Field 99, 109, 111, 120, 121, 127, 130,

Index

131, 139, 149, 167, 169, 170, 175, 184, 192, 193, 196, 203, 206, 209, 214, 216
Edwards, Bruce 176
Ekaitis, George 20, 22, 25, 26, 29, 32, 35, 36, 41
Elliott, Bob 98
Elson, Bob 103, 108
Engel, Joe 63, 64, 65, 66, 68, 69, 70, 106, 218
Ennis, Del 189, 191, 193, 198, 201, 209, 212, 216
Enroth, Dick 125
The Enterprise 11, 20, 21, 24, 29
Erickson, Paul 90, 104, 111, 112, 164
Erskine, Carl 211
Evans, Ed 42

Fairlee Elementary School 7, 10
Fallaw, Margaret 33, 221
Fancy Farm 6, 7, 9, 14, 15, 32, 221
Feller, Bob 46, 82, 97, 98, 102, 155, 173
Ferrell, Wes 47
Finney, Lou 45
Finoli, David 234
Fitzsimmons, Freddie 138, 146
Fleming, Les 165
Flowers, D'Arcy "Jake" 17, 101, 225
Flynn, Errol 79
Forbes Field 89, 134, 137, 138, 155, 197, 203, 210
Forman, Ross 143
Fox, Nellie 211
Foxx, Jimmie 12, 39, 57, 86, 101, 103, 110, 111, 134, 135, 136, 139, 143, 146, 149, 151, 228, 235, 236
Fraley, Oscar 156
Franklin, Benjamin 6
French, Larry 72, 76, 78, 86, 100
French Lick, Indiana, spring training 115, 116, 117, 132, 133, 146, 147
Frey, Lonnie 113, 176
Frick, Ford 112, 118, 204
Frisch, Frankie 89, 134, 194
Furillo, Carl 203, 209, 211

Gable, Clark 79
Galan, Augie 75, 78, 82, 83, 88, 100, 152
Gallagher, Jim 74, 92, 93, 94, 95, 100, 102, 103, 104, 106, 110, 115, 118, 121, 122, 132, 133, 138, 147, 152, 162, 163, 164, 166, 167, 171, 180, 181, 228, 229
Gallagher, Joe 87
Gammon, Wirt 64, 66, 67, 71, 125
Garrity, Vince 110
Gazette and Bulletin 55
Gee, Johnny 169
Gehrig, Lou 49, 66, 106, 139
Gessner, Otto 125
Gilbert, Charlie 95, 96, 106, 107
Giraitis, Jerry 23, 26, 27
Gleason, James J. 55
Gleeson, Jim 70
Goldsborough, Phillip S. Lee 33
Goldsborough, T. Alan 33
Goldstein, Louis 36, 38, 228, 231
Goliat, Mike 201, 203, 204, 209
Gomez, Lefty 154
Gonzalez, Mike 138
Gooding, Gladys 109, 184, 192
Goodman, Ival 108, 140, 143
Gordon, Flash 96
Graham, Rev. William L. 231
Grainger, Priscilla 13
Grant, Cary 79
The Grapes of Wrath 48
Grasso, Mickey 201
Green, Dallas 227
Greenberg, Hank 102, 103, 156, 157, 158, 159, 174
Gregg, Hal 88, 142, 149, 169
Greims, Arthur, Jr. 133
Grieb, W. Clark 218
Griffith, Calvin 31
Griffith, Clark 17, 31, 32, 63, 68, 71, 106
Griffith Stadium 30, 31
Grimm, Charlie 93, 127, 128, 135, 136, 138, 142, 145, 146, 147, 148, 150, 151, 152, 153, 154, 155, 156, 157, 158, 159, 163, 164, 165, 166, 168, 172, 173, 174, 177, 179, 181, 182, 190, 191, 194, 206
Grove, Robert "Lefty" 39, 45, 235
Gumpert, Randy 46, 49, 61, 62, 63
Gustine, Frankie 94, 134

Haas, Bert 113, 179
Hack, Stan 75, 87, 88, 93, 98, 99, 100, 104, 111, 114, 120, 121, 127, 133, 135, 136, 139, 140, 146, 153, 154, 155, 157, 159, 165, 169, 177, 179, 217, 225
Ham, Bus 49
Hamilton, Jimmy 68
Hamilton County Herald 71
Hamlin, Luke "Hot Potato" 78, 100
Hamner, Granville 182, 189, 191, 193, 203, 215
Hamner, Ralph 185
Hanson, Swede 139, 140
Hanyzewski, Ed 105, 117
Harder, Mel 47
Harlow, Dick 20
Hartnett, Gabby 69, 71, 72, 74, 76, 78, 79, 80, 81, 82, 83, 89, 92, 217
Hastings, Sen. Daniel O. 28
Hastings Cup 28, 36, 41
Hayworth, Rita 40
Hearn, Jim 214
Heintzelman, Ken 192, 199
Hemingway, Ernest 87
Hendricks, Elrod 155
Hendrickson, Don 154
Henline, Butch 184
Hepburn, Katharine 7

Index

Hepburn, Rev. Dr. Sewell S. 7
Herlihy, Ken 186, 228
Herman, Billy 75, 78, 86, 92, 93, 94, 95, 96, 99, 100, 109, 119, 120, 217
Hernandez, Chico 111, 112
Hewitt, Burke 57
Higbe, Kirby 75, 99, 111, 169
Higgins, Pinky 45
High, Andy 68
Hill, Jess 50
Hill, Patrick 130
Hitler, Adolf 65
Hobbs, Roy 196
Hodgson, Al 32
Hoerst, Frank 96
Hoffecker, Miriam Ford 12, 13
Hollmig, Stan 194, 200
Holmes, Kelly 60
Holmes, Tommy 167
Hopp, Johnny 150
Hornsby, Rogers 148
Horsey, Elmer 219, 225
Hostetler, Chuck 160
Houston, Francis 14
Hoyle, Harry 7
Hoyt, Morton 219, 220
Hubbard, Cal 46
Hubbell, Carl 76, 96, 99, 217
Huckleberry, Earl 39
Hudson, Johnny 95, 96
Huffman, Wilbert 35, 36, 38, 41, 42
Hughes, Don 155
Hughes, Roy 157
Hughson, Tex 138

Irvin, Monte 205
Isaminger, James C. 46

Jacobs, "Spook" 227
James, Bill 234
James, Harry 79
Jansen, Larry 194
Javery, Al 119
Johnson, Bob 45, 51
Johnson, Don 74, 108, 137, 140, 145, 148, 169
Johnson, Judy 235
Johnson, Roy 156, 157, 169
Johnson, Walter 64
Joiner, Alan 220, 221, 222, 226
Joiner, Emily 124, 130, 221, 222, 223, 225, 231
Jones, Sheldon 204
Jones, Willie "Puddin'head" 203, 206, 209, 211, 213, 214
Jorda, Lou 112, 142
Jordan, David 234
Jurges, Billy 187
Just, Ward 159

Kaline, Al 235
Kane, Dr. 61

Kazanski, Ted 215, 217
Keaton, Buster 13
Keller, Charlie "King Kong" 42, 66, 86, 161
Kelley, Harry 45, 54
Kerr, Buddy 171
Kibler, John Thomas 16, 17, 18, 19, 20, 22, 24, 25, 30, 32, 37, 38, 44, 101, 133, 225
Kibler, John Thomas, Jr. 133
Kieran, John 96, 97
Kiner, Ralph 215
King, Joe 153, 233
Konikowski, Alex 185
Konstanty, Jim 196, 201, 203, 206
Kosko, June 191
Koslo, Dave 178, 179, 186
Kott, Carl 49
Krausse, Lew 56
Kupcinet, Irv 160
Kurowski, Whitey 109

Lade, Doyle 177
Lafata, Joe 198
Lajoie, Napoleon 140
Lanahan, Dick 66
Landis, Kenesaw Mountain 102, 108, 115, 137
Lanfranconi, Walter 103
Langdon, Dot 192
Lanier, Max 183
Latrobe, John 225
Lavagetto, Cookie 96
Lawrence, Frank D. 57, 59, 60
Lee, Bill 93, 94, 107, 117, 154
Leiber, Hank 75, 78, 80, 81, 82, 83, 86, 87, 93, 94, 95, 96, 97, 98
Leonard, Dutch 188, 215
Levy, Lank 59
Lewis, Allen 229
Lieb, Fred 140
Life 146
Lindell, Johnny 188
Link, Alfred 191
Liska, Jerry 153
Litwhiler, Danny 119, 211
Livingston, Mickey 165
Lobert, Hans 210
Lodigiani, Dario 29
Logan, Bob 150, 154
Lohrman, Bill 113
Lopata, Stan 202
Los Angeles Times 80, 142, 148, 165
Lotshaw, Andrew Hemmingway 82, 94, 97, 104, 115, 156, 200
Lowrey, Harry "Peanuts" 103, 128, 149, 150, 152, 157
Lusby, Josiah 6
Lyons, Ted 81, 114

Mack, Connie *see* McGillicuddy, Cornelius Alexander
Mack, Earl 51
Mack, Michael 120

Index

Mack, Ray 180
Maddern, Clarence 187
Mailho, Emil 44
Malamud, Bernard 196
Mancuso, Gus 72, 78, 140, 146
Mantle, Mickey 47
Maranville, Rabbit 86
Marion, Marty 143, 171, 217
Marquardt, Ollie 55
Marsh, Earl 158
Marshall, Max 113
Marshall, Willard 176
Martin, Edward A. 137
Martini, Wedo 39
Mason, Frankie 71
Masterson, Walt 191
Mattick, Bobby 83
Mauch, Gene 82, 128
Mayo, Eddie 157, 160, 200
Mayo, Jack 194, 213
Mays, Willie 14
McCann, Gene 40
McCarthy, Joe 50, 191
McCauley, Pamela Yerkes 226
McCullough, Clyde 94, 100, 105, 106, 109, 112, 113, 115, 116, 128, 169, 177, 203
McDonald, Jeannette 13
McGillicuddy, Cornelius Alexander ("Connie Mack") 1, 29, 39, 44, 45, 46, 47 49, 50, 51, 52, 54, 59, 60, 62, 63, 64, 105, 109, 120, 182, 219
McGowan, Roscoe 142, 175, 211
McGrew, Ted 69
McHenry, Art 61
McInnis, Stuffy 29
McKechnie, Bill 86, 152
McKinney, Curtis 167
McMahan, Eddie 133
McManus, Marty 61, 63
McNutt, Paul 146
McPhail, Larry 68, 69, 76, 140, 152
Mead, Gilbert W. 33, 43
Medwick, Joe "Ducky" 64, 96, 99, 106, 112, 234
Melton, Cliff 97
Melville, Larry 57, 58
Memorial Stadium 221
Memphis Commercial Appeal 70
Merullo, Len 78, 109, 112, 113, 124, 127, 128, 135, 152, 166, 167, 168, 172, 176, 179
Mexico City, spring training 50, 51, 52, 54
Meyer, "Monk" 128, 162, 163, 181, 182, 185, 188, 190, 194, 195, 196, 197, 199, 201, 202, 209, 214, 215, 216
Miles, Dee 63, 71, 105
Miller, Eddie 171, 182, 193
Miller, Roger 126
Minner, Paul 170, 210
Mize, Johnny 90, 95, 177, 215, 217
Mooty, Jake 84, 173
Moses, Wally 29, 45, 105

Mulcahy, Hugh 168
Muncrief, Bob 165
Munger, George "Red" 174, 184, 209
Munzel, Edgar 116
Murtaugh, Danny 211
Musial, Stan 110, 120, 122, 217, 234
Mutiny on the Bounty 79
Myers, Billy 103
Myers, Roy 47, 49

Naktenis, Pete 46, 47, 62
The Natural 3, 196
Neun, Johnny 58
New York Daily News 153
New York Journal-American 141
New York-Penn League 54, 61
New York Times 49, 96, 142, 153, 175, 211
New York World-Telegram 143
Newcombe, Don 203, 209
Newhouser, Hal 155, 156, 158
Newsome, Bobo 47
Nicholson, Albert Earle 6, 14, 32, 34, 43, 143
Nicholson, Albert Kane 101, 220, 223, 225
Nicholson, Albert Tylden 6, 8, 10, 13, 61, 149, 162, 163, 221
Nicholson, Alverta Tylden Beck ("Miss Bertie") 6, 8, 32, 43, 143
Nicholson, James Laurence ("Larny") 6, 8, 9, 10, 34, 120, 228
Nicholson, Nancy Kane 40, 61, 62, 101, 103, 116, 137, 149, 151, 162, 163, 188, 217, 218, 219, 220, 222, 223, 225
Nicholson, William Beck "Swish": all-star games 86–87, 98–99, 120, 137–138; birth and early life 3–16; college career 17–43; death 228–231; debut with Philadelphia A's 44–46; diabetes 161, 205–208, 215–216, 225–227; draft status 118, 133, 145–147, 149–150; enrollment at Annapolis 32–34; intentionallly walked with bases loaded 139–141; marriage 61; minor league career 47–71; most valuable player votes 122, 143; nicknames 128–131; purchase by Cubs 68–70; retirement 217; statue dedication 228; tobacco chewing 85, 127; traded to Phillies 181, 187; World Series 155–160
Nicholson, William Beck, Jr. 40, 76, 149, 210, 220, 222, 223, 224, 226
Niehoff, Bert 47, 48
Norfolk Virginian-Pilot 57, 59
Novikoff, Lou 89, 90, 93, 94, 95, 105, 106, 107, 111, 114, 115, 116, 118, 119

O'Connell, Danny 203
Old St. Paul's Episcopal Church 7, 8, 222, 223, 225, 226
Olsen, Bernard 78
Olsen, Vern 90, 98, 99
O'Neill, Steve 214, 215
Oswalt, Mary Meyer 201

Index

Ott, Mel 87, 96, 109, 126, 130, 136, 138, 139, 140, 141, 148, 171, 234
Outlaw, Jimmy 159
Overmire, Stubby 157
Owen, Mickey 112

Pafko, Andy 133, 140, 143, 146, 150, 152, 159, 166, 167, 169, 173, 181, 182, 183, 184, 185, 224, 227, 235
Page, Joe 188
Parker, Clarence "Ace" 51, 52, 59, 60, 172
Passeau, Claude 81, 83, 87, 90, 94, 98, 99, 106, 107, 109, 113, 117, 120, 121, 133, 136, 145, 146, 149, 157, 159, 161, 168, 169, 175
Patkin, Max 173, 192
Pearson, Monte 49
Pesky, Johnny 191
Phelps, Babe 235
Philadelphia Evening Bulletin 205, 217
Philadelphia Inquirer 44, 46, 190, 229
Piedmont League 56
Pieper, Pat 74, 158
Pittsburgh Press 113, 216
Pollett, Howard 170, 175, 183
Polo Grounds 96, 97, 109, 121, 138, 139, 141, 169, 177, 178, 210, 213, 214
Poppleton, Ray 26
Porterfield, Bob 191
Povich, Shirley 71, 106, 201
Price, Johnny 173
Prim, Ray 150, 158
Pyle, Ewald 139

Queen Anne's Record-Observer 110

Raffensberger, Ken 137, 210
Ray, Bob 80
Reagan, Ronald "Dutch" 90
Reardon, Beans 141
Redford, Robert 3
Reese, Pee Wee 84, 86, 89, 119, 127, 168, 203
Reichler, Joe 148, 190
Reinhold, Fritz 21, 23
Reiser, Pete 236
Revord, Jim 124, 226
Reynolds, Carl 76
Rhodes, Gordon "Dusty" 45
Richards, Paul 70
Rickert, Marvin "Twitch" 165, 166, 167, 168
Rickey, Branch 92, 175
Riddle, Elmer 185
Ridzik, Steve 213
Rigney, Bill 171, 204, 205
Rinehart, Billy 43
Ripken, Cal, Jr. 228, 235
Ritchie, Gov. Albert C. 33
Roberts, Robin 84, 184, 189, 190, 192, 199, 202, 203, 204, 205, 210, 211, 214, 216, 217, 224, 227, 228, 229
Robinson, Frank 234

Robinson, Jackie 15, 175, 176, 179, 182, 184, 185, 187, 190, 209, 211
Robinson, Ollie 22
Rodgers, Bill 148
Rodricks, Dan 130
Roe, Preacher 209
Rogell, Bill 83
Romano, Jim 209
Roosevelt, Franklin D. 27, 30, 33, 98, 102, 147
Root, Charley 94, 99
Rose, Pete 234
Rowe, Schoolboy 112, 122
Rowell, 'Bama 196
Rowland, Clarence "Pants" 78, 118
Russell, Rip 76, 83, 88, 90, 93, 103, 110, 111
Ruth, Babe 86, 103, 122, 154, 177, 228, 234, 235
Ryan, Connie 137, 138

Sain, Johnny 177, 192, 209
St. Louis Post Dispatch 84
Salisbury Times 217
Sanicki, Ed 200
Sauer, Hank 235
Sawyer, Eddie 189, 190, 193, 196, 197, 198, 199, 201, 202, 203, 205, 208, 211, 212, 213, 214, 224, 227, 228
Scalisi, John 134
Schacht, Al 59, 120, 173
Scheffing, Bob 100, 105, 167
Schmidt, Fred 175
Schmitz, Johnny 109, 179, 181
Schumacher, Hal 113
Schupp, Charlie 57
Schuster, Bill 134, 139, 140, 149
Scully, Cornelius D. 137
Secory, Frank 154
Seminick, Andy 146, 191, 203, 204, 205
Sevareid, Hank 68
Severn School 33, 34, 37
Sewell, Luke 183
Sewell, Rip 105, 118, 138, 179, 182
Shenk, Larry 224
Shepherd, Will 71
Shibe Park (Connie Mack Stadium) 43, 44, 45, 49, 54, 88, 97, 120, 126, 143, 168, 184, 188, 189, 192, 193, 194, 198, 199, 202, 203, 205, 206, 209, 210, 211
Shipley, Burton 31
Shotton, Burt 198
Sianis, William 158
Silvestri, Ken 193
Simmons, Al 29, 39, 75
Simmons, Curt 84, 189, 199, 202, 211, 214, 215, 227
Sisler, Dick 196, 202, 203, 206, 212
Slaughter, Enos 170, 188, 224
Smith, Eddie 94
Smith, Frank 210
Smith, Captain John 5

Index

Smith, Red (coach) 157
Smith, Red (writer) 52, 137
Smith, William 225
Smith, Rev. William 6
Smoot, Roger 25
Snead, Sam 183
Snider, Duke 217
Sosa, Sammy 235
Sothoron, Norwood 26
Southern Association 63, 65, 66, 67, 68, 69, 70, 71
Southworth, Billy 137, 138, 154
Spalding, Dick 93, 103, 106
"Spite" Fence 45
Sport 178
The Sporting News 23, 97, 102, 103, 106, 132, 140, 143, 147, 149, 151, 162, 209
Sportsman's Park 86, 94, 99, 100, 107, 126, 154, 170, 174, 209
Stanky, Eddie 57, 60, 117, 118, 167, 168, 204, 205
Statz, Jigger 181
Steadman, John 228, 235
Stein, Pete 65
Steinbeck, John 48
Steinhagen, Ruth Ann (alias Ruth Burns) 194, 195, 196
Stengel, Casey 108, 109, 191
Stenger, W.J. 11
Stephenson, Riggs 213, 235
Stewart, Bill 84, 109
Stone, Billy 125, 178, 193
Stonebreaker, Steve 225
Stringer, Lou 89, 90, 93, 94, 100, 111
Sturgeon, Bobby 83, 100

Taft, William Howard 219
Taylor, Harry 183
Tebbetts, Birdie 48
Texas League 47, 48
Thomas, Ira 29, 30, 31, 39, 42
Thompson, Gene 177
Thompson, Hank 204
Thompson, Junior 113
Thomson, Bobby 185, 194, 211, 224, 234
Tignor, Hobart 30, 31, 36, 38, 39, 40, 41, 42, 43
Todd, Al 83, 89, 116
Torgeson, Earl 215
Tost, Lou 108
Travis, Cecil 102
Trout, Dizzy 143, 158, 159, 161
Trucks, Virgil 155
Tydings, Millard E. 33

University of Maryland 1, 12, 18, 21, 25, 26, 29, 30, 31, 34, 37, 38, 42, 43, 86
Usilton, Fred 27
Usilton, Herbert 24

Valo, Elmer 29
VanderMeer, Johnny 84, 107, 130, 179

Vaughan, Irving 75, 83, 86, 91, 135, 213
Veterans Stadium 224
Vickers, Harrison 22, 33, 220
Voiselle, Bill 139, 140, 153, 167, 177

Waitkus, Eddie 3, 84, 94, 126, 167, 168, 169, 172, 177, 178, 180, 181, 188, 193, 194, 195, 196, 198, 200, 201, 202, 205, 208, 209, 211, 212, 215, 231
Walker, Dixie 127, 148, 152, 168, 175, 176, 187, 196, 234
Walker, Harry "The Hat" 181, 187, 188
Walters, Bucky 120
Waner, Paul 76, 142, 143, 161, 217
Ward, Arch 127, 137, 150, 183, 187, 191
Ward, Ellery 26
Warneke, Lon 117, 121, 204, 211
Washington, George 5, 6, 33
Washington College 6, 11, 12, 16, 17, 18, 19, 20, 21, 22, 23, 24, 25, 26, 27, 28, 29, 30, 31, 32, 33, 34, 35, 36, 37, 38, 39, 40, 41, 42, 43, 46, 218, 225, 227
Washington Elm 23, 25, 26, 29, 33, 36, 38, 41, 51
Washington Evening Star 21
Washington Post 20, 21, 25, 26, 38, 71, 106, 201
Webber, Les 109, 142
Wehmeier, Herm 210
Welton, Betty Beck 40
Werber, Bill 50, 51, 52, 54
West, Max 86
Westcott, Rich 164
Whitworth, Dick 48
Wiechec, Frank 197, 200, 205, 206
Wilks, Ted 148
Williams, Billy 235
Williams, Ted 98, 99, 102, 107, 191, 215, 235
Willis, Rachel 22
Willis, Vic 38
Wilson, Bert 124
Wilson, Hack 89, 122, 135, 213, 235
Wilson, Jimmie 92, 93, 94, 95, 96, 100, 103, 104, 105, 107, 108, 109, 110, 111, 112, 116, 117, 119, 121, 134, 135, 136
Wittig, Johnny 120
Wood, "Smokey Joe" 236
Workman, Charley 150
Wrigley, Philip K. 67, 69, 71, 72, 74, 78, 88, 89, 92, 97, 103, 132, 172, 185, 187
Wrigley, William, Jr. 67, 79
Wrigley Field 2, 67, 68, 72, 74, 75, 76, 79, 83, 84, 85, 89, 90, 92, 93, 94, 95, 96, 97, 98, 102, 103, 107, 108, 110, 111, 113, 114, 117, 118, 119, 122, 124, 125, 127, 128, 136, 141, 145, 148, 150, 151, 152, 153, 158, 160, 165, 168, 169, 170, 171, 173, 174, 175, 176, 177, 178, 179, 183, 185, 186, 187, 191, 194, 196, 210, 225, 234
Wyatt, Whitlow 106, 121
Wyrostek, Johnny 215
Wyse, Hank 145, 156, 157

Yankee Stadium 139
Yeutter, Frank 205, 217
York, Rudy 96, 234
York, Tony 134
Yoter, Elmer "Rabbit" 57

Young, Babe 179
Young, Cy 137
Young, Gibby 36, 41
Yount, Floyd "Eddie" 51, 52, 55, 56

www.ingramcontent.com/pod-product-compliance
Ingram Content Group UK Ltd.
Pitfield, Milton Keynes, MK11 3LW, UK
UKHW041932140426
5217IPUK00014B/430